DATE DUE

JUL 1 9 2018

BRODART, CO.   Cat. No. 23-221

The Cartels

The Cartels

The Story of Mexico's Most Dangerous Criminal Organizations and Their Impact on U.S. Security

GEORGE W. GRAYSON

Praeger Security International

 PRAEGER

AN IMPRINT OF ABC-CLIO, LLC
Santa Barbara, California • Denver, Colorado • Oxford, England

Library of Congress Cataloging-in-Publication Data

Grayson, George W., 1938–
  The cartels : the story of Mexico's most dangerous criminal organizations and their impact on U.S. security / George W. Grayson.
    pages cm — (Praeger security international)
  Includes bibliographical references and index.
    ISBN 978–1–4408–2986–4 (hardback) — ISBN 978–1–4408–2987–1 (ebook)
  1. Drug traffic—Mexico. 2. Drug traffic—Government policy—Mexico. 3. Organized crime—Mexico. 4. Cartels—Mexico. 5. Corruption—Mexico. I. Title.
HV5840.M4G725   2014
363.450972—dc23   2013019550

ISBN: 978–1–4408–2986–4
EISBN: 978–1–4408–2987–1

18 17 16 15 14   1 2 3 4 5

This book is also available on the World Wide Web as an eBook.
Visit www.abc-clio.com for details.

Praeger
An Imprint of ABC-CLIO, LLC

ABC-CLIO, LLC
130 Cremona Drive, P.O. Box 1911
Santa Barbara, California 93116-1911

This book is printed on acid-free paper ∞

Manufactured in the United States of America

Contents

Preface and Acknowledgments

The United States has diplomatic relations with 194 independent nations. Of these, none is more important to America than Mexico in terms of tourism, trade, investment, natural resources, migration, energy, and security. While military revolts convulsed many Latin American countries in the 1930s, our southern neighbor maintained remarkable stability. A major factor differentiating Mexico from other hemispheric nations was the performance of President Lázaro Cárdenas del Río (1934–1940). He infused his nation with a sense of nationalistic cohesion by turning the railroads over to the workers, expropriating foreign oil companies, and expanding the number of communal farms known as *ejidos*.

Taking a page from Italy's Il Duce, Benito Mussolini, Cárdenas converted Mexico's dominant party into a corporatist entity—with participation based on one's occupational status—blue-collar, peasant, small businessperson, artist, professional, bureaucrat, or teacher. The state also exerted influence on chambers of commerce representing important industries and professions. In theory, the grassroots members of the "revolutionary party" channeled demands to sectoral leaders who in turn advanced their interests in the citadels of power. In practice, the president, prominent cabinet members, the chief of the Party of the Mexican Revolution (PRM), bosses of official unions, and other party stalwarts made decisions on a top-down basis.

Decision makers in Washington realized that cooptation, corruption, and control of dissidents permeated Mexico. However, the regime resembled more a *dicta-suave* ("soft dictatorship") than a *dicta-dura* ("hard dictatorship"). In any case, the Great Depression, World War II, conflicts in Korea and Vietnam, the Cold War, and energy challenges filled the United States' agenda. It was a godsend not to have to station large numbers of troops along the 2,000-mile-long border with our authoritarian but stable neighbor.

During the last decades of the twentieth century the Institutional Revolutionary Party Partido Revolucionario Institucional (PRI), successor to the PRM, suffered one blow after another. Among the most damaging were the October 1968 Tlatelolco Massacre of civilians, the bungling of an oil bonanza in the late 1970s and early 1980s, the mishandling of relief efforts in the wake of back-to-back earthquakes in 1985, the assassination of Guadalajara's Roman Catholic cardinal in 1993, a miniuprising by self-styled Zapatistas rebels in 1994, the murder of the PRI's popular presidential candidate in 1994, and a series of economic disasters at the conclusion of presidential terms in 1976, 1982, 1988, and 1994.

The last debacle—the "Christmas Crisis" of December 1994/January 1995—slashed the value of the peso. This sharp devaluation slammed the middle class with sky-high interest rates, home mortgage foreclosures, and massive unemployment. In 1997 citizens took revenge on the PRI by electing Cuauhtémoc Cárdenas, son of the iconic Lázaro and standard-bearer of a leftist coalition headed by the Democratic Revolutionary Party (PRD), as mayor of Mexico City. In 2000 (Vicente Fox Quesada) and 2006 (Felipe Calderón Hinojosa), standard-bearers of the center-right National Action Party Partido Acción Nacional (PAN) captured Los Pinos presidential residence.

One of the many problems confronting the PAN chief executives was narcotics trafficking. The interdiction of drug routes to Florida and other southeastern states in the 1980s and 1990s forced Colombian cocaine merchants to rely on Caribbean islands, Central America, and Mexico as super-highways to El Norte. Mexican drug syndicates eventually took possession of the shipments at the Guatemalan border, converting their million-dollar enterprises into billion-dollar operations. Mexican capos earned fortunes selling cocaine, marijuana, heroin, and methamphetamines to American consumers. The Sinaloa Cartel, headed by the redoubtable Joaquín "El Chapo" Guzmán Loera, and other powerful, well-armed criminal organizations dominated strategic geographic enclaves.

Although there was no grassroots outcry for a Mexican iteration of the "war on drugs," Calderón threw tens of thousands of Federal Police and armed forces into the battle, lest the country lose sovereignty over cartel-dominated regions. Between late 2006, when the *panista* was inaugurated, and 2012 when he left office, more than 47,000 people lost their lives and another 26,000 went missing in confrontations with organized crime.

Outraged over the mayhem, the electorate focused its ire on the PAN by selecting the PRI's Enrique Peña Nieto as its chief of state. The movie-star handsome former Mexico State governor became a perpetual motion machine on the campaign trail and as president after swearing the oath of office on December 1, 2012. The respected newspaper *Reforma* compared his continual movement to a Harlem Shake performer. As paladin of the "new PRI," he jailed a venal union leader, launched a trust-busting scheme aimed at media giants, and announced social programs to benefit crime victims, the homeless, the unemployed, the hungry, people with disabilities, older adults, women, young people, and indigenous communities. In an attempt to divert attention to other issues, he avoided mentioning the narco-mayhem and encouraged the media to do the same.

Meanwhile, he forged a "Pacto por México" ("Pact for Mexico") with major opposition parties as a mechanism to debate pressing issues and muster votes for social ventures, oil-sector reform, a new fiscal system, and implementation of a sweeping National Development Plan (PND), fashioned by his astute Finance Secretary Luis Videgaray Caso. Peña Nieto even found time to make four visits abroad during his first eight months in power, including trips to China and Japan.

On the hustings, the president had pledged to create a 40,000-cadre civilian-led Gendarmería Nacional, based on highly esteemed national law-enforcement agencies in France, Spain, and Chile. At the same time, he vowed to modernize the Judicial Police (PJ) under the watchful eye of the former police chief of the Federal District (DF), medical doctor, retired admiral, and karate ace Manuel Mondragón y Kalb. Still, the violence rose as bloodthirsty cartels continued to extort, kidnap, steal, torture, and murder—often in a grisly, sadistic fashion.

West-central Michoacán, Lázaro Cárdenas's bailiwick, boasted the hottest of the hot spots in late 2013. Frequent clashes erupted between and among vigilantes, cartels, gangs, self-defense units, ad hoc law enforcers, the judicial police, and the armed forces. The Tierra Caliente and other zones in the state resembled a Tolstoyan battlefield strewn with corpses. Will Peña Nieto be able to win, or at least manage, the drug war so that Mexicans can feel safe in their homes, schools, workplaces, and streets?

I am indebted to an array of experts and institutions for helping me address this question. Above all, scores of professionals from the military, law-enforcement, diplomatic, intelligence, and political communities from the United States and Mexico furnished trenchant insights into criminal organizations, their leadership, structures, assets, methods, allies, locations, and weaknesses. For obvious reasons, our conversations must remain off the record.

Similarly, courageous journalists who risk their lives to cover the crime beat privately shared remarkable insights. I look forward to attending their Pulitzer Prize ceremonies. I must mention Ildefonso Ortiz, an investigate reporter for the *Monitor* of McAllen, Texas, who courageously allows his by-line to appear in first-rate articles about the Gulf Cartel, Los Zetas, border atrocities, and related subjects. Longtime friend Dudley Althaus, who served as bureau chief for the *Houston Chronicle*, knows more about Mexico than I have forgotten and has been a gold mine of information. I apologize to other U.S. reporters who would phone with straightforward inquiries only to find themselves pummeled with questions. These Fourth Estate mavens included William Booth and Nick Miroff (*Washington Post*); Tracy Wilkinson and Marjorie Miller (*Los Angeles Times*); Randal C. Archibold and Ginger Thompson (*New York Times*); David Luhnow, Jose de Cordoba, and Nicolas Casey (*Wall Street Journal*); Sandra Dibble (*UT-San Diego*); Lynn Brezosky (*San Antonio Express-News*); David Agren (*USA Today*); David Graham (*Thompson Reuters*); Diana Washington Valdez (*El Paso Times*); Greg Flakus (*Voice of America*); Deborah Hastings (*New York Daily News*); Kathy Corcoran, Mark Stevenson, and Olga Rodriguez (Associated Press); and Jonathan Levin (Bloomberg).

Articles by Silvia Otero López and Ricardo Alemán (*El Universal*); Abel Barajas and René Delgado (*Reforma*); José Carreño Carlón, Leo Zuckerman, Jorge Fernández Menéndez, Francisco Garfias, and María Amparo Casar (*Excélsior*); Julio Hernández López (*La Jornada*); Julio Scherer, J. Jesús Esquivel, José González Olmos, and Anabel Hernández García (*Proceso*); and other Mexican journalists provided invaluable insights into security issues.

I would be remiss not to express appreciate to academic colleagues who are über experts on Mexico: Bruce Bagley (University of Miami), John J. Bailey (Georgetown University), David Shirk (University of San Diego), Agustín Basave Benítez (distinguished professor and administrator at the Ibero-American University and author of the incomparable *Mexicanidad y esquizofrenia*), Nathan P. Jones (James A. Baker III Institute for Public Policy, Rice University), Guillermo Suárez Mier (American University), Ambassador to Chile Otto Granados Roldán (formerly at the Instituto Tecnológico y de Estudios Superiores de Monterrey), and Tyler R White (University of Nebraska–Lincoln).

Professor White thoughtfully included in a book a revised version of a paper that I gave on "Mexican Governors: The New Viceroys" at the Great Plains National Security Education Consortium on March 1, 2012. The other editors of the volume are Courtney Hillebrecht and Patrice McMahon. It will be published by Routledge in late 2013 and is titled *State Responses to Human Security: At Home and Abroad*.

Among the Mexicans who agreed to extensive—and amazingly helpful—interviews were Ing. Guillermo Flores Velasco, Juan Gabriel Valencia Benavides, Fred Álvarez Palafox, Alejandro Hope, Óscar Aguilar

Asencio, and Cuauhtémoc Ibarra. During our meals together, they provided both intellectual and culinary nourishment.

Editors of previously published works have graciously allowed me to draw from these books and monographs. Above all, I wish to thank Virginia Curtis Horowitz, president of Transaction Publishing, who granted permission for me to quote from two books: *Mexico: Narco-Violence and a Failed State?* (2010) and *The Executioner's Men: Los Zetas, Rogue Soldiers, Criminal Entrepreneurs, and the Shadow State They Created* (co-authored with Samuel Logan in 2012). I also owe a huge debt of gratitude to her late husband, Professor Irving Louis Horowitz, a scholar's scholar, for his guidance, stimulation, and mastery of the English language.

Similarly, Dr. Antulio J. Echevarria II, director of research at the Strategic Studies Institute, the Army War College, allowed me to draw upon material from three SSI studies: *La Familia Drug Cartel: Implications for American Security* (December 2010), *Threat Posed by Mounting Vigilantism in Mexico* (September 2011), and *The Impact of President Felipe Calderón's War on Drugs on the Armed Forces: The Prospects for Mexico's "Militarization" and Bilateral Relations* (January 2013).

The staff at the Reference Desk and Inter-Library Loan Department of the College of William & Mary's Earl Gregg Swem Library is composed of latter-day James Bonds. There was nothing that they couldn't track down in Williamsburg or at libraries around the world. Computer gurus in the Information Technology Center adroitly came to my rescue on more occasions than I can count. Among those gifted specialists on whom I relied heavily were Joe Cunningham, Karin Juraszek, and Julie Martin. Let's hope Virginia's governor decides to give them—and their colleagues in the university—a raise after four lean years.

Steve Catalano, the senior editor for history, politics, and security issues at Praeger Publishers (ABC-CLIO), suggested the subject of this book and responded quickly, patiently, and inventively to all needs that arose during its writing, editing, and publication. ABC-CLIO's Nicole Azze also lent a helping hand whenever the need arose.

Project manager Bhuvaneswari Rathinam at PreMediaGlobal epitomized intelligence, courteousness, and sangfroid—even when tables got mixed up and deadlines were not met.

The manuscript editor Sarah Wales-McGrath proved herself to be an impeccable wordsmith, an amazingly thorough reader, and a painstaking champion of consistency. She is truly an editor's editor.

Without the many contributions of William & Mary stellar law student Lindsey C. Nicolai, the manuscript would never have seen the light of day. She meticulously researched, proofread, improved the prose, and even re-keyed portions of a chapter that the author (or a goblin) inadvertently erased.

My wonderful wife Bryan Holt Grayson provided unwavering encouragement, extraordinary forbearance, the patience of Job, and scrumptious meals that sustained me during hundreds of hours at the computer. This book is dedicated to our grandchildren Jake, Grady, Will, Liza, Maggie, and baby Owen.

With so many helping hands, any errors that crept into these pages rest with the author.

After an overview of twentieth-century Mexican political events, this book (1) examines the informal "Rules" of narco-trafficking, (2) describes the United States' interdiction of drugs from Colombia, (3) analyzes the Gulf Cartel and Los Zetas, (4) describes the Sinaloa Cartel and its allies and enemies, (5) evaluates Calderón's approach toward these and other mafias, (6) focuses on the impact of a militarized drug war on Mexican society, (7) homes in on Peña Nieto's strategy for combatting cartel violence, (8) focuses on the status of the rule of law in Mexico, (9) keys in on enablers of organized crime, and (10) offers conclusions about prospects for diminishing the bloodshed arising from Mexico's struggle with the underground.

Introduction

More than four decades after his death in 1970, former president Lázaro Cárdenas del Río remains an iconic figure to the Mexican people. More than 1,000 cities and villages bear his name, as do an untold number of streets such as the Lázaro Cárdenas Central Axis in Mexico City; highways in Guadalajara, Monterrey, and Mexicali were named for him; every state has dozens of statues that proclaim his glory; citizens venerate him as one of the nation's most admired politicians; Google records tens of thousands of hits for his name; authors have written scores of books, chapters, and articles about him; and March 18, the date in 1938 when he nationalized foreign oil companies, represents a "day of national dignity." Foreigners also revere his memory: Serbians named the Setaliste Lazaro Kardenasa promenade in Belgrade for him; the Spanish erected a monument dedicated to his admitting defeated Republicans after that country's civil war in the 1930s; Barcelona has its Calle Lázaro Cárdenas; and the Russians awarded him the Lenin Peace Prize in 1955.[1]

Who was this man whom historians sometimes refer to as Mexico's Franklin Delano Roosevelt? Why did his tenure (1934–1940) leave such an indelible mark on the nation and the challenges it confronts today? How did he help stabilize a large country—now threatened by criminal organizations, violent teachers, and anti-oil reform zealots—in a region beset by revolution, rebellions, and coups d'état. Can newly elected president Enrique Peña Nieto recuperate the power once enjoyed by the chief executive, but diminished greatly in recent years?

EARLY LIFE

The eldest son among eight children, when his father died 16-year-old Lázaro quit school to work as a printer's devil, a jail keeper, and a tax collector to support his lower-middle-class family in Jiquilpan, a sleepy town in the central-west state of Michoacán known for configuring jewelry from jade, turquoise, and other semiprecious stones. Meanwhile, the fragile Monarch Butterflies wintered 175 miles away at the opposite end of the state.

As a child he confessed that "I was fixated on the idea of achieving fame . . . liberating the country from the yoke of oppression."[2] As he grew into manhood, he found himself swept up in the fury and passion of the 1910 revolution when reformer Francisco I. Madero detonated the overthrow of long-ruling dictator Porfirio Díaz. Cárdenas, who sought a father figure, became a protégé of General Plutarco Elías Calles, a top commander of the triumphant "Constitutionalist" forces who welcomed disciples. After the four-year tenure of his ally Álvaro Obregón, Calles ascended to the presidency in 1924. As a result, the young officer won the accolade of "*bravo jefe*" for his valor in battle and eventually ascended through the ranks to become a major general. Earlier, as a colonel, he had observed the arrogance of U.S. and European oil companies who treated their holdings in the Veracruz area as a corporate fiefdom—with inferior dining facilities, living accommodations, medical facilities, and compensation for Mexicans. The multinational corporations had not built schools for Mexican children, but they did take advantage of underground pipelines to the coast to evade tax payments. Eager for powerful allies, the firms attempted to ingratiate themselves with Cárdenas in 1925 with a $50,000 gift and a luxurious Packard—both of which he rejected as he continued to navigate the area's rut-filled, unpaved roads in his aging Hudson.[3] He did take the side of the Petróleo Unión against a company-funded Single Union (Sindicato Único), but no satisfactory resolution of the conflict crystalized. At this time Cárdenas began to "toy with the idea of expelling the oil companies from Mexican soil and abolishing the existence of that 'state within the state.' "[4]

GOVERNOR OF MICHOACÁN

Calles, who attained the informal title of *Jefe Máximo* or (Maximum Chief), rewarded this *chamaco* (kid) by ensuring his election as Michoacán governor in 1928.

In this office the austere, arrogant, libidinous general put into practice revolutionary tenets embedded in the 1917 Constitution, which he had absorbed from another mentor, General Francisco J. Mújica. In accord with the socially progressive fundamental law, the state executive spurred unionization, educational reform, improved health care, and the break-up of haciendas. From large land holdings, he accelerated the creation of *ejidos*, which were communal farms inhabited mainly by the local Tarascan Indians and small farmers. After all, Tarascan blood flowed through his mestizo veins.

This indigenous community, known today as Purépecha, which had enjoyed the protection of Michoacán's first bishop, Vasco de Quiroga, conferred upon the handsome mustachioed leader the same appellation applied to the beloved holy father who fought their enslavement in the Colonial era—*Tata* (Father).

Tata embraced the cause of the Indians but deplored a master-supplicant relationship. As one of his aides wrote: "What impressed me most was the strict paternal commitment with which he rejected any attempts to kneel to him or kiss his hand, which . . . the village elders wanted to do in recognition of his authority. He would take them by the hand with cordial energy and raise them up so that they looked him in the eye."[5]

Unlike Múgica, a fierce Jacobin, Cárdenas did not persecute the Roman Catholic prelates, as occurred with a vengeance in states such as Tabasco, although he did limit the number of priests in Michoacán. In addition, he adhered to Free Masonry, which favored secular education, civil liberties, and the assistance of the poor peasantry. Today's Grand Lodge in Michoacán bears Cárdenas's name. His relative tolerance aside, Governor Cárdenas took a leave of absence from the statehouse to fight Cristeros, militant Catholics who revolted against Calles, an atheist and freemason, who in 1926 enforced anti-Church provisions in the 1917 Constitution. These moves included registering priests, banning the clergy's right to vote, outlawing public Masses, and forbidding the Church from owning property.[6] Bishops closed churches and priests were castigated during the three-year conflict known as the Cristero Rebellion. Its rallying cry "¡Viva Cristo Rey!" (Long Live Christ the King!). This showdown took the lives of some 40 priests and 90,000 combatants, a third of whom were Cristeros. During this confrontation, Cárdenas favored conciliation and compromise in lieu of hangings and firing squads. He befriended Luis María Martínez, bishop of Morelia, capital of Michoacán, and the two men often ironed out religious disputes to avoid bloodshed.

Large landowners and other powerful economic interests that Díaz had coddled took umbrage at the no-nonsense governor's redistributionist policies. He showed his contempt for them and for the industrialists when he ordered the expropriation of the plants that had shuttered their doors rather than implement labor regulations.[7] He curbed their influence by forging a phalanx of loyal allies. Not only were the Indians devoted to him, but he founded the Michoacán Revolutionary Confederation of Labor (CRMDT), which became the first mass structure created by a government and vertically linked to it. This corporativist organization, an echo of the viceregal past, would loom large in a few years.[8]

Public monies funded the mobilization of CRMDT "shock troops," which, in keeping with Cárdenas's manipulative style, fomented clashes over land ownership. Just when it seemed that violence would erupt, the governor would ride in by automobile or horse and benevolently resolve the dispute—invariably in favor of the peasant or small farmer. Through a "purifying commission," the CRMDT also endeavored to purge teachers who favored the Church and failed to advance the ideology of the Mexican revolution.[9]

Cárdenas's social initiatives proved costly, were often afflicted by mismanagement and corruption, and forced the state to borrow heavily to meet its obligation—a practice even more egregious today than in the 1930s.

A medley of events—an incredibly bloody revolution (1910–1916), the lethal struggle in the Cristero War (1926–1929), the assassination of president-elect Álvaro Obregón (1928), and a depleted treasury—encouraged the Machiavellian Calles to devise control mechanisms lest Mexico return to the Hobbesian state of the unfettered violence in which upwards of a million people may have perished.[10]

The venerable Jefe Máximo, who ruled personally and through minions for a dozen years, contributed greatly to stability and continuity in 1929 by forming the revolutionary party. In theory, this farrago of revolutionary generals, local machine bosses, small-party honchos, trade unions, and campesino groups allowed participants to retain their identities. In fact, Calles quickly emerged as *primus enter pares*, and the confederal structure of the National Revolutionary Party (PNR), a forerunner of today's Institutional Revolutionary Party (PRI). He fashioned a dominant party as a counterpoise to the ambitious revolutionary generals, many of whom served as governors to "force them to resolve their conflicts within an institutional context rather than on the battlefield."[11]

Calles, who once said, "I love Cárdenas like a son," paved the way for the activist governor to reach the presidency in 1934 under the auspices of the so-called revolutionary party.

POWER OF THE JEFE MÁXIMO

The Jefe Máximo selected party leaders, highlighted these worthies at public events, magnified the organization's accomplishments, and required public employees to donate a week's salary to the cause. These resources enabled the party to finance campaigns, trumpet public works and social activities, and recruit new cadres. From the beginning the party was the government and vice-versa. Needless to say, Calles handpicked candidates for major offices and in the early 1930s, three of his sons held governorships. As a *callista* provisional president admitted: "The PNR [National Revolutionary Party] is frankly a government party. . . . The

Government has the program of the Revolution; the party has the program of the Revolution and of the Government. . . . The party will be a sincere collaborator of the administration. . . . This is the mission of the PNR and for this I say that the PNR is a government party."[12]

In the run-up to the 1934 presidential election, Calles pondered whom to name as candidate among several aspirants, including Cárdenas, who had headed both the War Ministry and the PNR. The favorite of the powerful revolutionary general became evident when his son, Rodolfo, a federal deputy, extoled the merits of the *michoacano*. This informal Selection-by-proxy (*dedazo*) became the revolutionary party's nomination artifice until 1999, when President Ernesto Zedillo Ponce de León (1994–2000) organized a primary to select the PRI's standard-bearer.

Calles anticipated that the energetic, dashing Michoacán notable would allow him to continue pulling the strings from behind the scenes even as he revived the image of the regime whose commitment to land reform, labor rights, and educational advancement had waned. Although destined to amass great wealth, Cárdenas's reputation for honesty, political acuity, and moderate anticlericalism deemed important in unifying the party. He paid lip service to a Six Year Plan. Like the 1917 Constitution, this document resembled a sales prospectus inasmuch as "it was a patchwork of compromise, contradictions, and Utopian affirmations." As the nominee's platform, it was "an imprecise set of directives that provided neither central planning nor machinery for enforcement."[13]

The retired general had no intention of serving as anyone's puppet. He endorsed the party's nebulous program, but he ran a campaign designed to emancipate himself from the clutches of Calles and his retinue. He faced only token opposition. Still, he pursued the nation's highest office as if it were a life-or-death struggle. The 39-year-old traveled 1,600 miles by car, train, horseback, and on foot to visit every state and major city, as well as scores of small towns, ejidos, union halls, and social gatherings. Not only was he striving to throw off Calles's yoke, but he was eager to learn about the impoverished south and other parts of the country unknown to him, identify talent that would strengthen his entourage, and indelibly create the image as the people's national Tata. He was one of the few prominent politicians who disdained bodyguards, believing that the people would look after his well-being.

CÁRDENAS WINS THE PRESIDENCY

During his seven-month campaign Cárdenas crisscrossed the country, traveling more than 34,000 miles by plane, automobile, train, ship, and horse.[14] This venture enabled him to visit parts of the country he didn't know, recruit a team of his own, and vividly imprint his image on the psyche of his countrymen. He polled 98 percent (2,225,000) of the ballots cast compared with 24,395 for Antonio Villarreal González, the hapless candidate of the Revolutionary Confederation of Independent Parties. His victory ushered in a new style of leadership that refused to bow to dictates of the previous éminence grise. Distinguished scholars have detailed the collision between the new president and the Jefe Máximo, with the latter ultimately forced into exile in the United States.[15] Suffice it to say, Cárdenas acted with autocratic élan to seize control of the pulleys and levers of power. He raised salaries in the army to curry its favor, replaced Calles's allies with loyalist officers, extended the presidential term to six years (*sexenio*), forced the resignation of legislators who balked at his pro-union labor policies, asserted the right to ban the dissemination of newspapers and magazines that "denigrate the nation or the government," and imposed a state monopoly on the importation and sale of newsprint as a means to punish or reward publications. He also ousted 14 pro-Calles governors, including the Jefe Máximo's own son and namesake.

Cárdenas promoted a pragmatic truce to the church-state quarrel. No friend of Roman Catholicism—he criticized the Church for having "delayed the nation's social and economic evolution"[16]—the new president officially denounced Calles's merciless persecution of Catholics and no longer suppressed worship. The former Michoacán governor was fond of saying that he was "tired of closing churches and finding them full." He would have preferred to open them and "find them empty."[17] Nevertheless, he ordered all schools to teach socialism, Marxism, atheism, and sex education—a curriculum that outraged a number of prominent Catholics who, in 1939, created the pro-clerical, elite-led National Action Party (PAN).[18]

In fact, many of the regime's education inspectors notified Catholic schools of impending visits, which gave the teaching sisters an opportunity to reverse a picture that displayed the Virgin Mary to show the stern aesthetic face of president Benito Juárez, renowned for separating church and state, that graced the other side.

Cárdenas's devotion to the dispossessed highlighted his six-year tenure, during which he distributed some 44 million acres of land, more than all of his predecessors combined. He also established a credit bank to help fund projects for ejidos. In the process, he shattered the spine of the landowning elite, who excoriated him as a "socialist," a "Stalinist," and a "Marxist."

Establishment epithets aside, Cárdenas remained devoted to the working class. Amid the Great Depression, the government enacted the 1931 Federal Labor Law, which greatly enhanced the state's ability to regulate union activities and strikes.

Even though elected by a landslide, Cárdenas quickly showed that he was an inveterate reformer. Unable to manipulate his successor, the irascible Calles voiced the angst of businessmen when he condemned work stoppages, often backed by Cárdenas, as a threat to the "economic life of the nation" that constituted "acts of treason."[19] One of the strikes was against the telephone company in which Calles held stock.

Calles began to plot to depose the new chief executive. Enough was enough: On April 9, 1936, a military officer stormed into Calles's home and rousted him out of bed even as the ex-president was pouring over a Spanish version of *Mein Kampf*, Adolph Hitler's manifesto for Germany's aggrandizement. He was arrested, rushed to the nearest airport, and flown to Texas with a fist of lackeys. His reign of power abruptly ended, although he was allowed to return to Mexico before his death in 1945.

Led by the Electrical Workers' Union, most segments of organized labor threw their weight behind Cárdenas in his defiance of Calles. Their fealty encouraged the populist chief executive to support the formation of "a single organization of industrial workers that would end the inter-union strife that is equally pernicious to the interests of workers, employers, and the government."[20] In addition to promoting stability, Cárdenas sought to channel peasant and worker activists away from class conflict and toward strengthening the state and advancing "Revolutionary Nationalism," the amorphous social, redistributionist, and nationalistic goals enshrined in the 1917 Constitution.

Cárdenas tightened his control of trade unions by spurring the merger of the major labor centrals. These included the Regional Confederation of Mexican Workers (CROM), the "Purified CROM" headed by intellectual communist Vicente Lombardo Toledano, the General Confederation of Federal District Workers (CGOCM) led by Fidel "Don Fidel" Velázquez Sánchez, and small organizations. The pro-Cárdenas unions evolved into the Confederation of Mexican Workers (CTM) in February 1936. By the end of the year, the new umbrella grouping claimed to represent 1,200 organizations and some 200,000 workers. As was the case with campesinos, they were drilled as a "paramilitary" unit but not armed.[21] The CTM gave impetus to the nationalization of their nation's railroads, whose administration was turned over to the Railroad Workers' Union. This move backfired as the rail system suffered from poor management, insufficient maintenance, unreliable service, and a politicized workforce.

TAKEOVER OF THE OIL INDUSTRY

More dramatic was the nationalization of foreign oil companies in 1938 —an event touted as Mexico's declaration of economic independence from multinational giants. Article 27 of the Constitution stipulated that

"All natural resources in national territory are property of the nation, and private exploitation may only be carried out through concessions." The drafters of the 1917 Fundamental Law couldn't enforce this provision. Over the years, though, protracted disputes, involving wages and benefits between the Oil Workers' Union (STPRM) and management, sparked the takeover at a time when Mexico was the world's second largest producer of black gold. The crisis culminated at 9:45 p.m. on March 18, 1938, when the husky-voiced Cárdenas announced in a radio broadcast the nationalization of the Mexico's oil industry, including equipment and machinery belonging to 17 U.S. and European corporations, the most notable of which were the Mexican Eagle, Royal Dutch/Shell, and Standard Oil of New Jersey. As he said in a solemn speech:

It is the sovereignty of the nation which is thwarted through the maneuvers of foreign capitalists who, forgetting that they have formed themselves into Mexican companies, now attempt to elude the mandates and avoid the obligations placed upon them by the authorities of this country.[22]

The decree precipitated an overwhelming response. In reaction to the CTM's call for a show of support, some 200,000 people thronged Mexico's City Plaza de la Constitution (*Zócalo*). The call for contributions to honor Cárdenas's pledge that "Mexico will honor her foreign debt" met a resounding response: "State governors, high Church officials, patriotic grande dames, peasants, students—all the numberless and picturesque types of Mexicans—pitched in what they had, including money, jewels, even homely domestic objects, chickens, turkeys, and pigs."[23]

The demonstrators, hoisting banners such as "They shall not scoff at Mexican laws," screamed themselves hoarse as Cárdenas greeted them from a central balcony. Nearby hung the bell that Father Miguel Hidalgo had tolled 128 years earlier in the town of Dolores to proclaim the nation's fight for independence from Spain.[24]

Cárdenas took advantage of his popularity to reorganize the revolutionary party. He spurred its restructuring along corporatist lines —namely, automatic affiliation with the party through one's occupation. These group-focused "sectors" in the renamed Party of the Mexican Revolution (PRM) included peasants, blue-collar workers, white-collar and professional members, and the military—with the latter encompassing officers in an army grossly inflated by the revolution. Each collectivity exerted influence through a mass-membership organization with smaller constituent parts. These included the CTM, The National Peasant Confederation (CNC), and, later, the National Confederation of Popular Organizations (CNOP) for teachers, bureaucrats, artists, shopkeepers, doctors, lawyers, and other middle-class citizens. "Each sector's line of force reached from the centre through regions, states, and small localities, to provide candidates, ideas, power, and votes for the single, presidentially dominated party."[25]

In 1940 the military sector was discontinued mainly because politicians wanted to prevent the armed forces from becoming the mediator of disputes and the legitimator of each new administration. For their part, officers shied from the glare of public political involvement. Retired military men eager to remain active in partisan affairs gravitated to the CNOP.[26]

The chief executive extended the corporatist framework to domestic enterprises, which were formally barred from joining the revolutionary party. These "peak" bodies included chambers of commerce and associations for lawyers, bankers, insurance firms, large farmers, and stockbrokers. The leaders of these entities might not resonate to the dogma of Revolutionary Nationalism, but they were loath to alienate a government that could incite strikes, close down companies for real or perceived violations, and favor allies with contracts.

The PRM enabled Cárdenas to artfully divide and conquer to fortify the regime's sway over society. He separated the labor and peasant sectors lest their combined force exercise disproportionate influence. In the same vein, he placed unionized teachers and other public functionaries in the CNOP to spur creative competition for public posts rather than collaboration between blue-collar and white-collar unions. And while grassroots members of labor union locals theoretically exercised power from the bottom to the top, in reality the jefes of these units dominated their members in accord with the dictates of the president and the revolutionary party's bosses. In the case of the 300-member Congress (now 500 members), the sectors would vie for as many seats as possible. Once the party hierarchy with the imprimatur of the president allocated the candidacies, the sectors closed ranks. In other words, they endorsed the nominee of the revolutionary party regardless of his provenance. This spirit of "all for one and one for all" extended to the selection of governors, senators, mayors, and other elected officials.

In many ways, Cárdenas resembled Chicago's crafty mayor Anton F. Cermak—portrayed by Kelsey Grammar in the popular television series *The Boss*—for his prowess at balancing antagonistic interests and settling disputes. Cermak's tenure ended in 1933 when a shooter killed him while attempting to assassinate President Roosevelt.[27]

Meta-constitutional powers magnified presidential clout: the dedazo enabled him to discourage backbiting from presidential aspirants, who did not want to offend the incumbent. Meanwhile, this device allowed him to select his successor in consultation with other power brokers— in the party, the business community, the Church, and the military. Unaudited bank accounts ensured a princely life style, as well as millions of dollars in resources with which to shower largesse on family members and other allies. And his ability to approve and remove governors like toadies permitted him to influence affairs at the state level.

The capriciousness associated with a near monopoly on power and access to the state's wealth exacerbated the corruption, which had infused Mexican society since the colonial period. No segment escaped cancerous venality, which was carried out under informal rules of the game. Petróleos Mexicanos (PEMEX), the state firm established after the 1938 expropriation, became a cesspool of dishonesty, especially under Joaquín "La Quina" Hernández Galicia, the redoubtable head of the Oil Workers' Union (STPRM). Payment for tenured jobs, automatic access to work for family members and chums, the exploitation of retirees through forced labor on union farms, the suppression of foes to the "official" slate of candidates in intramural elections, and the enrichment of leaders became the norm. Traditionally, the government was complicit in or ignored such scandalous behavior as long as the STPRM chief exhibited obeisance to the president, did not embarrass the chief executive, delivered votes to the revolutionary party, and kept order within his ranks.

CÁRDENAS SELECTS A SUCCESSOR

Many observers expected Cárdenas to name his ambitious mentor, the strident Jacobin, Francisco Mújica, as his heir-apparent. Instead, the general-turned-politician selected the moderate Manuel Ávila Camacho, who "marked a distinctive shift from the populism of the 1930s. The institutionalization of the Revolution and the official party had begun."[28] In accord with his motto "National Unity," the chief executive eliminated the PRI's military sector as a means to curb the involvement of the armed forces in the affairs of the national government. Porfirio Díaz once said that "a dog with a bone in its mouth will not bite." In this spirit, ranking army officers opted for governorships, the accumulation of wealth, and the recital of tales to grandchildren about heroic exploits on battlefields.

He also greatly diminished the taxing authority of states and municipalities to ensure their dependency on the federal government.

Ávila Camacho healed several festering wounds. He propitiated the Church with the assurance that "I am a believer." He slowed the establishment of ejidos and inserted the more pragmatic Fidel Velázquez as head of the powerful CTM, replacing the Marxist Lombardo Toledano, who was expelled from the confederation in 1948. The redoubtable Velázquez, who served until 1997, took control of the organization. Although he epitomized Revolutionary Nationalism, Don Fidel undermined Marxists and prevented Communism from gaining influence among working people, even as his labor movement became more conservative, autocratic, and corrupt.

Ávila Camacho rejected Cárdenas's devotion to socialist education. He also stimulated the economy by creating a credit-dispensing National Development Bank (NAFINSA), acquiring the Monterrey-based Altos Hornos de México iron and steel complex, and created the Mexican Social Security Institute (IMSS), whose members have access to health care and pensions. By the mid-1940s he had resolved the oil companies' claims for compensation, and PEMEX petroleum once again flowed northward. In contrast to Mexico's neutrality during World War I, Mexico cast its lot with the Allies in World War II. He backed the 1942 formation of a joint U.S.-Mexican Defense Commission to co-ordinate military action and train Mexican officers at U.S. bases, and credits and discounts facilitated Mexican purchases of equipment to upgrade its unprofessional armed forces. The torpedoing of Mexican tankers by German U-boats provoked Ávila Camacho to secure a declaration of war on May 30, 1942. While it did not generate noticeable enthusiasm, this action excited little opposition.[29]

Ávila Camacho's older sibling Maximino became one of the many "inconvenient brothers" (*hermanos incómodos*) who have vexed Mexico's presidents. In the Cristero War, the fanatical Maximino had burned villages and shot prisoners; a convinced antileftist, he had balked at introducing Cárdenas's social reforms when he was governor of Puebla, and he thought that he, rather than Manuel, should have followed Cárdenas into the presidency. His extreme behavior, which included a threat on the life of Miguel Alemán Valdés and unbounded ambition, may explain his assassination.

As a result, the outgoing chief executive opted for someone who showed devotion to revolutionary principles, had experience as a governor, and had not served in the military. This man was Miguel Alemán Valdés, 46, who had managed Avila Camacho's presidential campaign, served as Gobernación secretary, and gained a reputation as a forceful and successful advocate for defending miners and other exploited workers against corporations.

With the emergence of a new nonmilitary leadership, the official party altered its name to the Institutional Revolutionary Party (PRI). This change reflected a shift of emphasis from peasant and union rights to the private sector, which—in concert with the state—would balance Mexico's dependence on primary product without giving a fillip to industrialization.

Hand-in-hand with this name change came what would be termed a Golden Age in bilateral relations. Especially noteworthy was the assignment of 300 volunteers, including 30 pilots, to train in the United States as the Mexican Expeditionary Air Force. In March 1945 Squadron 201—known as the "Aztec Eagles"—set off for the Philippines to help liberate the island of Luzon. Five Mexican pilots perished in combat, and their unit won praise from General Douglas A. MacArthur, commander of the Allied Forces in the South Pacific.

Mexico and Brazil, which sent an army unit to Italy, were the only Latin American states to dispatch military forces overseas on behalf of the Allies.

Bilateral relations had improved to the point that Harry S Truman (March 3–6, 1947) and Miguel Alemán (April 27, 1947) exchanged official visits. David McCullough writes that the acclaim received by the U.S. visitor was "thrilling." A beaming Truman returned the "¡Vivas!" of the throngs—one woman shouted, "Viva Missouri!" To the Mexican legislature, Truman said: "I have never had such a welcome in my life."[30]

On September 2, 1947, Mexico was among the signatories of the Inter-American Treaty of Reciprocal Assistance, known as the Rio Treaty, which outlined a system of mutual defense on the part of Western Hemisphere nations against the Soviet Union, its satellites, and other potential outside aggressors.

The new administration ushered in a fresh period in Mexican politics. Although his father had fought in the revolution, Alemán had not taken part in a single battle. Despite his record of crossing swords with the business tycoons in courtrooms, the handsome, mustachioed Veracruz native was determined to power economic growth.

He received economic assistance from Washington to construct schools, launched flood control and irrigation projects in the country's north to benefit agrobusinesses, extend the nation's rail and highway networks, and advance industrial development. When he left office in 1952 there were 9,920 miles of paved roads—four times as many as at the time of his inauguration. At the same time he encouraged inexpensive hydroelectric power, promoted massive irrigation initiatives, and shielded large landowners from the expropriation of their property. In addition, he completed a new campus for the keystone of the nation's university system, the National Autonomous University of Mexico (UNAM), and relied on a new generation of economists and other technocrats rather than political hacks.

Alemán's most notable accomplishment was attracting investment in plants and factories from abroad as the cynosure of Import-Substitution Industrialization (ISI). He spurred "stabilizing development"—a strategy that suppressed the wage demands of the CTM affiliates and provided a cornucopia of benefits to investors whom he cocooned from competition. As a result U.S. equity capital and loans cascaded across the border at an ever-faster pace, growing five-fold between 1950 and 1970, from $566 million to $2.8 billion. Kimberly-Clark, the Ford Motor Company, Sears Roebuck, Proctor & Gamble, Colgate, Goodyear, and John Deere were among the scores of major firms that helped constitute Mexico's "economic miracle."

Gaudy neon signs flashed invitations to "Fume Raleigh" ("Smoke Raleighs") and "Tome Coca-Cola—La Pausa Que Refresca" ("Drink Coca-Cola—the Pause that Refreshes")—as Madison Avenue stamped its imprint on Avenida Insurgentes, Paseo de la Reforma, and other shop-infested thoroughfares.[31]

At first Alemán depended heavily on tariffs to stimulate domestic and foreign investment in the country. He kept duties low on raw materials purchased abroad while imposing tax rates that often exceeded 100 percent on imported manufactures. By the late 1950s Mexico had replaced tariffs with import permits—licenses issued by the government to importers—as the principal protectionist tool. Revenues from these permits stimulated industrialization and, this tool limited Mexican purchases of foreign goods; the policy also conserved valuable foreign exchange for only the most essential items. Currency devaluations in 1949 and 1954 provided yet another safeguard to emerging industries by markedly undervaluing the peso, which further discouraged imports. Licensing in the economic sphere found a parallel in the licensing of interest groups, which kept them under the regime's corporatist thumb.

The government gave impetus to this economic miracle by providing investors with roads, rail spurs, airports, and improved seaports. The benefactors also received tax benefits, low-interest credit, subsidized oil and gas, cheap electricity, and the assurance by the CTM's Fidel Velázquez of a docile labor force, provided that jobs were plentiful, salaries satisfactory, fringe benefits available, and corruption ignored.

Although formally outside the revolutionary party, some members of the private sector affiliated with the PRI's Popular Sector. These Friends of Miguel flourished as long as they played ball with the movers and shakers of the system. In return for spurning strikes, union grandees dispensed jobs and perquisites to their members; meanwhile, sticky-fingered bureaucrats and politicians fattened their bank accounts from graft paid by businesses to satisfy unfathomable rules, regulations, and ad hoc requirements. They handed over the payola in order to consolidate and enlarge their lucrative monopolies and oligopolies.

The government's ubiquitous involvement in the economy provided ample opportunities for kickbacks and other forms of illicit enrichment. Alemán and his entourage turned a blind eye to official corruption that might find, for example, a middle-level functionary refusing to sign an import permit until the applicant forked over a generous "commission." "Public works in particular enriched many officials and Alemán himself bought up much of Acapulco before building a new airport and ocean front boulevard in the resort as well as a new road linking it to Mexico City." A subsequent president placed Alemán at the head of the National Tourism Council (CNT), and he proceeded to globetrot publicizing the industry that helped make him one of Mexico's richest men. In the words of Valentín Campa, a Communist railroad workers' leader: "Government is business and business is government."[32]

A reporter for *El Universal* who criticized the government's economic policy quickly found himself unemployed. The ubiquitous venality ignited criticism, and the PRI became the target of attacks. To restore popular faith in the ruling party, Alemán nominated Adolfo Ruiz Cortines, a former governor of Veracruz and ex-minister of Gobernación, and a man noted for his impeccable character, to succeed him in 1952.[33] He required functionaries to report their assets at the beginning and end of their government service, practiced vise-like control over state expenditures, led the drive to eliminate malaria, implemented a Rural Social Welfare plan to uplift the peasantry, and successfully worked to grant suffrage for women.

NATIONAL LIBERATION MOVEMENT

Cárdenas deplored Alemán's pro-capitalist policies. The unwritten rule of Mexican politics specified that new presidents did not expose questionable activities of predecessors, and former chief executives remained out of the news except for ceremonial events. Tata Lázaro maintained a relatively low profile for two decades after leaving the presidency except for brief service as Secretary of War (1943–1945). However, in light of President Adolfo López Mateos's (1958–1964) coolness toward Fidel Castro's revolution, the former chief executive formed the National Liberation Movement (MLN) a "civic organization" to unite the disparate elements of Mexico's left—a move regarded as radical by Washington policymakers, then in the throes of the Cold War. It was ironic that the president who had done so much to promote the dominance of the official party would launch a dissident force.

The PRI responded pragmatically. Several prominent intellectuals joined forces with Cárdenas, but the MLN never threatened to subvert the government. Instead, it lobbied for fairer income distribution, national control of oil and other natural resources, and an independent foreign policy. Its program, in the words of scholar Olga Pellicer de Brody, was "written within the vocabulary of reformist movements."[34] The regime co-opted the movement as it had done with most groups across a broad left-right spectrum. Still, Washington officials, rattled by Senator Joe McCarthy's anticommunist tirades, considered asking the University of Pennsylvania to retract a speaking invitation tendered to Cárdenas because they perceived the MLN as a subversive group. The CIA went ever further, characterizing the movement as "a rabidly anti–United States, pro-Cuba Communist front."[35]

Nevertheless, Mexico adhered to its pro-business course, and the chief executive often involved himself in investment initiatives. For example,

Gustavo Díaz Ordaz (1964–1970) phoned the head of Banamex, the nation's largest bank, and told him that "we must add value to sulfur produced in Mexico." The bank dutifully joined a Dutch firm to import phosphate rock from North Africa for use in making sulfur-phosphate fertilizer in Mexico. The venture proceeded smoothly until Díaz Ordaz's successor decided that the state should take over fertilizer output. The chief executive wasted no time in driving Banamex out of the business by forcing it to charge unrealistically low prices and banning its importation of phosphate rock.[36]

When the carrot failed to work, presidents used the stick—with the force of a bludgeon. Student dissatisfaction with both political conditions and economic inequality erupted in the mid-1960s. In early 1966 a movement at UNAM forced the resignation of the rector. In subsequent months the government dispatched shock troops to restore order at universities in Morelia and Sonora. Díaz Ordaz saw the mobilization as forming part of a cabal. He often quoted the French novel *Clochemerle* to reinforce his view that violence, however innocuous it might seem at the beginning, can cascade out of control.

As campus unrest mounted in 1968, the president perceived himself as the target of young, leftist conspirators whose counterparts in France and the United States, respectively, had challenged the regimes of Charles De Gaulle and Lyndon B. Johnson, ultimately forcing the arrogant leaders to step down. In mid-August, several months before Mexico was scheduled to host the International Olympic Games, the student strike committee shifted from desultory marches to a huge demonstration that attracted 150,000 people to Mexico City's Zócalo central plaza. The dissidents waved placards castigating Díaz Ordaz as a "Criminal," "Hated Beast," and "Assassin." The confrontation boiled over on October 2, 1968, when military and police units fired on several thousand unarmed students, homemakers, and office workers decrying their nation's lack of freedom. When the smoke cleared, several hundred protesters and innocent bystanders lay dead. The count is unknown because authorities buried dozens, perhaps hundreds, of the fallen in unmarked graves.

Gobernación secretary Luis Echeverría Álvarez and the president's consiglieri at the time of the so-called Tlatelolco Massacre, succeed Díaz Ordaz in Los Pinos presidential residence. As a populist, he believed that affluent countries of the northern hemisphere should transfer resources to the impecunious nations of the southern part of the globe. Needless to say, he offended the business community with his "dependency" ideas and erratic economic policy. Especially outraged at his behavior were members of the "Monterrey Group," powerful entrepreneurs whose multi-national firms produced cement, beer, steel, synthetic fibers, and other items. Eugenio Garza Sada, the most important businessman of his generation, detested Echeverría to the point that he planned to launch a well-funded hard-hitting national newspaper to expose the corruption and irresponsibility of the regime. Before he could accomplish his goal, he was assassinated on September 17, 1973. Although the government blamed the crime on guerrillas, Jorge Fernández Menéndez, a prize-winning reporter, claims that the shadowy Federal Security Directorate (DFS) conceived, planned, and orchestrated this murder at the behest of the presidency.[37]

Echeverría named José López Portillo, a lawyer who had served as finance secretary, to succeed him in the 1970–1976 sexenio. An oil boom highlighted his administration. Mexico's success became the envy of a world foundering in recession. Such glamour, though, diverted attention from mounting "petrolization." This neologism describes an economy's becoming overheated by large black gold reserves; an overvalued currency; growing reliance on external credits to import an ever-escalating quantity of food, capital, and luxury goods; and a moribund rural sector whose small farmers flock to cities.

Like a heroin addict who sells his blood in the morning to get a "fix" from a well-heeled dealer at night, the arrogant López Portillo reacted to the pressures of petrolization by borrowing ever-more heavily from financial center banks, whose vaults overflowed with "petrodollars" deposited by oil-rich Mideast sheiks.

When international oil prices sagged and then plummeted, Mexico was staggering under a $100 billion debt by the early 1980s. Blaming financial interests for the rapid depreciation of the currency, a disoriented López Portillo nationalized Mexico's 34 banks, with combined assets of $14.3 billion. The two major institutions—Banamex and Bancomer—held 47 percent of the total. Many, if not all, the banks held large stock holdings in corporations. The September 1, 1982, takeover extended the government's control over the most productive segments of the economy.

The president agreed to rendezvous with the distraught bankers. After a few minutes of lavishing compliments on his guests, the chief executive asked: "Now what may I do for you?" When they raised the question of the expropriation, he assured them that "it was nothing personal" and that he was merely "looking out for the best interests of the country." The incredulous bankers disagreed but said they would go to court rather than use force to regain their property. López Portillo informed them that they had made a wise decision because he had "dispatched troops to protect the banks," adding: "I know what I have done is unconstitutional, so I am going to change the Constitution [to legalize my action]."[38] This gambit shook the confidence of the financial and business sectors, and constricted the PRI's ability to work with a powerful segment of the economy.

López Portillo's successor, Miguel de la Madrid Hurtado (1982–1988), supported "Moral Renovation" to burnish the badly tarnished image of the presidency and the PRI regime that he headed. His good intentions to stanch electoral fraud and clean up PEMEX came a cropper with the devastating El Grande earthquakes that struck Mexico and four other states in September 1985.

Any ward politician worth his patronage allotment could have clamped on a hard hat, rolled up his sleeves, and waded into the smoking rubble after the shocks killed at least 10,000 people and left tens of thousands homeless. However, the president neither ventured into the streets to help those injured nor did he show up on the balcony of the National Palace to offer sympathy and succor to grieving families assembled in the Zócalo central plaza below. The disaster illuminated the sweetheart deals that the government had made with unscrupulous cronies who cut corners and used inferior building material. For example, the National Medical Center of the Mexican Social Security System, Latin America's largest and most sophisticated hospital, fell like a house of cards. The head of the Urban Development Ministry had approved plans for the Juárez Hospital, which collapsed during the cataclysm because of shoddy construction.

No wonder a majority of respondents to public opinion surveys believe that Carlos Salinas de Gortari, the PRI's nominee in the 1988 presidential showdown, lost the election to Cuauhtémoc Cárdenas, former Michoacán governor and son of the revered Lázaro. Cuauhtémoc and other traditionalists had defected from the revolutionary party the year before. They regarded the cosmopolitan Salinas (1988–1994) as threatening the PRI's hammerlock on power by phasing out subsidies, diminishing welfare programs, lofting energy prices, and deepening a local version of perestroika. In 1989 these dissenters spawned the leftist-nationalist Democratic Revolutionary Party (PRD).

Detractors joked about Salinas's diminutive size, bald head, and floppy ears. As a CTM affiliate, the *petroleros* were expected to support the PRI standard-bearer, a Harvard-educated paladin of modernization, in his hard-fought electoral showdown against Cárdenas. In the fraud-suffused 1988 presidential campaign, La Quina actually voted for Salinas, whom he detested.[39] Meanwhile, he passed the word that union members were free to cast ballots for Cárdenas. After the election, Hernández Galicia and a sidekick had the temerity to publicly oppose Salinas's plans to reorganize the economy, intimating that transferring even the smallest part of the industry to private hands would precipitate refinery fires, ruptured pipelines, strikes, and a downturn in production.

The feisty young president quietly listened to such threats. In response, however, he dispatched federal police and army units to La Quina's modest home just off Avenida Roosevelt in Ciudad Madero, Tabasco, on January 10, 1989. Following a brief armed exchange with bodyguards, the troops rushed into the dwelling and whisked the supposedly "untouchable" strongman to Mexico City. Authorities later claimed to have found a cache of weapons in the residence of La Quina and placed him and 53 union stalwarts around the country behind bars. The federal prosecutor arraigned the labor chieftain on charges of resisting arrest, illegal weapons possession, arms smuggling, and "qualified" homicide. Although the last charge was dropped, the supposedly untouchable cacique remained in prison until December 16, 1997. To gain his release, La Quina pledged to refrain from political activities. At age 90, he did cast a ballot for his son for mayor of Ciudad Madero in the July 7, 2013, contest.

Was Salinas attempting to reform the venal oil sector? Not at all, according to the late political gadfly Heberto Castillo: "The January 10 action did not open the door to democratizing the petroleum union. It was not an opening, but greater government control of the trade unions."[40] The president replaced Hernández Galicía with an overseer who would do his bidding, even as PEMEX overflowed as a sewer of corruption.

After the death of La Quina's first replacement, Salinas installed Carlos Romero Deschamps as the union's secretary general on June 25, 1993. The porcine-faced power broker has served in the Chamber of Deputies, now holds a Senate seat, and was elected to another six-year term as leader of the Oil Workers Union in October 2012. He won unanimously by voice vote against a half-dozen contenders; however, colon cancer may abbreviate his term.[41] Unlike La Quina's modest appearance, Romero Deschamps enjoys Rolex watches, an apartment in one of Cancún's most exclusive zones, a yacht named *El Indominable* (The Indomitable), and heaping presents on his daughter Paulina, a modestly paid PEMEX employee. Her Facebook account, now deactivated, highlighted a custom-made Louis Vuitton Lickit PM Suhali purse, meals in the Nobu restaurant owned by actor Robert de Niro, Vega Sicilia wines, jet-set travel to exotic places, and English Bulldogs—Keiko, Boli, and Morgancita.[42]

In an attempt at even-handedness, Salinas also arrested a scion of a well-known banking family accused of manipulating the stock market. In addition, he sold the state-owned airline, the national telephone company (TELMEX), and steel mills; reprivatized the banking system that López Portillo had nationalized seven years before; launched a reform of ejidos (communal farms) to permit the occupants to sell, divide, or rent out their land to boost output; and promised to reorganize PEMEX along business lines. Most striking of all, he negotiated the North American Free Trade Agreement (NAFTA) with the United States and Canada. This pact, which reached from the Yukon to the Yucatán, promoted lowering and eliminating tariffs and nontariff barriers to give impulse to trade and investment.

Profligate spending also became a hallmark of the SNTE Teachers' Union, headed by the redoubtable Elba Esther Gordillo Morales, whom the late M. Delal Baer called "Jimmy Hoffa in a dress." An anonymously published book bore the title ¿*Elba de Troya o Lady MacBeth Gordillo?*—and it was filled with intercepted phone calls revealing her behind-the-back treachery even to supposed loyalists. Job-buying, sinecures in the Education Ministry, the illicit diversion of union funds to personal acquisitions, payoffs to politicians, and the promotion of teachers and principals based on loyalty rather than merit abound. Gordillo, also referred to as "La Maestra," acquired her position when her predecessor and lover Carlos Jonguitud Barrios proved unable to quell dissident members who were demanding a 100 percent pay increase. The government may have sparked the demonstrations as an excuse to rid itself of Jonguitud, a crude, corrupt cacique who had formed Vanguardia Revolucionaria, an organization parallel to the SNTE that used clubs, guns, and Molotov cocktails to battle opponents in the union. Gordillo did ask Salinas to accomplish the removal of Don Carlos with "dignity."[43]

Frustrated with demonstrations for the salary hike, Salinas brusquely summoned him to the Los Pinos presidential palace, told him that after decades in his arduous post he deserved a vacation at government expense, and ushered the jowly cacique out of his office. Only after Jonguitud was ensconced in the backseat of a taxi on his way home did he learn from the vehicle's radio that had "resigned" as the SNTE kingpin. Don Fernando Gutiérrez Barrios, secretary of Gobernación and a former head of the Federal Security Directorate, subsequently phoned Jonguitud to say that an airplane was waiting at Mexico City's airport to take him and his family anywhere they wanted to go. Moreover, he would find a briefcase full of money to defray his expenses.[44] Although he rejected several ambassadorships as a consolation prize, the dethroned "moral leader" of educators was given a senate seat from San Luis Potosí, where he had previously served as governor. In a remarkable act of cynicism, upon her predecessor's death in 2011, La Maestra teared up as she offered condolences to the family and took a turn as "honor guard" next to his coffin, at the foot of which she had placed a floral arrangement.

As discussed in Chapter 7, newly elected president Enrique Peña Nieto has targeted public schools for major reforms. One of his first steps was to bring charges against the Machiavellian Gordillo of embezzling $200 million. She was immediately incarcerated.[45]

Salinas gained support for the accord from the National Action Party in *concertacesiones* (mutually beneficial deals) negotiated with the redoubtable Senator Diego "El Jefe" Fernández de Cevallos. The PAN backed NAFTA and other liberalizing initiatives in exchange for the government's jettisoning odious anticlerical provisions in the Constitution, creating a Federal Electoral Institute (IFE) to take charge of the electoral process, recognizing the victory of PAN candidates, and allowing for the election of the Jefe de Gobierno (mayor of Mexico City), whom the president previously appointed.

For nearly five years Salinas presided over an extremely successful administration, overcoming an uprising by the Zapatista National

Liberation Army (EZLN); a nasty squabble with Mexico City mayor Manuel Camacho Solís, who hoped to succeed him; and the March 23, 1994, assassination of his hand-picked successor, Luis Donaldo Colosio. Nonetheless, even while NAFTA began to liberalize Mexico's once-protected market, many of the bottlenecks remained intact: virtual monopolies and oligopolies in telecommunications, the mass media, cement, processed foods, oil, retail business, electricity, education, and petroleum.

Salinas replaced Colosio with the colorless Ernesto Zedillo Ponce de León, a technocrat who held a doctorate in economics from Yale but had little political experience and no campaign entourage. The outgoing chief of state was sitting on top of the world. Prominent politicians at home and abroad touted him to become executive director of the World Trade Organization or head of an equally prestigious institution. To maintain his status on the global stage, Salinas had allowed various state-run banks to make loans irresponsibly, giving momentum to brisk inflation and the flight of hard currency reserves. Three weeks after he left office, the so-called Christmas crisis slammed into the Zedillo administration like a typhoon. The Finance Ministry botched the devaluation, which devastated and antagonized the middle class, who had begun relying on credit cards, acquiring mortgages, and purchasing automobiles on installment plans. Voters savored their revenge in 1997 when the PRI lost its majority in Congress; Cárdenas, the standard-bearer of the leftist Democratic Revolutionary Party captured the mayorship of Mexico City; and the opposition picked up governorships in Jalisco (PAN/1995), Nuevo León (PAN/1997), Querétaro (PAN/1997), Zacatecas (leftist coalition/1998, Tlaxcala (leftist coalition/1999), and Baja California Sur (leftist coalition/1999).

Possessed of democratic instincts, Zedillo became known as the "nine fingered president" because he passed up the *dedazo* in favor of holding an internal PRI primary to select the party's 2000 presidential candidate. Ideology aside, the brainy economist turned politician simply did not have the political muscle to impose a nominee. Former secretary of Gobernación Francisco Labastida Ochoa won the four-way competition only to lose the general election to PAN standard-bearer Vicente Fox Quesada.

CONCLUSION

After one of the bloodiest revolutions in history, Mexican leaders pursued stability at all costs. Beginning with Calles, they brought as many constituencies as possible under the regime's broad tent; co-opted the army; cultivated good relations with past adversaries such as the Roman Catholic Church, the business and banking elite, and the United States; and complemented the nation's vast agrarian sector with an industrial base.

The state itself was weak, as evidenced by police venality, a shamefully corrupt judiciary, anemic tax collections, and the inability to curb violence in impoverished states such as Guerrero, Oaxaca, Michoacán, and Chiapas. As a result, informal rules were hammered out to promote mutually advantageous practices with the government in every realm of society. Groups defying these guidelines risked retaliation from Mexico City. The object was to avoid confrontations with the regime, evince loyalty to the PRI and the president, and express obeisance to "Revolutionary Nationalism," a vacuous, mercurial concept that often changed with every presidential election. A series of factors—the Tlatelolco massacre, the nationalization of the banking system, the ham-fisted reaction to the *El Grande* earthquakes, the Christmas crisis, the ubiquitous kleptocracy, the sweetheart relations with villainous union chieftains—undermined the precepts that allowed the revolutionary party to hold power for 71 years, longer than the Soviet Union's communists. A set of understandings also guided relations between authorities and drug kingpins, which is the subject of Chapter 1. Peña Nieto's top goal is to stanch the bloodshed, even as he diverts the public's attention from violence to foreign travel and programs designed to improve education, housing, benefits for older adults, investment, infrastructure, energy output, and nutrition. Meanwhile, he hopes to forge a new security apparatus that will help the PRI government recover the power that it once enjoyed.

CHAPTER 1

The Ten Commandments and "El Padrino"

INTRODUCTION: THE TEN COMMANDMENTS

The president, the government, and the Institutional Revolutionary Party imposed informal rules of the game on the educational system, the oil industry, the mass media, and other sectors of society. Similarly, federal officeholders, governors, mayors, police officials, and army officers demanded that paladins of the underworld, particularly narco-traffickers, adhere to a latter-day version of the Ten Commandments. Table 1.1 summarizes elements in these unwritten accords that often varied over time and from area to area.

In return for adhering to these strictures, the government did not impede the import, storage, processing, and export of products. In fact, official agencies often cooperated in the drug business.

If the narco-syndicates violated these strictures, they suffered reprisals at the hands of the PJF, DFS, or cunning military squads such as the *brigada blanca*.

EVOLUTION OF THE SYSTEM

Until the 1970s the army and law enforcement agencies generally boasted superior firepower over the cartels, whose operatives depended on handguns or machine guns.[1] But that did not matter. Relying on bribes (*mordidas*), the desperadoes pursued their illicit activities with the connivance of authorities, frequently through ad hoc pacts that might last days, weeks, or months. Loyal to the PRI, the armed forces bolstered the

Table 1.1

Ten Commandments

	Obligations of the Drug Traffickers
1	Capos paid the sums demanded of them upon demand; often more than one representative received payments
2	The size of payments was based on the *"plaza"* (area controlled by the DTO) and the earnings from the product
3	The cartel leaders showed deference to mayors, governors, and other political figures, sometimes attending social functions together; they respected the territories of competitors and had to obtain "crossing rights" ("derecho de piso") before traversing their turfs
4	The criminal organization did not sell drugs in Mexico, least of all to children; nor did it kidnap, extort, kill, or in any other way attack civilians, especially Americans
5	If a score had to be settled, the execution was accomplished in a remote area; north of the border if possible
6	Traffickers would do such "favors" for the government and PRI politicians as killing an adversary
7	Criminals did not obtain weapons more powerful than those used by the Army, the Federal Judicial Police (PJF), and the Federal Directorate of Security (DFS)
8	Certain cities were "sanctuaries" where the families of the narco-bosses could live peacefully without fear of attacks from rival cartels or authorities; the wives and girlfriends of traffickers were "untouchables"
9	Prosecutors and judges would turn a blind eye to cooperative criminals
10	While prepared to influence candidates and office-holders, Mafiosi did participate directly in elective politics

top-down control exercised by the state. Drug trafficking organizations (DTOs) sought protection from local police, from regional or zonal military commanders, and sometimes directly from governors or their representatives. Just as in other forms of corruption, authorities allocated *plazas*, which in the case of drugs refers to areas and corridors where the gangs held sway to produce, store, or ship narcotics. Reportedly, they followed a "1-2-3 system": a payoff to authorities of $1 million for an interior location, $2 million for a coastal zone, and $3 million for a U.S.-Mexico border crossing.[2] Rizzo García, former governor of Nuevo León (1991–1996), told an audience of law students that, without mentioning names, previous PRI presidents dictated the corridors for shipping narcotics to prevent attacks on civilians. "Somehow the problems with drug trafficking were avoided, there was a strong State control and a strong President and a strong Attorney General and a tight control of the Army," he stated. "This dilemma was lost due to problems of professionalism, it is natural that new officials [the Fox administration] come without experience ... the last thing they wanted to hear was anything from the PRI, they said that the PRI were the 'snake in the grass' and with that they refused counsel."[3]

His comments stirred a firestorm of denials: "Statements of this nature and superficiality do little to make a true diagnosis of the serious problem we have today, of crime and drug trafficking," said PRI strongman Manlio Fabio Beltrones. "We are all accountable for our statements and need to back them up with evidence."[4]

As is the case today, prominent and "legitimate" members of the business community and professionals aided the criminals by selling them goods and services, and even participating in joint ventures. Known drug dealers openly went to the theater, attended public functions, and found photographs of themselves hobnobbing with prominent local figures plastered on the society pages of newspapers.

Clashes among families or between traffickers and police happened in places such as Mi Delirio, Montecarlo, and other saloons in Tierra Blanca, a rowdy bar- and brothel-suffused neighborhood of Sinaloa's state capital, Culiacán. Small municipalities in states such as Oaxaca and Guerrero were also killing grounds. The inequality of power ensured that drug barons also paid danegeld to representatives of the federal government —with up-front payments of $250,000 or more.

In some cases, a military regional or zonal commander would keep the lion's share of the payola. However, such officials often received key assignments because of their close ties to superiors in Mexico City. Thus, the recipients would forward a portion of the payola upward through the chain of command.

In accord with the Ten Commandments, kingpins behaved prudently, were courteous to public figures, spurned kidnappings, appeared with governors at their children's weddings, and, although often allergic to politics, helped the hegemonic PRI discredit its opponents by linking them to narco-trafficking.

Unlike Colombia, where kingpin Pablo "Czar of Cocaine" Escobar won election as an alternate federal congressman in 1982, Mexico's barons did not pursue elective office. In addition, they did not sell drugs within the country (least of all to children), target innocent people, or invade the turf or product line (marijuana, heroin, cocaine, etc.) of competitors.

As Professor Leo Zuckerman has emphasized, each syndicate had its own geographic enclave. If one lord needed to cross the territory of another, he would first ask permission and, if granted, pay the appropriate fee, known as the right of transit (*derecho de piso*). Meanwhile, chiefs would not attack the families of their counterparts, notably in such "sanctuary" cities as the Federal District, Monterrey, and Guadalajara.

This practice had ceased by 1989 when authorities captured Héctor Luis "El Güero" Palma Salazar, who had risen from petty car thief to a gunman for Miguel Ángel "El Padrino" / "The Godfather" Félix Gallardo. Arrested in Arizona in 1978, Palma returned to Mexico to find that Venezuelan mobster Rafael Enrique Clavel, in connivance with Félix Gallardo, had forced his wife to withdraw $7 million from the bank. After this transaction, Clavel decapitated her and shipped her head to Palma before hurling his enemy's two children off a bridge. In retaliation, Palma executed Clavel's three children and bribed a PJF commander to allow him to hide in his house. Typically off bounds in the past, women no longer were "untouchables," as evidenced by the deaths, from January to August 2005, of 58 females throughout several states: 25 in Sinaloa, 17 in Tamaulipas, 11 in Chihuahua, 3 in Michoacán, and 2 in Guerrero.[5]

Moreover, the number of murders often rose at year's end in Sinaloa when gangsters returned home for the holidays and settled scores with their rivals in the state. In 2013 only Mexico City and Querétaro, 135 miles north of the capital, had attributes of sanctuary cities. However, gangs from the dangerous Tepito market and Buenos Aires neighborhoods, as well as petty drug dealers from Ecatepec and other nearby Mexico State megacities, have authored inhumane acts. For instance, on May 26, 2013, gangsters kidnapped a dozen young people from the Heavens nightclub in the DF's Zona Rosa tourist center. Observers believe the victims were killed.[6] As in other fields of national life, the government sought stability—with the Gobernación ministry acting as the regime's political interlocutor. If criminal activities threatened the tranquility of a municipality, the governor was expected to crack the whip, perhaps with the help of murky groups dispatched from Mexico City. If the state executive failed to restore order, he might find himself replaced by someone who could end the turbulence.

MIGUEL ÁNGEL FÉLIX GALLARDO

Miguel Ángel Félix Gallardo, alluded to earlier in this chapter, became a prominent figure who made millions of dollars while adhering to the regime's rules but finally felt the government's boot slam down on his neck when he broke them. Pedro Avilés Pérez, a marijuana entrepreneur who was the first drug lord to use airplanes to smuggle drugs to the United States, preceded him as the top drug don in Sinaloa. Nonetheless, Félix Gallardo became the first kingpin to dominate narcotics trafficking in Mexico, control the routes between his country and the U.S. border, and cut deals with the Medellín Cartel and other Colombian suppliers.

A scrawny, rail-thin youngster with the suggestion of a mustache, he was one of nine children whose hard-working parents and siblings scratched out a living on farms around Bellavista, where rainwater sluiced through unpaved streets and poverty manifest itself in many of the 467 shacks in which the inhabitants lived. When his father abandoned the family, Félix's mother was left to raise her brood in a ramshackle house purchased on a hacienda just outside Culiacán, Sinaloa, a state that straddles the jagged Sierra Madre, and—with the contiguous states of Durango and Chihuahua —forms the "Golden Triangle" where marijuana and cocaine flourish. In the late nineteenth century, partly because of the recent influx of Chinese settlers, Sinaloa became a significant source of opium derived from the cultivation of poppies. The state's proximity to the United States yielded a large market for the drug, which was legal at that time.[7]

As a teenager, the soft-spoken, entrepreneurial Félix Gallardo loaded a flimsy wooden cart with cloth, ribbons, thread, buttons, and toys and set forth each day bartering his wares for cheese and chickens, which he then hawked in Culiacán to supplement the family's anemic income. In addition to huckstering, he sold used automobile tires. In 1963, at age 17, he joined the inexorably corrupt State Judicial Police. His first assignment was to protect the family of Leopoldo Sánchez Celis, who formally governed Sinaloa from 1963 to 1968 but exerted influence long after his term ended. The young man's astuteness, discretion, austerity, and reliability impressed the state executive, who soon brought him into his entourage to protect his children. Sánchez Celis introduced the young man to businessmen, politicians, large farmers, journalists, judges, prosecutors, and members of other law-enforcement agencies. Among other mentors was Eduardo Lalo Fernández, who taught the young man the heroin business.

Félix Gallardo was like a member of the Sánchez Celis household. On May 28, 1983, when the former governor's son Rodolfo Sánchez Duarte got married, Félix Gallardo and his wife María Elvira served as godparents. In the 15 years between his functioning as Sánchez Celis's right-hand man and Rodolfo's nuptials, the so-called Boss of Bosses had developed links that made him one of the nation's top drug dealers. "El Padrino ensured that the right people all the way up Mexico's Pacific coast were in his pocket, from politicians to policemen."[8]

The intrepid young businessman also prospered under Sánchez Celis's successors: Alfredo Valdés Montoya (1969–1974), Alfonso G. Calderón (1975–1980), and, most of all, Antonio Toledo Corro (1981–1986).

Toledo Corro, a former secretary of agrarian reform and crony of President José López Portillo (1976–1982), gained infamy for the venality of the state's police and the strength of his lucrative ties to the underworld. "It's been amazing, the things that have been turned up," said one White House source. "Really amazing. It was the case where drug dealer X would talk to one of his distributors one minute, his wife the next, and a governor after that."[9]

When queried about burgeoning violence associated with the cultivation and sale of drugs in Sinaloa, Toledo Corro blithely responded: "Narco trafficking is a legacy of other generations. It is not a problem that arose yesterday nor will it be resolved tomorrow."[10] In fact, the drug business was flourishing to the point that, during harvests in the mountains, agents for the producers used loudspeakers to recruit harvesters not only from such poor Culiacán neighborhoods as 6 de Enero, Libertad, and Rosales, but from adjoining states. So enticing was the work that, during the period of cultivation, only women, children, and the elderly populated many of the local towns and villages. At one time, El Padrino, who typically flaunted his presence in the city, even hid out in the governor's Culiacán home, but Toledo Corro claimed not to know that there were outstanding warrants for the apprehension of his houseguest.

The relationships can be summarized as follows:

A popular *corrido* or ballad by the musical group Los Tucanes de Tijuana refers to three little animals—el gallo, la chiva y el périco—slang for marijuana, heroin and cocaine, and all were firmly rooted in the subterranean culture by the 1970's. In Sinaloa, each *animalito* had a master "wrangler"—Ernesto "Don Neto" Fonseca Carrillo in poppy and heroin production, Rafael Caro Quintero in producing and distributing marijuana—especially sensimilla, and Miguel Ángel Félix Gallardo, who would rise to become the most powerful "Jefe de Jefes" or "El Padrino," through cocaine importation and distribution. Each crime boss oversaw an underground and subterranean network rooted in violence, co-optation and bribery that touched most state institutions and local businesses . . . This trio of local men eventually forged an unholy, but uneasy alliance cemented by their shared origins in and around Badiraguato, Sinaloa. Their subterranean network became stronger and larger as it was extended by kinship through blood and inter-marriage, rituals of *compadrazco*, mutual connections with many public officials, and their unique reliance on traffickers from Durango and Chihuahua to transport their product. In particular, their alliance with a regional cacique, Pablo Acosta of Ojinaga, Chihuahua, allowed them to sell their contraband directly in the US market.[11]

The ubiquity of drugs in the Golden Triangle prompted Washington to put pressure on President Luis Echeverría. Until 1947 Mexico's Health Department oversaw Mexico's drug policy. Desultory initiatives to destroy illegal plants were largely undertaken to pacify Uncle Sam.

As chief executive, Cárdenas rejected a campaign against drugs; however, after World War II, Washington sought to curb the production of poppy and marijuana, lest returning members of the armed forces, who had become dependent on drugs while in Asia and the Middle East, have access to illicit substances.

As part of his outreach to the United States, in 1947 President Alemán shifted antinarcotics policies to the Attorney General's Office (PGR). At the same time he created the Federal Security Directorate, a political police force that one U.S. embassy employee analogized to the Gestapo.[12] "Some analysts further suggest that [the] DFS developed particularly strong relations to the drug trafficking organizations during the 1970s when it tolerated their activities in exchange for assistance with paramilitary operations against a leftist terrorist group, the 23rd of September Communist League."[13]

The DFS worked hand in glove with the Central Intelligence Agency, which had evolved from the Office of Special Services the same year. The DFS was also vested with authority in drug matters, as well as combatting subversives, including communists (even though Fernando Gutiérrez Barrios, one of the organization's directors, befriended Fidel and Raúl Castro and facilitated their return from his home state of Veracruz to ignite a rebellion against the authoritarian regime of Cuba's Fulgencio Batista). Officials in the U.S. embassy in Mexico City had misgivings about the honesty of DFS personnel such as Colonel Carlos I. Serrano, a confidant of President Alemán.

In 1948 the Mexican government announced a major drive to destroy the illegal plants in the country: This "campaign involved the military for the first time as a permanently assigned eradication force . . . [but] only between 100 and 400 were assigned to support police agents in the destruction of one third to one-half of the entire opium poppy crop."[14] The military, formally subordinate to the PGR in drug affairs, occupied a key position among producers, traffickers, the police, and politicians. There were more players in the drug trafficking camp. From then on and for decades, the military's hermetic attitude, the mutual protection of political families from the PRI, and the law of silence put the new mediators such as PJF and DFS agents in the vortex of drug-related corruption.[15]

The antidrug surge proved a Herculean challenge. The territory was vast and rugged, many roads no more than rutted dirt paths, the destruction of plants with machetes arduous, local leaders intractable. Army commanders bristled at orders from PJF agents, and the clannish population was hostile to the prospect of losing their livelihood. In the 1960s the United States provided the Mexican government with aircraft, jeeps, and spare parts to facilitate the eradication effort. According to Richard Craig, "It also made future campaigns more difficult as opium and marijuana cultivators, aware of the increased probability of aerial detection, began concealing their crops amidst legitimate ones and planting smaller plots in even more remote regions."[16]

Concerned about the continuing northbound flood of narcotics, President Richard M. Nixon launched Operation Intercept in September 1969. Some 2,000 Treasury agents and coast guard boats swarmed around the 2000-mile border as customs and border patrol agents scrupulously inspected cars, trucks, visitors, and workers crossing into Mexico. At the same time, the U.S. Army stationed mobile radar units from El Paso to the Pacific Coast to interdict small planes ferrying marijuana to the Southwest. Torpedo boats also pursued smugglers.

Nixon applauded the venture as "very, very successful." While the operation was in effect, the flow of narcotics and marijuana from Mexico into this country was substantially curtailed. "Marlbuena [Marijuana] is still in short supply in the United States, and in most places where it is available, at least the Mexican form, the prices have doubled and in some cases tripled."[17] The U.S. ambassador to Mexico, Mexican officials, and entrepreneurs on both sides of the border disagreed with this assessment. After 20 days, Operation Intercept gave way to Operation Cooperation, which relaxed the burden placed on persons and firms engaged in lawful and unlawful commerce.

Still, drugs poured into the United States, and Washington increasingly exhorted Mexico, whose leaders were eager for investment and capital from their northern neighbor, to stanch the influx of narcotics. By 1974 it was said that Mexico was the principal source of heroin for U.S. addicts, and two years later 5,000 soldiers and airmen were involved in Mexico's drug eradication campaign.[18]

OPERATION CONDOR

The flow of drugs accelerated, and their sale became yet one more profit center for the PRI. "Controlled, tolerated or regulated by mighty politicians in northern states, drug trafficking seems to have been a business that was developed from within the power structure. . . ." The traffickers were not autonomous specialized groups, but rather "a new class of outlaws that depended closely on political and police [protection and was banned from political activity]."[19] Under mounting pressure from Uncle Sam, Mexico's Attorney General Pedro Ojeda Paullada met in Culiacán with Governor Alfonso G. Calderón from Sinaloa, Governor Héctor Mayagoitia Domínguez from Durango, a representative of Chihuahua state, state attorneys general, and relevant military zone commanders. These officials committed themselves to combatting "narco-trafficking," a term coined in the 1980s.

The dealers had long since broken the rules of the game by employing R-15, 38- and 45-calibre weapons, and high-powered machine guns. Meanwhile, the perfidious Manuel Salcido Uzeta, known as "Cochiloco" (or "Crazy Pig") because of his violent rages and extreme cruelty, had the run of Culiacán. In September 1973, for example, he paid 250,000 pesos to three PJF agents to capture and incarcerate six young men employed by a rival. Two years later, he brazenly walked out of the capital's jail one November Sunday night after dishing out more than 500,000 pesos to the guards. The following April, he attended his father's funeral in Mazatlán in the company of a dozen bodyguards. No one raised a finger to arrest him. Gobernación minister Mario Moya Palencia said that the drug criminals constituted a "Trojan Horse" inside the walls of Culiacán.[20]

Echeverría's administration (1970–1976) launched Operation Condor, which the U.S. Drug Enforcement Administration (DEA) referred to as Operation Trizo. General José Hernández Toledo (no relation to the governor) headed this foray for the military, while Carlos Aguilar Garza took charge for the PGR. The initiative involved 10,000 troops slashing away with machetes, torching stacks of drugs, and dousing illegal crops with the toxic herbicide Paraquat. Hernández Toledo, who had taken part in the 1968 Tlatelolco massacre and the subsequent suppression of students in Morelia and Hermosillo, predicted that drug trafficking would be terminated in six months. The invasion destroyed large quantities of drugs and curbed output, yet prices rose and drugs continued to reach U.S. consumers.[21]

This military operation had several unintended consequences. To begin with, nearly 100,000 residents of the drug-growing sierra, where 30 percent of the population earned their livelihood from the coca trade, migrated to the Sinaloan municipalities of Guasave, Guamúchil, and Culiacán. Sinaloa's capital became known as "Little Chicago" because of raging gang warfare that woke residents with gunfire at all hours of the night. The troops arrested, tortured, and jailed hundreds of small farmers and villagers. In 1977 the first of 15 warrants was issued for Félix Gallardo's arrest for drug trafficking, but a judge dismissed the charge.

Both Washington and Mexico City collectively broke their arms patting themselves on the back for the success of the venture. Jerry Kelley, a DEA pilot told prize-winning journalist Elaine Shannon that the Americans "flew every inch of the country and we knew what they were doing and what was there. It didn't matter who was corrupt. There was no way they could hide what was going on."[22]

Jon R. Thomas, the deputy assistant secretary of state for international narcotics matters said in 1985 with respect to Mexico's antidrug drive: "The program ... has had a lot of success during the past 10 years. We are aware of the efforts that have been made by Mexico, and of the deaths of Mexican agents."[23]

Mexican leaders were even more effusive. Despite the death of key police officials in the state, Sinaloa's governor and Culiacán's mayor declared that "narco-trafficking has been totally eliminated."[24]

In contrast, scholar Luis Alejandro Astorga Almanza characterized the putative military and political success as nothing more than a "mirage." "In the long term," he wrote, "the social cost of the military operation was more important for a large number of people, whose negative attitude towards Federal Police and the military was reinforced, than the spectacular destruction of illegal plants which made Mexican and American anti-narcotics officials so happy and optimistic."[25]

Félix Gallardo lived in luxury outside Culiacán on a sprawling ranch filled with his collection of electronic gadgetry, Italian designer shoes, and priceless watches. Although he later returned to Sinaloa, he and other big shots gathered their belongings and moved to Guadalajara to avoid being swept up in the antidrug action. They were alerted to move to another place by Federal Security Directorate agents Esteban Guzmán Salgado and Daniel Acuña Figueroa, who helped the newcomers find posh homes in the colonial "pearl of Western Mexico." The transplants lived like minor royalty, displacing the local marijuana trafficking chief, driving chrome-laden expensive automobiles, carousing with voluptuous young women, and holding wild, all-night parties.

In addition to El Padrino, notable leaders included Avilés Pérez, mentioned earlier in this chapter, who transported cocaine via an air bridge from Culiacán through the Baja California cities of Tijuana and Mexicali. His life ended in a shootout with federal police in 1978. Ernesto "Don Neto" Fonseca Carrillo, the group's treasurer, may have alerted authorities to Avilés Perez's whereabouts. Rafael Caro Quintero, Avilés Perez's lieutenant in Chihuahua, acquired large marijuana and poppy plantations. Like Félix Gallardo, Cochiloco projected the image of a Robin Hood. He bought uniforms for a municipal volleyball team, paved a rural road, and became godfather to numerous children who were growing up in poverty as he had. Pedro Orozco García, as he called himself, lived on a 900-acre ranch; owned 1,200 head of cattle; rode his palomino in the annual Independence Day parade; and delighted in his stable of thoroughbred horses before falling under a hail of bullets on October 9, 1991.[26] Félix Gallardo struck up a friendship with Honduran chemist Juan Ramón Matta Ballesteros, who helped the Sinaloan forge ties with Pablo Escobar, the bloodthirsty capo of the Medellín Cartel. Matta Ballesteros, who was arrested in 1988, acted as a key player in the establishment of the "Mexican Trampoline"—the vaulting of cocaine from Colombia to the United States via Guadalajara.

THE CAMARENA AFFAIR

On February 7, 1985, five armed men snatched DEA agent Enrique "Kiki" Camarena and wrestled him into a car in broad daylight near the U.S. consulate general in Guadalajara, considered the cynosure of Mexican drug trafficking. The 37-year-old law enforcement official had infiltrated several groups and gained the confidence of Fonseca Carrillo, El Cochiloco, and Félix Gallardo while working on Operation Godfather. Camarena believed that El Padrino and fellow Sinaloan Caro Quintero were exporting between $3.2 and $8 billion worth of marijuana from a two-square-mile farm replete with a sophisticated irrigation system, drying sheds, an airstrip, armed guards, and 10,000 workers.[27] This plantation, *el Búfalo*, lay on the eastern side of the Sierra Maestra and was owned by Sonora Cartel chief Caro Quintero. The initiative flourished as an agricultural oasis in the Chihuahuan Desert thanks to the blatant connivance of the federal and local police, as well as Defense Secretary Juan Arévalo Gardoqui.

Camarena blew the whistle on the lucrative venture, and 450 Mexican soldiers reinforced by helicopters destroyed the marijuana plantation. The kingpins were livid at the blow to their bank accounts and turned heaven and earth to learn who had revealed their lucrative initiative. Félix Gallardo concluded that Camarena was the Benedict Arnold. The DEA agent was seized and savagely tortured, and his skull was crushed like an eggshell. He may have been killed weeks before his decaying corpse, along with that of his Mexican pilot Alfredo Zavala Avelar, was found in a rural area near La Angostura, Michoacán, on March 5. U.S. authorities not only accused Dr. Humberto Álvarez Machain, a physician for the DFS of having given Camarena injections to prolong his punishment, but they paid bounty-hunters to abduct the officer in Guadalajara, bring him into the United States, and place him on trial in Los Angeles. After several years of legal wrangling, he gained acquittal.

Also implicated and sentenced in connection with the Camarena slaying was Rubén "Don Rubén" Zuno Arce, a wealthy cattleman, an alleged Caro Quintero compadre, the former brother-in-law of ex-president Echeverría, and the erstwhile owner of the house where the DEA agent was mutilated.

NBC aired a miniseries on the Camarena affair, based, in part, on conversations with Shannon, author of the book *Desperados*. Mexico's consul general in Los Angeles said: "Some of the assertions made by the interviewer, reporter and guests are the product of sheer ignorance, imprecise, unfair, lacking any evidence and, maybe, in bad faith." Mexican spokespersons also denounced interviews during the series that equated drug corruption in their country with that of the Panamanian government headed by Manuel Noriega.[28]

Camarena's former colleagues were outraged. "Kiki's killing symbolized corruption at its worst in Mexico," said Phil Jordan, a retired DEA special agent in Dallas and former director of the organization's El Paso Intelligence Center. "We know why Kiki was taken from us—because the [Mexican] government was working in complicity with the godfathers of the drug trade..."[29] In the largest homicide venture ever undertaken, the DEA dispatched 25 agents to Mexico as part of Operation Leyenda (Operation Legend), which was designed to capture their colleague's murderer. Meanwhile, the agency requested that the Mexican federal police investigate Caro Quintero, Félix Gallardo, and Fonseca as the possible culprits.

Mexico's Attorney General's Office placed Guillermo González Calderoni, the highest ranking federal police commander and an experienced narcotics officer during the Salinas presidency (1988–1994), in charge of the case. He was told to nab the outlaw alive in three months—after all, Mexico faced the prospect of decertification and economic sanctions if the U.S. Department of State deemed that the country was not cooperating fully with Washington's policies and taking adequate steps to curb drug proliferation. Congress had enacted this punitive legislation in 1986 in the aftermath of the Camarena tragedy.

In cooperation with the DEA, Calderoni's team used wiretaps to locate El Padrino's home and rented an apartment across the street. When a deliveryman brought ice and food to the capo's residence, guards opened the door to retrieve the items, enabling law-enforcement officers to storm the premises. They caught the multimillionaire in his pajamas, rammed the barrel of an AK-47 in his mouth, and placed him under arrest. The don offered Calderoni, with whom he had enjoyed a long-standing friendship, $5 or $6 million for his release. A bribe was out of the question in this high-profile takedown. Mexican and U.S. authorities charged him with the kidnapping and murder of Camarena, drug smuggling, racketeering, and multiple violent crimes. "Félix Gallardo had become the most wanted drug trafficker both at [the] national and international level," according to the PGR. "This shows the willingness of ... Carlos Salinas to fight this social cancer to whatever end."[30]

At the time of Félix Gallardo's arrest, the army detained and disarmed all 600 police officers in his bailiwick of Culiacán—an indication of the prodigious corruption in the state capital.

The mass media delighted in reporting the wealth of a kingpin, especially one who never managed to finish high school. His possessions included some $900 million, 90 houses, 3 jet aircraft, a dozen thoroughbred horses, 16 ranches, 14 motorcycles, 2 hotels, 100 head of cattle, 25 fighting cocks, and 25 automobiles, among which were a Jaguar, a Mercedes, a Porsche, and a Cadillac.[31] In addition, he reportedly owned property in every Mexican state. He lived in one house in Guadalajara, while his 17 children lived in two nearby residences.[32]

The Boss of the Bosses began his 40-year prison sentence in 1989. He allegedly operated his empire from behind bars using cell phone and fax for three years until authorities transferred him to the Almoloya high-security penitentiary near Toluca in Mexico State. While in captivity, he reportedly allocated plazas among his allies to minimize conflict.

CONCLUSION

Félix Gallardo does not have Internet access in his cell. Yet, in August 2008 his large family—he fathered 17 children—created the website www.miguelfelixgallardo.com. A son took charge of erecting the so-called narco-billboard that sought medical attention for his father, who allegedly suffers from near-blindness, difficulty in walking, a chronic ear infection, and a severe throat disease. In early 2007 a judge allowed an otolaryngologist to treat the 63-year-old inmate. Although the web page featured a robust young man on a motorcycle, the Boss of Bosses appeared gaunt and sallow-faced.[33]

The relatives of Ernesto Fonseca Carrillo, 77, a fellow resident of Almoloya and another infamous drug don who participated in the killing of Camarena, have also pled for their loved-one's treatment. "We're not asking that he be freed," his daughter Arcelia Fonseca told reporters in April 2008. "We are asking that he given medical attention or he will die [of cancer]."[34] No change occurred.

More fortunate was Caro Quintero who, much to the consternation of U.S. officials, won release 12 years before completing his 40-year sentence for his involvement in killing Camarena. In early August 2013, Mexican judges ruled that the infamous drug lord was improperly tried in a federal court for a state offense.

By participating in the capture, torture, and murder of the DEA's Enrique Camarena, the men paid a hefty price for breaking the Ten Commandments.

CHAPTER 2

The United States Seeks Interdiction of Drugs from Colombia

INTRODUCTION

Authorities have covered the origins of Mexico's drug exports to the United States, and this chapter will not revisit this terrain. Rather, Appendix A sets forth major developments with respect to controlled substances

It's useful to begin with the U.S. government's critical need for an alternative source of opium with which to make morphine during World War II. Turkey's alliance with the Axis powers combined with Japan's occupation of poppy-growing regions in Asia forced Washington into a *sub rosa* move to obtain supplies from Mexico. Deprived of illegal psychedelics from the Orient and the Middle East, the United States acquired limited supplies of low-quality opium from Mexico, but they proved insufficient to satisfy demand.

On the one hand, Washington continued urging Mexico to curb the drug trade; on the other hand, it purchased low-grade "black tar" opium from its southern neighbor. "We were concerned that our supply of opium or morphine would be cut off because the world was at war. So we needed a supply close by. But, this was one of those black box things. Who knows when it happened, who did it, and why," stated Edward Heath, who later headed the Drug Enforcement Administration office in Mexico for 10 years. "It was a good agricultural place for it. And generation after generation the people just did it, they perfected it," explained Heath.

During this period of a government-tolerated opium trade, many Sinaloans made their fortune. "Everybody was growing it, it was institutional.

Some government officials bought the harvest from the farmers to export themselves. There were even soldiers up in the hills caring for the plants," explained Dr. Ley Dominguez, a 77-year-old life-long resident of Mocorito, a fly-specked village whose name means "place of the dead" and Sinaloa's most notorious poppy-producing municipality after Badiraguato. After Japan's defeat, however, the United States no longer needed Sinaloa's inferior strain of opium. But many farmers continued to produce opium and heroin; operations became more clandestine, and smuggling networks, often congruent with those used to ship whiskey during Prohibition, were set up.[1] As indicated in Chapter 1, Mexico became an increasingly popular source of narcotics, especially when tens of thousands of military personnel returned from overseas with a taste for, if not a full-blown addiction to, drugs. It was during this "era of good feelings" that President Miguel Alemán complied with Washington's request and established the Federal Security Directorate to help the Federal Judicial Police and Army crackdown on the planting, harvesting, and transport of illicit substances. Some members of the DFS transferred to the PJF because of the latter's greater involvement in drug affairs and the opportunity for more graft.

So-called recreational drugs became fashionable among young people—in part because they were more available; in part because they symbolized a protest against the system in an era of political and social cleavage between the Depression/World War II generation and their children; and because many regarded marijuana use as a means to protest the Vietnam conflict.

President Lyndon B. Johnson's administration (1963–1969) consolidated various agencies that had vied for bureaucratic turf into the Justice Department's Bureau of Narcotics and Dangerous Drugs (BNDD).

However, what would become the "war on drugs" gained momentum under President Richard M. Nixon (1969–1974). To begin with, he appointed a national commission, headed by Pennsylvania's conservative former governor Raymond P. Shafer, to study the effects of marijuana and other substances—with a view to proposing appropriate drug policies. The Shafer Commission funded more than 50 projects, ranging from a study of the effects of marijuana on humans to a field survey of the enforcement of marijuana laws in six metropolitan areas. The body found: "No significant physical, biochemical, or mental abnormalities [that] could be attributed solely to their marihuana smoking."[2]

Dismayed by such findings, the chief executive excoriated Shafer in a White House conversation with his aides. "You see, the thing that is so terribly important here is that it not appear that the Commission's frankly just a bunch of do-gooders, I mean, they say well they're a bunch of old men who don't understand, that's fine, I wouldn't mind that, but, but if they get the idea you're just a bunch of do-gooders that are going to come out with a quote soft on marijuana report that will destroy it, right off the bat."[3]

The president recognized neither the merits of Governor Shafer's thorough study nor the domestic turmoil and brutal conditions in Southeast Asia that inspired the use of narcotics. In December 1970, Comedian Bob Hope generated a tsunami of laughter from a crowd of U.S. troops by telling jokes about marijuana and the use of drugs in Vietnam. Sent to boost morale as part of the United Service Organization (USO), Hope sarcastically proclaimed, "Is it true the officers are getting flight pay? I saw a Sergeant before the show standing on a corner with a lampshade on his head waiting to be turned on. . . . At one barracks, everyone was watching 12 O'Clock High. And they didn't even have a TV set." He added, "I hear you guys are interested in gardening security. Our officer said a lot of you guys are growing your own grass." Hope drew the greatest cheers when he declared: "Instead of taking away marijuana from the soldiers, we ought to be giving it to the negotiators in Paris."[4]

In late 1970, Congress passed the Comprehensive Drug Abuse Prevention and Controlled Substances Act, which consolidated existing drug laws. While reducing penalties for marijuana possession, it also embraced the Controlled Substances Act. This provision established five "schedules" for regulating drugs depending on their medicinal value and potential for addiction. In addition, the legislation broadened the power of police to conduct "no knock" searches.

The following year, Nixon proclaimed "a new all-out offensive" against drug abuse, which he condemned as "America's public enemy number one." A medley of factors—the chief executive's law-and-order orientation, anti-Semitism and other personal prejudices, the burgeoning number of pot-smoking "flower children" who berated his war in Southeast Asia, widespread campus demonstrations, and the number of marijuana users returning from Vietnam—help explain his crusading zeal.[5]

Beginning in mid-1971, the government went so far as to require urinalysis of all returning members of the armed forces. This project, which became known as Operation Golden Flow, found only 4.5 percent of soldiers tested positive for heroin.[6]

The dissemination of the "White House tapes" revealed that Nixon's views on marijuana sprang from personal prejudice rather than evidence. He can be heard saying to Chief of Staff H. R. Halderman: "That's a funny thing, every one of the bastards that are out for legalizing marijuana is Jewish. What the Christ is the matter with the Jews, Bob, what is the matter with them? I suppose it's because most of them are psychiatrists . . .," adding "By God, we are going to hit the marijuana thing, and I want to hit it right square in the puss . . ." When Nixon was talking with TV personality Art Linkletter, whose 20-year-old daughter jumped to her death after taking LSD, about "radical demonstrators," he said "They're all on drugs."[7] He added that you "see homosexuality, dope, [and] immorality in general. These are the enemies of strong societies. That's why the Communists and the left-wingers are pushing the stuff, they're trying to destroy us."[8]

The forced resignation of Nixon in August 1974, the domestic oil short-age, the Iran hostage crisis, and double-digit inflation deflected Washington's attention from drug-related issues. In 1976 Democratic candidate Jimmy Carter campaigned in favor of eliminating federal criminal penalties for the possession of up to one ounce of marijuana. Carter's "drug czar" Peter Bourne, an urbane British-born psychiatrist, did not regard marijuana, or even cocaine, as a serious public health threat.

THE "COCAINE COWBOYS" STORM MIAMI

By the late 1970s, Colombia's Cali and Medellín Cartels had begun to make South Florida their number-one destination for cocaine exports. Mafiosi from Medellín and Cali developed a labyrinth of trafficking corridors through the Dominican Republic, Haiti, and the Bahamas to South Florida. They showed ingenuity in moving their product, including air-drops of 500 to 700 kilograms in the Bahamian island chain and off the coast of Puerto Rico. They also engaged in mid-sea boat-to-boat transfers of 500 to 2,000 kilograms—with some large cocaine shipments destined for Miami.

Their vendors, the "cocaine cowboys," answered to their principals in Colombia as they turned Miami into the "murder capital of the 1980s." They operated through specialized "cells," composed of 10 or more employees, in distinct geographic zones. These units, whose members were unknown to each other, devoted themselves to different facets of the cocaine business: transport, storage, wholesale distribution, and money laundering. The head of each cell was responsible to a manager who oversaw several cells. In accord with a rigid top-down chain of command and control, the regional director reported to a drug lord or his designee. The DEA found that loyal lieutenants had some discretion with day-to-day operations, but ultimately they reported via sophisticated communications to the Colombian dons and their families.

José (Chepe) Santacruz Londoño (Cali Cartel) presents an interesting case. In the late 1970s, he and his wife entered the United States illegally. They set up shop distributing Colombian cocaine from Atlanta, Georgia, an ideal smuggling location because of its function as a transportation hub. Eventually Chepe went back to Colombia as the Mexicans replaced Colombians as wholesalers in the United States. In turn, the Mexicans were later largely supplanted by Jamaicans and Dominicans. After Chepe was captured, three of his children, wanting to avoid guilt by association, let Ambassador Myles Frechette know that they were U.S. citizens by birth and held U.S. passports.[9]

One of the original cocaine cowboys was Conrado "El Loco" Valencia Zalgado. In April 1979, he was racing along the Florida Turnpike Extension in his Audi when he opened fire with a MAC-10 on rival drug couriers trying to outrun him in a Pontiac Grand Prix. Once the smoke cleared, the police found a handcuffed corpse of "Jaime" in El Loco's abandoned car. Authorities charged the shooter, who in his prime made Al Pacino's "Scarface" look like Tommy Tune,[10] with attempted murder and threw him behind bars. His lawyers bailed him out with $105,000 in cash, and he moved to California, played the role of a laid-back Valley guy, and tooled around Topaganda Hills in a red 1948 DeSoto.

Max, as he began calling himself, ran out of luck when police discovered numerous calls to Miami on a phone bill in his garbage can. A California judge slammed him with a 30-year prison term before he was returned to Miami. There the judge gave "Jose Ramon Ruiz," El Loco's most recent sobriquet at the time, a 125-year sentence.[11]

Appendix B describes the major Colombian cartels.

DADELAND MALL EVENT

Back to the turnpike episode: Jaime's friends retaliated in a dramatic event that occurred at Dadeland Mall on July 11, 1979. Two men stepped out of a truck bearing the logo of a party supplies store. The vehicle turned out to be a "war wagon" jammed with weapons. The driver and his sidekick nonchalantly walked over to the Crown Liquors store, yanked two submachine guns from a paper bag, and unleashed a fusillade of bullets. They killed two of El Loco's allies, a Colombian drug trafficker and his body guard, while wounding two store employees.[12]

Men were not the only gunslingers navigating the blood-soaked streets of South Florida. Griselda Blanco, a stalwart of the Medellín Cartel, may have masterminded the Dadeland Mall massacre. In any case, she became a skilled pickpocket, kidnapper, and prostitute before age 20. In the mid-1970s, she moved to the United States and, reportedly, was generating $8 million per month in cocaine sales.

Only her cruelty eclipsed her financial acumen. She is believed to have ordered more than 40 murders while in Dade County, including the slaying of drug dealers Alfredo and Grizel Lorenzo, who failed to pay $250,000 for five kilos of cocaine. Another incident sparked the death of two-year-old Johnny Castro, shot twice in the head when riding with his father, Jesús "Chucho" Castro, a former hit man for her organization. Appropriately, she named one of her three sons after Michael Corleone of *Godfather* movie fame.[13]

A plea agreement enabled her to return to her hometown in 2004. Eight years later, two gunmen on motorcycles shot her in her square, jowly head after she stepped out of a butcher shop. Ironically, observers credit the 69-year-old "Cocaine godmother" with inventing the concept of the "motorcycle assassin," who speeds by and sprays his victim with bullets.

Even more notorious was Pablo Escobar. Before he died in a hail of bullets, the Medellín "extraditable," so called because he headed the list of a dozen capos sought by the United States government, directed operatives to blow a Colombian airliner out of the sky. The November 27, 1988, explosion killed 101 passengers and 6 crew members. Why the carnage? He thought that five police informants were aboard the domestic flight. A judge, operating in secrecy, charged Escobar with masterminding the assassination of Liberal presidential candidate Luis Carlos Galán in Soacha, in a poor neighborhood on the southern edge of Bogotá in mid-August 1989. Galán had championed a crackdown on organized crime.[14]

The drug kingpins ultimately brought destruction on themselves. Operations by the South Florida Task Force, formed in 1982 and headed by Vice President George H. W. Bush, spearheaded the interdiction of cocaine shipments to Florida and other Southeast states. This gambit forced the Colombians to pursue new corridors to the United States, with Central America and Mexico becoming their preferred thoroughfares.

By the mid-1990s many of the big shots were dead or behind bars, and cartels had fragmented into *cartelitos* strewn around coca-producing zones. These less notorious groups maintained lower profiles and concentrated their activities in medium-sized cities and small towns where officials were vulnerable to graft in exchange for protection. Such "boutique" players—Los Rastrojos and las Aguilas Negras—are extremely violent but pose less of a threat to the Colombian state.[15]

PLAN COLOMBIA

The violence associated with Florida's drug epidemic thrust Colombia to the center of the Clinton administration's foreign-affairs agenda. The "balloon effect" spurred Colombia's emergence as the number one cocaine producer; successes by the U.S. government and grower countries reduced production: specifically, Bolivia (Operation Blast Furnace in 1986 and Plan Dignidad 1998) and President Alberto Fujimori's interdiction of the "air bridge" between Peru's Alto Huallaga growing region and Colombia in the mid-1990s. These initiatives shifted Andean coca output to Colombia. While cultivation in Peru and Bolivia plummeted, Colombia accounted for approximately 90 percent of the world's coca leaf supplies by 2000.[16]

Rumors swirled that President Ernesto Samper (1994–1998), nominee of the Liberal Party, had raked in millions of dollars from the Cali Cartel to win a runoff election for the presidency. Once in office, however, the extremely ambitious politician vowed to detractors and the United States that he would lower the boom on drug activities. Samper did so, but only under pressure from Uncle Sam.

Ambassador Myles R. R. Frechette arrived in Bogotá only days before Samper was sworn in as chief executive on August 7, 1994. The U.S. administration had told the envoy that his highest priorities were to get General Rosso José Serrano named national director of the Colombian National Police (PNC), bring down the Cali drug syndicate, and persuade Colombians to reinstate the extradition of criminals, a process not included in the country's 1991 constitution. Without the legal surrender of fugitives, it was virtually useless to fight narco-trafficking within the Colombian legal system because of the high degree of corruption and impunity.

Upon taking office, Samper shipped General Serrano off to Washington as police attaché and appointed General Ricardo Vargas Meza as PNC director. He did so because Serrano had a reputation as being tough, successful, and incorruptible, while Vargas was considered corrupt and an accomplice in Galán's murder. It took three months of intense pressure from Ambassador Frechette to persuade Samper to make Serrano the national police chief. Under Serrano's leadership, the Cali Cartel top leadership either surrendered or was captured in 1995. Still, Colombia's congress did not amend its constitution to provide for extradition until December 1997.[17]

Despite such progress, officials in Washington had strong misgivings about the honesty of Colombian leaders. Samper's long-time friends, defense minister and former campaign manager Fernando Botero Zea and former campaign treasurer Santiago Medina corroborated the earlier allegations that Samper and his minister had conspired with corrupt congressmen to spike important antinarcotics bills even as he had taken $5.9 million in covert donations from drug dealers in his run-off for the presidency. Gift-wrapped packages of $200,000 were regularly flown from Cali to Bogotá, and cartel bank accounts even paid for some of Samper's TV ads.

In a subsequent trial, Guillermo Pallomari, the accountant for the Cali syndicate, recalled his entourage's jubilation over the bribe. "We've got ourselves a president!" boasted Miguel Rodríguez Orejuela, a top boss of the cartel.[18] The witness revealed that Rodríguez Orejuela and his brother Gilberto hosted a secret dinner for Samper during a campaign stop in Cali. The drug chiefs proposed turning themselves over to Colombian authorities in exchange for light sentences. Much to the dismay of U.S. ambassador Frechette, a skilled and veteran diplomat, the mobsters received sentences of only five years behind bars, less than a quarter of the maximum term. The envoy characterized the outcome as "really, really regrettable."[19]

Specifically, Botero accused the president himself of having known and approved of the decision to go to the cartel for funds during the final days of the campaign. Botero's testimony broke the case wide open. Colombia's chief prosecutor, Alfonso Valdivieso Sarmiento, formally charged Samper with illegal enrichment, with violating Colombia's campaign spending limits, and with attempting to cover up his crimes. Colombia's house of representatives dismissed the charges. When Samper claimed to have known nothing of the payola, Bogotá's feisty bishop Pedro Rubiano called his denial tantamount to ignorance of an elephant "in one's living room." Pundits began referring to Samper's campaign as the "Elephant."[20]

Ambassador Frechette recalls that at the time of Samper's impeachment, Rubiano was still a bishop and president of the Conference of Colombian Bishops. Subsequently he was elevated to cardinal. "He was a wise man and had a wonderful sense of humor. I met with him several times to explain U.S. policy. But he was also a realist. He knew that if he ever supported any aspect of U.S. policy, he would be criticized not just by the Samper government, but also by some within the Church."[21] Many drug traffickers, like Pablo Escobar, gave money to Catholic charities and also for the construction or renovation of churches, monasteries, and convents. The Catholic Church took the position that the provenance of money didn't matter so long as it was put to a use approved of by the Church. That said, the scandal that surrounded Samper and his acceptance of narco-trafficker money dominated the media for months. Rubiano's pachyderm metaphor confirmed what everybody already believed about the chief executive.

It was against this backdrop of allegations and growing scandal that President Bill Clinton decided to decertify Colombia. This action signified that the Colombian government was not cooperating with Washington in the drug war and impelled the cutting off of aid. The U.S. State Department also revoked Samper's visa to visit the United States. In announcing this decision, Secretary of State Madeleine Albright said the measure sprang from the "result of our concern that corruption remains rampant at the highest levels of the Colombian government and that senior officials are failing to cooperate with us in the fight against drugs."[22]

Shocked by decertification, Samper rebutted this charge, saying that "all programs of joint cooperation, especially those dealing with the eradication of [coca and poppy] crops, will be redesigned in their operations and content."[23] He suggested that in light of the alleged environmental damage done by spraying glyphosate, the United States pay farmers not to grow either coca or poppy—a suggestion never considered seriously in Washington.[24]

Although not interfering in the campaign, official Washington delighted in Andrés Pastrana's victory in the August 1998 presidential race. Clinton wasted no time in inviting his Colombian counterpart to the White House, where they explored "the possibility of securing an increase in U.S. aid for counternarcotics projects, sustainable economic development, the protection of human rights, humanitarian aid, stimulating private investment, and joining other donors and international financial institutions to promote Colombia's economic growth." Washington made a big fuss over Pastrana because trying to work with Samper had been a nightmare. It was such a welcome relief to see Samper pass from the scene and be able to help Colombia avoid becoming a failed state.

Diplomatic contacts regarding this subject continued during the rest of the year and into 1999.

In October 1999, the PNC, the Colombian Attorney General's Office, the U.S. Attorney General's Office, and the DEA initiated Operation Millennium, described as "a long-term, complex investigation targeting the inner working of several of the largest international drug trafficking organizations operating in Colombia and Mexico, and smuggling their product into the United States." Among the early successes was the seizure of more than 13,000 kilograms of cocaine during the last two weeks of August.[25]

A NEW BREED OF GUCCI-WEARING NARCO-ENTREPRENEURS

Another achievement was the arrest of Alejandro "Juvenal" Bernal Madrigal, who epitomized the upper-middle-class "legitimate" professionals who aided and abetted the drug trade. *Newsweek* described him as a "light-complexioned, blue-eyed businessman, 40, [who] lavished millions of dollars on his pampered stable of top-of-the-line show horses." He also delighted in taking Caribbean cruises aboard his yacht, the Claudia V, with "bosomy young models;" his children attended one of Medellín's best private schools; his wife stroked a tennis ball at the posh Ceylan Racquet Club; and he circulated without body guards among the city's elite, who also enjoyed an occasional puff or two of marijuana.[26]

Unlike the earlier, trigger-happy coke lords, these young professionals exuded intelligence and urbanity. "These new guys don't flaunt jewels or drive flashy cars, and they are more educated and less violent," says General Serrano. "You have to use a lot more intelligence and surveillance to nab them." Law enforcement officers reported that he deftly used high-tech devices—satellite phones and the Internet—to export tons of cocaine every month that equaled roughly 25 percent of Colombia's total production.

And they were phenomenally successful. Their drug shipments dwarfed the amounts that were sent north by the old Medellín and Cali cocaine cartels at the peak of their bloody machinations a decade before. In 1990 the country's traffickers produced about 65 metric tons of cocaine—a quantify that shot up in the following years according to the DEA and the CIA.

Only persistent, dogged police work gave rise to the capture of Bernal. Colombian police seized him on October 13, 1999, during an Operation Millennium raid, the culmination of a joint U.S.-Colombian investigation spanning a year and two continents. In a single night, some 30 of Colombia's most wanted individuals were rounded up, including Fabio Ochoa

Vásquez, a leading member of Medellín's reputed first family of cocaine. Even so, Bernal was the one who got top billing in the DEA's announcement of the mass arrests.[27]

CLINTON VISITS COLOMBIA AND PROVES A "SAINT" TO ANTONIA SARMIENTO

Conservative Andrés Pastrana Arango narrowly captured the presidency in a mid-1998 run-off against a candidate of the Liberal Party, which had lost support because of alleged financial linkages between President Ernesto Samper (1994–98) and the Cali drug organization. Pastrana, whose father had been the nation's chief executive in the early 1970s, earned a law degree from San Carlos College in Bogotá before studying at the Center for International Affairs at Harvard University. The younger Pastrana lost his presidential bid, but attracted national attention when the Medellín cartel kidnapped him on January 18, 1988. The national police rescued him a week later, and in March he became Bogotá's first popularly-elected mayor.

Pastrana ran on a good government platform. As Charles Krause noted in a PBS interview with the chief of state, his campaigned focused on several issues: ending the 30-year guerrilla war that had left nearly half of the country in the hands of leftist rebels; destroying the cartels that provided 80 percent of the cocaine consumed by Americans; and igniting economic growth.

On the heels of his victory, Pastrana met with the FARC guerrillas in a jungle hideaway. Both sides pledged to begin formal peace parlays by year's end. Still, negotiations were characterized by fits and starts through 1999, even as the FARC and the smaller National Liberation Army stepped up attacks on towns.

In October 1998, Pastrana visited President Clinton at the White House to examine mutual security concerns.[28]

In August 2000 Clinton became the first U.S. president to travel to Colombia in a decade. He placed his seal of approval on Pastrana's "Plan Colombia"—a multipronged initiative designed to help the Andean republic regain sovereignty over vast drug-growing regions in the country's south, diminish widespread violence, and stanch the flow of cocaine entering the United States, especially South Florida. The cost was projected to be $7.5 billion over a three-year period, with Colombia pledging to contribute $4 billion and the United States providing $1.5 to $2 billion— with the remainder coming from international financial institutions and the European Union. Bruce M. Bagley, the leading expert on Colombian affairs, observed that the target for support was Washington inasmuch as Plan Colombia was initially written in English and first circulated among U.S. policymakers before it was made available in Spanish to the Colombian Congress in Bogotá.[29]

At a news conference, the American chief executive vehemently challenged the notion that the venture would thrust U.S. combat troops into the Andes. "This is not Vietnam; neither is it Yankee imperialism," Clinton stressed in defending the controversial $1.3 billion U.S. aid package, part of a $7.5 billion scheme to break the hammerlock that narco-lords held on his host's nation. "A condition of this aid is that we are not going to get into a shooting war," he added. Pastrana reiterated that "we will not have a foreign military intervention in Colombia" during his four-year administration. He also vowed to seek a peace agreement after years of fighting the 20,000 cadre Revolutionary Armed Forces of Colombia (Fuerzas Armadas Revolucionarias de Colombia—FARC), impel economic growth, and fortify the rule of law. "I hope the people of Colombia will understand it and be patient with him," said the visiting dignitary. Clinton lauded Pastrana's efforts to accomplish two objectives that none of his predecessors had attempted: "He's trying to fight the narcotrafficking and find a way to have a diplomatic solution to the civil unrest that has dogged Colombia for 40 years. It is a massive undertaking."[30]

Security concerns dictated that the bilateral parlays take place not in violence-plagued Bogotá, but in the church-infested Spanish colonial port of Cartagena that Sir Francis Drake had sacked in 1586. This change of venue delighted snaggle-toothed Antonia Sarmiento, whose rickety clapboard house was refurbished to make a good impression on the visiting dignitary. "Bill Clinton is a saint brought to me from Heaven," she grinned.[31]

Although Colombians prepared the social provisions of the plan, Washington took the lead in crafting its antidrug and security elements.[32]

The White House's national security adviser for Latin America, Arturo Valenzuela, claimed that the new U.S. aid had "nothing to do" with the antiguerrilla struggle. Nevertheless, Drug Czar General Barry McCaffrey admitted that the money would make an "important" contribution. "In practice Washington's continuing rhetorical efforts to maintain a strict diversion between U.S. anti-narcotics aid and the Colombian military's anti-guerrilla operations are both futile." In a late January 2000 trip to Washington to lobby for the aid package, Pastrana openly recognized that to the extent that the FARC are "in the business," U.S. antinarcotics funds and equipment would be used against the guerrillas.[33]

Clinton went to great pains to include Representative Dennis Hastert in deliberations over Andean affairs. The speaker of the house applauded, and Congress approved the assistance, which included the provision of U.S. helicopters and military trainers. At a news conference in Cartagena, Hastert extolled his hosts: "The people of the United States and the people of Colombia have a great deal in common. There's the distance of an ocean, but there is a tradition of democracy—here, the oldest democracy in the Southern Hemisphere, and in the north, a democracy [that] has strived for over 200 years to ensure that people have human rights, that they can determine their future, that they can work to better themselves in an economic way."[34]

It was interesting that Hastert talked about human rights in Colombia in 2000. In late 1996 or early 1997, the speaker, accompanied by a number of Republican congressmen and Democrat Rod Blagojevich, visited Bogotá. In a private meeting with Frechette at the Embassy to discuss the decertification of Colombia in 1996, the legislators complained that I reported to the State Department too much about violations of human rights. The Speaker said to the diplomat, "we all believe in human rights, but why do you have to pay so much attention to those issues?" The Ambassador explained that I worked for the Executive Branch and that "my instructions were very clear about reporting on human rights."[35]

Briefing reporters on Clinton's visit, National Security Adviser Samuel R. "Sandy" Berger again sought to allay the fear that Americans would be dragged into another Vietnam-type debacle:

You should learn from what happened before. But the fact is this is nothing similar what-so-ever. We're talking about a few hundred American people going to train some Colombia army battalions—vetting them for human rights, training them in human rights as well—who will have a greater capability to provide security for the Colombian [N]ational [P]olice when they go to destroy crops. These are the parameters of our understanding.[36]

As it crystallized, Pastrana predicated his six-year scheme on forming three anti narcotics battalions, trained and equipped by U.S. Special Forces and complemented by 60 helicopters to provide troop mobility. The units would focus on eradicating 60,000 hectares of poppy in the southern department of Putumayo, a province of mountains and tropical savannah, a FARC bastion and home to the rebels' most fearsome fighting force, the 3,000-cadre Southern Block. "We are ready for the gringo imperialists. We will turn this into another Vietnam for them," Southern Block leader Comandante Christian bragged.[37] Apart from meeting strong armed resistance, the proposed aerial eradication program posed a danger to poor vulnerable peasants. "Most peasants are involved in growing coca not for a love of money or the desire to be a multimillionaire, nor to be a drug dealer, just to survive and maintain their children," insisted the president of a local support group seeking to help campesinos find an alternative to producing coca.[38]

Pastrana made a valiant effort to negotiate a peace with the FARC; however, the insurgents' veteran leader, Manuel "Sure Shot" Marulanda, failed to appear at the opening round of the talks, desultory conversations broke down, and the 20,000-strong guerrillas continued the tsunami of kidnappings and attacks on remote towns. Critics demeaned Pastrana, the charming scion of a privileged family, as "light." Among other things, he allowed the guerrillas unfettered access to a Switzerland-sized "demilitarized zone" covered by a vast range of mountains and tropical savannah where the rebels could go about their business free of intrusion by police, the armed forces, or local authorities.[39] Frechette commented that "90,000 Colombians living in this enclave were left to the mercies of the brutal, totalitarian guerrillas."[40]

After four years without a cease fire, political opposition mushroomed amid rampant violence exacerbated by the emergence of 10,000 paramilitary vigilantes, the United Self-Defense Forces of Colombia (AUC).

The rebels claimed control of 100 of the country's 1,093 municipalities, the number of kidnappings was among the highest in the world, and assassinations and other crimes soared. AUC was also gaining influence, expanding its massacres, and producing illicit drugs in competitions with the FARC, the National Liberation Army (ELN), and other narco-traffickers. To his credit and U.S. assistance, Pastrana did make strides in professionalizing the Colombian Army.

Ambassador Frechette remembers that throughout Pastrana's presidency, the Colombian National Police under General Serrano continued to register notable successes against the narco-traffickers. A key intelligence officer, General Oscar Naranjo Trujillo, would later became a bit player in Enrique Peña Nieto's successful campaign for Mexico's presidency in mid-2012. "Serrano was a delight to work with. I met frequently with him and his intelligence chief, then Colonel Naranjo, and admired their dedication and professionalism. Both he and Naranjo spent a great deal of time studying the personalities of criminals they were up against to understand their weaknesses and use them to take them down."[41] Serrano, who is short and stocky, is incredibly agile with lightning reflexes. "We played tennis from time to time, and I never once beat him. He loved it when people on the street recognized him. One time, visiting a police training facility, we walked past two small boys who recognized me and called me by my first name."[42] Serrano pretended to be indignant that they didn't remember his name. He pressed the boys until one jumped up and shouted out "Rosso José." Serrano's eyes twinkled, and he gave each of them a candy. Serrano was so popular, he began to wonder whether he should run for president. He soon discovered, however, that popularity was one thing, but support for the presidency quite another.[43]

On another occasion, Serrano asked Frechette to travel with him and Defense Minister Botero to southern Colombia to fly over a triple canopy rain forest, which hid many cocaine processing labs. At the airport, the ambassador saw he had also invited the heads of the army, navy and air force. They set off in two helicopters and, once they got to the area, Serrano ordered the helicopters to fly only a few feet above tree level. The jungle was so dense it was impossible to see anything on the ground.

"Soon I heard buzzing and some noises in the body of our helicopter. I asked Serrano about the noises, and he said that the narco-traffickers were shooting at us."[44] When the party got back to Bogota, Frechette's wife told him that the State Department had been calling urgently. Officials in Washington had read a wire service story saying that the helicopter in which he was flying had been shot down.

Still, as author Bert Ruíz wrote: "Pastrana is someone who tackled a job he wasn't big enough for. He promised hope, dared to dream of peace and wasn't able to deliver."[45]

Symbolic of his failure was the ransacking of the building in Los Pazos, a village of 400 people deep inside the jungle, where the peace negotiations took place. Vandals smashed windows, scattered ashes, and covered with graffiti walls that had once been adorned with posters promoting harmony.

Álvaro Uribe Vélez, Pastrana's successor, entered office with "blood in his eye"—that is, a fierce determination to battle the FARC, which had killed his father in 1983. "I hold no bitterness," he said before his election,[46] "I just want to serve Colombia." And serve he did. Recent presidents had virtually "let a thousand flowers" bloom in their ministries. Not Uribe. He micromanaged cabinet operations, worked closely with the army and PNC, and reached out to the people. In the past, weekends were sacred for high officials, but not under Uribe. With his entourage in tow, the congenial workaholic made Saturday and Sunday visits to towns throughout the country.[47]

Strongly backed by the public, the erstwhile Antioquia governor mobilized the masses in waging all-out war against the FARC. Marulanda, the FARC's maximum leader, died of a heart attack in March 2008 in the jungle where he had led guerrilla attacks for more than 50 years. But between March 2008 and 2010, the Colombian armed forces killed three other senior FARC leaders. Uribe proposed talks with the insurgents on the condition that they lay down their weapons. Washington embraced him fully, providing not only equipment and training, but also up-to-date intelligence.

Middle-class Colombians praised his success in driving insurgents out of cities, although the FARC still held sway over southern jungle regions and rural zones.

In addition, on July 15, 2003, Uribe negotiated a peace with the AUC paramilitary chiefs, who agreed to demobilize 31,000 of their cadres in exchange for reduced prison sentences and protection from extradition.

Between 2002 and 2008, kidnappings declined 83 percent, homicides by 40 percent, and terrorist attacks by 76 percent. In addition, police are now in all of the nation's 1,099 municipalities, including those once held by rebels.[48]

To his credit, Uribe did not seek to amend the Constitution to run for a third term, which he would have won. Rather, he basked in the reputation of being the staunchest U.S. ally in the fight against the underworld.

CONCLUSION

As conservative columnist Max Boot said:

Álvaro Uribe is one of the most consequential world leaders of the past decade. He is the man primarily responsible for what I have called the "Colombia Miracle"— the amazing turnaround that has taken his country from being a dysfunctional narco-state to a flourishing democracy where drug dealers and Marxist rebels are on the run, and most of the people live in secure conditions.[49]

Boot correctly applauds Colombia's success, but he may be indulging in hyperbole by employing the word "miracle." Enormous progress has been made, especially in securing urban areas. However, as a distinguished former envoy has observed, Juan Manuel Santos (Uribe's successor) inherited a plateful of problems: deeply embedded corruption in the executive branch and in Congress; an inadequate, costly health-care system; street crime in urban areas; charges of human rights abuses; and the quest for ending the FARC and National Liberation Army (ELN) insurgencies. For example, at a late 2012 meeting in Oslo, Colombian negotiators made clear their interest in a peace accord provided the FARC halted military operations. The next day, the guerrillas killed five Colombian troops and wounded 10 more in a bomb attack in the southern province of Putumayo.[50] The 5,000-member ELN agreed to lay down its weapons, and the FARC engaged in parlays with the Colombian representatives in Havana in mid-2013. Guerrilla spokesman Victoria Sandino floated the idea of the election of a constituent assembly that would discuss the "minimum 11 proposals for the democratic restructuring of the state and political reform." This proposal may be a nonstarter because only Congress can approve a referendum, and the rebels do not want legislators involved.[51]

All told, the U.S. government has contributed approximately $7 billion to Plan Colombia and drug eradication. The scheme also gave Peña Nieto's security team an idea of what happens when large cartels metastasize, as is occurring in Mexico. Budgetary issues reduced by 15 percent the aid that Washington contributed to the Andean nation in 2013. The U.S.-Colombia Free Trade Agreement should give a fillip to that country's economy, which is projected to grow 4.4 percent in 2013. Unlike many Latin American leaders, Santos did not blister the Obama administration for attempting to thwart intelligence leaker Edward Snowden's unsuccessful attempt to gain asylum in Bolivia. Instead, the Colombian leader further ingratiated himself with the Obama administration by extraditing Daniel "El Loco" Barrera Barrera, one of the largest cocaine distributors in Colombian history, who pled not guilty on July 10, 2013, in a New York federal court to producing drugs and funneling revenues to terrorist organizations. Santos called him "the last of the great capos."[52]

CHAPTER 3

Shift in Cocaine Flows, the Gulf Cartel, and Los Zetas

INTRODUCTION

Mexico advanced from the minor to the major leagues in drug trafficking because of several factors that shifted the flow of Colombian drugs in the late twentieth century: the successes of the South Florida Task Force (1982–1990), Operation Impunity (1997–1999), Operation Millennium (1998–1999), and Plan Colombia (2000 to present) sharply diminished cocaine shipments to South Florida. The PAN's Vicente Fox Quesada, who assumed the presidency in 2000, halted the dispatch of shadowy police and army squads to punish kingpins who broke the rules of the game. Unlike his successor Felipe Calderón, Fox did not make combatting drugs his number one objective. Higher priorities were a sweeping immigration agreement with the United States, protecting the rights of Mexicans living in El Norte, constructing a new airport to serve Mexico City, and laying to rest the grievances of the indigenous people associated with the Zapatista Army of National Liberation (EZLN). Although following orders, Secretary of Defense Gerardo Clemente R. Vega García had misgivings about using the armed forces to fight criminal elements, possibly because such an offensive could reduce the military's standing as one of the most respected institutions in the nation. In addition, the constitution stipulated that civilian law-enforcement agencies were responsible for fighting crime.

Nonetheless, in 2002 Fox's administration did arrest AFO boss Benjamín Arellano Félix soon after police in Sinaloa killed his brother Ramón. The following year, federal police captured Gulf Cartel big shot

Osiel Cárdenas Guillén and his accomplice Adán Medrano Rodríguez. Overall takedowns of drug mafiosi reached a peak of 28,651 in 2005—a number that rose to 36,332 in 2009 before falling to 11,197 drug-related incarcerations in 2011.[1] In all fairness to the PAN chief executive, human rights considerations impeded the resort to extralegal methods to hammer these barons, who had not only multiplied in number but, in many cases, no longer exerted iron discipline over their cadres. However, without muscular backup from Mexico City, local police were vulnerable to corruption and intimidation. The concept of *plata o plomo* ("pocket bribes or be killed") was by no means a cliché. Authorities who failed to cooperate with the gangsters risked their lives and those of their families.

Meanwhile, the advent of the North American Free Trade Agreement (NAFTA), which took effect on January 1, 1994, proved a godsend for Mexico's macroeconomy—the trade among Canada, Mexico, and the United States surged from $288 billion in 1993 to $918 billion in 2010, a 218% increase.[2] At the same time, the trilateral pact sharply drove the southbound cascade of weapons and transborder export of drugs to what one analyst called "America's big nose." Profitability rose inasmuch as "in the early 1980s, white powder [cocaine] that had once been a white-collar drug exploded into American inner cities in the form of crack cocaine."[3]

The total number of northbound traffic through the two commercial bridges in Laredo (World Trade Bridge and the Laredo-Colombia Solidarity Bridge) reached the highest point of 1.7 million trucks in 2011 even though there was a significant drop in 2009 due to the economic downturn.[4]—with only 8 to 10 percent stopped for random searches by the U.S. Immigration and Customs Enforcement agency (ICE). In addition to the Nuevo Laredo connections, there are 11 other spans connecting northern Mexico with Texas. They are often jammed with automobiles, tractor-trailer trucks, and rail cars 24 hours a day. Delivery techniques range from the bizarre to the quixotic. At least twice, desperados used a catapult in an attempt to propel 45 pounds of marijuana across the fence dividing the countries; on another occasion, authorities in Nuevo Laredo discovered a woman whose car trunk held a statue of Jesus comprised of 6.6 pounds of cocaine mixed with plaster.[5] More successful have been reliance on torpedo-sized semisubmergible vessels, which can move up to 2 tons of drugs from offshore to Mexican ports.[6] Border Patrol agents have discovered radios, cell phones, and GPS tracking devices used by drug runners. "These guys are very ingenious," said Rafael Reyes, chief of global enforcement operations for the U.S. DEA. He pointed out that the criminals know a certain quantity of drugs will be seized. "They line up 10 loads, and if you pick off two or three, well, that's the cost of doing business. 'I got seven across.' So it's that shotgun mentality."[7]

The narco-traffickers became so adept at burrowing under the U.S.-Mexican border that in 2003 ICE created a multiagency task force to thwart these criminal moles.

JUAN GARCÍA ÁBREGO AND CHANGE IN DELIVERY STRUCTURE

At first, the Mexican crime organizations picked up shipments at the Guatemalan frontier or at an isolated spot in Mexico and handed them off to Colombian wholesalers at the U.S. border. The Mexicans acted like FedEx, UPS, DHL, or some other delivery service. Juan García Ábrego,[8] who headed the Gulf Cartel until early 1996, revamped this business model. He was a crony of Raúl, the kleptocratic younger brother of President Carlos Salinas (1988–1994), and Tamaulipas's corruption-drenched governor Tomás Yarrington Ruvalcaba (1999–2005). In 1994 the drug lord's narco-trafficking brother, Humberto, helped organize the prime fund-raiser in the north for PRI presidential candidate Luis Donaldo Colosio, who was later assassinated.[9] The putty-faced García Ábrego became the first Mexican to appear on the FBI's Ten Most Wanted list largely due to his path-breaking accord with Colombian cartels in the early 1990s, and President Clinton's determination to lower the boom on the multibillion-dollar illicit drug flow.

As examined in Chapter 2, mounting pressure from the Americans in South Florida convinced the Colombians to change their supply route. They found the Mexican Federal Judicial Police too brutal and corrupt to trust.[10] Thus, they agreed to turn over half of their shipments to the Gulf Cartel, which incurred the risk of guaranteeing delivery of cocaine in return for banking the earnings from sales. The formula soon became the model for all major Mexican syndicates. "This deal was a major turning point in the fortunes of the Mexican cartels. With this new arrangement, the power and wealth of the Mexican drug cartels exploded."[11]

By renegotiating this pact with the Cali Cartel, García Ábrego succeeded in deriving 50 percent of a shipment from the Colombians as payment for delivery, instead of the less attractive $1,500 per kilogram previously received. The new business model came with a price: the Mexicans had to guarantee that Colombian exports reached their destinations. While risky, this deal generated estimated wholesale revenues at $1.1 to $1.6 billion per year, giving rise to $500 to $800 million in profits annually.[12] Mitigating the risk was García Ábrego's close ties to the presidency, as well as to the Ministry of Communications and Transportation, whose responsibilities included oversight of airports, seaports, highways, communications networks, and the egregiously venal Federal Highway Police.[13]

In the wake of this transformation, García Ábrego accumulated large quantities of cocaine along Mexico's northern frontier. The new configuration exacerbated corruption because stockpiling as much as 100 tons of cocaine meant there were more palms to grease.

At the same time, the agreement enabled the Gulf Cartel honcho to design his own distribution network and with newfound profits, expand his political influence. He collaborated with Guillermo González Calderoni, the devious Federal Judicial Police commander who had won fame for killing drug honcho Pablo Acosta and later capturing Félix Gallardo.[14] This linkage vouchsafed the organization's success and shielded its leaders from arrest. The crooked cop never needed to prove his loyalty to the organization; he had grown up in Reynosa and was a boyhood friend of García Ábrego's older brother Mario. In a world where trust is worth more than life, he drew upon their shared history, transcended only by blood relations.

DEA administrator Thomas Constantine stated: "These sophisticated drug syndicates from Mexico have eclipsed organized crime groups from Colombia as the premier law-enforcement threat facing the United States. Today ... bosses have at their disposal airplanes, boats, vehicles, radar, communications equipment and weapons in quantities that rival the capability of some legitimate governments."[15]

The Gulf Cartel took advantage of large Mexican American communities to establish drug distribution centers in Chicago, Dallas, Denver, Houston, New York, and Los Angeles. The Colombians agreed to the arrangement as long as the Mexicans left them selected East Coast markets. The windfall allowed García Ábrego to make additional investments to insulate his organization from law enforcement. In the early and mid-1990s, he showered millions of dollars on Mexican officials, the army, and politicians.

The syndicate's corruptive influence stretched across the Gulf of Mexico to Quintana Roo, where Ábrego and Governor Mario "Chueco" ("Crooked Face") Villanueva Madrid facilitated the passage of drugs from the Yucatán Peninsula through Campeche, Tabasco, Veracruz, Tamaulipas, and ultimately to Nuevo León. This corridor provided the initial framework for what would become the states where his organization exercised significant territorial control and political influence.[16] Still, President Salinas's successor and nemesis, Ernesto Zedillo, brought a swift end to the handy work of García Ábrego, who was taken into custody outside of Monterrey, Nuevo León, on January 14, 1996, and immediately delivered to the FBI in Houston.

In closed proceedings, the prosecution revealed that the Gulf Cartel had smuggled more than 15 tons of cocaine and 46,000 pounds of marijuana into the United States and laundered approximately $10.5 million. His cousin testified that García Ábrego routinely spent up to $80,000 on pricey watches and expensive suits for Mexican police and prosecutors during frequent shopping trips in Texas. A government witness alleged that the defendant paid $1.5 million a month to Javier Coello Trejo, the assistant attorney general in charge of combatting narcotics—an accusation that Coello Trejo denied, much to the disbelief of ranking American diplomats. After a four-week trial, the jury needed only 12 hours to convict García Ábrego on 22 counts, including money laundering, drug trafficking, intent to distribute, and operating a criminal enterprise. The defendant choked back tears as the presiding judge, eager to make him the poster boy in the drug war, decreed the seizure of up to $350 million of his assets—$75 million more than the prosecution requested, and sentenced him to 11 consecutive sentences at the federal ADX prison in Florence, South Carolina. Meanwhile, the PJF commander who made the arrest allegedly received a bulletproof Mercury Grand Marquis and $500,000 from a competing cartel for accomplishing the takedown.[17]

Osiel "The Friend Killer" Cárdenas Guillén took the reins of the Gulf Cartel. His paranoia that allies and enemies were plotting his assassination prompted him to recruit approximately 30 deserters from Mexican army's special forces, known as the Airborne Special Forces Group (GAFES). These intrepid commandos became known as Los Zetas and are discussed later in the chapter. They terrorized, killed, and tortured Cárdenas's foes, but they could not prevent their employer's capture when an informer divulged Osiel's whereabouts. The army seized him at a party in Matamoros on March 14, 2003.

EVOLUTION OF THE GULF CARTEL

After Cárdenas's takedown, the Gulf syndicate's leadership was composed of Osiel's brother Ezequiel "Tony Tormenta"/"Tony the Storm" Cárdenas Guillén, the Friend Killer's confidant in Tamaulipas Jorge Eduardo "El Coss" Costilla Sánchez, and Zeta chief Heriberto "The Executioner" Lazcano Lazcano, also referred to as "El Lazca." The troika repulsed a move by the Sinaloa Cartel, commanded by the notorious Joaquín "El Chapo" Guzmán Loera, to seize Nuevo Laredo and other northern entry points into the United States. Joining the Sinaloans in this venture were the Beltrán Leyva Organization (BLO) and its bloodthirsty gunslinger Édgar Valdez Villarreal, called "La Barbie," a nickname acquired because his light complexion and corn-flower blue eyes resembled those of Mattel's Ken doll.

This Gulf Cartel victory aside, the organization's fragmented and dysfunctional leadership experienced one setback after another. The demonic Miguel Ángel "El 40" Morales Treviño had risen to number-two in the ranks of Los Zetas. A Nuevo Laredo native who spent his youth in Dallas,

El 40 joined Los Tejas gang before becoming a Jack-of-all-trades for the Gulf Cartel. A sadist, he encouraged Los Zetas to commit grisly acts of cruelty to brand themselves as the most venal criminal outfit in the country, if not all of the Americas. His readiness to decapitate enemies was bad for business for the corporate-oriented Gulf Cartel. The renegades also struck situational alliances with the Beltrán Leyva Organization, made up of Sinaloans who had broken ties with El Chapo.

The Gulf-Zeta divorce became conclusive in early 2010 when El Coss acquiesced in Samuel "Metro 3" Flores Borrego's plan to kill Sergio "Concord 3" Peña Mendoza, El 40's right-hand man. When Costilla Sánchez refused to hand over Metro 3, Treviño Morales rounded up and executed 16 Gulf Cartel members in Reynosa. This murder exacerbated fissures in the narco-clan.

On November 5, 2010, soldiers and marines, the navy's infantry, downed Osiel's brother Tony Tormenta in a gun battle in Matamoros, reportedly benefiting from information supplied by Costilla, who had been scheming to seize the cartel's reins. In March 2011, Rafael "El Junior" Cárdenas Vela, Osiel's nephew managed to replace José Luis "El Wicho" Zuñiga Hernández as boss of Matamoros, but fear of assassination by El Coss's hit men prompted his flight to the United States, where his career ended when federal authorities arrested him in Port Isabel, Texas, on October 20, 2011. Partial control of the organization fell into the lap of another Cárdenas Guillén brother, Mario "El Gordo"/"Fatso" whom the marines apprehended in Tamaulipas on September 3, 2012. Just over five weeks later, the military, perhaps relying on a tip from El Junior, nabbed Costilla. An astute journalist's description of double-chinned, mustachioed El Gordo's appearance before the media symbolized the state of the Gulf Cartel: "Wearing an armored vest and his shirttail hanging out, the balding, chubby Cárdenas mostly cast his eyes downward, occasionally glancing to the side."[18] One week later, the armed forces detained Juan Gabriel "Gabi" Montes Sermeño, one of the syndicate's top commanders in southern Tamaulipas. Montes led the organization's strike team known as the Kalimanes. As a regional leader, he focused on money laundering, moving drugs, and managing the organization's ranches. Before entering the underworld, he worked as a cattleman.

In late September 2012, the navy and the Federal Police Support Forces apprehended José Inés Medina Rodríguez, in Cadereyta, just outside Monterrey, Nuevo León. In addition to a 9-millimeter (mm) pistol, the alleged plaza boss of Ciudad Juárez had in his possession 24 bullets, four bags of marijuana, 14 doses of cocaine, and 17 psychotropic pills. They also discovered an image of Santa Muerte, the so-called Saint of Death, a boney-fingered, scythe-carrying female cult figure whom some traffickers worship.[19]

In early 2013, authorities further weakened the Gulf Cartel by sentencing El Wicho to seven years in prison on federal immigration and weapon charges. They also took into custody Juventino "El Secre" Palacios González, and two other cell leaders along with 13 of their accomplices. They confessed to having committed 12 executions in the Monterrey metropolitan area.[20]

Amid intrigue that found one honcho betraying another, the syndicate fragmented—with the strongest currents being a pro–Cárdenas Guillén faction, Los Rojas, led by Homero "Los Orejas" Cárdenas, a family member; and pro–El Coss acolytes, Los Metros, headed by Mario Armando "El Pelón" Ramírez Treviño. El Chapo has urged reconciliation between the two blocs—to the point of dispatching toughs from the Jalisco New Generation Cartel (CJNG), a vicious Guadalajara-based anti-Zeta gang to bolster the forces of El Pelón, whose lieutenant is an original Zeta, Cruz Galindo Mellado. Yet an outbreak of intra-mural violence erupted in Reynosa on March 10, 2013, when Miguel "El Gringo" Villarreal, the plaza jefe in Miguel Alemán, Tamaulipas, who also ordered kidnappings and assassinations along the South Texas frontier, challenged "El Pelón" for supremacy of the syndicate. At the end of three hours of mayhem, several dozen Gulf members were killed, including El Gringo and his lieutenant Jesús "El Puma" García Román.[21]

In the fall of 2013, the Gulf Cartel held sway in Reynosa and Matamoros, while sharing control with Los Zetas over San Fernando, a strategic, dangerous crossroads 30 miles south of Matamoros.

The Gulf Cartel made common cause with the Sinaloa Cartel in hopes that it could help El Chapo oust El 40 from his Nuevo Laredo stronghold in return for the less lucrative plazas of Matamoros and Reynosa. El Chapo paid Los Tejas thugs to attack Treviño Morales's gunmen and assets to weaken his once-iron grip on Nuevo Laredo.

Appendix C describes the evolution of the Gulf Cartel and Los Zetas.

The Gulf Cartel never recovered from the capture of Osiel Cárdenas. Even though no fewer than 39 lawyers registered to defend him, in a closed trial in a Houston federal courthouse, Cárdenas was convicted and sentenced to a 25-year term. His readiness to "sing like a canary" about Los Zetas should diminish his prison stay, a federal agent told me off the record. By 2014, he will have spent 11 years locked up, reducing his remaining time behind bars to 14 years—possibly fewer if he proves even more helpful to U.S. authorities. For example, he used a government-provided cell phone to contact a leader of La Familia Michoacán with advice about that deadly cartel's policies.

Yet, the Gulf Cartel's fortunes could improve with the debilitation of Los Zetas combined with the mid-2013 movement of more drugs crossing into the United States not just at Nuevo Laredo but also along the border between Nuevo Laredo and Reynosa.

EMERGENCE OF LOS ZETAS

As mentioned, Osiel was convinced that enemies were out to kill him, and indeed, he had given them ample reasons to do so. He told a confidant in the army, Lieutenant Arturo "Z-1" Guzmán Decena, that he "wanted the best men possible" to safeguard him. Guzmán, who himself had deserted, replied: "They are in the Army," and spearheaded the recruitment of GAFES.

This contingent emerged when France's National Police Intervention Group instructed a Mexican Rapid Intervention Force to provide security for the 1986 World Cup matches held in Mexico City amid difficult economic conditions. On June 1, 1990, the group adopted its current name, Special Forces Airmobile Group (GAFEs). American and Israeli experts instructed members of this elite unit in rapid deployment, aerial assaults, marksmanship, ambushes, intelligence collection, surveillance techniques, prisoner rescues, sophisticated communications, and the art of intimidation. Eight years later the GAFES saw action against the Zapatista National Liberation Army (EZLN), a rebel force in the southern state of Chiapas. They also began to participate in the war against drug cartels—distinguishing themselves by capturing Benjamin Arellano Felix head of the Tijuana Cartel and, of course, Osiel Cárdenas. It is ironic that loyal GAFES helped to apprehend Osiel, the kingpin whom the apostate GAFES-turned-Zetas had been hired to safeguard.

Contrary to conventional wisdom, there is no evidence that any of the original Zetas trained in the United States. El Lazca recruited Germán "El Tatanka" Torres Jiménez, who began his criminal career in Veracruz, as an instructor. The original Zeta, known as "Z-25," displayed expertise in logistics and kidnapping. He also executed five members of La Familia Michoacán, described in Chapter 4, before the federal police arrested him in Poza Rica, Veracruz, in late April 2009.[22] The army turncoats set up at least six camps to train older adolescents and men in their early twenties, as well as ex-federal, state, and local police officers. Los Zetas allegedly conducted exercises at locations southwest of Matamoros, across the border from Brownsville; just north of the Nuevo Laredo airport; near the town of Abasolo, between Matamoros and Ciudad Victoria; and at the "Rancho Las Amarillas" outside the rural community of China, which lies near the Nuevo León–Tamaulipas frontier. When the Calderón administration began to capture and kill experienced Zetas, rumors spread that the criminals might move their boot camps into the United States.[23] In fact, the FBI reported that a cell of Los Zetas had acquired a ranch in an isolated Texas county that it used for both training and "neutralizing" foes.[24] In view of the no-holds-barred battle against Los Zetas and the loss of its top men, they are more likely to conduct out-of-country training in Central America.

Many of the Benedict Arnolds acquired advanced instruction from foreign experts in marksmanship, intelligence, communications, propaganda, jungle warfare, sabotage, and other key areas. They provided several rings of protection for the Friend Killer, who rewarded them with attractive compensation, better food than was dished out at military canteens, high-powered weapons, small amounts of drugs, and the knowledge that they belonged to a closely knit "Army of Narcos" that looked after comrades. They assumed the "Zeta strut."

Once Osiel was out of the pictures, Los Zetas, like Frankenstein, gradually turned with a vengeance on their masters. They entered into situational alliances with the rival Beltrán Leyva Organization. Moreover, Osiel Cárdenas never tutored Los Zetas in narco-trafficking. Unschooled in the arcane narcotics business and lacking Colombian contacts, the cartel made a concerted effort to diversify its activities after authorities seized their first major drug load. The 11.7-ton container of cocaine captured in Altamira, on October 5, 2007, was intended for El 40. Although eight of his heavily armed cohorts were apprehended, Morales Treviño fled when he realized that law-enforcement officials were on the scene.[25]

In addition to some drug commerce, Los Zetas turned to a dozen or more felonious activities. These include extortion, murder-for-hire, kidnapping, human smuggling, contraband, petroleum theft, money laundering, prostitution, arson, sale of body parts, hijacking automobiles and trucks, loan-sharking, paying small farmers to grow poppies, providing protection, and taxing rivals who want to cross their territory. Their penchant for obscene cruelty gave the cartel "cred" (credibility) in the underworld. Several examples appear later in the text.

Los Zetas, which the White House had labeled a "global menace" comparable to the Camorra in Italy, the Yakuza in Japan, and the Circle of the Brothers in Russia, achieved the status as the second most powerful criminal group in Mexico. There are several explanations for their success. Los Zetas developed a reputation derived from sadistic and savage acts. A friend cautioned the author not even to utter the word "Zeta" aloud when walking in the streets of Xalapa, the colonial capital of Veracruz, a state penetrated by these bandits. Their inhumane cruelty meant if the outlaws sought "protection" payment from, say, an auto dealer, he knew that failure to comply would lead to the bombing of his showroom and, very likely, the abduction and the horrific death of a loved one. For instance, El 40 mastered the preparation of a *guiso* ("stew"). The recipe was simple: he and his brigands sliced and diced a child or adult, plunged his blood-soaked body into a pig cooker or rusty 55-gallon oil drum, and doused the victim with gasoline. In some cases, burning the corpse to a crisp obviated taking reliable DNA samples of the body.[26]

Authorities could identify the charred remains of Rodolfo Rincón Taracena, whom the killers abducted in 2007. According to the Committee to

Protect Journalists, the seasoned reporter's offense was to have exposed criminals targeting slot-machine patrons at *"narco-tiendas"* or small stores selling drugs in Villahermosa, Tabasco's capital. The alleged culprits belonged to a Zeta cell headed by José Akal Sosa.[27]

As one veteran reporter expressed it: "The elderly are killed. Young women are raped. And able-bodied men are given hammers, machetes and sticks and forced to fight to the death." He referred to a report that Los Zetas have forced passengers dragged from busses to engage in gladiatorial fights to determine who could qualify to be one of their ruffians.[28]

Roman-like combat, guisos, castrations, butchery, skinnings, incinerations, beheadings, and other gruesome practices serve several purposes. They spark fear in enemies, who shy from confrontations with these villains; they bolster Zetas' chances to extort money from their targets; they gain widespread media attention, which generates an ambience of fear and distrust; they dissuade all but the most valiant journalists from covering their behavior; they originally maintained discipline in their ranks; they increase the likelihood that, for example, petroleum specialists will aid and abet their theft of oil and natural gas—a crime that earned them 5,125 million pesos ($427 million) between 2007 and mid-2012.[29] Coal has become another lucrative commodity that the commandos are stealing.[30] An informal motto was that you had to kill to become a Zeta, and you had to die to leave the organization. The early Zetas kept records on their members; if one deserted, he might achieve freedom, but family members, including children and women, were likely to suffer a ghastly death because of the escape.

After a withering gun battle, marines killed Lazcano in Progreso, Coahuila, on October 7, 2012 while he was nonchalantly watching a baseball game. What ensued is worthy of a best-selling "Who done it?" After forensic experts examined Lazcano's corpse, the marines—believing they had gunned down a common criminal—deposited the capo's remains at a private funeral home in Sabinas, Coahuila, 80 miles from the U.S. border.

A day after the slaying, a gang of masked, heavily armed hoodlums burst into the parlor, overpowered the staff, shoved Lazcano's decaying body into a hearse, and forced the owner to drive to a yet-to-be-discovered venue. What explains this ghoulish action?[31]

As ruthless as they are, veteran Zetas originally claimed to adhere to the tradition, begun by the U.S. Marines in 1775, of never leaving a fallen brother behind, especially if he was in the hierarchy.

For example, in early March 2007, Zeta gunmen broke into a cemetery in Poza Rica, Veracruz; used hammers to smash open the gravestone of their comrade Roberto Carlos Carmona; and carried away the casket containing his body.

Los Zetas find other ways to honor their dead. Three months after the army killed Guzmán Decenas, the lieutenant who recruited many members of the original force, a funeral wreath and four flower arrangements appeared at his gravesite with this inscription: "We will always keep you in our hearts: from your family, Los Zetas." A U.S. source indicated that a fingerprint match revealed that Lazcano had been killed. Lest rumors persist that The Executioner is alive and well, his family agreed to have a relative exhumed from a cemetery in his native Hidalgo to carry out DNA tests, which affirmed the identity of the Los Zetas's chieftain.[32]

As a result, leadership passed to Treviño Morales, the most sadistic member of the hierarchy. "Now Lazcano was a brutal task master and extremely violent. However, Miguel Treviño is 100 percent more violent that Lazcano ever was," said Mike Vigil, former DEA chief of international operations.[33]

For instance, El 40 believed that small-time drug sellers who worked for his organization had skimmed cash they were supposed to turn over to a collection agent. Accompanied by several thugs, the Zeta honcho barged into the boarding house where the vendors lived. They lined the men up against the wall. Then El 40 ferociously wielded a two-by-four, pummeling the first alleged cheat to death. The second experienced a more gory fate. The Zeta strongman slashed his throat with a razor-sharp butcher's knife, plunged his hand through the victim's bloody thorax, and yanked out his heart. Los Zetas demand every peso they believe owed to them, and don't want to be cheated out of even a widow's mite.[34]

HOW LOS ZETAS REMAINED POWERFUL FOR SO LONG

In view of the death of El Lazca and the many setbacks suffered by Los Zetas, how did they remain the second most powerful cartel in Mexico with a presence in 21 states, in Central America, and in the northern Andes?

Below are factors that, while still practiced, are less relevant because of the cartel's fragmentation.

First, their readiness to inflict excruciating cruelty enhanced their ability to instill fear in average citizens and criminal rivals. Among their more heinous actions were: massacring 72 illegal aliens near San Fernando (military found the mass grave on August 24, 2010); killing 52 clients and employees in the fire-bombing of the Casino Royale in Monterrey (August 25, 2011); instigating a riot at the Apodaca penitentiary in Nuevo León in which 44 inmates died and 30 Zetas escaped (February 19, 2012); and mutilating the bodies of 49 people in Cadereyta, Nuevo León (May 13, 2012).[35]

Second, they are past masters at bribing and intimidating local police, thousands of whom receive one paycheck from their municipality and another from the cartel. Third, diversification of criminal acts provides them with more than a score of revenue sources, with their recent foray into "petroleum rustling" proving especially lucrative. Moreover, the brigands have hijacked tractor-trailers and livestock trucks even as they expand the sale of protection to table-dance cafes, brothels, bars, and discotheques.

Fourth, unlike the army, Los Zetas have shown an amazing ability to make quick decisions and marshal the appropriate weapons and equipment, particularly when attempting strategic attacks and retreats.

Fifth, they engaged in desultory alliances with the Beltrán Leyva Organization, the Juárez Cartel, and Los Mazatlecos, the Mazatlán-based ally of BLO, as well as La Resistencia, a Jalisco State gang. Other "force multipliers" included ties with the Mara Salvatruchas, which concentrates its criminality in Central America and the Mexican-Guatemalan border, the Barrio Azteca, the Texas Syndicate, and smaller drug merchants Guatemala, El Salvador, Honduras, Colombia, and Venezuela.[36]

Sixth, they proved proficient in using narco-banners and such social media as the Internet, Twitter, and YouTube to recruit cadres, disseminate information about their horrendous deeds, and denounce competing organizations.

Seventh, they've relied on safe houses and smuggling corridors in key regions of the country, as well as sophisticated operations in other countries, especially in Guatemala, El Salvador, and Honduras where they are competing with the Sinaloa Cartel. The Mexican-Guatemalan border resembles a sieve blasted by shotgun pellets, and Los Zetas have taken advantage of some 300 pedestrian crossings to penetrate its southern neighbor. Its ambassador to Mexico, Fernando Andrade Díaz Durán, lamented that Guatemala's government "is extremely concerned because during the last three or four years, Los Zetas has consolidated its presence in all of our country."[37] The country's president, Otto Pérez Molina, has announced the possibility of joint maneuvers with Mexico and the United States at the border, which will include posting a brigade at the frontier, especially in San Marcos department, similar to a state in the United States.[38] Similarly, Colombia's chief executive Juan Manuel Santos has ordered the PNC to investigate whether Los Zetas are active in his country.

Eighth, they operate on U.S. soil. For example, they have smuggled guns and grenades from Mexico through the Falcon Dam and then move them to the U.S. side of the border to Roma, Texas, and then back to Miguel Alemán, Tamaulipas, to evade Gulf Cartel checkpoints.[39] The commandos reportedly have recruited young Hispanic gangs in Laredo, Texas—the so-called *zetitas*—to broaden their activities in the United States.[40] Some would-be thugs identify themselves as Los Zetas as if it were a franchise like McDonald's. This tactic elevates the fear of potential victims. "It's gotten to the point where you get drunk, shoot at some cans and paint your face black, and that makes you a Zeta. . . . A lot of it is image and myth."[41] The desperados are quick to take revenge on copycats. Above all, they do not want amateurs taking a slice of their market. In addition, the ersatz Zetas may not carry out threats, diminishing the credibility of the organization. In October 2007 Zeta imposters demanded first 1 million dollars than 1 million pesos from a restaurant owner. Although they shot up the façade of his home, no one was injured, and the family quickly moved to another state.[42] In May 2008 a 35-year-old man was found in Monterrey. He had been tortured, an ice pick was plunged through his thorax, and a note dangled in his hand: "This is one of those who carried out extortions by telephone trying to pass for 'Z.' "[43] In February 2009 the brigands executed two "false Zetas" in Reynosa, leaving behind a handwritten note saying that "this is what will happen to those who attempt to pass themselves off as Zetas."[44]

Ninth, newspaper sellers, street vendors, taxi-cab drivers, and other denizens of city streets serve as couriers and lookouts, which means there are even more eyes available to signal threats to Los Zetas. The hundreds of thousands of youngsters known as "Ni-Nis"—they neither work nor study—are ripe for recruitment The prospect of a few thousand pesos in their blue jeans, access to a weapon, and the ability to live for the moment makes Los Zetas attractive. They seem to follow the Sinaloan adage: "Better to be a king for five years than a beggar all your life." At the same time, Los Zetas finance hip-hop narco-corridos, which are far more appealing to young people than traditional ballads.

Tenth, the government of the last governor of Veracruz allowed the gangsters to become entrenched in his bailiwick. As a consequence, the navy has taken over the lion's share of law-enforcement in the coastal state's major cities.

Finally, they use women more skillfully than other cartels. Las *Panteras* ("The Panthers") are linked to the organization's myriad financial and criminal structures. These Panthers are females concentrated in Nuevo León with *jefas* in most states. Their leader, believed to be Ashly "La Comandante Bombón" Narro López, was captured in Cancún on February 9, 2009, in connection with the murder of General Tello Quiñones. Their task is to negotiate deals with police, politicians, military officers, and others who can assist Los Zetas. Should talks break down, La Pantera may kill her interlocutor. First identified at a party thrown by El Lazca in mid-December 2006, these women change their makeup and the color and style of their hair according to the assignment they are undertaking.[45] One quarter of Los Zetas apprehended in early 2011 were females, according to the PGR. In addition to seduction and murder, these women traffic in arms and drugs, launder money, and undertake kidnappings. Their weekly salaries range from $305 for defending a Zeta plaza to $1,525 for murdering a rival cartel member or law-enforcement agents. "We cannot play down or ignore the increase in the participation of women in the cartels, with time they will be converted into leaders," said UNAM analyst José Luis Piñero.[46]

Table 3.1

January to September 2007 Expenditures by Zetas' Monterrey Plaza

Expenditure	Amount in Dollars	Percentage of Total
Administration and lookouts	18,400	2.85
Security	1,100	0.17
Gifts	50,000	7.73
Raffle (five Rolex watches)	25,000	3.86
Payoffs to police	552,350	85.39
TOTAL	646,850	100.00

Source: Confidential

In addition, Las Panteras may function as financial agents. In these cases, they rent a well-protected home or apartment and report not to the plaza boss but directly to the cartel's leadership. They either turn over the proceeds on a regular basis to a courier or deposit them in a local bank account to which the cartel's leaders have access. They demand receipts from cartel members who buy cars, rent apartments, or incur other major expenses. A floating auditor makes unannounced visits to cells to ensure that finances are in order. Table 3.1 indicates nine months of the Monterrey plaza's expenditures in 2007.

CONCLUSION

Every law-enforcement agency and most cartels are eager to eliminate Los Zetas—the former because inhumane acts are bad for business, the latter because of the mayhem that the paramilitaries cause. The killing of Heriberto Lazcano the apprehension of El 40, and the take-down of scores of founders and recruits have fragmented Los Zetas, just as took place in Colombia with the Medellín and Cali Cartels.

Among fallen Zetas who operated key plazas, command-and-control, and financial structures were Jaime "El Hummer" González Durán (November 7, 2008), Sigifredo "El Canicón" Nájera Talamantes, (March 23, 2009), Germán "El Tatanka" Torres Jiménez (April 25, 2009), Braulio "El Gonzo" Arellano Dominguez (November 3, 2009), Jesús Enrique "El Mamito" Rejón Aguilar (July 4, 2011), Carlos "La Rana" Oliva Castillo (October 12, 2011), Raúl Lucio "El Lucky" Hernández Lechuga (December 12, 2011), Francisco "El Quemado" Medina Mejía (April 4, 2012), Alberto José "El Paisa" González Xalate (April 29, 2012), Iván "El Taliban" Velázquez Caballo (September 26, 2012), Salvador Alonso "La Ardilla"

Martínez Escobar (October 7, 2012), and accountant Alfonso Zamudio Quijada (May 9, 2013).

El Lazca's death proved a major reversal because of his knowledge of military strategy. Equally devastating was the split between Lazcano and El 40. The former's ally, "El Talibán," arrested in late September 2012, accused El 40 of betraying comrades in order to get better treatment for his family members captured in the United States. These family members include his brother José and José's wife, Zulema, who laundered money through the purchase and racing of thoroughbred quarter horses in Oklahoma, New Mexico, and California;[47] and a nephew, Juan Francisco Treviño Chávez, whom the Nuevo León state investigative agency, caught in mid-June 2012 along with a cousin who also belonged to Los Zetas, Jesús Chávez García.[48] Mamito also divulged information to authorities about the organization's operations. As the armed forces and police removed top dogs from the scene, Los Zetas were forced to rely heavily on green-as-grass newcomers, who lacked the savvy of veterans in staging operations and combatting foes.

In addition, they were turning little or no profit inasmuch as they had to purchase weapons and pay recruits.

Even more devastating was the apprehension of El 40. At 3:15 a.m. on July 15, 2013, marines flying a Black Hawk helicopter swooped down on a grey 2013 Ford Super Duty truck. They took only 7 minutes to snag their prey, his bodyguard, and an accountant on a dirt road outside of Nuevo Laredo without firing a shot. Treviño Morales and his confederates were carrying $2.18 million in cash and a small arsenal of weapons.[49] The Mexican newspaper *La Jornada* reported the U.S. security agencies had supplied an un-manned drone to facilitate capture.[50]

Los Zetas are crippled but alive. As late as the spring of 2013 and before El Lazca's imprisonment, the Dallas-based consulting firm Stratfor called them "the most powerful criminal organization in Mexico."[51] Several months later, they still were the 800-pound gorilla in Nuevo Laredo and had cadres in San Fernando (where the Gulf Cartel was also present) and Southern Tamaulipas. In addition, they were a force to be reckoned with in; Piedras Negras, Torreón, and other regions of Coahuila; Tuxpan and Coatzacoalcos, Veracruz; La Huasteca of San Luis Potosí; Zacatecas; Villahermosa and other municipalities in Tabasco; Hidalgo (where they are battling the Knights Templars), the north of Sinaloa in league with the BLO, and Central America. Besides brutal deaths, the paramilitaries have left a legacy of "zetanization"; namely, that competing cartels began to decapitate, castrate, and dismember their prey to emulate Los Zetas's tactics as a means to cower police, extort money, and obtain ransoms from the families and friends of kidnap victims.

With Treviño Morales behind bars, the Sinaloa Cartel will step up its assault on northern bastions of Los Zetas. "As a cohesive group there is probably not much left of them," observed Mexican security consultant Alejandro Hope. "But there will continue to be people who call themselves Zetas, act like Zetas and belong to gangs that use their letter." More pessimistic was Father Pedro Pantoja Arreola, a Catholic priest in Saltillo, Coahuila, the stronghold of Omar Treviño Morales, El 40's brother who seeks to head the organization. "No matter who is in charge," the priest said. "[T]he system will remain in place as poverty and criminal logistics combine, often with violence used as a way to maintain control."[52]

Chapter 4 discusses the origins, leadership, and growth of the Sinaloa Cartel and the diaspora, impelled by Miguel Ángel Félix Gallardo, of other syndicates that operate in the north and northwest of the country and regard Los Zetas as evil incarnate. The Sinaloa Cartel and Los Zetas are the largest and most dangerous criminal organizations in Mexico.

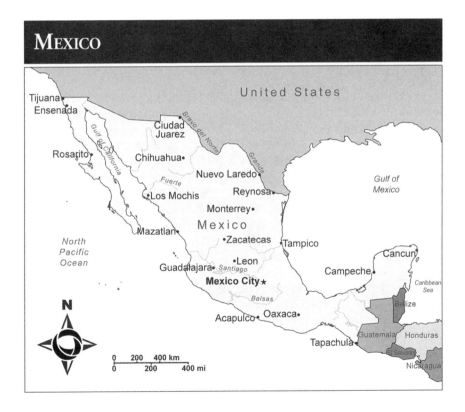

CHAPTER 4

The Sinaloa Cartel: Its Allies and Adversaries

INTRODUCTION

As indicated in Chapter 1, on April 8, 1989, the pajama-clad, unshaven Miguel Ángel Félix Gallardo, was puttering around in the kitchen when a squad of federal police, led by PJF commander Guillermo González Calderoni, arrested him in his suburban Guadalajara home. No shots were fired because the kingpin's young wife (he had two) refused to cook for the three slovenly bodyguards, who were compelled to eat breakfast elsewhere.[1]

A judge convicted the crafty Sinaloan of drug trafficking, bribery, and illegal possession of weapons. When first thrust behind bars, he directed his lucrative empire via mobile phones, lawyers, and intermediaries visiting his well-appointed apartment above the warden's office. One of the striking features of his quarters was a large framed photograph of the drug don with the stern-faced Pope John Paul II. The so-called *capo culto* read voraciously, prized a bulging collection of books, and contributed generously to the Autonomous University of Sinaloa. He financially supported the works of José Luis Cuevas, Martha Chapa, and other artists, who autographed pictures that were given to him. While in the DF's Reclusorio Sur (Southern Penitentiary), he took up painting. He concentrated on portraits of Napoleon and Don Quixote—short men who had made an impact on history. He also enjoyed a stereo, television, and other electronic items. His indulged career suffered when, after two years, he was transferred to the high-security Almoloya prison near Toluca, Mexico.[2]

The attorney general's office insists that to minimize internecine fighting, he distributed plazas to lieutenants either at a meeting in Acapulco before his capture or from behind bars. Although subject to kaleidoscopic changes and continual intrigue, the ultimate sorting out of plazas involved the following territories:

- Joaquín "El Chapo" Guzmán Loera, who had learned the trade from Pedro Avilés Pérez, and Héctor Luis "El Güero" Palma Salazar, received Mexicali and San Luis Río Colorado, Sonora, which lies along the along the U.S. border at the intersection of Sonora, Baja California, Arizona, and California
- DFS commander Rafael Aguilar Guajardo was sent to Ojinaga, Chihuahua, to learn the ropes from incredibly powerful Pablo Acosta Villarreal, who was killed in April 1987; soon thereafter, Aguilar Guajardo was murdered by Carrillo Fuentes[3]
- Amado "Lord of the Skies" Carrillo Fuentes became the don of Ciudad Juárez
- Héctor Luis "El Güero" Palma Salazar received Nogales and Hermosillo
- Jesús "El Chuy" Labra Avilés, mentor to the Arellano Félix brothers, was dispatched to Tijuana
- Ismael "El Mayo" Zambada García became active in Sinaloa and would join forces with El Chapo

Chapter 3 homed in on the Gulf Cartel and Los Zetas. Here we provide an overview of other notable cartels, emphasizing their (1) leadership, (2) organization, (3) assets, (4) alliances, (5) enemies, and (6) current status—with occasional references to gangs and other criminal organizations with which they cooperate or compete.

SINALOA CARTEL

Leadership

The modus vivendi configured by Félix Gallardo depended on several drug syndicates playing by the rules of the game that governed the behavior of the government and the underworld—above all, respecting the turf of their counterparts, whether friends or enemies. Like his mentor, Sinaloa Cartel leader Joaquín Guzmán Loera graduated from the school of hard knocks—with honors. Born into a poor family in La Tuna, Badiraguato, a municipality in the rugged mountains of Sinaloa, he was estranged from his father, a farmer and opium producer. Poorly educated, Guzmán, who later became known as "El Chapo" ("Shorty"),[4] even relied on friends to compose love letters to his many sweethearts, including three wives. As a youngster, Shorty admired Pedro Áviles Pérez, who pioneered the use of airplanes to haul cocaine to the United States. Erstwhile car thief "El Güero" Palma gave impulse to Guzmán Loera's career by placing him in charge of shipping drugs from the Sierra to cities and the border.[5]

El Chapo did not shy from confronting the Arellano Félix Organization (AFO), or Tijuana Cartel, which was composed of middle-class Sinaloans who shattered Félix Gallardo's attempted entente by seeking to dominate all of Baja California, in addition to areas of Sinaloa and Durango. Battles raged between the Sinaloa Cartel and its Tijuana rivals. In November 1992 El Chapo dispatched 40 sicarios who killed nine adversaries in a raid on an AFO party in Puerto Vallarta. The AFO responded by trying to assassinate Guzmán Loera at the Guadalajara Airport on May 24, 1993, where they mistakenly killed Guadalajara Cardinal Juan Jesús Posadas Ocampo, forcing El Chapo to flee to Guatemala, where he was arrested two weeks later.

Organization

Although Guzmán Loera called the shots, the Sinaloans formed a "Federation" rather than a vertical, top-down syndicate. "El Mayo" Zambada, a native of El Álamo, Badiraguato, is a seasoned narco-trafficker, an inseparable ally of El Chapo, and virtual co-leader of the enterprise. His financial and political acumen enabled the mustachioed strongmen to knit close relations with Félix Gallardo and Amado Carrillo Fuentes in their heyday. Since the 1990s, El Mayo has had his own *pistoleros* force, which helps him enforce agreements with interlocutors. He profits from a degree of autonomy. While his gunman Gustavo Inzunza reportedly killed more than 50 people in Sinaloa, spilling blood is not El Mayo's forte—except when agreements with him remain unfulfilled. He also has a benevolent side. Before the DEA and PGR placed a $5 million bounty on his head, Zambada García returned to his hometown of El Álamo every Christmas to distribute beer and cash to ensure his friends and neighbors had a happy holiday.[6] Javier Torres "JT" Félix long served as El Mayo's top bodyguard until JT's teenage daughter, overjoyed at his return home for Christmas, posted his picture on her Facebook page.

Ignacio "Nacho" Coronel Villarreal, Guzmán Loera's cousin, was on nearly the same footing in Guadalajara as Mayo was in Sinaloa. Born in Durango State, Nacho was a protégé of Amado Carrillo Fuentes, the redoubtable chief of the Juárez Cartel, who died undergoing plastic surgery in mid-1997. The latter's nickname derived from his imaginative use of planes to transport drugs. Coronel conducted business from one of his two homes in Zapopan, an upscale colonial suburb in the Guadalajara area. His specialty was hallucinogens. The secretive Coronel was allegedly "the forerunner in producing massive amounts of methamphetamines in clandestine laboratories in Mexico, then shipping it to the United States," according to the FBI, which offered a $5 million reward for the number three leader in the Sinaloa Cartel. In addition, Coronel controlled trafficking through Jalisco, Colima, and areas of Michoacán—the "Pacific route" for smuggling.[7]

In an action reminiscent of the withering assault against Osama bin Laden, the army used ground forces and helicopters to kill Nacho in mid-2010, delivering what the DEA called a "crippling blow" to the Sinaloa Cartel.[8] The blitzkrieg contradicted rumors that the Calderón administration was devoting fewer resources to the Sinaloans than to other syndicates. There was also speculation that El Chapo gave the military Coronel's location because of the latter's increasing arrogance.

In any case, the demise of Coronel opened Guadalajara to warfare among the Sinaloa Cartel; the Beltrán Leyva Organization; Los Zetas and an allied gang, La Resistencia; and the New Generation Jalisco Cartel, which are linked to the Sinaloa Cartel. The BLO, comprised of better educated sinaloans, split with El Chapo in 2008.

Jesús "El Rey" Zambada García, El Mayo's brother, handled the cartel's operations in Central America until his capture in a gun battle in Mexico City in October 2008. The following May, soldiers arrested Roberto "El Doctor" Beltrán Burgos, another insider who took orders directly from El Chapo.[9]

Assets

JT's brother Manuel "El M1"/"Ondeado" Torres Félix operated some 30 ships that supplied Andean cocaine to the Sinaloa Cartel. He purchased older vessels in Brownsville, Texas;, dispatched them to Tampico for repairs, repainting, and reflagging; sent them to a Colombia port for pick-ups; and, after they had passed through the Panama Canal, unloaded their cargo in Altata, Sinaloa, a tranquil fishing village 45 miles west of Culiacán. He also functioned as a cunning hit man. In mid-October 2012, soldiers killed El Ondeado, whose extravagant exploits were glorified by balladeers.[10] The Sinaloa Cartel continues to benefit from a robust flow of cocaine from Colombia; methamphetamines delivered overland, by air, or through Lázaro Cárdenas (Michoacán), Manzanillo (Colima), Altata, and other ports; and homegrown marijuana and poppy. El Chapo endured a setback when army and marine units arrested his security chief Jonathan "The Ghost" Salas Áviles in Sinaloa in early February 2013.[11]

Support among the poor represents another important asset for El Chapo, who poses as a benevolent Godfather. He provides jobs for thousands of people; repairs roads, sidewalks, and churches; and keeps the peace in the Golden Triangle, where the jagged mountains and verdant forests of Sinaloa, Durango, and Jalisco merge. Author Malcolm Beith suggests the region should be known as the Bermuda Triangle—at least for enemies of El Chapo. It's also a part of "México bronco"—an untamed region where you can have someone murdered for $35.[12]

El Chapo prides himself on being a "Gentleman Narco." Stories abound of his entering fancy restaurants and schmoozing with elegant diners before feasting on fist-sized shrimp and blood-red steaks in a backroom. He then leaves unobtrusively, while his bodyguards pick up the tabs of other patrons and return their cell phones. American publications have magnified his image: in early 2009 *Forbes* magazine listed El Chapo as one of the wealthiest people in the world, with an estimated fortune of $1 billion. Not to be outdone, *Time* magazine named him one of the "most influential people" of 2009, labeling him "the new Pablo Escobar, a king-pin testing the ability of a nascent democracy to control organized crime." He appeared in the category of "leaders and revolutionaries" along with President Barack Obama, Secretary of State Hillary Rodham Clinton, French president Nicholas Sarkozy, and German chancellor Angela Merkel.[13]

Guzmán Loera occasionally dons disguises. He prefers decking himself out as a priest or army officer to minimize questions about his identity. He surrounds himself with bodyguards. Some of the gangs that protect him are Los Chachos, Los Negros, Los Tejas, and Los Lobos, which suppos-edly have committed more than 1,000 murders throughout Mexico. (14)

"Beneath the disguises, the entourages and the layers of security lay the real Chapo, a man who was always more comfortable in a baseball cap and jeans than in the flashy gold jewelry and designer suits worn by other narcos."[14]

Under his baseball cap is an extraordinarily innovative mind. "Cocaine Alley" represents a particularly impressive brainchild. This term referred to a bunker, buttressed by concrete walls and featuring a 200-foot pas-sageway from a warehouse crammed with drugs, arms, and money to the home of El Chapo's attorney in Agua Prieta, Sonora, adjacent to Doug-las, Arizona. The corridor was wide enough to accommodate a small truck that smuggled goods back and forth across the border.[15] An ability to recruit and exploit cheap labor facilitates the construction of structures such as Cocaine Alley and a labyrinth of other cross-border tunnels.

One of El Chapo's more adroit colleagues is Juan José Esparragoza Mor-eno. This man, known as "El Azul" ("The Blue One") because of the blu-ish tint of his face, goes largely unnoticed, which is exactly what he wants. Born in Chuicopa, Sinaloa, in February 1948, he is one of the few survivors of a generation now sleeping the eternal sleep or languishing behind steel bars: Félix Gallardo, Ernesto "Don Neto" Fonseca Carrillo, Rafael Quintero, Emilio Quintero Payán, and Manuel "Crazy Pig" Salcido Uzeta.[16]

El Azul combines the bargaining skills of a Talleyrand, the strategic instincts of a Henry Kissinger, and the low-key personality of a squint-eyed accountant. He aligned himself with the Juárez Cartel until the July 1997 death of Amado Carrillo Fuentes. Meanwhile, he developed close ties with the Beltrán Leyva Organization and El Mayo Zambada. Once El Chapo escaped from the Puente Grande prison in January 2001, El Azul cast his lot with the Sinaloa Cartel. However, his talent as a negotiator and his fealty to his word enables him to sit at the same table with rival kingpins. Despite occasional sightings, El Azul remains a mysterious figure, much like devilish Keyser Söze in the neonoir film *The Usual Suspects*. A protagonist in the movie repeats the words of Charles Baudelaire, who said: "The greatest trick the devil ever pulled was convincing the world he didn't exist." This is followed by his earlier description of Keyser Söze: "And like that, he's gone."[17]

Esparragoza Moreno presided over one such parlay in Monterrey in September 2004. The session involved El Chapo, El Mayo, and BLO chief Arturo Beltrán Leyva among others. Their goal was to liquidate Rodolfo Carrillo Fuentes (Amado's brother) and exterminate Los Zetas en route to forging a hegemonic monopoly over drug trafficking; namely, the Sinaloa Cartel, which would overshadow and dominate the smaller, weaker Gulf Cartel. A key player was La Barbie, who had been El Chapo's chief enforcer before casting his lot with the Beltrán Leyvas. For some 14 months, the Sinaloans tried in vain to seize the north. So determined was El Chapo that he allegedly recruited Colombian guerrillas and Mara Salvatrucha cutthroats to assist in the conflict.[18] The turning point was the June 8, 2005, assassination of Nuevo Laredo's newly installed police chief. On the same day, seven masked gunmen stormed into a Chihuahua hospital and killed a federal agent who was recovering from gunshot wounds. Under pressure from the government, and with no clear vision of victory, La Barbie and the Sinaloans reluctantly sought a rapprochement with the Gulf Cartel. They realized that incessant bloodletting was harmful to the bottom line.[19] They did, however, manage to liquidate Rodolfo Fuentes, a powerful adversary, Amado's brother, and chief of the Juárez Cartel.[20]

Although seen in Mexico City and elsewhere, Esparragoza Moreno dresses like a regular middle-class citizen, hiding his preference for gaudy bracelets and chains, Ray Ban sunglasses, shiny hair, extravagant watches, and tailor-made suits. His discretion allowed him to go unrecognized when then-attorney general Antonio Lozano Gracia and he exchanged pleasantries when the two men dined at the same restaurant the DF's stylish Polanco neighborhood.[21] In mid-2013, the Federal Institute for Access to Information (IFAI), which seeks greater transparency in government, petitioned the Attorney General's Office to disclose information about El Azul and other most wanted criminals.[22]

El Azul has carved out a fiefdom in Cuernavaca, Morelos, a state contiguous to Mexico City. He also has operatives in Guadalajara

(Brenda Guadalupe Esparragoza Gastélum) and Puebla (Juvenicio Ignacio González Parada). Law-enforcement units and army units have been
at his beck and call. Police patrols have even escorted planeloads of drugs
that he transported by truck to other parts of the country.[23] The U.S.
Treasury Department has designated him a Foreign Narcotics Kingpin,
which means that his properties are subject to confiscation and a large fine
for every violation. Stiff penalties also apply to anyone who does business
with him. Esparragoza Moreno again became a press item in August 2013.
Enrique Álvarez del Castillo, former governor of Jalisco (1983–1988),
identified El Azul as the publicity agent for Rafael Caro Quintero, who
obtained an early release from Mexican prison on August 9, 2013, an
event discussed in Chapter 7.[24]

One observer attributed his success and longevity as follows: "He is a
very skillful capo. He is liked by all. He murders but does not murder
senselessly. He dislikes violence. He only kills for the money. He is a
kingmaker of drug traffickers, to be respected."[25]

Alliances

Above all, El Chapo's wealth has enabled him to clamp a hammerlock
on local police, prosecutors, the judiciary, politicians, and elements of
the army. In the drug world, he cooperates with the Gulf Cartel and the
Knights Templars against Los Zetas. In addition, he works with the ever-
more powerful CJNG, remnants of El Nacho's organization in Jalisco, as
well as the Nueva Federación, also called the *Matazetas*, who serve as
shock troops against his paramilitary nemesis.

THE BELTRAN LEYVA ORGANIZATION (BLO)

Leadership

Four brothers launched the BLO in Sinaloa: Marcos Arturo "El Barbas"/"The Beard," Héctor "The Engineer"/"H," Carlos *"El Jefe de los
Jefes"*/"Chief of the Chiefs," and Alfredo "El Mochomo"/"Red Stinging
Ant." Arturo took pride in his culinary hospitality; he frequently served
diners the meat of victims, the plates brimming with spicy sauces. He
and his brothers specialized in infiltrating law-enforcement agencies to
obtain classified information about upcoming initiatives. As mentioned
in Chapter 3, the cartel aligned with the Sinaloa or Pacific Federation until
early 2008, when Arturo Beltrán Leyva negotiated the control of plazas
with Los Zetas without informing his cartel allies. Arturo also accused
El Chapo of facilitating the January 20, 2008, arrest of Alfredo, who oversaw large-scale smuggling and money-laundering projects. Too, there
was a clash over a drug shipment in Chicago. The Red Stinging Ant

reportedly directed two teams of assassins, Los Pelones in Guerrero and Los Güeros in Sonora. When authorities arrested him and three members of his security detail in a house in Culiacán, they found an AK-47 and other firearms, 11 fancy watches, a luxury SUV, and two suitcases crammed with approximately $900,000.[26] El Mochomo's own Colt pistol bore the mantra "I'd rather die on my feet than live on my knees." American ambassador Tony Garza said, "Today was a significant victory for Mexican Armed Forces. This arrest demonstrates once again the ongoing commitment of President [Felipe] Calderón and his administration to hit the criminal organizations where it hurts."[27]

Assets

At one time, the BLO controlled airports in Mexico City, Monterrey, Acapulco, Toluca, and Cancún; accumulated a large stock of cocaine; and, above all, bribed the assistant attorney general for organized crime, Mexico's Interpol representatives, and army bigwigs, paying some of its informants as much as $450,000 per month. They had also contested trafficking corridors with El Chapo through Sinaloa, Durango, Sonora, Jalisco, and Michoacán, as well as dominance over Guerrero and Morelos, over which they had purview before the rupture with the rival mafioso.[28]

In addition, Arturo had befriended General Ricardo Escorcia Vargas, commander of the 24th Military Zone Region until late 2007, who allegedly closed his eyes to drug-laden King Air flights arriving from Colombia and landing near his Cuernavaca headquarters. In mid-2013, the PGR dropped charges against Escorcia because of the unreliability of the protected witness who testified against him and other officers. The BLO boasted two of the nation's most deadly gunmen: La Barbie Valdéz Villarreal, who was identified in Chapter 3, and Sergio "El Grande" Villarreal.

Organization

A publication that focuses on Mexican criminal bands indicated: "The Beltrán Leyva organization has quickly become one of the most powerful drug trafficking organizations in Mexico. Not only have they shown themselves capable of trafficking drugs and going toe-to-toe with the Sinaloa cartel, they also have demonstrated a willingness to order targeted assassinations of high-ranking government officials."[29]

What a difference a year makes! In August 2009 federal police apprehended the BLO's Ever Villafane Martínez in his posh home in the Jardines del Pedregal neighborhood of Mexico City. On the lam since he escaped from a Colombian prison in 2001, the 51-year-old Villafane was an important figure in Colombia's Northern Valley Cartel and the main cocaine supplier to the Beltrán Leyvas. In the aftermath of his arrest, the BLO knitted ties with Víctor and Dario Despinza Valencia of the same syndicate.

A much more resounding blow to the organization took place on December 16, 2009, when the navy/marines killed Arturo in a luxury condo in Cuernavaca. During the protracted firefight, Gonzalo Octavio Araujo, a key *pistolero*, committed suicide. The cartel suffered a further loss two weeks later when the federal police apprehended Arturo's brother Carlos, who was using the alias Carlos Gámez, in Culiacán.

Then La Barbie struck out on his own, continuing his sybaritic parties with entertainment provided by "Pesado," "Intocable," and the late actress, producer, and recording star Jenni Rivera, whom he plied with cocaine and abused.[30] Ironically, "Hurts So Bad" was the last song she recorded before dying in a plane crash. An aperçu reveals a good deal about the killer's warped persona. He delighted when Arturo fed meat from their victims to dinner guests. The dominoes continued to fall when authorities nabbed Valdez Villarreal, who had severed ties with the Beltrán Leyvas, on August 30, 2010. The marines also apprehended strongman El Grande on September 12, 2010.

In November 2012 the federal police in Mexico City arrested a Beltrán Leyva boss, Aldo Ramos de la Cruz, who was "suspected of being responsible for designing logistics for the running of drugs from the state of Tamaulipas" to the United States, controlling operations at the Sonora border with the United States, handling the planting and harvesting of marijuana and poppies in Guerrero, and overseeing BLO operations in violence-wracked Acapulco.[31]

Allies

The BLO occasionally makes common cause with Los Zetas, which have taught them military tactics in return for helping the paramilitaries establish a beachhead in Sinaloa. In addition, they have at times undertaken joint ventures with the Juárez Cartel and the AFO. Héctor also works with the Mazatlecos, a minor gang named for its home base of Mazatlán, a busy port and resort on the Pacific coast. Los Mazatlecos, which previously took orders from El Mochomo, also cooperate with Los Zetas. Chapo Isidro Meza Flores (Guasave and surrounding villages) and Samuel "El Torillero" Lizárraga Ontiveros (Mazatlán) have cooperated with the BLO in northern Sinaloa, although Chapo Isidro is considered a loose cannon. Avalos Sánchez "El Güero-Saba" works directly under El Torillero and his number one enforcer. Patrón Sánchez Juan Francisco (or "H-2") holds sway over Nayarit, a longtime barony of the Sinaloa Cartel. H-2's reputation for ruthlessness and derring-do soared after he executed a clever ambush that destroyed a convoy of well-armed

Sinaloan gunmen, killing 25 of its members.[32] In addition to the areas cited, the BLO crosses swords with El Chapo in Culiacán and maintains a lower profile in the DF, Morelos, Mexico State, and Pueblo.

Status

Although the Beltrán Leyvas still import cocaine from Colombia, Peru, and Ecuador, setbacks since 2009 have severely crippled them. Their survival increasingly depends on reinforcements from Los Zetas and Los Mazatlecos, as well as the few remaining spies they are believed to have in the government's security bureaucracy. They have recently lost their contacts in the army. A "hydra effect" has found more than a half-dozen *cartelitos* and dangerous gangs springing from the enfeebled BLO. These include Los Mazatlecos (Sinaloa and Nayarit), the Independent Cartel of Acapulco (Guerrero), La Barredora (Guerrero), La Mano Con Ojos (DF and Mexico State), the Cártel del Centro (DF and Mexico State), Los Rojos (Morelos and Guerrero), Los Pelones (Morelos), and Guerreros Unidos (Morelos and Guerrero). These gangs often prove a financial burden inasmuch as Héctor must pay the fees of their lawyers, lest their leaders spill the beans on the BLO.

JUÁREZ CARTEL

Leadership

After Operation Condor, five small organizations battled to control cross-border drug flows between Ciudad Juárez and El Paso. Félix Gallardo's ally, Guadalajara Cartel leader "Don Neto" Fonseca Carrillo, ordered former DFS chief Rafael Aguilar Guajardo to Ojinaga near the border in the early 1980s. As indicated in Chapter 3, he apprenticed himself to Pablo Acosta, the scar-faced *padrino* who dispatched 60 tons of cocaine per year to "El Norte." "Pablo Acosta was the first 'modern' drug capo to emerge in Northern Chihuahua—ruthless, single-minded, cruel, and completely dedicated to consolidating his power and eliminating enemies and competitors at all costs."[33] The flamboyant Acosta took advantage of the nightclubs, gambling parlors, brothels, and drug dens. In the 1960s a female reporter asked President Gustavo Díaz Ordaz what he thought about the city's functioning as a "springboard" for illegal narcotics. "Don't forget, miss," the chief executive responded, "that if a diving board exists, then there must be a swimming pool."[34]

Amado Carrillo Fuentes, who deployed a fleet of Boeing 727s to move drugs, forged an alliance with the Cali Cartel's Gilberto and Miguel Rodríguez Orejuela. Transporting Colombian cocaine to municipal airports and unpaved airstrips around Mexico and other countries enabled him to multiply the tonnage of the product delivered and amount of profit. El Mayo Zambada worked closely with this airborne capo.

Carrillo Fuentes co-opted General Jesús Gutiérrez Rebollo, the "drug czar" of President Ernesto Zedillo (1994–2000). The payoffs led the three-star general to concentrate antidrug campaigns on Tijuana's Arellano Félix Organization and other antagonists of Carrillo Fuentes. The DEA described Amado as the "most powerful of Mexico's drug traffickers," making him an even more inviting target for law-enforcement agencies and rival criminal organizations. At its high point, the Juárez Cartel operated in 21 states, with its major strongholds in Culiacán, Monterrey, Ciudad Juárez, Ojinaga, Mexico City, Guadalajara, Cuernavaca, and Cancún.

As authorities closed in on him, the mighty capo flew to Cuba, Russia, and other countries seeking asylum. When these efforts failed, he resorted to changing his appearance.

The *jefe* of the Juárez Cartel died in mid-1997 while undergoing cosmetic surgery and liposuction to remove 3.5 gallons of fat from his body. During the eight-hour procedure at the Santa Mónica Hospital in the DF, the patient apparently succumbed either of an overdose of the sedative Dormicum or a malfunctioning respirator. One of the three surgeons who performed the procedure, Pedro López Saucedo, entered a witness protection program in the United States after he provided information about the Juárez Cartel.[35] The other physicians soon lost their lives.

Local residents swarmed to the Lord of the Skies' elaborate funeral at his mother's property in Guamuchilito, Sinaloa, where he had cultivated a reputation as the local Robin Hood. Sidekicks of Carrillo's recent years—gun-toting gangsters or affluent and mighty associates—did not appear to make up the bulk of the crowd that trudged through the guarded metal gates of his family compound and past the magnificent rose gardens to pay their last respects. "Rather, it was the peasants and farmhands who inhabit this dusty village of about 1,200 people who attended the services throughout the day at the modest blue stucco house, where funeral wreaths the size of refrigerators wilted in sweltering heat."[36] In 2006 Governor Eduardo Bours asked the federal government to tear down Carrillo's mansion in Hermosillo, Sonora. Dubbed "The Palace of a Thousand and One Nights," this castle-like structure exemplifies nouveaux riche "narcotechture" and still sits unoccupied.[37]

Vicente Carrillo Fuentes, Amado's brother, defeated the Muñoz Talavera brothers for control of the syndicate. The new don formed a partnership with his brother Rodolfo Carrillo Fuentes, his nephew Vicente Carrillo Leyva, and Ricardo Garcia Urquiza. He retained the services of several of his late brother's lieutenants such as the notorious Arturo "El Chacky" Hernández González (captured in April 2005). According to the FBI and the PGR, Vicente also allied with the Beltrán Leyvas

(Monterrey), Mayo Zambada García (Sinaloa and Baja California), and El Chapo (Nayarit, Sinaloa, and Tamaulipas).

Once El Chapo escaped from prison in 2001, a number of Juárez Cartel cadres migrated to the camp of the Sinaloan, who reportedly had the viceroy's brother Rodolfo gunned down in the heart of Culiacán on September 11, 2004. Vicente rejoiced at the assassination of Guzmán Loera's brother, Arturo, in La Almoloya three and a half months later. These killings ignited all-out warfare between the Sinaloa and Juárez Cartels to the point that in 2009 President Calderón sent thousands of troops to Juárez, which had become an even more blood-drenched killing arena.

Organization

This is a family-oriented syndicate with Vicente "El Viceroy" Carrillo Fuentes serving as the principal leader after his brother Amado's death. Vicente Carrillo Leyva, 32, who was second only to his uncle in the cartel's structure, disguised himself as a young businessman and lived in the DF's upscale Bosques de las Lomas section, using the name Alejandro Peralta Álvarez. Licenciado Álvarez epitomizes a new breed of "narco-puppies" who sport Armani suits, live in exclusive areas, rub elbows with the elite, and are conversant with the latest technology.[38] Just a week before, Mexico's government posted a 30 million peso ($2.1 million) reward for Carrillo Leyva and 23 other top cartel suspects. When apprehended, the young man was wearing an Abercrombie and Fitch jogging outfit.

Assets

At one time the country's most powerful criminal organization, the Juárez Cartel still benefits from its knowledge of and proximity to the border. Taking advantage of their symbiotic relationship with La Línea and El Barrio Azteca, the organization has co-opted police officers and intimidated foes. In early 2012 it unfurled banners accusing hard-nosed police chief retired army Lieutenant Colonel Julián Leyzaola —"a criminal with a badge"—of corruption and connivance with the Sinaloa Cartel. The organization also threatened to kill a policeman each day so that the "citizens will know how corrupt you are."[39]

Allies

The Juárez Cartel depends heavily for support from two vicious cross-border enforcement gangs: La Línea, composed of current and former policemen from Chihuahua, and El Barrio Azteca, which functions in Mexico and major cities in Texas and New Mexico. An alliance with Sinaloa Cartel collapsed when Vicente refused to allow El Chapo to use

his smuggling corridors. Reportedly, in 1997 El Chapo proposed a rapprochement to promote business, but La Línea vetoed the overture. La
Línea's chief, José Antonio "El Diego" Acosta Hernández, admitted to
personally ordering 1,500 murders, he was also sentenced to life in prison
for having orchestrated the 2010 killing of a U.S. consulate employee, her
husband, and another worker at the U.S. mission in Ciudad Juárez.[40] The
badly debilitated Juárez Cartel cooperates with Los Zetas, the BLO, and
remnants of the Tijuana Cartel.

Current Status

Although Vicente remains in hiding, police captured Benjamin "El
Cachitas" Valeriano Jr., one of the main operators of the syndicate.
According to authorities, he worked for Guillermo "El Pariente" Castillo
Rubio, who was also taken into custody in 2012 and who was considered
the second in command after Vicente Carrillo Fuentes. Born in the United
States, he was arrested on July 21, 2012, in Mexico City, according to
federal police reports.[41]

A medley of factors have reduced killings in Ciudad Juárez: the growing influence of the Sinaloa Cartel, the use of the city as a laboratory for
the U.S.-funded Mérida Initiative community-building initiatives, cooperation from Governor César Duarte Jáquez, the presence of a tough-
as-nails police security director (Leyzaola), and what might be called
"battle fatigue" after thousands of murders in several years. Even as Ciudad Juárez cools down, 215 miles to the south in Chihuahua City, the
state's capital, shootings continue unabated. During the third weekend
in June 2013, nine individuals died and others suffered wounds.[42]

LA FAMILIA MICHOACÁN AND THE KNIGHTS TEMPLARS

Leadership

Carlos "Carlitos"/"El Tísico" Rosales Mendoza paved the way for La
Familia Michoacana. He originally collaborated with the cousins who
ran the Milenio Cartel, an early entry into the Pacific coast trade in methamphetamine ("meth" or "ice"). The alliance broke down, and Rosales
Mendoza sent an SOS to the Gulf Cartel's Cárdenas Guillén requesting
the dispatch of Los Zetas in battling his rivals.

Mendoza went on to create "La Empresa" along with Nazario "El
Chayo"/"El Más Loco" Moreno González and José de Jesús "El Chango"
Méndez Vargas. Enrique "Kike" Plancarte Solís handled the acquisition of
and sale of narcotics, and Servando "La Tuta" Gómez Martínez concen-
trated on drug activities in Arteaga, Michoacán, and along the coast of
Guerrero and Michoacán.

After the arrest of Carlitos in August 2004, La Empresa morphed into La Familia Michoacán. Its leaders were Bible-toting of fanatics of Nazario "El Más Loco" Moreno González and Jesús "El Chango" Méndez Vargas. La Tuta presented himself as the spokesman for the organization, and Plancarte took care of commercial chores.

La Familia burst into the limelight on September 6, 2006. On that sweltering night the organization's gunmen crashed into the seedy Sol y Sombra nightclub in Uruapan, Michoacán, fired shots into the air, ordered revelers to lie down, ripped open a plastic bag, and lobbed five human heads like bowling balls onto the beer-stained black and white dance floor. The desperados left behind a note hailing their act as "divine justice," adding: "The Family doesn't kill for money; it doesn't kill women; it doesn't kill innocent people; only those who deserve to die, die. Everyone should know this; this is divine justice."[43]

The day before the macabre pyrotechnics in Uruapan, the killers had seized their prey from a mechanic's shop and hacked off their heads with bowie knives while the men writhed in pain. "You don't do something like that unless you want to send a big message," said a U.S. law-enforcement official, speaking on condition of anonymity.[44]

La Familia's stated "mission" was to eradicate trafficking in methamphetamines and other narcotics, kidnappings, extortion, murder-for-hire, highway assaults, and robberies.[45] The group also committed itself to "defending citizens, merchants, businesses and farmers from all crimes, thus filling the security void left by the central government."[46]

Public relations man La Tuta Gómez Martínez claimed that through kidnappings and executions the cartel was ensuring "a peaceful climate for law-abiding citizens." In addition, he cited as his organization's principal targets El Chapo Guzmán and the Beltrán Leyva brothers because they were responsible for meth addiction in Michoacán communities.[47]

Organization

Journalist Richard Ravelo asserted that the 4,000 members of La Familia were born and raised in Michoacán; that they earned between $1,500 and $2,000 per month; and they were well connected with state and local officials. They reportedly attended church regularly, carried Bibles, and distributed the Good Book in local government offices.[48] In fact, Moreno even prepared his own version of the Bible—*Pensamientos de la Familia* (Maxims of the Family), which was required reading for members of the organization. The narco-evangelicals courted grassroots support by assisting campesinos, erecting schools, donating books, preventing the sale of adulterated wines, and employing "extremely strong strategies" to bring order to the Tierra Caliente, a fertile region that embraces parts of Michoacán, Guerrero, and Mexico State.

Assets

"Location, location, location" doesn't apply only to the real estate market. La Familia operated principally in Michoacán, the major port of which—Lázaro Cárdenas—furnishes an open sesame for cocaine and precursor chemicals for methamphetamines. To the north, Manzanillo, Colima, provides another entry point for illegal substances; to the south, Salinas Cruz, Oaxaca, is another option. Lázaro Cárdenas, which ranks among the country's largest container recipients, commands a strategic location: Half of Mexico's population lives within a radius of 186 miles of this coastal city, and in 2008 it handled more cargo (22,128,000 tons) than any other of the country's other 21 ports. In 2012, 1,522 ships arrived with cargos; by 2015 the port will receive 6 million containers annually.[49]

Lázaro Cárdenas and other cities and municipalities teem with young men from other parts of the country who are jobless, uneducated, and hooked on alcohol and drugs. Through an intensive religious indoctrination program, La Familia swept these youngsters into its folds and, provided that they cleaned up their lives, gave them food, jobs, and shelter. These youngsters escaped deracination and addiction only to enter one of the most savage precincts of the underworld. Official records indicate that both Moreno and Gómez converted to evangelical Christianity while working in the United States in the 1990s. "Returning to Mexico, they found that religious discipline was a useful tool to keep criminal troops in line."[50]

Hand-lettered, poorly spelled, enigmatic missives showed up next to the decapitated heads in Uruapan as part of the group's intense propaganda campaign designed to intimidate foes, terrorize the local population, and inhibit action by the government.

Like Los Zetas, La Familia disseminates news of its ghastly deeds nationally by conventional media as well as by Internet, Facebook, Twitter, and carefully placed banners.

On the heels of the Uruapan bestiality, La Familia took out a half-page advertisement in newspapers. The sadists claimed to be crime fighters determined to cleanse Michoacán of methamphetamines, kidnappings, extortion, and other criminal activities. *El Sol of Morelia*, a newspaper published in the capital of Michoacán—which lies 135 miles west of Mexico City—confirmed that it published the half-page ad that was carried on September 22, 2006. *La Voz de Michoacán* also ran the group's manifesto.

Some zealots in the organization carry arms and drive vehicles similar to those of the federal police. This allows them greater freedom to move around their areas of interest.[51] Still, leaders have become so brazen that they have designed their own outfits to mark their identity and distinguish their cadres from adversaries. Another cartel asset is that some of its members speak the language of the Purépecha, an indigenous people in northwestern Michoacán, notably in the area of the cities of Cherán and Pátzcuaro.

Allies

What may have begun as a small group of armed men on the prowl to protect their children from methamphetamines has turned into a cruel criminal force that is just as well armed and organized as any drug smuggling organization in Mexico. It also learned from Los Zetas how to butcher adversaries. The attorney general's office claims that elements of La Familia not only dominate narcotics sales in many of the 77 of the 113 municipalities of their home state, but also the distribution route to the U.S. border that snakes through territory that has traditionally been in the hands of the Sinaloa Cartel. To this end, they have established safe houses as refuges at strategic points along the route northward. They also cast their lot with the Sinaloa and Gulf Cartels in an effort to extirpate Los Zetas, particularly in northern Mexico.

While originating in Michoacán, the cartel has a presence in several dozen municipalities in neighboring Mexico State, as well as in Guanajuato, Guerrero, and Jalisco.

Status

After federal police shot El Chayo in late 2010, confounders Gómez Martínez, Plancarte Solís, and a majority of votaries abandoned La Familia to form the Knights Templars (Caballeros Templarios), pledging to "fight and die" for their interpretation of social justice. Their name derives from militaristic crusaders who defended pilgrims bound for the Holy Land between the years of 1119 and 1312. The current zealous desperados, who want to be considered more than a drug Mafia, wear Roman warrior–style helmets during induction ceremonies and disseminate propaganda depicting themselves as champions in the fight against "materialism, injustice, and tyranny."

The Knights made their debut with the following text:

To the society of Michoacán we inform you that from today we will be working here on the altruistic activities that were previously performed by the Familia Michoacán, we will be at the service of Michoacán society to attend to any situation which threatens the safety of the Michoacanos. Our commitment to society will be: to safeguard order, avoid robberies, kidnappings, extortion; and to shield the state from possible rival intrusions.[52]

They greeted Peña Nieto with "narco-banners" in Michoacán (18 municipalities), Guerrero, and Guanajuato. These "cordial" messages expressed support for his anticrime actions—an indirect plea to eradicate their nemesis, Los Zetas.[53]

This self-proclaimed brotherhood broadcast a cease-fire in the run-up to Pope Benedict XVI's visit to Mexico in March 2012.[54] La Tuta has even said that the Knights would lay down their arms if federal, state, and local authorities would crush criminal elements in Michoacán.

The Knights Templars eclipsed La Familia after police apprehended the latter's number two, El Chango Méndez, whose son has tried to patch together remnants of his father's organization. Both La Familia and Los Templars continue to suffer loses as indicated by the arrest of both Christian Enrique "El 18" Lara Hernández, the latter's plaza boss in Uruapan, and Javier "El Chivo" Beltrán Arco, the Templar's top gunman. Within hours of the capture of El Chivo and two accomplices, 100 protesters believed to have been bankrolled by the Knights Templars swarmed into the streets of Apatzingan in protest. The federal police reported the capture of 43 members of this cult-like clan during three weeks in mid-2012.[55]

An alliance with La Corona, a brutal gang headed by El Nacho's nephew José Ángel "El Changel" Carrasco Coronel, which appeared in November 2011 in Zapopan, opened Jalisco to the Templars.[56] The cartel's strength in Jalisco increased after the army captured El Changel in Sinaloa in early 2013.[57]

"But the rise of the Knights Templars from the ashes of La Familia shows the fundamental problem of the drug war: whenever one set of bad guys is taken down, another steps up to take its place, largely because Mexico has few if any real investigative police institutions to halt the vicious cycle."[58] These "bad guys" contributed to the strife that engulfed Michoacán in the fall of 2013. The state looked like a Tolstoyan battle field with armed units striking out in all directions: local auto-defense groups battled La Tuta's forces; the Knights Templars warred against the CJNG; cartels shook down mayors for the public works budgets; and community police sprang up in municipalities such as Buenavista, Tepalcatepec, and Coalcomán; and Peña Nieto dispatched troops in an effort to bring order out of chaos in what appeared to be a "failed state" within the state.[59]

ARELLANO FÉLIX ORGANIZATION (AFO/JUÁREZ CARTEL)

Leadership

The middle-class couple Francisco Arellano Sánchez and Alicia Isabel Félix Azueta raised 11 children in the Culiacán area. Five of these siblings—Francisco Rafael, Carlos, Benjamín, Ramón Eduardo, and Francisco Javier—smuggled clothing and electronics before entering the drug business. Caro Payán, to whom Félix Gallardo had allocated the Tijuana plaza, was forced to flee the country only to be arrested in Canada. Jesús "El Chuy" Labra Avilés and Benjamín Arellano Félix rushed to fill the vacuum left by Caro Payán's departure. This bloodless coup against Payán sparked a lingering and intense enmity between the AFO and its Sinaloan and Sonoran counterparts.

Organization

After the arrest of El Chuy in March 2000, the AFO became a family affair. Benjamín served as the chief strategist, and Ramón Eduardo directed blood-curdling violence against the syndicate's foes in a manner reminiscent of Sonny Corleone in the *Godfather* films. Another pivotal cartel figure was Ismael "El Mayel" Higuera Guerrero, chief operations officer, money launderer, and the boss in Ensenada, a coastal city south of Tijuana. Arturo Everado "El Kitty" recruited violent youths from Tijuana and San Diego.

A native of Sinaloa, Teodoro "El Teo" García Simental made common cause with the AFO. The obese sadist quickly emerged as a diabolical kidnapper and killer. David Shirk, director of the Trans-Border Institute at the University of San Diego, reported that El Teo "allegedly exercised what must be the most openly insane regime in the history of the drug war: He is said to have dismembered 300 victims and had henchmen dissolve them in barrels of lye. At one point, he allegedly configured nine of his victims, several of them uniformed police officers, on a street, so that they spelled out his nickname."[60] By 2010, though, just as his own side prevailed, Garcia Simental was arrested in a Baja California resort town, and the wars in Tijuana have since receded, with the Sinaloa Cartel controlling the traffic and the city, almost astonishingly, settling back into something approaching normality.

Assets

Ready access to drugs, a reputation for brutality, proximity to the border, and an army of lookouts greatly benefited the AFO. Their smuggling corridor across the southwest U.S.-Mexico border gave rise to the shipment of hundreds of tons of cocaine and marijuana over a two-decade period. They used their princely earnings to bribe politicians, policemen, and army personnel. "Those who couldn't be bought were often killed by AFO enforcement teams; heavily armed assassins who drove around Tijuana and other Baja California cities in convoys of armored SUVs equipped with sophisticated radios and other communications gear tuned to Mexican police frequencies."[61] The Arellano Félix Organization also recruited young toughs eager to make money from San Diego's Logan Heights gang. David "D" Barrón, a gangster from this band, enabled one or more brothers to escape from Christine's discotheque in Puerto Vallarta when Héctor Palma Salazar, a Sinaloa Cartel stalwart, rained bullets on the club.

They also constructed tunnels to move product, money, and weapons across the border. The longest tunnel stretched 2,400 feet from a warehouse near the Tijuana airport to a warehouse in San Diego's Otay Mesa industrial zone. Authorities discovered more than 2 tons of marijuana in the sophisticated structure. The DEA says the gang is responsible for the smuggling of tons of marijuana, cocaine, heroin, and methamphetamine over the past decade.[62]

Alfredo "Popeye" Araujo Ávila, an AFO hitman, allegedly coordinated the killing of Cardinal Posadas Ocampo in 1993. The assailants pumped dozens of bullets into the prelate, whom they mistook for the Arellano Félix Organization's nemesis El Chapo Guzmán. Popeye was also suspected of shooting prize-winning Tijuana journalist Jesús Blancornelas.[63]

Their money, skill at bribery, murders, and fearsome reputation aside, the AFO's fortunes began to decline in 2000. The capture or death of the most experienced brothers presaged a split in the organization between El Teo, formerly the syndicate's top enforcer, and Fernando "The Engineer" Sánchez Arellano. El Teo attempted to broker an alliance with the Sinaloa Cartel's El Mayo Zambada García even as he sought to control the Baja California peninsula. He, his brother Manuel "El Chiquilín"/ "Tiny" García Simental, and close ally Raydel "El Muletas"/"The Crutches" López Uriarte had some 400 gunmen on their payroll. López Uriarte got his sobriquet from the number of victims whose legs he had smashed. Foes who suffered only broken bones were lucky. El Teo and El Muletas dismembered a young woman, mutilated and decapitated a state functionary, assassinated police, and killed competing drug dealers.[64]

The DEA reported that these gangsters financed their activities by bribing or cowing Baja California Sur's government secretary, its public security secretary, its attorney general, the state police chief, and other notables. Then-governor Narciso Agúndez Montaño was also suspected of collaborating with El Teo and his stalwarts.[65]

The extent of García Simental's cruelty turned all elements of society against him. Elements of the army, navy, and federal police captured García Simental in La Paz, Baja California Sur, on January 13, 2010. The following month authorities captured El Chiquilín and El Muletas.

Allies

The AFO reached its zenith when Luis Fernando Sánchez Arellano was firmly allied with the psychotic El Teo and his cutthroats. Not only did they dominate the Baja Peninsula, but the DEA found them operating in

Tennessee (Nashville, Memphis, and Knoxville), South Carolina (Columbia, Greenville, Charleston, and Florence), as well as Indianapolis, Charlotte, and Phoenix.[66] The AFO now has only limited alliances with the Juárez Cartel and Los Zetas.

Current Status

Factors in shattering the AFO included the adroitness of 2nd Zone Commander Alfonso General Duarte Múgica, who aggressively pursued his prey and won the confidence of the local community until he was transferred in early 2012. Equally important was Duarte's ability to work in tandem with tough-as-nails secretary of public security Lieutenant Colonel Julián Leyzaola, a retired general who reportedly used harsh tactics to pry information from local policemen about El Teo and the AFO. Indeed, the highly regarded weekly news magazine *Zeta* named both Duarte and Leyzaola as Men of the Year. Also important was the backing received from PAN governor José Osuna Millán, who encouraged the president and SEDENA to dispatch first-rate cadres to Tijuana.

In addition, one must consider the growing dominance of the Sinaloa Cartel, which has taken over most of Baja California and reduced the AFO to a shadow of its former self. Unable to obtain cocaine from Colombia, the cartel must depend on shipping homegrown marijuana. All transactions are subject to the supervision and consent of El Chapo and El Mayo.

Shirk, who keeps a sharp eye on Tijuana, believes that the pattern of violence rejects the official narrative of a slow triumph of the police over the gangs.[67]

Instead, he sees a clear pattern of spikes and declines in violence as an indication that in the midst of this violence was a kind of rational deal-making, with truces made and broken between the cartels and perhaps the police. (The cynical view is that the AFO simply offered Garcia Simental up once his madness had become more liability than asset.) The long current lull, Shirk says, likely reflects the Sinaloa Cartel's triumph. Murders are down and public safety has been restored, and yet the Sinaloa Cartel has only been strengthened. "If what you've done in the end is hand control from one trafficking organization to another, then was it worth it?" Shirk asks. "You can have a debate about that."[68] In any case, killings are down from 844 (2008) to 364 (2012).

Thanks to assiduous research by David Shirk, Nathan Jones, and other scholars, there is more reliable information in the public domain about the AFO than other DTOs. These "Phases" appear in Appendix D. Appendices E, F, and G detail losses incurred by the Arellano Félix clan, an overview of cartels, and their characteristics.

CHAPTER 5

Calderón's Approach to the Drug War

INTRODUCTION

During the 1962 gubernatorial campaign of Jorge Eugenio Ortiz Gallegos, a pregnant woman walked along the side of a stage in Morelia, Michoacán, gently bouncing a baby in her arms. She was María del Carmen Hinojosa, and her child-to-be was Felipe de Jesús Calderón Hinojosa. Running on the National Action Party (PAN) slate with Ortiz Gallegos was María del Carmen's husband, Luis Calderón Vega, a founder of the party who—all together—lost eight races for Congress. Felipe Calderón was virtually born into politics. As youngsters, he and his sister and four brothers distributed pamphlets, attended party rallies, and railed against the dominant and demonic PRI. As his elder brother Juan Luis recalls: "We went to great pains to avoid PRI brigades, composed of ruffians, who chased us, ripping down our campaign posters . . . we also had to stay out of the way of the police who threatened us. It was either the imprudence of adolescents or adrenaline, but we weren't scared. . . ."[1]

In 1962 Felipe left Morelia, his birthplace, to move to Mexico City, where he received a law degree from the respected conservative Escuela Libre de Derecho. Meanwhile, many of his PRI counterparts studied law at the highly politicized National Autonomous University of Mexico (UNAM). He later earned a master's degree in economics at the Autonomous Technological Institute of Mexico (ITAM) and a master's in public administration at Harvard University's John F. Kennedy School of Government. A devout Roman Catholic, he opposed homosexuality and held a pro-life stance on abortion—except in cases of rape, danger to the mother's life, and prospect of fetal deformity. He followed a liberal line in economics, favoring balanced budgets, low taxes, and free trade. He told an interviewer that "the best public policy was to take care of the rich because wealth trickles down, and the government should enforce conservative and reactionary Catholicism."[2] He was a disciple of the respected, pragmatic intellectual Carlos Castillo Peraza, a politician and writer whom Calderón succeeded as party president. Castillo Peraza, his role model who resigned from the PAN, urged him to avoid authoritarianism and have "confidence" in his entourage.[3]

He joined the PAN as a teenager and became president of the party's youth. In addition to myriad party positions, Calderón served on the Representative Assembly of the Federal District (1988–1991), the capital's city council, and twice as a federal deputy (1991–1994; 2000–2003). He met his wife, Margarita Zavala, when she was also a member of the Chamber of Deputies and proposed to her during a 1994 campaign swing. The couple went on to raise three children. Even though he lost the governorship of Michoacán in 1995, as national party president (1996–1999) he helped impel PAN gubernatorial victories in Nuevo León, Querétaro, Baja California, and Aguascalientes.

His opening to win the PAN's nomination for Los Pinos came in May 31, 2004. On that date he resigned as secretary of energy in light of scorching criticism of his political ambitions by President Vicente Fox, who was backing another wannabe, Senator Santiago Creel Miranda. The ballyhooed rupture with a weak, extremely ineffectual chief executive enabled the *michoacano* to break with an unpopular administration, forge his own identity, and assemble a team for the upcoming election.

Nonetheless, it can be argued that the outcome of the mid-2006 election constituted more of a loss for the messianic Andrés Manuel López Obrador (AMLO), candidate of a leftist coalition, than a victory for Calderón, who was characterized by prize-winning journalist Dudley Althaus as a "bespectacled, short and balding ... [man] who looks more like a book-keeper than a barnburner."[4] In the run-up to the mid-July 2006 balloting, AMLO watched his once-double-digit lead evaporate as a result of his own missteps. Much to his credit, he refused to explore an endorsement from Elba Esther Gordillo, the corrupt union leader. However, he was a "no-show" at the first national televised debate in which the PAN standard-bearer exhibited competence and confidence. And he enabled Calderón's strategists to shrewdly link López Obrador to Venezuelan strongman Hugo Chávez, a bitter Fox critic who was unpopular in Mexico.

On March 10 López Obrador demanded that Fox "shut up," and berated him with colloquial language. Even though Fox was an inept leader, Mexicans have a reverence (or at least an affinity) for their chief executives. In the epitome of demagogy, Calderón warned of "the existence of Bolivarian cells" financed by the Venezuelans, by embassy personnel, or by the government of Hugo Chávez. If these references were too subtle, the PAN "war room" accentuated the purported López Obrador-Chávez nexus in a fusillade of TV spots. One ad took language from a diplomatic squabble in 2005, when the Venezuelan jefe warned his Mexican counterpart, "Don't mess with me, sir. You'll get stung." Then it cut to video footage of AMLO saying, "Shut up, *chachalaca*"—a reference to a constantly chattering rare bird. The message concluded with the admonition: "No to intolerance."[5] Just as his electoral war room had contained a handful of young activists, Calderón preferred to work with a small entourage for mapping anticartel strategies. His virtual alter ego was presidential office chief Juan Camilo Mouriño Terrazo, the 36-year-old scion of an affluent Spanish family residing in Campeche, one of Mexico's oil-producing states. Mouriño Terrazo and Margarita Zavala, the authoritarian candidate's politically savvy wife, might challenge Calderón's positions. Other members of the team were loath to do so. These included Communications Director Max Cortázar, Private Secretary César Nava Vázquez, General Coordinator of Media and Communications Alejandra Sota Mirafuentes, Administrative Coordinator General Patricia Flores Elizondo, PAN president Guillermo Martínez Mora, brother-in-law Juan Ignacio Zavala, and Arturo Sarukhán Casamitjana, later ambassador to Washington who virtually ran the Foreign Affairs Ministry under Calderón.

The chief executive had a short fuse and did not invite criticism. He was overly self-confident and believed that he knew more than others around him. Newspaperman and scholar Jorge Zepeda Patterson said, "There is an element in his persona that is rigid, belligerent, vertical, almost authoritarian . . . [b]ut he has tried to work on these defects."[6]

As much as the chief executive favored young nondissenting admirers, he harbored a visceral dislike for the Institutional Revolutionary Party, which harassed him and his family in Michoacán. Calderón proved incapable of working with his nemesis when it won 237 out of 500 seats in 2009 mid-term elections. His animus was deep-seated. A former deputy who was elected to Congress along with Calderón in 1991 said that the young *panista* was not merely aloof from the PRI but looked upon the ruling party as hopelessly corrupt and illegitimate. As was the case with his PAN predecessor Vicente Fox, his family's economic fortunes had also suffered at the hands of venal PRI officials. So great was his antagonism that when he walked into the spacious San Lázaro legislative palace at the beginning of a session, he would keep to the opposition's side of the aisle, lest he encounter the devils in red, white, and green, the PRI's colors. He strictly avoided the handshakes, embraces, and bicep-squeezing with *priístas* that most elected officials engage in as part of the superficial bonhomie of the legislative culture.[7] His 2006 campaign was a virtual crusade against the PRI. And before leaving office, he accused a PRI governor of leaving a state (Veracruz) in the hands of a drug gang. When asked whether Peña Nieto would strike a bargain with the underworld, he said, "There are many in the PRI who think the deals of the past would work now. I don't see what deal could be done, but that is the mentality that many of them have."[8]

CALDERÓN AND THE DRUG WAR

Mexico's version of the drug war had taken more than 2,000 lives during the last year of Fox's sexenio. Yet, while the army concentrated on its traditional role of crop eradication, Fox relied heavily on the federal police to pursue the narco-Mafias. In view of the relatively low death rate in 2006, it is questionable whether Calderón needed to launch a no-holds-barred fight against the cartels, which were a thorn in his side but not a dagger in his heart. Just as there was no casus belli for Lyndon B. Johnson's dispatching thousands of troops to Southeast Asia in the 1960s, there was no hue and cry from the populace to go to war against the narco-syndicates.

During his campaign, the PAN standard-bearer had concentrated on education, energy, job-creation, and other social goals. Upon taking office, the new president and his inexperienced advisors over-reacted to the degree to which many areas of the country had succumbed to the drug cartels. Among areas of supposedly lost or compromised sovereignty were the Golden Triangle (Chihuahua, Durango, and Sinaloa); enclaves of the Tierra Caliente (Michoacán, Mexico State, and Guerrero); much of Oaxaca; vast neighborhoods in such cities as Reynosa, Matamoros, Nuevo Laredo, Ciudad Juárez, Nogales, Tijuana, and Ensenada; and parts of the Isthmus of Tehuantepec. Table 5.1 indicates the number of drug-war casualties in recent years.[9]

A medley of factors escalated the amount of bloodshed that Calderón inherited. As discussed earlier, the implicit arrangements between PRI-run administrations and narco-mobsters had long-since broken down, and Fox couldn't have revived them if he had wanted to. There was a downturn in killings in the late 1990s, but murders, kidnappings, and extortion continuously increased after 2000. The worsening situation prompted Fox to dispatch the armed forces to Nuevo Laredo and Tamaulipas to confront the cartels. Fighting escalated in 2005 when El Chapo Guzmán unsuccessfully attempted to seize Nuevo Laredo from the Gulf Cartel, even as he sought control of Tijuana and other corridors into California. The drug-related death toll for the year rose to 1,537 before reaching 2,119 in 2006 as beheadings, torture, homicides, and grenade attacks beset Acapulco, Monterrey, and Michoacán, the new chief executive's home state.

Table 5.1

Drug Related Deaths, 2006 through October 4, 2013

Year	Number of Drug War–Related Deaths
2013	6,150 (through October 4)
2012	9,158
2011	12,366
2010	11,583
2009	6,587
2008	5,207
2007	2,275
2006	2,119
TOTAL	47,268

Source: A major Mexico City newspaper publishes a weekly tally of violent deaths in the country. See "Muertos Violentos en el País: Ejecutómetro," see, *Reforma*, October 7, 2013.

Acapulco's mayor, Alberto Lopez Rosas, told Reuters, "This is completely new for us" and "It is an upsetting situation which has surprised all of us in Acapulco."[10]

Lack of confidence in Mexican police meant that 92 percent of all crimes went unreported.[11] In light of the corruption infusing law-enforcement agencies, Calderón sought advice from Joaquín Villalobos, a leader of the Farabundo Martí National Liberation Front in El Salvador. He made a splash April 1993 when the Mexican media publicized his presenting to President Salinas an automatic weapon given to the commando by Fidel Castro.[12] After the 1992 signing of peace accords ending the Salvadoran civil war, Villalobos studied in England Oxford University, where he befriended ex-president López Portillo's son. Later, with dubious credentials, Villalobos set himself up as a "consultant for the resolution of international conflicts." The former guerrilla, whom U.S. officials called "the baby-faced killer"[13] during the warfare in Central America, developed a professional relationship with Public Security Secretary Genaro García Luna and, especially, the new attorney general, Eduardo Medina Mora.

The design of the war strategy lay with Calderón. Yet, Villalobos, who first began consulting for Mexico's government in 2005, furnished a narrative and served as an interpreter of the strategy to the public, often relying on such bromides as: "The imperative is to restore state authority, order, where the government has lost it. The growth of the state is a slow process, and only then will the violence diminish." The chief executive gave lip service to these tenets and saw Villalobos "as some kind of guru," stated a senior government analyst who disagrees with the Salvadoran and who spoke on the condition of anonymity because of the sensitivity of the topic.[14] Table 5.2 displays the 12 myths and salient criticism of them.

Table 5.2

Villalobos's 12 Myths of Combatting Organized Crime

Myth	Criticism/Comments
1. You must not confront organized crime.	Criminal syndicates have compromised the sovereignty of important areas of the nation and intimidated police, mayors, and governors with "silver or lead" threats.
2. Mexico is "Colombianized" and in danger of becoming a failed state.	As brutal as organized crime has been, Mexico has not suffered widespread car and truck bombings, explosion of an Avianca Airways passenger jet, and assassination of political candidates, including a presidential nominee, Luis Carlos Galán in 1989.
3. The intense debate over insecurity is a sign of deterioration.	Debates over strategy are normal in a plural society and should be encouraged, not discouraged.
4. Deaths and violence indicate that you are losing the war.	Violence inevitably arises when combatting an enemy. A retired Colombian national police general who is now a Peña Nieto adviser said that "when we know that drug trafficking has strongly penetrated into society, the main problem is not violence, but non-violence because it implies that the drug traffickers control society."
5. Three years is enough time to defeat the cartels, and the struggle has been lost.	The time to manage a problem is directly proportional to the size and historical roots of the challenge, which—in the case of Mexico—is exacerbated by its contiguity to the world's largest population of consumers.
6. Attacks by narco-syndicates prove that they are powerful.	With few exceptions, cartel attacks spring from revenge, such as the deadly conflict between Los Zetas and the Gulf Cartel in January 2010 when the former kidnapped Víctor "Concord 3" Peña Mendoza—a confidant of El 40—and sought to convince the ranking Zeta in Reynosa to switch allegiance. When Concord 3 refused to change sides, he was executed, presumably by Gulf Cartel gunman Samuel "Metro 3" Flores Borrego. In return, Los Zetas's Treviño Morales seized 16 Gulf Cartel members in Reynosa.

(continued)

Table 5.2 *(continued)*

Myth	Criticism/Comments
7. Corruption and poverty must be ended before winning a conflict.	Intense fighting impedes the ability to carry out social and economic reforms. Drug commerce is based on greed and recruits the poor, but depends primarily on production areas and trafficking corridors.
8. Powerful politicians and businesses are behind the narco-trafficking.	While smugglers arise from the lower middle class and are poorly educated, their ability to infuse fear in the well-to-do facilitates kidnapping and extortion. Professionals such as real estate brokers, investment counselors, and vehicle distributors often do business with syndicates without asking the provenance of the funds used in their transactions.
9. The only solution is negotiating with the narco-traffickers.	The idea of negotiating with a cartel is a fantasy. When it was attempted in Colombia, Pablo Escobar and his colleagues converted prisons into luxurious headquarters that he turned into command and operations posts that mocked the judicial system even as he continued to orchestrate operations from behind bars.
10. Any strategy must include the legalization of drugs.	A strong argument can be made for legalization; however, even if the drug trade were to vanish—a big if—the cartel and gang members would not disappear. Rather, they would devote their criminal skills to kidnapping, extortion, money-laundering, prostitution, and other crimes.
11. The participation of the army against cartels is negative, and troops must be withdrawn.	The army, which is trained to pursue, capture, and kill, represents a "broad sword" (massive force) when a "scalpel" (intelligence, informants, drones, etc.) is required; however, the corruption and cooptation of federal, state, and local police obviates withdrawing military personnel from the battle against cartels.
12. The most effective and rapid means to combat crime is through extra-judicial means.	The idea of eliminating criminals in the most expedient way possible—even deploying paramilitary units—undermines Mexico's Sisyphean effort to create to judicial system based on Anglo-Saxon legal precepts rather than suborning judges, prosecutors, and others involved in the resolution of cases.

Source: Joaquín Villalobos, "Nuevos mitos de la guerra contra el narco, *Nexus*," January 1, 2012; Border Beat reporter Gerardo "12 Myths of the War against the Drug Cartels, Parts 1 and 2," *Borderland Beat*, September 23, 2010 and September 24, 2010; Tracy Wilkinson, "A Top Salvadoran ex-Guerrilla Commander Advises Mexico's Conservative President," *Los Angeles Times*, October 22, 2010.

Soon Calderón's speeches began to channel the adviser's phrases. At times it was as if a puppet were regurgitating the words of a ventriloquist. For examples, a soaring death toll reflects the "self-destruction" of the cartels, "The criminals would prefer to be at peace, doing business," "We will never negotiate with narco-traffickers," and "Deaths indicate that we are winning the fight against the cartels." The president realized that he could not engage in this crusade alone.

THE MÉRIDA INITIATIVE

When President George W. Bush visited Guatemala City on March 12, 2007, his host Óscar Berger voiced alarm over the mounting violence besetting his country. According to a diplomat who attended the session, he said, in effect: "We are a poor country. We lack the resources with which to protect our citizens from cartels. We need the U.S. military to come in and help us." The urgency of this lament seized Bush's attention. Although he had not arrived with a security proposal in his briefcase, the guest and his host agreed that the scope of the challenge called for a multinational venture. As the visiting chief executive said about the drug trade, it is a "serious problem because narco-trafficking destabilizes areas. It's in our interest ... to promote prosperity and peace and stability."[15]

Bush heard the same tale of woe even more forcefully from Calderón, whom he visited in Mérida on the Yucatán peninsula. Although pledging to combat narcotics activities, the Mexican leader emphasized Washington's responsibility for widespread consumption because "while there is no reduction in demand in your territory, it will be very difficult to reduce the supply in ours."[16] He also took umbrage at the cross-border flow of cash and weapons. Any action plan, he insisted, would have to rest on "shared responsibilities."[17]

Members of the U.S. House of Representatives felt they had received too little information about any new scheme with Mexico, and there was concern over the failure to include Central America and Caribbean nations. Representative Elliot L. Engle, chair of the subcommittee on the Western Hemisphere, said that the $50 million originally earmarked for Central America was no more than a "drop in the ocean," especially when the isthmus was a freeway for U.S.-bound cocaine. As a result, Congress increased funding for this area to $61.5 million.

The letter of agreement for the Mérida Initiative signed in December 2008 embraced Mexico, Central America, the Dominican Republic, and Haiti. The initial price tag was $1.4 billion for training, equipment, and intelligence sharing for three years. The disbursement process was slow, and U.S. legislators insisted on holding back 15 percent as an incentive for the recipients to address human rights abuses in their nations.

The U.S. State Department announced the architecture of the accord in terms of Four Pillars: disrupting the capacity of organized crime to operate; developing the capacity of judicial and security institutions to sustain the rule of law; building a twenty-first–century border that facilitates legitimate trade and movement of people while thwarting the flow of drugs, arms, and cash; and building strong and resilient communities.[18]

Washington earmarked 41 percent of Merida resources for the acquisition of 21 aircraft, including Casa-245 twin-engine planes and five Bell-412 helicopters to support interdiction activities and facilitate rapid response by Mexican law-enforcement agencies. Secretary of State Hillary R. Clinton also promised $80 million for Black Hawk helicopters. The balance of the assets would be used to professionalize the police; to purchase night-vision goggles, drug-sniffing dogs, and ion scanners; and to stanch commerce in narcotics, weapons, and illegal aliens.

The Mérida honeymoon ended quickly. More than two years after the signing of the accord, the United States has dispersed only $24 million— less than 2 percent—of the $1.3 billion that Congress approved for the bilateral war on drugs, according to the U.S. Government Accountability Office (GAO).[19]

Why the delay?

U.S. policymakers have difficulty focusing on more than two or three issues at a time.

In addition to the protracted recession and health-care legislation, the White House had been weighing whether and how many additional troops, if any should be sent to Afghanistan. Never mind that continued successes by the Mexico-based cartels would have had graver consequences for the United States than thrusts by al-Qaeda and the Taliban.

Another key factor rested with a labyrinthine bureaucracy. The GAO found that three separate Department of State (DOS) bureaus were administering Mérida allocations. Each employed different budgeting terms as well as separate spreadsheets for the monies it handled. The DOS had no consolidated database for these expenditures. Cooperation over the Mérida accord took several years because there was no robust history of military-to-military interaction as was the case with Colombia and Honduras.

Congress continued to throw up road bumps. Legislators required the DOS to submit detailed reports on the progress of the Mexican and Central American governments in addressing human rights abuses in their countries. Legislators vetoed the release of 15 percent of funds approved for Mexico until the Calderón regime provided assurances that alleged civil rights transgressions by the federal police and military were appropriately investigated and prosecuted.

Nongovernmental organizations (NGOs) continued to lobby lawmakers about "atrocities and torture" committed by the Mexican military.

Critics of the Mérida Initiative have been quick to compare it to Plan Colombia. The Mexicans vigorously reject this analogy because Colombia has accepted the presence of U.S. military personnel in its country.

There are, of course, similarities. Corruption abounds in both countries, the armies have played a role in drug eradication, Nongovernmental organizations have thundered against human rights violations, cartels and "cartelitos" plague both the Mexico City and Bogotá regimes, private sector enablers have fattened their bank accounts by selling goods and services to the underworld, elements of the Roman Catholic Church have taken contributions from Colombian and Mexican criminals, and many affluent members of the private sector have moved their businesses and families to the United States.

However, the differences are much greater. Mexico's toxic nationalism, exacerbated by contiguity, militates against allowing U.S. troops into its country. Colombia has a national police force, while Mexico has hundreds of law-enforcement agencies embracing 459,000 sworn officers, and there is far less friction between the PNC and the Colombian Army. In addition, more than half a dozen major cartels operate in Mexico, a much larger country, compared with the now-defunct Medellín and Cali organizations. Colombia is a unitary, not a federal state, and department heads don't have the clout and vast authority of Mexico's governors. Recent chief executives—Vicente Fox and Felipe Calderón—did not evince the dynamism and skill of Álvaro Uribe Vélez (2002–2010). Even though its cities are far safer than before Uribe's tenure, smaller Colombian organizations, the so-called cartelitos, export more cocaine than ever. Table 5.3 presents differences between the drug wars in the two countries.

The contract for the five Bell helicopters was signed on April 22, 2009. Even though the manufacturer has promised to expedite what is usually a two-year production process, the aircraft would not be ready until late 2010. An additional year was needed before the brace of Black Hawks rolled off the assembly line.

Was it possible that congressional representatives from Connecticut, where the Textron Corporation produces Bell aircraft and their colleagues from Texas, where United Technology manufactures Black Hawks, were at odds over which firm should produce the fixed-wing combat aircraft? Such lobbying had increased the price tag and slowed delivery of helicopters included in the Plan Colombia in the late 1990s. The Mérida Initiative has also unwritten the creation of state-level law enforcement capacity known as Model Police United (MPUs).

Moreover, the numerous U.S. agencies involved in the Mérida program indicated that they needed "dozens of additional staff members . . . at the sprawling American Embassy in Mexico City to handle administrative matters," the *New York Times* reported.[20]

Table 5.3

Differences between Drug Wars in Mexico and Colombia

1. Mexico's intractable resistance to U.S. troops in its country
2. Although far from a paragon of law-enforcement ability, Colombia has a national police force (PNC), and Mexico has some 3,000 municipal, state, and federal police agencies
3. Mexico is much larger in terms of population and territory
4. Mexico is contiguous to the United States
5. Mexico has a half-dozen or more cartels; Colombia had only two major cartels—Medellín and Cali—in addition to the North Valley Cartel, which rose to prominence after the break-up of the "Big Two," and now there are 300-plus cartelitos
6. Strong, decisive leadership under Álvaro Uribe Vélez (2002–10)
7. Army and police more prone to cooperate in Colombia
8. Colombia is not a federal state—department heads have neither the clout nor the impunity of Mexican governors
9. Although growing, a much weaker vigilante/autodefense presence in Mexico than in Colombia, where the AUC constitutes an important player
10. Colombia's electoral system, which has two strong parties, allows for reelection

Ambassador Carlos Pascual averred that the United States had actually spent more than was reflected in the July 2010 GAO document. For example, he told the *Washington Post* that there has been funding for the new federal police academy, which has graduated more than 3,000 cadets, but the contractor providing the U.S. instructors has not yet submitted an invoice for the training.[21]

Former U.S. ambassador to Mexico Jeffrey Davidow said, "I don't think the slowness in outlay is any kind of indication of policy failure . . . it is better to take the time and get it right."[22]

The Mérida monies represent 2 percent of Mexico's own antidrug budget.

Other U.S. programs complement the Mérida Initiative:

- The U.S. Agency for International Development (AID), with a $33 million budget in 2012, has concentrated development assistance on enhancing private sector competition, encouraging sustainable energy, and forming partnerships between U.S. and Mexican universities to address the rule of law and climate change.
- The U.S. Global Health and Child Survival program endeavors to prevent and treat HIV/AIDS and other infectious diseases. It was not funded in 2012.

- The U.S. Department of Defense (DOD) provides counterdrug assistance under the auspices of the U.S. Northern Command (NORTHCOM), located at Peterson Air Force Base in Colorado. DOD funds increased from $34.2 million (fiscal year [FY] 2009) to $89.7 million (FY 2010). Funding then decreased to $84.7 million (FY 2011). Overall, the Pentagon's allocations to Mexico reached $100.4 million (FY 2012) and may be more than $75 million in FY 2013.

Observers have written a library of books, monographs, and articles on the Mérida Initiative. Rather than revisit this terrain, the author provides suggested readings.[23]

Suffice it to say that the plan has gone through two stages and may be on the verge of a third as Peña Nieto grapples to design his own security blueprint. The first involved the Calderón administration's muscular military attack on the crime organizations while it negotiated its priorities for Mérida funding with Washington—a process that sparked turf warfare within the turgid Mexican bureaucracy. Nevertheless, working with Mexico City was a "walk in the park" compared to bargaining with Central Americans, whom one diplomat analogized to "herding cats." As discussed later, Calderón did manage to capture or kill a number of "kingpins," but cocaine, marijuana, heroin and methamphetamines continued to flow northward even as drug-related deaths soared.

While Mexico continued to rely on the army, navy, and federal police, its decision makers decided to modify this approach, which led to a "new stage." In late March 2010 a second high-level consultation took place in Mexico City. Secretary Clinton led the U.S. delegation, which included Defense Secretary Robert M. Gates, Chairman of the Joint Chiefs of Staff Admiral Michael G. Mullen, Homeland Security Secretary Janet Napolitano, and other ranking officials.

The secretary of state avoided arrogance when she addressed Mexicans' concern about weapons cascading southward from the United States. "We know that the demand for drugs drives much of this illicit trade, that guns purchased in the United States . . . are used to facilitate violence here in Mexico. And the United States must and is doing its part to help you and us meet those challenges."[24] Calderón expressed outrage at the botched operation known as Fast and Furious whereby the U.S. Bureau of Alcohol, Tobacco, Firearms, and Explosives allowed cartels to obtain hundreds of high-power weapons purchased in the Southwest in a muddled sting operation.[25]

The second phase, which was begun in 2009, continued to focus on military hardware, intelligence sharing, and police reform. However, the United States reallocated $310 million requested for 2011 military needs to backing Mexico's judicial reforms, good governance, and social cohesion. Now, said U.S. Bureau of Narcotics and Law Enforcement Affairs assistant secretary William R. Brownfield in remarks reported by the *El Paso*

Times, "the emphasis will shift to Mexico's border and their state and local police forces. That would be the best way [of] advancing the goals of the initiative's four pillar strategy of disrupting the ability of the cartels to operate, enhancing Mexico's capacity to sustain the rule of law, creating a modern border infrastructure, and building resilient communities."[26] Tijuana, Monterrey, and Ciudad Juárez were prime targets for improving social infrastructure.

A persistent problem was identifying specific measures with which to evaluate the program. Mindful of this challenge, Calderón identified 37 important capos, 24 of whom had been killed or arrested by the time he left office (as seen in Table 5.4).

Another metric was the murder rate in Ciudad Juárez. The number of fatalities fell from 3,115 (2010) to 2,086 (2011) to 784 (2012) in this city of 1.3 million inhabitants. Although arising from several factors, the steep drop in violence in Ciudad Juárez owes at least part of its success to the fourth pillar of the Mérida Initiative. Funds have been used to illuminate playgrounds, create soccer leagues, establish after-school programs, install street cameras, and cooperate with the Somos Ciudad Juárez citizens' venture.

Arturo Valenzuela, president of the Ciudad Juárez Security Table, attributed the impetus for change to the killing of 15 youngsters at a party in January 2010. He said antagonism gave way to cooperation between that the private sector and the government. In contrast, human rights spokesman Gustavo de la Rosa Hickerson explained the fall in the murder rate to a severe crackdown by law-enforcement agents. "The authorities have had to use a strong hand to control the incredible indices of violence ... We had to put up with check-points, arbitrary arrests, vacating our homes ..." he added.[27]

Yet, as late as May 2012 the city's outspoken PRI mayor, Héctor Muguía Lardizabal, asserted: "We don't see any benefit of Mérida ... [t]he U.S. is the biggest consumer of drugs and their aid package is not enough for us to do what they expect us to do, yet the American media is so critical of Juárez. These people need to be more responsible and not criticize what they don't know."[28] In support of his comment, the *New York Times* published 15 articles on violence in Mexico in 2012 and only three on Honduras and two on Colombia—despite murder rates in these nations that are higher than Mexico's.[29]

A Realpolitik theory holds that dominance of an area by a single criminal organization reduces bloodshed. Although the Juárez Cartel still exists, it has been eclipsed in Ciudad Juárez by the Sinaloa Cartel. In addition, Ciudad Juárez was a showcase for the Mérida Initiative, and the state capital of Chihuahua continued to incur an epidemic of ghastly violence, to the point that in mid-2012 citizens expelled from the Ascención municipality federal police assigned to highway security. The mayor of nearby

Table 5.4

Prominent Kingpins Arrested/Killed during Calderón Administration

Name of Criminal	Affiliation	Date/Place Arrested/ Killed	Agency Accomplish- ing the Arrest/Killing	Observations
Heriberto Lazcano Lazcano "Z-3"	Leader of Los Zetas	Oct. 7, 2012/Progreso, Saltillo/Killed	Navy/Marines	
Iván "El Talibán/Z-50" Velazquez Caballero	Top leaded of Los Zetas, who feuded with Treviño Morales; responsible for violence in SLP, Zacatecas, and Coahuila	Sept. 26, 2012/SLP/ Captured	Navy/Marines	
Eduardo Costilla Sánchez "El Coss"	Leader of the Gulf Cartel	Sept. 12, 2012/ Tamaulipas/Captured	Navy/Marines	
Mario Cárdenas Guillén	Brother of Osiel Cárdenas, historic leader of the Gulf Cartel	Sept. 3, 2012/Captured/ Altamira, Tamps	Army/Altamira,	
Erick Valencia Salazar "El 85"	Leader of the Cartel de Jalisco Nueva Generación	March 9, 2012/ Zapopan, Jalisco/Captured	Army	
Flavio Mendez Santiago "El Amarillo"	Founding member of Los Zetas	Jan. 18, 2011/Oaxaca/ Captured	Federal Police	
Martín Beltrán Coronel "El Águila"	A top leader of Sinaloa Cartel	May 12, 2011/Zapopan, Jalisco/Captured	Army	
José de Jesús Mendez "El Chango" Méndez Vargas	Succeed El Chayo as leader of La Familia Michoacán	June 21, 2011/ Aguascalientes/Believed killed	Federal Police	

(continued)

Table 5.4 (continued)

Name of Criminal	Affiliation	Date/Place Arrested/ Killed	Agency Accomplish- ing the Arrest/Killing	Observations
Francisco "El 2000" Hernández García	Beltrán Leyva Organization	Nov. 4, 2011/Ciudad Juárez/Captured	Federal Police	
Ezequiel Cárdenas Rivera "El Junior"	Nephew of Osiel Cárdenas and son of Ezequiel Cárdenas Guillén "El Tormenta"	Nov. 25, 2011/ Matamoros/Captured	Army	
Raúl Lucio "El Lucky" Hernández Lechuga	Founding Zeta and ran its activities in Veracruz, Puebla, and Oaxaca	Dec. 12, 2011/Córdoba, Veracruz/Captured	Navy/Marines	
Teodoro García Simental "El Teo"	Arellano Félix Organization	Jan. 12, 2010/La Paz, BCS/Captured	Federal Police	
Ignacio Coronel Villarreal "El Nacho"	Number 3 in the Sinaloa Cartel	June 29, 2010/Zapopan/ Killed	Army	Nacho's death sparked a free-for-all in Guada-lajara involving major cartels and their allied gangs
Édgar Valdez Villarreal "La Barbie"	Broke away from the BLO	Aug. 30, 2010/Captured	Army	

Name	Description	Date/Location/Status	Captured by	Notes
Sergio Villarreal "El Grande"	BLO	Sept. 12, 2010/Puebla/ Captured	Navy/Marines	May 23, 2012; extradited to U.S. and may cooperate with the DEA
Ezequiel Cárdenas Guillén "Tony Tormenta"	Gulf Cartel leader	Nov. 7, 2010/ Matamoros/Killed	Navy/Marines	
Nazario Moreno "El Chayo"/"The Monkey"	Founder to La Familia Michoacán Cartel	Dec. 9, 2010; Killed in western Michoacán	Federal Police	His protection was the responsibility of twelve gunmen he called the "Twelve Apostles"
Vicente Zambada Niebla "Vicentillo"	A key member of the Sinaloa Cartel	March 19, 2009/Mexico City suburb/Captured	Federal Police	
Vicente Carrillo Leyva	Leader of the Juárez Cartel and son of legendary kingpin Amado Carrillo Fuentes	April 2, 2009/Mexico City/ Arrested	Federal Police	
Raymundo "El Gori 1" Almanza Morales	Zeta leader in the Cancún area and believed have been involved with the murder of a general	May 22, 2009/Killed/ Monterrey	Army	

(continued)

Table 5.4 (continued)

Name of Criminal	Affiliation	Date/Place Arrested/ Killed	Agency Accomplishing the Arrest/Killing	Observations
Arturo Beltrán Leyva "jefe de los jefes"	Leader of BLO	Dec. 16, 2009 / Cuernavaca / Killed	Navy / Marines	
Alfredo "El Mochomo" Beltrán Leyva	Ally of El Chapo's Sinaloa Cartel	Jan. 21, 2008 / Culiacán / Arrested	Army	
Jesús Zambada García "El Rey"	Sinaloa Cartel operative for Central America	Oct. 19, 2008; Mexico City / Arrested	Federal Police	
Eduardo Arellano Félix	Youngest of the brothers who founded the Tijuana Cartel	Oct. 25, 2008 / Tijuana / Captured	Army and SSPF	Extradited to the U.S.; Aug. 31, 2012.

Delicias stated: "We see that in lieu of pursuing people linked to organized crime, federal police agents engage in extortion, and exacting 'quotas' from farmers, people who sacrifice a great deal to attend to their animals and land . . ."[30]

Even with 10,500 deaths in Ciudad Juárez since 2008, the city is attracting investment by large American and Japanese companies—a development that augurs well for economic growth and employment opportunities. Thanks to low pay and an abundant workforce, the number of export-related jobs jumped from 166,000 in mid-2009 to 215,000 three years later. Some 85 multinational firms—including Johnson & Johnson, Delphi, Siemens, and Foxconn—have major manufacturing activities in the city. "It's the Mexican paradox," said Claudio X. González, the venerable chairman of the Mexican subsidiary of Kimberly Clark, referring to the cascade of capital into a city that had undergone an epidemic of crime.[31]

There is no reason for complacency. "Juárez has been traumatized and so badly damaged that the many scars and mental damage left behind should never be underestimated. The ones who have endured so much pain to get through it all are heroes. The Juárez people are tough, resilient and deserve their city back. This is a war they never asked for or deserved. We will all look back at this tragedy as something so stunning that we may never grasp what truly happened."[32] In 2012 Acapulco, once the playground for Elizabeth Taylor, Frank Sinatra, Eddie Fisher, and Brigitte Bardot, replaced Ciudad Juárez as Mexico's most deadly city on a per-capita basis. Some 80 percent of "spring-breakers"—mostly scantily-clad, beer-drinking American college students—cancelled their reservations to stay at the resort in 2013.[33]

The Mérida Initiative has benefited Mexico's armed forces in terms of equipment, training, and intelligence. Military-to-military relations during the Calderón era were closer than at any time since World War II. Nonetheless, occasional contretemps have flared out as in the case with Wikileaks, described in the next chapter.

In addition, a *New York Times* front-page article asserted that the Pentagon and the DEA helped scuttle the selection of General Moisés García Ochoa as Peña Nieto's secretary of defense. The move allegedly sprang from concerns that the three-star officer had links to drug traffickers, misused military supplies, and skimmed cash from multimillion-dollar defense contracts when he headed the army's weapons acquisition program. American officials had reportedly given García Ochoa the nickname of "Mr. Ten Percent" because of the payola he allegedly received on projects. During the summer of 2012 the Mexican press reported that general had authorized payments totaling more than $355 million for sophisticated surveillance equipment without reporting those payments to civilian authorities or explaining how that equipment would be used.[34]

The U.S. envoy to Mexico rejected the idea that he interfered in the García Ochoa case. A memorandum issued by the embassy indicated that "Ambassador [E. Anthony] Wayne neither exercised pressure nor lobbied with respect to the President's selection of military members of his cabinet. To the contrary, Washington's policy is that the United States government will work with whomever President Peña Nieto selected."[35]

Rather than cashier the veteran military man as was the case in the Gutiérrez Rebollo scandal in the Zedillo administration, García Ochoa was named commander of the 11th Military Zone that embraces the violence-wracked states of Coahuila and Durango. This transfer appeared as a non-so-subtle reminder that General Salvador Cienfuegos Zepeda, whom the president named secretary of defense, was calling the shots. Despite grumbling about interference in Mexican affairs, Uncle Sam may have done his neighbor to the south a favor inasmuch as an exposé of García Ochoa's alleged business transactions after Peña Nieto's inauguration would have hugely embarrassed the new PRI regime.

Even though Washington is now prepared to move into its third phase, the Calderón-negotiated Mérida Initiative has disappeared from the vocabulary of the new administration's security team.

RELIANCE ON THE ARMED FORCES

Calderón called on Secretary of Defense Guillermo Galván, a fervent nationalist, to wrest contested areas from the ever-more vicious, wealthy, and numerous narco-syndicates. High-ranking U.S. officials courted Galván, to the point of hosting him at a Major League Baseball game in the Midwest. The chief executive went out of his way to ingratiate himself with the armed forces. Before taking office, a cadet from the Heroic Military College (Mexico's version of West Point) presented him with the presidential sash in an impromptu midnight ceremony. After his formal investiture by Congress, he went to the Campo Militar, the Defense Ministry headquarters, where he, along with Galván and Navy Secretary Admiral Mariano Francisco Saynez, reviewed the troops, received a 21-gun salute, and raised an enormous flag. At a breakfast with the military's top brass, Calderón praised the army for defending the nation and battling organized crime. "I will propose a substantial increase in troops' wages in recognition of the unquestionable effort and loyalty of our armed forces," he said.[36] He later announced he would cut his own salary to show a contrast with military pay raises.

On January 3, 2007, the chief executive even visited the 43rd Military Zone in Apatzingán, a no-man's-land in his home state of Michoacán. There he donned a floppy military tunic and sported an olive-green field hat emblazoned with five stars and the national shield—all symbols of the commander in chief—to accentuate his solidarity with the forces confronting the narco-criminals. He reiterated to his audience that "this is not an easy task nor will it be quick, but it will take much time. It will imply enormous resources of Mexicans, including the lamentable loss of human lives. This is a job which may not bear fruit rapidly, but it is indispensable to assure the future of Mexico." He went on to articulate an ambitious goal: "We are determined to recover the security, not only of Michoacán or Baja California, but of every region ... that is threatened by organized crime."[37] In addition to the military attire, Calderón frequently rode in a vehicle with the Mexican national eagle and five stars to underline his solidarity with the armed forces.[38]

THE KINGPIN STRATEGY

The Drug Enforcement Administration originally developed the "kingpin strategy" to disrupt and dismantle Colombia's Medellín and Cali cartels in the early 1990s. This approach sprang from an analysis of the business organizations that engage in production, transportation, distribution, and funding of their enterprises. The DEA concluded that[39]

it was futile to attack the cartel's business activities per se, and that the common thread among all of the critical nodes was the command-and-control elements that provided the leadership, authority, management and direction for those activities. It was decided that better success could be achieved by focusing on the people committing the crimes, and not the crimes themselves, especially given that many transnational criminal activities [take place] around the world.

The Calderón-García Luna-Galván-Saynez version of decapitating capos was to deploy large numbers of cadres—federal police and military—against the cartels to eliminate their leaders. Through mid-2009 the government had undertaken some 30 such offenses—seven in Michoacán alone—in the country's hotspots.[40] In a January 2007 interview with the *Financial Times*, the president exuded optimism about his crusade against criminal elements. He boasted, for example, that the assassination rate had fallen 40 percent in Michoacán and that public support for his policy had grown. He repeated a familiar refrain in blaming Uncle Sam for the mayhem besetting his nation: "The truth is that the U.S. is clearly responsible for what is going on here ... it is an economic and mathematics equation. It is impossible to reduce significantly the flow of drugs if there is not a reduction in demand ... by the world's largest consumer ..."[41]

Five weeks after the crackdown on criminal gangs, soldiers and federal police took down their first culprit. In mid-January 2007 they arrested Pedro Díaz Parada, chief of the Oaxaca Cartel and El Chapo's number one ally in the state. The savage criminal had escaped from prison in 1985 after serving just days of a 33-year trafficking sentence. Two years later the judge that put him behind bars was riddled with 33 bullets—"a bullet a year," according to a note left beside the victim's body.[42] All told, authorities killed or captured more than three dozen Mafiosi during Calderón's administration.

Despite these numbers, the kingpin approach suffered from severe weaknesses. To begin with, there is the Hydra effect, which derives from Hercules having decapitated the reptilian water beast only to find it regenerating one or more heads. In the context of the drug war, assassinating the top cartel figure often gives rise to lieutenants battling to succeed the fallen don.[43] Meanwhile, foes take advantage of the setback to invade the territory of the fallen doyen. At the same time, gangs associated with cartels often tried to enhance their influence in the organization. The upshot was generally a surge of deaths after most takedowns. Equally troubling was that the new chief might be younger, less confident, and more vicious than his predecessor.

Eliminating the top dog can incite fissures in the organization. As discussed earlier, the death of Arturo Beltrán Leyva on January 16, 2009, splintered the BLO. Notably, La Barbie established his own band that used extreme violence to bolster its position in Acapulco. The August 30, 2010, arrest of the blue-eyed cutthroat pulverized his organization, according to his would-be successor and brother-in-law Carlos "El Charro" González. A weaker group arising out of the BLO split was the Independent Cartel of Acapulco (CIDA), which concentrated on small drug sales (*menudeo*). The Sinaloa Cartel wasted little time before jumping into this strife over plazas. This free-for-all produced 28 deaths, including 15 decapitations, on January 8, 2011—a one-day record for Acapulco, which pundits began calling "Narcopulco."[44]

Other CIDA activists had no love lost for El Charro, against whom they spearheaded a campaign that wound up with his apprehension on November 23, 2010.[45] Within nine months, the army and federal police had arrested the next CIDA chief, Moisés "El Koreano" Montero Álvarez.[46] The October to December 2011 Operation Guerrero Seguro accomplished the arrest of 145 thugs, which further debilitated the CIDA. It's impossible to classify the affiliation of captives because groups like CIDA lack formal structures, undergo kaleidoscopic changes in bosses, and bring aboard freelance thugs who participate in its criminality when it suits them.

As alluded to in Chapter 4, the military's killing of El Nacho Coronel, number three in the Sinaloa Cartel, set off bloody confrontations in Guadalajara that involved the Sinaloa Cartel, the New Generation Jalisco Cartel (CJNG), Los Zetas (via La Resistencia), the Beltrán Leyvas, and La Familia Michoacán.

In a similar vein, the death of La Familia Michoacán's Nazario "El Chayo" Moreno González in December 2010 prompted Servando "La Tuta" Gómez Martínez and Enrique "Kike"/"La Chiva" Plancarte Solís to separate into the Knights Templar.

As mentioned earlier, the most brutal cartel-versus-cartel clashes involved the Gulf Cartel and Los Zetas—with the most casualties occurring in Nuevo León, Tamaulipas, and Veracruz.

Largely as a result of intercartel competition, 49 percent of the executions nationwide, including 15 decapitations, took place between April 16 and June 17, 2011, in nine states.[47]

A successful kingpin approach requires cooperation between and among military and law-enforcement agencies. At first, Calderón's entourage demonstrated more harmony than President Fox's staff, which pundits lampooned as a "Montessori cabinet." This was a puckish allusion to its participants' preference for self-expression over cooperation. It did not take long for disagreements to erupt in Calderón's security team, with angry exchanges filling the air. Defense Secretary Galván was hostile to the proposed combining of two federal police forces—the Federal Investigative Agency (AFI) and the Federal Preventative Police (PFP)—lest the move siphon resources from the military without cleaning up civilian law enforcement. Roberto Campa Cifrián vehemently fought García Luna over the merger—to the point that he resigned as executive secretary of the National Public Security System (SNSP), which coordinates, administers, and doles out money to federal, state, and local security forces. So strident was the clash that journalist Raymundo Jiménez García referred to an "underground war" between the two men. In fact, the verbal skirmishes were not sub rosa. The infighting had less to do with strategy—than a fight for power, status, and budgets among political rivals. Meanwhile, Calderón had to threaten, cajole, and beg to get the army, navy, and police agencies to share intelligence with Guillermo Valdés Castellanos, a Calderón confidant who headed the Center for Investigation and National Security (CISEN), Mexico's iteration of the CIA.

García Luna also clashed with Attorney General Eduardo Medina Mora, now Mexico's ambassador to the United States, and General Galván. The García Luna–Galván conflicts often arose over who deserved credit for successful anticartel ventures. Finance Secretary Agustín Carstens had to ward off García Luna's efforts to take command of the SHCP's Office of Financial Intelligence (UIF), which investigates money laundering and other financial crimes. In November 2008, Calderón named former deputy and distinguished lawyer Fernándo Gómez Mont as Gobernación secretary to referee and minimize rivalries and backbiting.

OPERATION HOUSE-CLEANING

Corruption constituted a giant impediment to successfully combatting the underworld. Operación Limpieza (Operation House-Cleaning) turned up princely payments to key Mexican government "crime fighters." In mid-2008 a protected witness in the United States alleged that from 2006 to August 2008, the head of the PGR's office for the Specialized Investigation of Organized Crime (SIEDO) Nöe Ramírez Mandujano, pocketed $450,000 per month in bribes from the Beltrán Leyva Organization. In return for this compensation, the SIEDO purportedly alerted the cartel to impending law-enforcement maneuvers. All told, Ramírez Mandujano and a baker's dozen of security officials landed behind bars.[48] This episode made the military and other civilian agencies even more wary of cooperating with the PGR. In mid-April 2013, a judge threw out the charges against the former SIEDO chief. "With regard to the principal witness by the code name of 'Jennifer' it was found that she acted with a lack of probity since she admitted that she lied in giving statements," according to the Federal Judicial Council.[49]

POLITICIANS AND THE KINGPIN THEORY

Politicians often gave lip service to attacking the capos only to change their tune when elected officials were charged with drug-related crimes. After five armed incursions into Michoacán with, at best, limited success in curbing the carnage, Calderón began to complement a military approach with a focus on politicians, including PRD's Michoacán governor Leonel Godoy Rangel (2007–2011), who was enabling La Familia and other cartels to act with impunity. On May 26, 2009, federal authorities captured Michoacán's former secretary of public safety, various law-enforcement personnel, police officers, a judge, and a dozen mayors allegedly linked to La Familia. The wily Godoy, who was also accused of receiving funds from the local cartel during his campaign, raised unshirted hell about not being informed of the arrests in advance. Except for PAN officeholders, politicians from across the spectrum excoriated the government's move.

PRD president Jesús Ortega Martínez accused Calderón of trying to curry the favor of voters in the run-up to the mid-2009 legislative elections, saying that the chief executive was "pursuing votes that would permit him to win this area."[50] In the final analysis most, if not all, of those jailed were freed—largely because witnesses feared testifying against La Familia. "It is important [the arrests], but it won't have an impact on the amount of drugs going to the United States," said Alberto Islas, a Mexico City security analyst. "At the end of the day, the mayors and politicians are just another instrument in the cartels' business."[51]

Governor Godoy turned hypocrisy from an art form into an exact science by vouchsafing the honesty of his half-brother Julio César Godoy Toscano, who won a seat in the Chamber of Deputies. Despite objections from the Ministry of public safety, the Michoacán native managed to get himself sworn in—only to be the subject of an impeachment procedure. Mexican authorities and Interpol have tried to locate the short-term legislator, who dropped out of sight. On October 14, 2010, the SSP charged Godoy Toscano with money laundering, and a local radio station aired a conversation between the erstwhile deputy and La Tuta Gómez Martínez, a chieftain of La Familia Michoacán.[52]

Calderón's strike against politicians backfired as constituents of mayors, possibly paid and manipulated by cartel activists, protested the arrest of their municipal leaders. Especially vigorous mobilizations took place in such La Familia strongholds as Apatzingán, Zitácuaro, and Buenavista.[53]

At this point, the president began to make reference to the imperative for social reforms, but expenditures as a percentage of budgets devoted to such programs changed little during his sexenio.

Defense Secretary Galván could not restrain himself from expressing dismay with politicians. Pronouncements by a Mexican defense secretary typically resemble a Kabuki dance—with reliance on nuances to convey meaning. In the classic highly stylized Japanese dance, the artist expresses meaning by lifting an eyebrow, flicking a fan, or giving a tilt of the head. Galván, who spoke at an observation of the ninety-seventh anniversary of the Loyalty March on February 9, 2011, spurned such subtlety to read the riot act to Mexico's self-serving political muckety-mucks.

The four-star commander did not attempt to disguise his disenchantment with officeholders: "We understand that political power is complex and generates various interests. . . . Nevertheless, it is incumbent [on politicians] at all times and in all circumstances to put the national interest first." In another mordant sentence, he said: "Social cohesion is an indispensable and crucial factor to advance our country . . . [and to attain] development, security, and the well-being of the population." He warned those who seek to divide members of the armed forces in the air, on the ground, and at sea: "Never will there be dissension among those who share the same cradle, the same forge and the same destiny: Mexico."[54]

Galván has pooh-poohed any friction with either Calderón or the navy, saying, "Under the orders of our supreme commander, marines and soldiers remain united, prepared and disciplined . . . which means serving the nation."[55] With these reassuring words, the defense secretary replaced his Kabuki mask, which hid an angry scowl.

What explains this remarkably frank expression of discontent, if not downright anger, by the chief of a military known for obeying civilians rather than questioning their directives?

Table 5.5

Examples of Military Personnel Accused, Arrested, Charged, or Convicted of Crimes

Individual	Date Arrested	Crime/Alleged Crime	Trial Court	Current Status
Gen. Ricardo Escorcia Vargas (commander of 24th Military Zone in Morelos)	May 15, 2012	Provided information to the Beltrán Leyva Organization (BLO) in late 2007 when they were allies of the Sinaloa Cartel	Did not stand trial	Incarcerated in Almoloya high-security prison in Mexico State on July 31, 2012; on July 4, 2013, a judge ordered his release because of unreliability of protected witnesses
Tomas Ángeles Dauahare (formerly number two in SEDENA);	May 15, 2012	Provided information to the Beltrán Leyva Organization (BLO) in late 2007 when they were allies of the Sinaloa Cartel	Did not stand trial; Ángeles Dauahare produced documents indicating that he was in Germany at the time of the alleged crime	Incarcerated in Almoloya high-security prison in Mexico State on April 17, a judge ordered his release because of unreliability of protected witnesses; on May 1, he became an adviser to the secretary of defense

Brig. General Roberto Dawe González; commanded an elite unit assigned to the 20th Military Zone headquartered in Colima*	May 15, 2012	Provided information to the BLO in late 2007 when they were allies of the Sinaloa Cartel	Did not stand trial	Incarcerated in Almoloya high-security prison in Mexico State on July 31, 2012; on July 4, 2013, a judge ordered his release because of unreliability of protected witnesses; plans to continue his military career
Gen. Manuel de Jesús Moreno Aviña; ex-commander of garrison in Ojinaga, Chihuahua, on the Texas border	January 30, 2012	Collaboration with narco-traffickers in torture, execution, and clandestine burials of civilians	Military	Pending
Brig. Gen. Rubén Pérez Ramírez	May 2012	Aiding narco-traffickers	Military	Imprisoned; on July 4, 2013, a judge ordered his release because of unreliability of protected witness

(continued)

Table 5.5 (*continued*)

Individual	Date Arrested	Crime/Alleged Crime	Trial Court	Current Status
Lt. Col. Silvio Isidro Hernández Soto	May 18, 2012	Provided information to the BLO in late 2007 when they were allies of the Sinaloa Cartel	Military	Imprisoned; on July 4, 2013, a judge ordered his release because of unreliability of protected witness
Maj. Iván Reyna Muñoz (represented Mexico in Panamerican Games in 1991 and 1993)	November 2011	Extortion; accused by La Barbie Valdez Villarreal of cooperating with the BLO	Military	Imprisoned; on July 4, 2013, a judge ordered his release because of unreliability of protected witness
A captain, four lieutenants, and two sergeants	Mid-October 2011	The army accused them of warning the BLO of pending military operations against the cartel in Morelos	Military	Confessed and were confined in the federal prison in Villa Aldama, Veracruz
Carlos Fidel Ábrego	2011	Altering the scene where soldiers, working with Nuevo León police, killed an innocent young man, Jorge Otilio Cantú, on April 18, 2011	Civilian court placed him under the jurisdiction of a military tribunal	Seeking amparo from Mexico's Supreme Court (SCJN)

Sgt. Evencio "El Batman" Castillo; ex-member of GAFES special forces	March 17, 2011	The only GAFES soldier captured in connection with safe-guarding Los Zetas in COAH; he allegedly received 3,000 pesos ($240) every two weeks for reporting troop movements	Military	Imprisoned
Pedro "El Gaucho" Toga Lara	March 12, 2011	Recruited 21 military personnel, including a general in the 6th Military Zone in Saltillo, COAH, to protect Los Zetas in return for generous bribes	Military	Imprisoned
Retired military officers Francisco Ortega Zamora and Juan Carlos Cruz Espinoza who served, respectively, as police chief and assistant police chief in Tijuana, Baja California	February 2010	Allegedly protected notorious killers and traffickers José Manuel "El Teo" García Simental and Raydel "The Crutches" Muletas"/"López Uriate	N.A. (retired officers still come under the jurisdiction of military tribunals)	N.A.

(continued)

Table 5.5 (*continued*)

Individual	Date Arrested	Crime/Alleged Crime	Trial Court	Current Status
Major Elfego José Luján Ruiz; commander 35th Infantry Battalion in Nuevo Casas Grandes, Chihuahua	March 2010	Eyewitnesses claimed that he ordered two deserters smothered and their bodies burned	Military; seeking an amparo or injunction from SCJN	Imprisoned in military penitentiary in DF
Lt. Col. Alfredo Bravo Alcaraz: sub-commander of 35th Infantry Battalion in Nuevo Casas Grandes, Chihuahua	March 10, 2010	Committed atrocities against civilians	Military; seeking an amparo from SCJN on the grounds that he was following orders; case under consideration	Imprisoned in military penitentiary in DF
Sgt. José Félix Flores Camacho	2007	Killing three people while driving a military vehicle in EDOMEX	Seeking an amparo from SCJN	Pending
Silvia Hernández Tamari (military nurse)	N.D.	Sexual abuse of a minor	Military (after a PGR investigation)	No information

*Major Iván Reyna Muñoz, subordinate of Escorcia Vargas, was convicted for the same crime and imprisoned in Querétaro; Defense Secretary Galván, who was unaware of the investigation into Dawe's activities, had planned to promote the general.

Sources: Gustavo Castillo García, "Militares acusados de *ejecutar* a 7 en Chihuahua buscan apoyo de SCJN," *La Jornada,* May 20, 2012; Benito Jiménez, "Suman 290 militares presos por abusos," *Reforma,* May 12, 2012; Benito Jiménez, "Tienen en prisión a cinco Generales," *Reforma,* February 19, 2012; "Pagaba a General narco en Coahuila," *Reforma,* February 18, 2012; "Ordenó quemar a dos desertores," *El Heraldo de Chihuahua,* February 15, 2012; Randal C. Archibold, "Mexican General Is Charged in Killings and Abuses," *New York Times,* February 1, 2012; Abel Barajas, "Planeaba Sedena ascender a Dawe," *Reforma,* July 28, 2012; Victor Fuentes, "Prevé Corte acotar el fuero militar," *Reforma,* July 28, 2012; Benito Jiménez, "Transladan a Generals a penal," *Reforma,* July 31, 2012; "Mexican Judge Orders Release of 5 High-ranking Army Officials Accused of Aiding a Drug Cartel," *Associated Press,* July 4, 2013.

This aggressive training—combined with an acutely inadequate intelligence system—has sparked more than 1,000 charges of human rights abuses from Amnesty International, Human Rights Watch, and the Miguel Agustín Pro Juárez Human Rights Center.

NGOs have continually publicized the army's human rights abuses in international forums, and former attorney general Diego Valadés and other eminent jurists claim that the military's drug war involvement violates Article 21 of the Constitution, which specifies that public security lies in the domain of civil authority. And Congress has balked at amending the fundamental law to legalize the policing actions of the army and navy. Still, it is unlikely that an effort to put military officers and the ex-president on trial for war crimes in some international tribune would prosper. Table 5.5 displays military personnel who have been imprisoned in recent years.

At the conclusion of his tenure, Calderón tried to put the best face on his struggle against the underworld even as drug-related killings declined in 2012 and the president's public opinion rating improved. In his final *Informe* (state of the union address), he said, "In these six years, our nation has waged an unprecedented fight for the rule of law, justice and freedom for our families," adding that the fight against the narcos was a still-evolving "process." Needless to say, he excoriated the United States for the southbound flow of high-powered weapons and the robust appetite for drugs produced in, or passing through, Mexico.[56]

CONCLUSION

Legal issues, strategic priorities, human rights invective, and interservice rivalries aside, Calderón left an important legacy in security matters.[57] To begin with, he expanded the size of the armed forces, doubled the security budget, and increased the pay of cadres. A leading newspaper reported that in 2012 the army had 541 generals (one for every 386 troops) compared with the United States' 620 (one for every 911 troops), China's 365 (one for every 6,301 troops), and Spain's 250 (one for every 520 troops).[58] The growth in personnel, resources, and engagements with narco-traffickers intensified wrongdoing in an institution where corruption is endemic.

In addition, he tripled the size of the federal police and, by the end of his administration, one-fourth of its cadres held college degrees—most of whom worked in telecommunications, forensic science, DNA analysis, fingerprint examination, electronic eavesdropping and voice detection, and other technical fields. No public figures exist on the number of well-trained police officers working the streets.

Moreover, his administration boosted from three to 12 the number of federal penitentiaries—even though inmates exert substantial control in most of these facilities where guards are poorly trained, underpaid, and subject to threats and corruption. At the same time, the PAN government supported gradually changing the judicial system from one based on the rigid written Napoleonic Code to open oral adversarial procedures—a reform evaluated in Chapter 8 and not scheduled to affect all states until 2016.

Calderón's regime severely weakened both the Arellano Félix Organization and the Beltrán Leyva Organization, while sharply increasing the number of extraditions. From December 1, 2006, to the end of 2011, the PAN government extradited 502 suspects, 478 to the United States.[59] During his tenure bloodshed fell sharply in Ciudad Juárez and Tijuana, border cities that are once again attracting tourists and investors.

Finally, under the Mérida Initiative, Mexico's ties with the United States improved substantially as demonstrated by Washington's provision of equipment, intelligence, and training. Alejandro Hope argued that "the security and intelligence communities of both countries work[ed] more closely than at any point since World War II."[60] In the final analysis, the kingpin strategy failed. Nonetheless, Calderón's dogged determination to cling to this star-crossed approach evoked memories of Lyndon Baines Johnson's insistence on escalating the Vietnam conflict despite the ever-larger number military personnel returned in body bags to the United States amid growing public opposition to the fighting.

CHAPTER 6

Impact of the "Militarized Drug War" on Mexican Society

INTRODUCTION

Critics of Felipe Calderón's Mexican version of the "war on drugs" warned that he was "militarizing" the nation by deploying tens of thousands of troops against drug trafficking organizations (DTOs) when there was no hue and cry from the public to undertake this crusade. Anthropologist Abel Barrera Hernández, director of the Human Rights Center of Tlachinollan, has excoriated the "violence expressed in militarization and the seizure of land and natural resources" in impoverished, indigenous areas. Poet and essayist Javier Sicilia, whose son was captured, brutalized, and murdered by thugs, has accused politicians of complicity in the criminal activities. "We cannot cry out," he said, "because this government is the same as members of organized crime and can think only in terms of violence and the wish to militarize the country ..." Along the same lines, students in Cuernavaca formed the National Coordinating System against Militarization and sponsored a forum called Young People and the National Emergency.[1]

Alexandro Poiré Romero, former technical secretary of the National Security Council and later Gobernación secretary (2011–2012), denied any trend toward militarization. He insisted that most of their operations do not involve fighting criminal bands. "Neither the Army nor the Navy ... is supplanting police agencies. At present the elements deployed, together with the Federal Police, are temporarily ... assisting civilian authorities, not acting alone," he affirmed. "The use of the armed forces to combat organized crime will be less necessary when local police forces improve their professionalization and [achieve] certification," Poiré added.[2] Improving the quality of local police is a slow process at best, a chimera at worst.

THE DRUG WAR HAS CHANGED THE ARMED FORCES

The seminal problem lies in Mexico's seldom if ever having had an effective, uncorrupted, and professional police force, whose members knew their communities, could referee barroom brawls and other relatively minor disputes, and gain the confidence of average citizens.[3] As a result, Presidents Fox (2000–2006) and Calderón (2006–2012) relied heavily on the men and women in khaki to combat the cartels that import, store, process, sell in the domestic market, and export narcotics. Although involved in drug eradication for four decades, Mexican soldiers are trained to pursue, capture, and kill—with little experience in urban settings. The violence associated with these activities, which took more than 47,000 lives between 2006 and 2012, has continued under Calderón's successor, Peña Nieto, some 6,150 deaths related to organized crime during his first ten months in office.[4] This chapter (1) provides an overview of the military's participation in Mexico's version of the drug war, (2) focuses on the recruitment of military men and women to serve in traditionally civilian law-enforcement posts, (3) indicates tasks that the armed forces have assumed or expanded in recent years, and (4) examines the emerging role of the navy.

OVERVIEW

President Fox committed an average of 19,293 troops annually to battling drug trafficking. This figure soared 133 percent to 45,000 during the Calderón sexenio. In 2009 alone the army assigned 48,750 men to combatting narcotics syndicates—with approximately one-quarter of these cadres involved in joint operations with the navy, the federal police, the U.S. Drug Enforcement Administration, the U.S. Homeland Security Department, the Federal Bureau of Investigations, and other agencies.[5] The emphasis on the military produced mixed results. The National Defense Ministry announced that between December 1, 2006, and late December 2011, it had arrested 41,023 suspects, while killing 2,321 criminals.

In a separate report, SEDENA published an annual review of criminals whose lives it had taken: 22 in 2007; 78 in 2008; 211 in 2009; 734 in 2010; and 1,246 through December 20, 2011.[6]

As part of the government's "kingpin strategy," the military apprehended or killed several dozen important capos, whose names appear in

Table 6.1

Deaths, Woundings, and Kidnappings of Army Personnel, 2007 to November 2012

Year	Deaths	Wounded	Kidnappings
2012	24 (through November 18)	NA	NA
2011	48	NA	59 (through December 7)
2010	61	NA	69
2009	44	NA	34
2008	54	NA	28
2007	22	NA	6
TOTAL	253 (133 died in non-combat situations)	744*	196

*The author found a gross figure of wounded army personnel, but not a year-by-year count.

Source: Benito Jiménez, "Crecen levantones . . . pero de militares," *Reforma*, January 2, 2012; "Mueren 18 sicarios por cada military," *Reforma*, December 20, 2011; "224 militares asesinados durante la 'guerra' de Calderón; la mayoría en Tamaulipas," *Aristegui Noticias*, January 7, 2013. Different sources provide conflicting data; however, the last item appears to be the most up-to-date.

Appendix H. The navy (SEMAR), which includes the marines, has substantially increased its participation and efficiency in battling narcos.

During the conflict the army has suffered kidnappings and deaths of its own elements, as reported. Although fewer confrontations between the cartels and the military have reduced the deaths of soldiers, the number of kidnapped military personnel has gradually risen.

LAW ENFORCEMENT

Various states and large cities have recruited ex-members of the armed forces to fill traditional civilian posts in law enforcement—appointments usually recommended and assuredly approved by National Defense Secretary Guillermo Galván Galván, often in consultation with the local zonal commander. As indicated in Table 6.2, the number of military men in these roles rose from six in February 2009 to 36 in April 2012—with six military officers in charge of state police forces. Of the dozen governors elected in 2010, seven opted to install a general at the head of the State Security Ministry: Carlos Lozano de la Torre (Aguascalientes), Roberto Borge Angulo (Quintana Roo), Mario López Valdéz (Sinaloa),

Table 6.2
Military Personnel in Public Safety Posts: July 2013

State/Municipality	Position	Incumbent	Date Appointed
Acapulco (Guerrero)	Secretary of Public Security	Col. (Ret.) Manuel Paz Espinosa; Gen. (Ret.) Héctor Paulino Vargas López (took over after Brig. Gen. (Ret.) Serafín Valdéz Martínez resigned on Feb. 16, 2010)	Late July 2011
Aguascalientes	Secretary of Public Security	Div. Gen. (Ret.) Rolando Eugenio Hidalgo Eddy	Oct. 6, 2008
Armería Colima	Director of Municipal Police	Capt. (Ret.) Jorge Mario Mercado Larios	Feb. 3, 2011
Baja California	Director of State Ministerial Police	Brig Gen. Florencio Raúl Cuevas Salgado; former commander of II Military Zone headquartered in Tijuana	March 27, 2008
	Director of State Preventative Police	Lt. Col. (Ret.) Eusebio Alecio Villatoro Córtez	Feb. 20, 2009
Boca del Río Veracruz	Director of Transit	Rear Adm. Saúl Cotarelo Díaz	Jan. 23, 2012
Chiapas	Secretary of Public Security	Maj. Rogelio Hernández de la Mata	Dec. 30, 2010
Chihuahua	Director General of Unified State Police	Div. Gen. (Ret.) Julián David Rivera Bretón	Oct. 3, 2010
Ciudad Juárez	Director of Public Security	Lt. Col. Julián Leyzaola Pérez*	March 10, 2011
	Police Chief	Div. Gen. Julián David Rivera Bretón	March 16, 2009
	Director of Security Operations	Col. (Ret.) Alfonso Cristóbal García Melgar	March 16, 2009
Ciudad Victoria, Tamaulipas	Chief of Public Security	First Capt. Rafael Lomelí Martínez	April 18, 2011
	Chief of Public Security	Gen. (Ret.) Ubaldo Ayala Tinoco	Jan. 1, 2011

Coahuila	Secretary of Public Security	Civilian Jorge Luis Morán Delgado resigned on Oct. 26, 2012 in the wake of the assasination of ex-Gov. Humberto Moreira Valdez's son and Morán was replaced by Ríos another civilian, José Gerardo Villarreal Ríos on Nov. 26, 2012.	Aug. 12, 2008 Feb. 24, 2009
	Director General of State Investigative Police	Brig. Gen. (Ret.) Jesús Ernesto Estrada Bustamante resigned on July 20, 2010	
	Undersecretary of Prevenion and Social Readaptation	Gen. José Luis García Dorantes	
Colima	Chief of the State Preventative Police (Equivalent to Secretary of Public Security)	Brig. Gen. (Ret.) Raúl Pinedo Dávila	Dec. 6, 2010 Dec. 6, 2010
	Coordinator of Intelligence in the Center of Control, Command, Computation, and Communications (C-4)	Adm. Andrés Humberto Cano	
Ensenada, BC	Commissioner (in charge of security and director of Municipal Police)	Div. Gen. (Ret.) Florencio Raúl Cuevas Salgado	Sept. 21, 2011 April 1, 2011
		Div. Gen. Juan Heriberto Salinas Altés (Ret.); former Army Chief of Staff	

(continued)

Table 6.2 (*continued*)

State/ Municipality	Position	Incumbent	Date Appointed
Federal District	Secretary of Public Security	Rear-Adm. Manuel Mondragón Y Kalb (Physician)	July 8, 2008 (Resigned December 1, 2012, to join the Peña Nieto administration)
Gómez Palacio (Durango)	Director of Municipal Public Security	Lt. Col. (Ret.) Antonio Horacio Ramírez Morales	Feb. 14, 2008
Guadalupe (Nuevo León)	Secretary of Public Security	Col. (Ret.) Enrique Alberto Sanmiguel Sánchez	April 6, 2011
	Director of Police	First Sgt. (Ret.) Florencio Santos Hernández	
	Coordinator of C-4	Capt. (Ret.) Alejandro Almazán Hernández	
	Coordinator of Recruitment, Instruction, and Training	Paymaster (Ret.) Hermelindo Aquileo Sánchez Castellanos	
Guanajuato	Secretary of Public Security	Gen. Miguel Pizarro Arzate	March 2, 2010
Guerrero	Secretary of Public Security and Civil Protection	Civilian Ramón Almonte Borje, who promised to promote tourism by hiring 18- to 25-year old female cops dressed in sexy uniforms for beach patrol duties in Acapulco	April 1, 2011
		Div. Gen. Juan Heriberto Salinas Altés (Ret.)	April 1, 2005 to April 1, 2011

Location	Position	Name	Date
Manzanillo Colima	Director of Municipal Police	Col. Gustavo Jiménez González	Jan. 24, 2011
	Director of Transit and Transportation	Capt. Miguel Ángel Urióstegui Trujillo	Jan. 31, 2010
Matamoros (Tamaulipas)	Secretary of Public Security	Lt. Col. Gabriel López Ordaz	Jan. 18, 2011
	Operations Director of Secretary of Public Security	Lt. Rafael Antonio Huerta Méndez	Jan. 18, 2011
	Director of Transit	Lt. Roberto Guerrero Roldán	Jan. 18, 2011
Michoacán	Secretary of Public Security	Div. Gen. (Ret.) Manuel García Ruiz	Aug. 8, 2010
	Coordinator of State Preventative Police	Capt. (2nd) Manuel García Ruiz	Oct. 26, 2010
Monterrey		Gen. (Ret.) José Pablo Leonel Vargas Martínez	Jan. 4, 2012.
Morelos	Secretary of Public Security	Div Gen. (Ret.) Gilberto Toledano Sánchez**	April 10, 2011
		Div. Gen (Ret.) Gastón Menchaca Arias; former commander of Tenth Military Region (Yucatán)	May 17, 2009
Nuevo Laredo	Secretary of Public Security	Brig. Gen. (Active) Manuel Farfán Carreola	Jan. 1, 2011

(continued)

123

Table 6.2 (*continued*)

State/Municipality	Position	Incumbent	Date Appointed
Nuevo León	Secretary of Public Security	Div. Gen. Jaime Castañeda Bravo	Feb. 3, 2011
Oaxaca	Secretary of Citizen Protection	Lt. Col. (Ret.) Javier Rueda Velásquez	March 31, 2008
Puebla	Secretary of Public Security	Div. Gen. Mario Ayón Rodríguez (Ret.); former director-general of personnel for National Defense Ministry	March 1, 2005
Querétaro	Secretary of Public Security	Capt. Adolfo Vega Montoto	Oct. 4, 2009
Quintana Roo	Secretary of Public Security	Brig. Gen. (Ret.) Carlos Bibiano Villa Castillo***	April 5, 2011
		Vice Adm. Miguel Ángel Ramos (Replaced Salvador Rocha Vargas who was arrested on charges of cooperating with drug traffickers)	Sept. 4, 2009
Rosarito, BC	Secretary of Public Security	Maj. (Ret.) Magdaleno Vázquez Ruiz	Nov. 26, 2010
Saltillo (Coahuila)	Director General of the Municipal Preventative Police	Brig. Gen. (Ret.) Marco Antonio Delgado Talavera	Jan 29, 2009
San Luis Potosí	Secretary of Public Security	Brig. Gen. (Ret.) Heliodoro Guerrero	Jan. 15, 2011
Tabasco	Secretary of Public Security Acting Secretary of Public Security	Div. Gen. Audomaro Martínez Jiménez Maj. (Ret.) Sergio López Uribe	Dec. 27, 2012 Feb. 1, 2009
Tamaulipas	Secretary of Public Security	Brig. Gen. (Ret.) Ubaldo Ayala Tinoco	Dec. 30, 2010
Tijuana, BC	Municipal Secretary of Public Security	First Capt. (Ret.) Gustavo Huerta Martínez****	Nov. 26, 2010

Tlaxcala	Secretary of Public Security	Brig. Gen. (Ret.) Valentín Romano López *****	Jan. 15, 2011
Veracruz	Secretary of Public Security Director of Public Transit	Lt. Arturo Bermúdez Zurita****** Rear Adm. Rodolfo Pallares Herrán	July 3. 2011 Feb. 23, 2012
Zacatecas	Secretary of Public Security Director of State Preventative Police	Gen. (Ret.) Jesús Pinto Ortiz Gen. (Ret.) Víctor Manuel Bosque Rodríguez	Sept. 11, 2010 Nov. 3, 2010

*Leyzaola replaced Col. Laurencio Rodríguez.

**Replaced Div. Gen. (Ret.) Gastón Menchaca Arias (14 days after seven people were killed in the state, including the son of writer and social activist Javier Sicilia.

***Bibiano replaced Vice-Adm. Miguel Ángel Ramos Real.

****Replaced Lt. Col. (Ret.) Julián Leyzaola Pérez, who became secretary of public security in Ciudad Juárez.

*****Replaced Div. Gen. José Leopoldo Martínez González (Ret.).

******Replaced Div. Gen. Sergio López Esquer: former commander for Coahuila, Baja California, Baja California Sur, and Veracruz.

Source: Jésica Zermeño, "Toman generales mandos policiacos," *Reforma,* February 15, 2009; Jésica Zermeño et al. "Optan estados por mando militar, *Reforma,* February 15, 2009; Encabezan los hermanos Ayón Rodríguez mandos policiacos en el país." *E-consulta,* February 15, 2009; "Gastón Menchaca, de Yucatán a Morelos, siempre en acción," *NotiSureste.com.mx,* May 17, 2009; Silvia Hernández, "Nombran a militar titular de SSP en Q. Roo," *El Universal.com.mx,* September 5, 2009; Roberto Aguilar, "Torre Cantú nombra a general titular de la SSP," *El Universal.com.mx,* December 31, 2010; Mauro de la Fuente, "Asume militares policía de Matamoros," *Reforma.com,* January 19, 2011; "Nombran a militar titular de policía de Armería, Colima," *Guerra Contra el Narco,* February 4, 2011; Juan Cedillo, "NL: general asume cargo de titular de Seguridad," *El Universal.com.mx,* February 5, 2011; Óscar Guadarrama. "El gobernador de Morelos cesa al secretario de Seguridad pública," *CNN México,* April 10, 2011; Andro Aguilar, "Militarización sin resultados," *Reforma* ("Enfoque"). April 10, 2011 (The author relied heavily on this source); Édgar Ávila Pérez, "Arturo Bermúdez Zurita fue designado a la dependencia luego de la renuncia del general Sergio López Esquer," *El Universal,* July 3, 2011; José García, "Toma General mando de la Policía regia," *Reforma,* January 4, 2012; "Asumen marinos Tránsito en Veracruz," *Reforma,* January 23, 2012; "Designan a ex militar como secretario de Seguridad Pública en Tabasco," *Notimex,* December 25, 2012; "Crisis en Coahuila, dimite secretario de Seguridad," *El Universal,* October 26, 2012.

Egidio Torre Cantú (Tamaulipas), Mariano González Zarur (Tlaxcala), Javier Duarte de Ochoa (Veracruz), and Miguel Alonso Reyes (Zacatecas).

Meanwhile, men with military backgrounds hold the position of secretaries of public security in 36 percent of the municipalities with the most homicides in the country, according to the National System of Public Security. Retired generals have assumed this role in the five cities that have registered the most killings: Acapulco, Chihuahua, Ciudad, Juárez, Culiacán, and Tijuana. On January 13, 2011, nine retired officers were named chiefs of nine municipalities in war-torn Tamaulipas: Altamira, Ciudad Victoria, Madero, Mante, Matamoros, Nuevo Laredo, Reynosa, Río Bravo, and Tampico.

While by no means new to Mexico, this approach appeared to offer several advantages.

First, the military men fill a void opened by the execution or resignation of more than a score of state and municipal security chiefs in dangerous posts. Three officials stepped down in Nuevo León municipalities: Allende, and Linares; another five civilians died at the hands of narcotraffickers.

Second, many of the officers selected have commanded one or more of the army's 12 regions and/or 45 zones and boast years of experience struggling against drug mafias.

Third, they are likely to have ties to—and the confidence of—current regional and zonal military chiefs who may have been consulted on their appointment and with whom they often coordinate assaults on DTOs.

Fourth, whether retired or on leave, military officers may be familiar with the tactics of Los Zetas, the original contingent of which served in the army's elite Special Forces Airmobile Groups, from which Los Zetas deserted. General Rolando Eugenio Hidalgo Heddy, public security secretary in Aguascalientes, also headed these commandos. Nuevo León's safety chief, Jaime Castañeda Bravo, had previously served on SEDENA's general staff, headed armored regiments, and functioned as commander of the 38th and 43rd Military Zones.[7]

Fifth, generals, admirals, colonels, and majors have emerged from a culture of discipline that needs to be inculcated in civilian police.[8] Members of such law-enforcement units have often acted in a venal, freewheeling manner—to the point that the great majority of serious kidnappings and other felonies go unreported because many citizens believe that the cops are in league with the miscreants. Even if military leaders cannot change behavior, they can oust incompetents and malefactors. For instance, General Salinas Altés removed 200 elements of Acapulco's Municipal Preventive Police when he took over as security boss in Guerrero, a poverty-stricken state plagued by lawlessness. Still, General (Ret.) Ernesto López Portillo, executive director of the Institute for Security and Democracy, admitted: "Military personnel can fill a vacuum, but are not trained to modernize the police; we do know how to strengthen, possibly discipline them, but not reconstitute them as is necessary."[9] Soon after becoming security chief in Monterrey, General José Pablo Leonel Vargas Martínez arrested 106 policemen and prosecutors accused of *halconeo*, that is, acting as a "falcons" or lookouts for cartels.[10]

Sixth, officers are in good positions to recruit active-duty or retired members of the armed forces as police officers in the jurisdictions that they serve.

Seventh, every public opinion survey shows that the armed forces enjoy a much better reputation than do the police. Such praise centers on their efforts in disaster relief, as well as their anticrime missions. As one anonymous source indicated, "even if military security chiefs are as corrupt as their civic counterparts, they give a psychological lift to the public."

Finally, in light of the relatively low pensions received by retired officers, assuming a civilian post supplements their income and reduces pressure to increase retirement income in some other way. Overall security expenditures have skyrocketed; yet, Mexico's Finance Ministry reported that the military budget shot up 74.2 percent between 2007 (32,200 billion pesos) and 2012 (55,610 billion pesos), as indicated in Appendix J.[11]

PRELIMINARY RESULTS

How have the officers in mufti fared?

Upon taking office, retired generals, colonels, or captains often clashed with local police forces, especially when they attempted to cleanse their ranks. In fact, as described in Table 6.3, by November 2009 military units had crossed swords with local, state, or federal law-enforcement agencies at least 65 times—up from two confrontations in 2008.[12]

After all, Los Zetas, the Sinaloa Cartel, the Knights Templars, and other cartels often demand the appointment of a "reliable" security chief in municipalities that lay along trafficking routes. Soon after reaching Tijuana to head the municipal police on March 10, 2009, Lieutenant Colonel Julián Leyzaola Pérez oversaw the dismissal or resignation of 600 law-enforcement agents, including 84 who were arrested for allegedly cooperating with organized crime. Meanwhile, 2,325 people, among them 43 police officers, died in the line of duty during these three years. Crime-related deaths did fall on his watch due to a confluence of factors: the city's population is relatively compact; former PAN governor José Guadalupe Osuna Millán (2007–2013) cooperated in the fight against DTOs; and the increasing dominance of the Sinaloa Cartel, which supplanted the Arellano Félix Organization, contributed to stabilizing the sprawling border city. The drop in violence aside, the state human rights commission and the National Human Rights Commission charged the police chief with torture before the Inter-American Human Rights Commission.

Table 6.3

Clashes between Military and Civilian Police

Date/Place	Police Agency	Military Agency	Nature of Conflict	Outcome
January 4, 2011 San Nicolás, NL	Municipal Police	Army	Police officers helped members of crime group escape by obstructing the military's chasing the armed suspects.	Three military personnel were hurt; a civilian killed.
March 25, 2011 San Luis Potosí	Municipal Police	Army	Mexican Army detained three police officers San Luis Potosí DGSP for involvement in a robbery of two civilians; police allegedly took 32,330 pesos.	
November 22, 2010 Apodaca, NL	Municipal Police	Marines	Suspicious activities; Marines investigated police officers.	Three outlaws and four policemen arrested.
October 26, 2010 Monterrey, NL	Municipal Police	Army	The Army stopped to investigate four policemen from Monterrey accused of following the military personnel of the the Public Security Ministry and the Federal Investigative Agency.	Only one policeman was taken into custody because he was carrying illegal radio equipment.
October 3, 2010 Monterrey, NL	Municipal Police	Army	Army investigated Guadalupe police officers for helping criminals escape after they threw a grenade into the city's main plaza.	Twelve people hurt.
August 20, 2010 Santiago, NL	Municipal Police	Army	Police accused of spying on, kidnapping, and killing Mayor Edelmiro Cavazos Leal.	Six municipal police arrested.

| July 29, 2010 Veracruz | Municipal Police | Army | Federal judge in Veracruz ordered military to arrest 40 municipal police officers, 16 ministerial officers, and 6 former law-enforcement officials suspected of involvement in organized crime. |
| January 13, 2010 Monterrey, NL | Municipal and State Police | Army | Police officer arrested for involvement in a kidnapping; after his incarceration, the suspect sought help from fellow officers who stopped the army from taking the detainee to a military facility. | After exchanging verbal insults and stopping traffic for 40 minutes, the state police allowed the municipal officer to be taken to the Procuraduría General de Justicia (PGR); after the incident the government secretary of Nuevo León, Javier Treviño, claimed that the state police arrived to support the military. |

(*continued*)

Table 6.3 (*continued*)

Date/Place	Police Agency	Military Agency	Nature of Conflict	Outcome
August 31, 2009 Monterrey, NL	Municipal Police	Army	Municipal police supporting crime. Army detained an armed man with drugs. Army transported person towards the military camp, but were stopped by police officers.	One police officer tried to flee the scene and was shot in the leg by a soldier; the man was transported to a military camp; three police officers arrested a couple of days later.
September 2, 2009 Monterrey, NL	Municipal Police State and Federal.	Army	After an incident in August, military inspected documents of law enforcement agent.	Municipal cop incarcerated for not having proper ID.
June 16, 2009 San Pedro de la Garza, NL	Municipal Police	Army	Army took away firearms from the police officers of the Ministry of Public Safety.	
May 9, 2009 Cuernavaca, Morelos	Municipal Police	Army	Army arrested 27 police officers from Yautepec, including the secretary of Public Security; believed to be protecting drug sellers.	
May 5, 2009 Aguascalientes	Municipal Police	Army	Police officers and military officers found associated with the Gulf Cartel. SIEDO stepped in to investigate the situation.	Six policemen and 12 military men arrested.

Date and location	Police	Military	Description	Outcome
April 13, 2008 Municipalities of Monterrey and Escobedo, NL	State Police	Army	The local police resisted an investigation that sparked a fight in Escobedo; on a different occasion, state police resisted investigation and surrounded the four military units in Monterrey.	Six injured; during the second encounter, four policemen suffered wounds and several state police were arrested. An arrangement freed the law-enforcement officers, and the military left the scene as police pelted them with insults. Offending officers were taken before a military tribunal.
April 8, 2008 Ciudad Juarez	Municipal police	Army	Army shot at a police vehicle after it failed to stop for inspection; police were attending to an emergency; Army arrested municipal cop.	One police officer Received a gun shot in the head and was in critical condition. The other two officers disappeared.

(continued)

Table 6.3 (continued)

Date/Place	Police Agency	Military Agency	Nature of Conflict	Outcome
June 6, 2007 Mexicali, BC international airport	PFP (Federal Preventive Police)	Army	Military took control of the airport; the PFP agents had allowed a smuggler to bring 26 kilograms of cocaine into the country; 14 people were investigated.	The military arrested seven officials of the PFP and three agents of Instituto Nacional de Migración (INM); suspects turned over to the Assistant Attorney General for Specialized Investigation of Organized Crime (SIEDO) in DF.

Sources: "Ejército detiene a tres policías de SLP," ("Army Detains Three Police in SLP"), *El Universal*, March 25, 2011; "Narcobloqueos en cuatro municipios de Nuevo León por la detención de un capo" ("Blockades by Municipal Police in Four Nuevo Leon Municipalities to Arrest Capo"), *La Jornada*, November 22, 2010; "Ejercito Mexicano detiene a 27 policías en Morelos" ("The Mexican Army Detains 27 Police Officers in the State of Morelos"), *Televisa*, May 9, 2009; "Ejército retira armas a policías de San Pedro Garza, NL" ("Army Takes Firearms Away from Police Officers of San Pedro Garza, NL"), *Televisa*, June 16, 2009; "Ejército revisa armas de 500 policías en NL" ("Army Inspects Firearms of 500 Police Officers in NL"), *El Universal*, November 28, 2011; "Policías y Militares se enfrentan en Nuevo León" ("Police and Soldiers Confront each Other in Nuevo León"), *El Universal*, January 13, 2010; " 'Cacería' de policías espías en la metrópoli" ("Hunt for Spying Police Officers in the City"), *revistacodigo21* magazine, October 26, 2010; "Investigan a policías por narcoterrorismo en Guadalupe; se recuperan heridos en granadazo" (" Police Investigated for Narcoterrorism in Guadalupe, Injured Recover After Grenade Explosion"), *revistacodigo21* magazine, October 3, 2010; "Confirman autoridades detención de 56 policías" ("Authorities Confirm Detention of 56 Officers"), *El Mexicano*, July 29, 2010; "Reportan balacera entre policías y militares en Nuevo León" (" Shootout between Police Officers and Military Soldiers Reported in Nuevo León"), *El Informador*, August 31,2009; "Controlan los 'Zetas' a la policía de Aguascalientes," ("The Zetas control the Police in Aguascalientes"), *Entre Líneas*, May 5, 2009, "Enfrentamiento entre militares y policías en Monterrey deja seis heridos," ("Confrontation Between Military and Police in Monterrey leaves six wounded"), *Chihuahua al Instante*, April 13, 2008; "Militares balean a policías de Ciudad Juárez," ("Military Shoot Police in Ciudad Juárez"), *La Jornada*, April 8, 2008; and "Arraigan a agentes federales adscritos al aeropuerto de Mexicali," ("Federal Agents Assigned to Mexicali Airport Detained"), *La Jornada*, June 6, 2007.

In addition, the NGO Human Rights Watch criticized Leyzaola for 390 disappearances, including four young *tiajuaneses*.

"The case of Julián Leyzaola is a rare mirage in which tough action in response to a security crisis has other costs: human rights' abuses. He has transgressed the fundamental principle of democracy whereby civil authority must control the military," stated Erubiel Tirado Cervantes, a security specialist at Mexico City's prestigious IberoAmerican University.[13]

These accusations did not prevent the convulsed city of Ciudad Juárez from hiring Leyzaola as its public security secretary on October 10, 2011, in a latter-day example of a sheriff facing down desperados at High Noon. In this office, he leads a force of 2,400 police working in six crime-ridden districts where 456 murders were recorded from January 1 to June 1, 2011. Bureaucratic restraints held up the ouster of crooked cops in this border city. Yet, almost a year later, Calderón announced a 60 percent fall in homicides as drug-related deaths declined from 300 each month to 120 as part of the "We are all Juárez" initiative, which involves economic, social, political, and safety elements.[14] The muscular public security director in Torreón, Coahuila, Carlos Bibiano Villa Castillo also believes in an ultra hard line toward law-breakers. A Pancho-Villa descendant and one of 36 children, the retired general told a reporter that he preferred to kill members of organized crime rather than interrogate them: "I like to feel the flow of adrenaline. On patrol, when I capture a Zeta or Chapo, I kill him. Why interrogate him? Here we beat the hell out of a bad actor. I have no confidence in the Federal Police because they do not kill [suspects], only arrest them. The Army and Navy kill them," he said six days after the March 2, 2011, confrontation with cartel gunmen.[15] Either because of or despite his stance, the mustachioed retired brigadier general was appointed secretary of public security by Quintana Roo's new governor Borge Angulo.

Upon leaving Torreón, he emphasized his loyalty: "My father is the Army, my mother is the Patria," he affirmed. He also claimed to have been "sleeping with the enemy ... of the 1,100 elements under his command, 1,000 were corrupt; they sold uniforms; they sold gasoline; even when on patrol they carried out their dirty business everywhere," he stated.[16] Soon after arriving in Cancún, a "narco-message" threatened death to the general. It was signed by the "Zetas Special Forces." Appendix I portrays examples of clashes between the military and civilian police forces.

Although conditions vary from state to state, overall the presence of a military man in a top security role has not diminished the violence afflicting their areas of responsibility as evinced in Table 6.4. In view of venal police forces, governors and mayors may have had no choice other than to reach into the barracks for public safety czars. Such appointments also enable state and municipal executives to appear to be "tough on

Table 6.4

Crimes Committed in States with Military Law-Enforcement Chiefs

State	Robberies	Kidnappings	Homicides	Executions
Aguascalientes	13%	-54%	1%	85
Chiapas	20	92	-6	n.a.
Chihuahua	4	-39	-3	1,0008
Coahuila	n.a.	n.a.	n.a.	n.a.
Colima	18	518	73	n.a.
Guanajuato	-7	-55	9	128
Michoacán	7	18	46	216
Morelos	7	160	15	433
Nuevo León	12	n.a.	27	n.a.
Querétaro	32	60	28	21
Quintana Roo	n.a.	n.a.	n.a.	n.a.
San Luis Potosí	n.a.	n.a.	n.a.	n.a.
Sinaloa	-3	278	1	n.a
Tamaulipas	-3	123	-9	n.a
Tlaxcala	n.a.	n.a.	n.a.	n.a.
Veracruz	-37	-100	-37	357
Zacatecas	3	27	17	18

Source: Monthly reports of the Executive Secretariat of the National System of Public Security (SESNSP) as compiled by Andro Aguilar, "Militarización sin resultados" ("Militarization without Results"), *Reforma* ("Enfoque"), April 10, 2011

crime" even as they cut deals with cartels or turn a blind eye to their illegal activities. One problem facing the retired officers is that they assume the civilian position without the benefit of the staff members who assisted them when they were on active duty.

When troops attempted to stop a suspicious looking SUV that was being escorted through Monterrey, they found themselves under fire from state policemen, who enabled the suspects to escape. "The moment they shoot at us, get in our way, use their guns to protect criminals, they become criminals themselves," said General Guillermo Moreno Serrano, the regional commander in Tamaulipas and Nuevo León, which lie along the Texas border.[17]

WikiLeaks's publication of a conversation between Galván and a U.S. official revealed the defense secretary's attitude toward the law-enforcement agencies. He complained about joint operations with the police because "leaks of planning and information by corrupted officials have compromised past efforts."[18] Moreover, in Nuevo Laredo, Los Zetas' sadistic paramilitary cartel hire unofficial "police"—an estimated 3,000 young people—who far outnumber the regular force. The mid-July 2013 arrest of Treviño Morales is certain to change this dynamic. These ubiquitous "spotters," as local residents refer to them, prefer crew cuts, adorn themselves with gold chains and earrings, press cell phones to their ears, and wear shorts well below their waists.[19]

MILITARIZATION DENIED

On May 6, 2011, the federal government launched a campaign to attract candidates for 422 positions at the new Accredited State Police (PEA). "We believe that with your talent, your ethical integrity, you, young people . . . can contribute to this force that is so important to the Mexican State," averred Education Secretary and presidential aspirant, now deceased, Alonso Lujambio Irazábal. Police academy students explained their lack of interest in terms of "corruption," "bad image," "fat," "drug addicts," "danger," and other pejoratives.[20]

Just as Los Zetas have relied on Guatemala's tough-as-nails Kaibiles for training and support, the Mexican government has backed Project Sparta, which reportedly involves the L-3 MPRI paramilitary consortium based in Alexandria, Virginia. The respected *Reforma* newspaper indicated that the corporation has deployed ex-U.S. military personnel who will establish 12 Virtual Military Training Centers where they will teach counterinsurgency, urban warfare, infantry tactics, and defense against improvised explosive devices. When contacted by telephone, Rick Kiernan, the company's senior vice president of strategic communication, denied that his firm had an arrangement with Mexico. He said, "There has been no contract awarded that I know of."[21]

STREET PATROLS

In addition to naming former armed forces chiefs to top security posts, mayors and governors are sedulously recruiting new law-enforcement officers from the ranks of military retirees. After purging half of the city's 400 police officers in Santa Catarina, one of 12 municipalities that make up metropolitan Monterrey, Mayor Gabriel Navarro Rodríguez made clear his determination to hire "elements with a military profile" to undertake patrol and surveillance duties. In essence, politicians have more confidence in men and women who have learned discipline, order, and teamwork in the armed forces. Nonetheless, Governor Rodrigo Medina de la Cruz said the arrival of several hundred soldiers did not signify the militarization of Nuevo León.[22] In September 2011, the state executive began the recruitment in Mexico City and other states outside of Nuevo León of a new law-enforcement agency, the Fuerza Civil. The original ranks of 422 members is projected to grow to 14,000 elements. For her part, the mayor of Monterrey, Margarita Alicia Arellanes Cervantes, "opened the doors of her municipality to God as the maximum authority."[23]

INFORMAL MILITARY-CIVILIAN GROUPS

In several areas, local leaders have initiated combined civilian-military groups. For example, at the naval base in Tapachula, Chiapas, weekly meetings that focus on combatting drug crimes include the navy, army, state attorney general, and elements of the business community. Similarly, in Tijuana and Ensenada, Baja California, the army and navy regularly hold sessions with representatives of the state government and the tourist sector. Mexico State governor Eruviel Ávila Villegas has penned an accord with the secretary of Gobernación to establish a coordinating body formed by the commanders of Military Zones 1 (Tacuba, DF), 22 (Santa María Rayón, Mexico State), and 37 (Santa Lucia, Mexico State); a representative of the attorney general's office (PGR); a representative of Mexico's version of the CIA, the National Security and Investigation Center (CISEN); along with four state officials: the governor, secretary of citizen security, government secretary, and attorney general.[24]

In other areas, so-called purple groups have been formed to overcome "stove-piping" by exchanging information during regular gatherings of the army, navy, and federal police. At land crossings, the army frequently cooperates with—or oversees the functions—of Mexican customs agents (who are often subjected to bribes).

"COLLATERAL DAMAGE" AND HUMAN RIGHTS VIOLATIONS

Professional police officers are taught to gain the confidence of citizens, separate adversaries, listen to their complaints, negotiate, bargain, and compromise before using force against troublemakers. In contrast, soldiers learn to use lethal force. The result is what the Pentagon euphemistically calls "collateral damage:" that is, the inadvertent wounding or killing of innocent civilians. Early in Calderón's drug war, nongovernmental organizations inveighed against the trampling of human rights in Mexico. They homed in on the 200,000-member army, as well as the government's indifference with respect to the approximately 140,000 migrants apprehended at the country's border in 2010, not to mention the tens of thousands who avoided capture. Mexico's zealous National Human Rights Commission (CNDH) claimed to have received

5,055 complaints, many against the military, during Calderón's tenure. The same group asserted that 5,300 people disappeared in this period.[25]

A statement by the Washington Office on Latin America epitomized the ever more caustic invective: "For years, organizations and shelters in Mexico have documented the abuses suffered by migrants traveling through the country. Every day along the principal transit routes, migrants, primarily Central Americans, are beaten, extorted, sexually abused and/or kidnapped by criminal groups, at times with the direct participation or acquiescence of Mexican authorities."[26]

The drumbeat of international outrage finally grabbed the attention of Mexico's brass, who instituted human rights training for soldiers and opened the door a crack on tribunals before which members of the armed forces stand trial. In 2008, SEDENA created the position of general director for human rights in its command structure, "a milestone that passed relatively unnoticed by most media and analysts."[27] In 2011 Mexican lawmakers approved a new statute that guarantees the rights of migrants, regardless of their immigration status. The legislation, which intended to prevent misconduct toward foreigners, created a 180-day visa for illegal aliens. The law also called for a new border police force to prevent crimes and conduct surveillance at airports, ports, bus terminals, and frontier areas. How effective this statute will be remains to be seen.

Pollsters for the *Reforma* newspaper found that a majority of citizens (58 percent) and opinion leaders (67 percent) recognized that the army committed human rights abuses. Indeed, 72 percent of the latter claimed to have known a victim of some crime. At the same time, average people (81 percent) and elites (64 percent) favored deploying the armed forces against criminal organizations.[28]

To raise spiritual consciousness and enhance concentration, the commander of the 24th Military Zone in Morelos, General Édgar Luis Villegas Meléndez, has taken a novel approach by requiring some 200 troops to undergo courses in meditation.[29]

PUBLIC RELATIONS: OUTREACH

Even though the populace backs its fight against DTOs, the army suffered a slight decline in support for this role—from 83 percent in 2009 to 80 percent in 2010. In early 2012, 70 percent of respondents to a Consulta Mitofsky survey favored the military's continuing to pursue criminal organizations, and 78 percent supported incorporating soldiers into the police. The results bristled with irony inasmuch as 49 percent of interviewees called Calderón's anticartel policy a "failure."[30]

Among institutions combatting drug cartels, respondents to a September 2011 National Survey of Victimization and Perception of Public

Table 6.5

Mexican Attitudes about Drug War

Use of Mexican Army to Fight Drug Traffickers	2011%	2012%
Support	83	80
Oppose	14	17
Don't Know	3	3
Campaign against Drug Traffickers is		
Making Progress	45	47
Losing Ground	29	30
Same as Past	25	19
Don't Know	1	3

Source: Pew Research Center, "Mexicans Back Military Campaign against Cartels," Pew Global Attitudes Project, June 20, 2012.

Security expressed the greatest confidence in the navy (83 percent), army (83 percent), federal police (55.4 percent), state police (42.3 percent), judiciary (38.2 percent), prosecutors (36.9 percent), municipal police (36 percent), and transit police (32.9 percent).[31]

As shown in Table 6.5, in mid-2012 the Pew Research Center found that four out of five Mexicans backed using the army against DTOs, although more respondents (49 to 47 percent) believed that the government was either losing ground or making no progress. Those interviewed favored U.S. training police and military (75 percent), and Washington's provision of money and weapons (61 percent). Yet only a third of those interviewed endorsed the deployment of U.S. troops in their country.[32] However, the Americans came out well in willingness to cooperate with Mexico.

Late in Peña Nieto's successful campaign, he named a tough-as-nails Colombian as his security adviser. The selection of General (Ret.) Oscar Naranjo Trujillo, nemesis of the Medellín and Cali Cartels and ex-director general of the Colombian National Police (2007–2012), was met with silence in SEDENA. However, Josefina Vázquez Mota, candidate of Calderón's National Action Party in the presidential contest, emphasized her faith in Mexico's armed forces and underlined that the country did not require "foreigners" in public safety posts.[33] In retrospect, the naming of Naranjo was a campaign gimmick, for the retired officer has played no role in fashioning the government's security policy.

To preserve its approval rating, defense and navy ministries have stepped up efforts to curry favor with the population. After the September 16, 2009, Independence Day parade, naval personnel mixed with the crowd, and an area on la Calle de Sevilla between Reforma and Avenida

Chapultepec in downtown Mexico City became a "gigantic photography studio." A mob of children, men, women, tourists, and whole families clamored to have their pictures taken with some 200 obliging members of the armed forces and their 40 vehicles. "Look Papa!" shouted a nine-year-old boy, who sat proudly in an armored vehicle with both hands grasping the controls of an antiaircraft weapon.

What may have begun spontaneously now forms an integral part of the annual march through the heart of the capital when the armed services show off their precision drills, new equipment, and recently acquired technology. Some youngsters even color their faces with combat grease and clamp on helmets. During the bicentennial of independence in 2010, the president announced that the armed forces would present miniature Mexican flags to every household in the country to symbolize their unity with the people.

In early February 2011 the army and air force again attempted to win friends and influence people. They sponsored an exposition called the Great Force of Mexico at the old Military College at Popotla, outside of Mexico City. At this event, children and adults strapped on parachutes, stepped into the cockpits of helicopters, and mounted Humvee personnel carriers. Some youngsters darkened their faces with cream worn in jungle combat, wriggled into field jackets, rappelled a low wall, and even took target practice. "The lack of rapport that usually characterizes contacts between civilians and the military disappeared. Smiles were the common denominator," according to a journalist on the scene.[34]

To promote both their achievements and recruitment, the army hired Servicios Profesionales y Asistencia Creativa, a Mexico City public relations firm headed by Alejandro Fernández Carrillo, and McCann World Group, whose clients include such multinational entities as Coca-Cola and the U.S. Army. Running television advertisements, trumpeting achievements on Twitter and YouTube, and airing brief recruiting videos before the beginning of motion pictures proved expensive. In 2007, SEDENA earmarked 111,246 pesos (approximately $10,000) for promotional activities in the media—with most of the funds dedicated to videos along with TV and radio commercials. Moreover, the polling firm of Beltrán y Asociados has conducted surveys for the military. Outlays for these advertising ventures soared to 46 million pesos in 2011 (approximately $3.8 million), as evidenced in Table 6.6.

Acclaimed director Rafael Lara is making a film depicting the valor of the army in the May 5, 1862, Battle of Puebla in which General Ignacio Zaragoza Seguín led the army to an unexpected triumph over the French. SEDENA assisted the venture with guidance, vintage uniforms, and extras.[35]

These efforts appear to have succeeded. Spontaneous applause greeted soldiers who marched in the September 2011 Independence Day parade.

Table 6.6

SEDENA's Expenditures on Publicity

Year	Outlays on Publicity (in Pesos)	% Change
2007	111,246	
2008	47,000,000+	421.49
2009	43,138,000	(8.95)
2010	14,688,000	(193.70)
2011	46,000,000	213.18

Source: Luis Brito, "La SEDENA invierte más en publicidad para mejorar imagen ante Ciudadanos," CNN México, September 7, 2011.

Earlier in the year, Norberto Rivera, the cardinal archbishop of Mexico City, invited worshippers to pray for the generals, chiefs, officials, and troops of the army, reaffirming their vocation of peace and assistance to a society that they serve with honor and loyalty. Meanwhile, he excoriated those who had "negated the love of God by abusing and mistreating boys and girls . . ."[36]

As part of the DN-III-E disaster-relief initiative, launched in 1966, army units in the north are rebuilding houses, rendering medical care, and providing dental services. On a typical day in a northern city, army professionals register some 397 medical check-ups, conduct 110 dental examinations, and distribute 847 pharmaceutical drugs. They also carry out projects involving masons (112), plumbing (38), electricity (21), carpentry (524), and haircuts (962).[37]

General Raymundo Balboa Aguirre co-chairs an organization called Unidad de Vinculación con la Ciudadania (UNIVIC), or Citizens Relations Unit. Officially, this body, which includes former Social Alternative Democratic Party deputy Marina Arvizu Rivas (an acquaintance of General Galván), seeks to bolster collaboration between the army and civilians, promote respect for human rights, and resolve conflicts arising from the drug war. In fact, it sprang to life to dampen criticism of the military after a fragmentation grenade killed two youngsters, aged five and nine, aboard a pick-up truck in a confrontation between the army and cartel members on the Guerrero–Ciudad Mier highway in Tamaulipas on April 3, 2010. A human rights activist claimed that soldiers reconfigured the scene in an effort to absolve themselves of responsibility for the deaths.[38] Incidents such as this may explain why no folk ballads—the so-call *corridos* that often extol the merits of traffickers—have circulated to laud the armed forces. In all fairness, UNIVIC has made reparations to victims, paid for funeral expenses, covered medical expenses, and funded psychological therapy.[39]

INCREASING ROLE OF WOMEN IN MEXICO'S ARMED FORCES

Recent military ceremonies have provided a showcase for the ever-greater visibility of women in uniform. Only in 1938 did the army admit women and then just to the Military Nursing School. They were admitted to the Military Medical School in 1973 and the Military Odontology School in 1976. For years, women were only allowed to be in the medical arts, secretaries, translators, drivers, communications specialists, and other support personnel. Females gained admission to the Colegio Heroico Militar, Mexico's version of West Point, for the first time in 2007. Even then, of 537 general officers, only five were women.[40] As seen in Table 6.7, the Defense Ministry claims that opportunities have increased substantially.

Under SEDENA's Equal Opportunities Program for Women and Men, 2008–2012, distaff members may enroll in all of the army's 17 schools, including those for combat instruction, basic and advanced military police training, and the preparation of sergeants, as well as the formation of officers at the Heroic War College. The Defense Ministry has also organized conferences, seminars, and courses to raise the consciousness of troop with respect to gender equality.

On December 16, 2011, the military launched a magazine titled *Observatorio para la Igualdad entre Mujeres y Hombres en el Ejército y Fuerza Aérea Mexicanos* (Observatory for the Equality between Women and Men in the Mexican Army and Air Force) to highlight actions taken to advance

Table 6.7

Women in the Mexican Army in Recent Years

Year	Number of Women in the Army	Total Number in Army	%Females
2006	6,309	196,767	3.21
2007	6,831	196,710	3.47
2008	7,980	202,355	3.94
2009	8,714	206,013	4.23
2010	10,234	206,013	4.97
2011	10,301	206,013	5.00
2012	11,810	211,000	5.60

Source: "Pide diputada una mujer al frente del Ejército mexicano," *El Universal*, December 16, 2008; Secretaría de Defensa Nacional, *Fourth Annual Report*, 2010; "Exaltan labor de mujeres militares," *Reforma*, March 6, 2012; "Impulsan sin plazas a mujeres militares," *Reforma*, April 23, 2012.

the careers of female members of the armed forces and to eradicate violence and discrimination against them.[41]

Greater chances for women in the *machista* army spring from social and international pressure, the presence of more skilled women prepared to enter the armed forces, and the need to recruit more elements in an institution plagued by desertions. Leftist deputy Maricela Contreras Julián even looked to the not-too-distant future when a woman could become secretary of defense—a wil-o'-the-wisp for decades to come.[42]

Female recruits and officers still face discrimination. While recognizing advances, Colonel Clementina Espíndola Zetna, who entered the military medical school in 1973, stated: "The atmosphere was extremely difficult ... [and] hostile. In the beginning, we were soundly rejected: 'women [should] remain in the home and wash dishes' ... 'you belong in the kitchen,' but as time went by integration [of women into the military] progressed."[43]

The army has had a difficult time placing women, and only six females have reached the rank of general, five of whom have retired. The Defense Ministry attributes the slow mobility to the military's lack of expansion. Spokesman General Ricardo Trevilla Trejo emphasized that distaff soldiers and officers must wait until more men leave the service to obtain assignments and promotions. As a result, it took eight months to incorporate 1,852 trained women into the ranks, and the objective, announced in 2007, of doubling the number of females in uniform by the end of 2012 proved illusory.[44]

Few reports have surfaced about sexual harassment, a headache for the U.S. armed forces. The small number of women in combat and fear of turning in abusers may explain the situation. Human rights organizations regularly report that Mexican soldiers humiliate, strip, grope, and have sexual relations with vulnerable females, especially migrants and indigenous girls. The Foreign Relations Ministry asserts that there are few transgressions. In late July 2012, 50 military personnel, including a captain, sergeants, and corporals, participated in a group marriage ceremony in the southern states of Chiapas and Tabasco. Volunteer coordinator Yolanda Martínez explained that the mass wedding would ensure that the brides would enjoy the benefits to which military families were entitled.[45]

In a somewhat related subject, the status of gays in uniform is in limbo. Homosexuality is not considered a crime, and the army follows a "Don't Ask, Don't Tell" policy. In the past, openly gay soldiers and officers faced dismissal and, no doubt, taunts and abuse from macho comrades.[46]

MILITARY PERSONNEL AND CIVILIAN COURTS

NGOs have long complained that trials of army and navy personnel in military tribunals are secret, the punishment lenient, and the results often unknown. Article 13 of the Mexican Constitution specifically provides for military jurisdiction over all military crimes and indiscipline; military tribunals execute jurisdiction over military personnel in accord with the Uniform Code of Military Justice (COJM). At the same time, Article 129 stipulates that "in peace time military authority can discharge only functions that are directly connected to military discipline." In July 2011 Mexico's Supreme National Court of Justice (SCJN) ruled that members of the armed services accused of torture, extrajudicial killing, and other abuses should be tried in civilian courts. "This is a very significant advance," said Andrés Díaz Fernández, a lawyer for the Miguel Agustín Pro Juárez Human Rights Center in Mexico City. "It creates very clear principles for Mexican judges."[47]

Enacting a law or rendering a judicial finding does not ensure resolution of the problem at hand. A cause célébré involved Lieutenant Colonel Alfredo Bravo Alcaraz, who on March 19, 2009, opened fire with a submachine gun on a vehicle carrying two civilians, one of whom died. When the survivor tried to escape, the lieutenant colonel asked why a lieutenant had failed to shoot him, saying, "Fucking mothers! Why are you bringing him in alive? Take him over there and kill him." Which the subordinate did.[48] The SCNJ's ruling aside, Bravo Alcaraz remains incarcerated in a military prison under an *arraigo* (detention order). With respect to the case, SEDENA issued the following statement:

The Defense Ministry assures society in general that it will in no form tolerate actions contrary to the military laws and regulations, and when one of its members fails to conform to the Law, his behavior will be investigated … and he will be punished according to the strict application of the law without regard to his rank, assignment, or commission without impunity nor opaqueness.[49]

At the early February 2012 Loyalty March, a military ceremony, General Galván admitted that the armed forces had made mistakes during the drug war even as he praised the chief executive as "an intelligent, brave, honest commander who has identified himself with the troops." At the same time, the defense minister urged clarification of the legal framework in which troops battled organized crime.[50]

Activists' pleas aside, legislators from the Institutional Revolutionary Party have blocked reform of the Code of Military Justice that would transfer jurisdiction over alleged crimes against civilians by members of the armed forces to civil courts. In late April 2012 the chairman of the Justice Committee in the Senate claimed that SEDENA doesn't want the change and that his incredibly influential PRI colleague in the Chamber of Deputies, Manlio Fabio Beltrones, posed the most formidable obstacle to change.[51]

In response to freedom-of-information petitions, SEDENA has begun to shed light on judicial actions. In February 2012 it reported that

344 members of the army were behind bars, while others were either standing trial or under arrest.[52] This figure, which did not include deserters, embraced five generals, two colonels, six lieutenant colonels, and five majors. General Manuel de Jesús Moreno Aviña was convicted after subordinates testified that he had ordered the execution of civilians, their torture, and clandestine burials. He committed these crimes, along with collaboration with narco-traffickers, when commanding the military garrison in Ojinaga, Chihuahua, between April 2008 and August 2009. Thirty-one other members of the army were convicted because of links to organized crime—19 of whom were tried in response to recommendations from the CNDH. Several generals joined their ranks. In mid-March 2011 military authorities arrested Pedro "El Guacho" Toga Lara in Saltillo, who reportedly served as Los Zetas' number two in the city. He and 16 colleagues were incarcerated when their names were found on the payroll (*narcolista*) of Los Zetas In addition to the chief of the General Staff for the military zone, those taken into custody included Sargent Evencio "El Batman" Castillo, a former member of the Special Airborne Forces Group (GAFES), from which the original Zetas deserted. Reportedly, El Batman recruited for Los Zetas who, in return for information about troop movements, received 3,000 pesos or more every two weeks at an OXXO convenience store, a 7-Eleven, or a Walmart. The prisoners alleged that they confessed only after being tortured.[53]

While moving slowly to put its house in order, the army still encompasses senior brass who have at least one foot, if not two, firmly planted in the past. This was evident when SEDENA held a ceremony in the DF's Military Camp No. 1 to pay homage to General Mario Acosta Chaparro, who died at the hands of an assassin in Mexico City on April 20, 2012. During 45 years in the military, the deceased had commanded parachutists, infantry battalions, the 27th Military Zone in Guerrero, and the Judicial Military Police. Still, his career was tainted by persistent accusations that he had protected the enormously powerful drug trafficker Lord of the Skies Carrillo Fuentes. He was also linked to the disappearance in Guerrero of 143 alleged subversives during the "dirty war" of the 1970s. A colonel who had served under Acosta spoke at his memorial service and stated: "I wish that many generals were like him."[54]

Apart from brutal killings and collaboration with cartels, the army has been cited for the mismanagement of funds. The Superior Auditor of the Federation (ASF), Mexico's version of the U.S. General Accountability Office, has charged a SEDENA sector that handles $64 million with letting large no-bid contracts. In addition, the Defense Ministry paid Russia approximately $1 million to void an order to repair five helicopters. A Ukrainian firm received $1.6 million to transport the aircraft but cancelled the agreement without paying a penalty. In 2009 the army purchased 54 Humvees, which had been used only two times as of July 2010.[55]

Invoking national security, the Defense Ministry rejected a request from the Mexican Academy of Science to test the GT200, a molecular detector purchased from the United Kingdom's Global Technical Ltd. The army, which has 738, and other security agencies have acquired 940 of these devices, which are known as the Devil's Ouija, at a cost of $28 million for use in antinarcotics operations. Physicist Dr. Luis Mochán Backal asserted that proponents were only describing the GT200's positive qualities while omitting its failures.[56]

In 2012 the Defense Ministry was negotiating with Boeing to purchase a 787 Dreamliner as the new presidential airplane to replace the TP-01 acquired in 2009. The price of such an aircraft is approximately $750 million, more than double the cost of Air Force One used by President Barack Obama.[57] The 4,400-member Presidential General Staff (Estado Mayor Presidencial (EMP) is in charge of logistics for the chief executive's travels. Recent military budgets appear in Appendix J.

To strengthen the esprit de corps and discourage desertions, SEDENA has initiated 21-gun salutes at burials of soldiers, made certain a military band was on hand to honor the fallen, provided a memorial flag to the spouse, authorized a life pension for widows and widowers, and furnished them with broader insurance coverage. In late 2012 the president celebrated the erection of a canon-shaped Defenders of the Patria monument to honor the soldiers and sailors who had died while serving their country.[58]

To compensate for desertions, the army reached out to young peasants devastated by their country's sluggish economic growth amid a recession in the United States. Although training may be rigorous and assignments challenging, campesinos from dirt-poor states such as Oaxaca, Guerrero, and Chiapas experience a better quality of life in the military. "There is recruitment throughout the Republic, principally in marginal and economically vulnerable areas to take advantage of the human resources necessary to integrate the [recruits] into the Army as soldiers," said Brigadier General Sergio García Vera, subdirector general of personnel at SEDENA. He reported recruiting 80,808 elements during the first four-and-a-half years of Calderón's administration.[59]

SEDENA has not followed César Duarte Jáquez's recommendation that it draft so-called Ni-Nis, the roughly 7.5 million young Mexicans who neither work nor study, but live aimless, sometimes violent, lives. In making this proposal, Chihuahua's governor asserted that these youngsters were "easy marks to be recruited by organized crime." The late secretary of education Alonso Lujambio quickly rejected the idea, stating that there were only 285,000 such young people and stressing how important it is that these individuals pursue educational opportunities.[60]

Security firms in Mexico are booming. In recruiting bodyguards, skilled drivers, technical experts, and consultants, they often look to former members of the military not only because of their training and discipline, but also because of their legal right to carry firearms. Ricardo de León Dorantes, president of the National Council of Public Security (CNSP), which embraces 200 firms, estimated that 40 percent of bodyguards hired by private parties are former members of the armed forces, while half are ex-policemen. In late 2008 their salaries ranged from 12,000 pesos ($1,200) to 20,000 pesos ($1,667) per month. In 2010 outlays on private security increased 11 percent over the previous year nationwide—with a 33 percent rise in states along the U.S.-Mexican border.[61] Although security providers are supposed to register with authorities, hundreds of such corporations ignore this requirement, which gives them greater flexibility to hire cashiered cops and soldiers.

MANUFACTURING

The army has expanded its manufacturing of munitions, uniforms, shoes, and other items. In August 2010 a SEDENA spokesman indicated that the military was 90 percent self-sufficient in the output of much of its equipment. In addition, the SEDENA Military Factories in Mexico City produce, under license, the Heckler and Koch family of small arms and light weapons. They have begun turning out the FX-05 Xiuhcóatl assault rifle and are moving away from the 7.62-millimeter (mm) G-3 to smaller and more effective weapons. The factories are also assembling the Oshkosh SandCat protected patrol vehicle, a 4-by-4 armored truck renowned for its speed and maneuverability.[62]

SEDENA plans to manufacture its own version of a homemade armored tank, nicknamed El Monstruo 2011, which is employed by Los Zetas for urban warfare. The steel-plated "Monster," also referred to as the Batimóvil, operates at up to 68 miles per hour, carries a dozen shooters, and provides small openings through which they can fire high-powered weapons. "El Monstruo 2011 is a homemade armored tank, the latest weapons innovation from Los Zetas, one of Mexico's largest and most brutal drug trafficking organizations."[63]

In mid-2012 El Universal reported that the ministry signed a contract for 5,000 million pesos ($379 million) to purchase state-of-the-art communication interception equipment from Security Tracking Devices, a Jalisco-based firm. The agreement raised questions because of its secrecy, the potential for the army to eavesdrop on innocent civilians, and the inability of journalists to find the contractor's alleged office in Mexico City.[64]

POLITICAL INVOLVEMENT

Although Mexico's generals have obeyed rather than deliberated, the absence of coups d'état does not mean that the army is indifferent to political decisions. Traditionally, they have expressed their views to the president or secretary of Gobernación behind closed doors. Such sub rosa contacts ended during the Fox administration (2000–2006) when Defense Secretary de la Vega García, followed the practice of civilian cabinet members by appearing before a congressional committee to discuss his ministry's interests, goals, and performance. In contrast, General Galván shunned public sessions in favor of private meetings with legislators from various parties in military installations. As mentioned in Chapter 5, he did not shy from upbraiding politicians on their performance; notably in his 2011 Loyalty Day speech. Galván's successor, General Salvador Cienfuegos Zepeda, met with key legislators soon after taking office on December 1, 2012.

Key officers have spoken out on political matters. General Sergio Aponte Polito, commander of the II Military Region in northwest Mexico, publically excoriated the ubiquitous involvement of elected and appointed officials in drug trafficking in the Tijuana area. He claimed that the police were cooperating with migrant smugglers, bank robbers, and drug lords. "The jowly, silver-haired 64-year-old general speaks in severe tones and writes as if he's inscribing his epitaph," observed a seasoned journalist. "What he's doing is completely unprecedented," stated Roderic Ai Camp, an expert on the Mexican military at Claremont McKenna College.[65] Aponte Polito's persistent criticism upset the National Action Party administration and led to his being transferred to Mexico City. After all, the PAN governor's replacement would be chosen on July 7, 2013 (He won by a narrow margin).

Three years later, another commander of the II Military Region was less reticent to condemn unprofessional behavior. After the September 16, 2011 Independence Day celebration, General Alfonso Duarte Múgica publically upbraided Government Secretary Cuauhtémoc Cardona Benavides. At a gathering organized by the military, Duarte said, "I do not want to see [Cardona] in any military installation, and he is an ugly and disrespectful drunk." Both Governor Osuna Millán and a television camera crew observed this contretemps.[66]

PENITENTIARIES

The government euphemistically calls a number of its prisons Centers of Social Readaptation (CERESOs). Wardens, their subordinates, and guards nominally control Mexico's penitentiaries, especially the nine high-security federal facilities. In reality, payoffs by inmates to their keepers, combined with the proliferation of organized gangs behind bars, give well-heeled convicts unparalleled influence. Wealthy "deluxe prisoners" grease the palms of guards, who—for the right price—will permit them to exit the facility for a few hours to conduct business, lovemaking, or criminal ventures. These prisoners use every tactic—including fear, intimidation, money, and sex—to compromise the prison staff and administration.[67]

Inmates sometimes settle scores with adversaries behind bars. This was most notoriously exemplified in the 2004 murders of El Chapo's brother Arturo "El Pollo"/ "The Chicken" Guzmán Loera (December 31) and his associate Miguel Ángel "Ceja Güera"/ "White Eyebrow" Beltrán Lugo (October 6) inside La Palma prison.

Drug lords also carry on negotiations behind bars. The late assistant attorney general José Luis Santiago Vasconcelos acknowledged that Los Zetas' patron Osiel Cárdenas cut a deal to cooperate with Tijuana Cartel honcho Benjamín Arellano Félix to decimate the Sinaloa Cartel while both were "locked up" in Almoloya prison outside Toluca in Mexico State.

In January 2005 gangsters seized six employees of the Matamoros penitentiary and handcuffed, blindfolded, and shot them, leaving their cadavers in a white sport utility vehicle parked opposite the facility. This savagery may have been a response to the siege six days earlier of La Palma prison by 750 federal police and military. Clearly, drug dealers had corrupted the guards and were overseeing violent networks from inside. In early December 2008 enemies are believed to have executed two Zetas in the Mazatlán detention center.[68]

Thanks to widespread access to cell phones, prisoners find it easy to engage in extortion. A committee of the Chamber of Deputies estimated that convicts had extorted 186,620 million pesos between 2001 and 2007. The equipment installed in 2007 to block telephone signals in 11 prisons has fallen into disrepair and no longer functions.[69] This situation prompted Mexico State to invest 10 million pesos (roughly $770,000) to block telephone signals in its four largest penitentiaries, Neza-Bordo (Nezahualcóyotl), Barrientos (Tlalnepantla), Chiconaultla (Ecatepec), and Almoloya de Juárez (Santiaguito).[70]

Just as in the United States, drugs flow freely inside Mexico's prison walls. Of the 37,000 inmates in Mexico City's penal institutions, an estimated 25,900 are addicts. Authorities admit that the availability of the substances, which may generate 15.5 million pesos a month, represents a convenient way to minimize melees and curb other violent outbursts. As a prison official told a city councilman, "Sir, if I cut off the flow of drugs, there will be a mutiny the next day."[71] In late 2008 authorities discovered 51 packets containing 119 kilograms of marijuana covered with sacks of toilet paper and boxes of soft drinks aboard a truck seeking to enter the the Reclusorio Sur, a prison in the southern part of the capital.[72]

So ubiquitous were drugs in the Detention Center (CEDES) of Reynosa that it gained fame as a *narcopenal* run by the convicts. La Suburban, a gang linked to Los Zetas, not only handled the intramural drug trade, but extorted money from their foes who lived in an adjoining structure known as the Sinai in the two-building compound.[73]

Overcrowding accentuates turmoil. Of Mexico's 439 federal, state, and local penal institutions, 228 are stuffed with an excessive number of inmates. In Mexico City's Reclusorio Oriente, 70 prisoners occupy 1 six-by-five square meter cell. They must sleep standing up, lie in hallways, vie for green spaces to stretch out, or pay for access to a bunk.[74] Exacerbating the crisis is that 80 percent of federal prisoners (34,952) are in state prisons, with the remainder (9,494) in federal institutions. In 2010, according to the Ministry of Public Safety, Mexico had 222,771 men and women behind bars.[75]

An especially brazen escape happened in Zacatecas on May 16, 2009, and all of it is available for public viewing on YouTube. Before dawn, 30 or more heavily armed thugs believed to be Zetas, riding in trucks adorned with Federal Investigative Agency logos, stormed into the Cieneguillas penitentiary as one of their helicopters whirred overhead. In the blitzkrieg assault, they extricated 53 prisoners, including Zetas, members of the Beltrán Leyva crime family, and other narco-felons. State and federal authorities immediately began apprehending escapees even as they investigated the director and his 50 subordinates to determine who fostered the escape.[76] One of several recaptured was Osvaldo "The Vampire" García Delgado, a kidnapping specialist whose Los Cotorros gang coordinates activities with Los Zetas in the state of Hidalgo.

When incarcerated, Los Zetas threaten to beat other convicts if they do not fork over 5,000 pesos or more. In addition, the paramilitaries provide women, drugs, and food to inmates who are forced to pay off debts incurred behind bars by working for Los Zetas even after they have completed their sentences. "There are few cases when men exit prisons clean," explained one expert. "I can assure you that practically no one under 30 does so."[77]

In October 2009 actions of Los Zetas precipitated a riot in the Topo Chico prison in Nuevo León that the state police had to put down. Some 100 Zetas controlled the 400 other inmates in the facility through extortion and shakedowns for protection. Before the uprising, PRI governor Natividad González Parás had brushed off friction in the penitentiary as "A squabble between one group of friends against another group of friends over personal problems."[78]

As in other facilities, Los Zetas practice virtual "self-governance" in the federal prison in Apodaca, Nuevo León (Cereso), where they have brutalized members of the Gulf Cartel and other foes.[79] Such conditions have prompted the government to dispatch army unit to conduct searches in penitentiaries and sometimes take control of the institutions. Examples abound: In early June 2009 elements of the army and federal police riding in small tanks, armored vehicles, and troop transports swept into Xalapa's Ignacio Allende prison, one of the oldest detention centers in Veracruz. The authorities did not disclose how many of the serious felons were moved to other facilities.

In mid-August 2009, General Felipe de Jesús Espitia, commander of the Fifth Military Zone, announced that troops would replace civilian administrators and guards at the Cereso of Aquiles Serdán, located in the heart of Chihuahua state. This action followed the resignation of the warden after three of his bodyguards were killed.[80] During the night of August 29, 2010, units of the 24th Military Zone took charge of Morelos's Atlacholoaya Cereso after a series of violent incidents that took the life of the facility's director. Soldiers also assumed control of district jails in Cuautla, Jojutla, Jonacatepec, Telecala, and Pueten de Istia.[81]

Military men now serve as directors of the penal facilities in the three largest cities in Quintana Roo. In late April 2011 General Carlos Bibiano Villa Castillo, the state's secretary of public security, placed officers in charge of the Cereso in Chetumal (Captain José de Jesús Moreno Abad), the Cereso in Cancún (General Eulalio Rodríguez Valdivia), and the jails in Playa del Carmen (Second Captain José Luis y Peniche Novelo) and Cancún (Captain Higinio Sánchez Baltazar). The state director of prisons is a civilian attorney, Ricardo Tejada de Luna.[82] Army personnel now control access to the principal entrances to three Monterrey-area penitentiaries—Topo Chico, Cadereyta, and Apodaca—inside of which more than 50 killings have taken place.[83] Military police have also taken over security duties for the PGR's Center of Federal Investigations in Mexico City, where some 250 suspects were being held in mid-2012.[84]

In a volte face, Defense Secretary Galván ordered 52 soldiers who were being held prisoner at the Campo Militar 1-J to be transferred to a federal penitentiary in Villa Aldama, Veracruz, in April 2011. He feared that their underground allies might attempt to free the inmates from the SEDENA lockup in Mexico City.[85]

CUSTOMS

In recent years, presidents have sought to fight corruption among customs officials—a Herculean challenge that they have lost because of the lucrative payments to officials who either close their eyes to smuggling or take part in the crime. In mid-August 2009 the armed forces took over the functions of the fiscal police in 49 land ports across the northern border. For its part, the navy has begun overseeing customs operations in seaports. Two years earlier, the army assumed the inspection of passengers at the Rodolfo Sánchez Taboada airport in Mexicali because of suspicion that seven Federal Preventative Police agents were facilitating cocaine shipments to the United States.[86]

GUARDIANS OF ELECTIONS

The Federal Electoral Institute (IFE), a citizen-run body that registers voters, organizes balloting, and announces preliminary results, formally requested that the army guarantee the security of elections in 2012, as it had done in previous balloting. So narrow was Calderón's 2006 victory that the army, at least until mid-2012, guarded the ballots 24 hours per day, seven days a week. In Querétaro alone, 21 soldiers fulfilled this assignment. In Guerrero, the electoral packets were secured in a building once known for table-dancing in Chilpancingo.[87] The vulnerability of politicians to narco-assassins became evident in the mid-2010 contest for governor in Tamaulipas, a state beset by fighting between Los Zetas and a group of syndicates supporting the Gulf Cartel. In the run-up to the July 4 election for the statehouse, Los Zetas executed PRI candidate Rodolfo Torre Cantú as he was traveling to the Ciudad Victoria airport on his final campaign swing. Although any politician may be targeted, the syndicates are especially eager to influence the voting in municipalities in which they store, process, and transport drugs.[88] During Calderón's administration, thousands of functionaries and 31 serving mayors died at the hands of cartels—with Durango (five) and Michoacán (five) suffering the most fatalities. Of those killed, 19 belonged to the PRI; five to the PAN; two to the PRD; and five to other parties. The most vulnerable officials were those living in small municipalities—87 percent of those who died were living in jurisdictions of fewer than 50,000 people. Only 239 of the countries' 2,457 municipalities receive so-called "security subsidies" from the federal government to help them combat crime.[89]

FIREFIGHTERS

On August 25, 2011, a group of Los Zetas set fire to the Casino Royale in Monterrey. The conflagration took 53 lives. In the aftermath of the tragedy, SEDENA announced the formation of a brigade of firefighters. Although the army has long acted in accordance with its DN-III strategy of disaster relief, these efforts have typically focused on floods, volcanic eruptions, forest fires, tropical storms, earthquakes, and other catastrophes. The tragedy in Monterrey produced a broader view of this function and involved activating an Immediate Response to Disasters and Emergencies Team, composed of seven officers and 45 enlisted volunteers, which was formed in the aftermath of the September 1985 earthquakes that struck Mexico City and adjoining areas.[90]

ROLE OF THE NAVY

The navy and its infantry, the marines, have received accolades for their actions against drug syndicates. Even before 2009, marines were involved in limited skirmishes with criminal organizations. However, their actions made national headlines on December 16, 2009, when a detachment of leathernecks from Mexico City successfully killed Arturo "El Barbas" Beltrán Leyva, head of the eponymous cartel. Ski-masked commandos took him down after a prolonged frenzied firefight in his luxurious bunker in Cuernavaca, Morelos, a colonial gem located 47 miles from the Federal District. The army had shown no interest in attacking the site even though its 24th regional headquarters lay only a few blocks from El Barbas's bailiwick. The regional commander had apparently bonded with the so-called boss of bosses.

The episode marked one of the first—but by no means the last—land engagements against traffickers by a naval force. Long regarded by the army brass as its "little brother," the navy has emerged as the most efficient ally of U.S. security agencies. In February 2009, the navy even signed a pact to keep secret all communications with the U.S. Department of Defense.

In addition to the El Barbas takedown, the navy/marines have distinguished themselves in successful efforts against Gulf Cartel co-boss Antonio Ezequiel "Tony Tormenta" Cárdenas (killed), regional chief of the sadistic Los Zetas cartel, Lucio "El Lucky" Hernández Lechuga (captured), Zeta chief Heriberto "The Executioner" Lazcano Lazcano (killed), and Lazcano's successor Miguel "Ángel "El 40" Treviño Morales (captured).

The 200,000-plus member army has registered successes, but the navy with 50,000 cadres, including 18,000 marines, has captured or killed disproportionately more kingpins. It is fortunate that Fox's defense secretary did not succeed in eliminating the navy's infantry. The July 28, 2013, ambush of Vice-Admiral Carlos Miguel Salazar Ramonet and a marine guard will sharpen this service's animus toward the cartels.

What accounts for the navy's rise in stature? To begin with, many mossback generals exhibit a toxic nationalism toward the United States that is exemplified by speeches and ceremonies that revive memories of the War of North American Aggression when Mexico lost nearly half its territory to Uncle Sam in the mid-nineteenth century. In mid-2013 Defense Secretary Cienfuegos told a group of Mexican officials, more or less, that "the major problem facing their country was the infusion of American values." Rather than have his official portrait made with a Mexican flag, as is the custom, he chose Chapultepec Castle, emblematic of the conflict with the United States as his backdrop. As the first president to live in this spawling edifice, Lázaro Cárdenas would have been proud of the image and ideas that Cienfuegos is projecting.

Nor will visitors to the country find statues of General John J. "Black Jack" Pershing, who in March 1916 led the 10,000-soldier Punitive Expedition in a vain attempt to apprehend the iconic Pancho Villa, whose forces had raided Columbus, New Mexico. In 1914 a misunderstanding involving U.S. sailors in the oil-exporting harbor of Tampico morphed into a six-month occupation of Veracruz; however, the navy incurred neither the losses nor the humiliation suffered by the army at the hands of the invaders. One reason may be that the navy did not become a separate force until 1939. Before then it existed jointly with the army in the War Ministry.

Since becoming an independent service, the navy has cooperated with the U.S. Coast Guard on rescue and relief missions, tracking down criminals at sea, and interdicting migrants trying to reach the United States.

The imperative for sea duty enables superiors to buffer subordinates from criminals. Port calls give Mexican seaman a chance to hobnob with foreigners—an opportunity unavailable for most army personnel. In addition, conducting land operations, staffing highway checkpoints, patrolling airports, and occupying cities exposes army units to ubiquitous corruption. The culture of graft long prevalent in the military combined with human rights abuses forced action by Calderón's defense secretary. As indicated in Chapter 5, at least five retired senior generals accused of accepting lavish bribes from the BLO were placed behind bars in the Almoloya maximum-security prison before they were released because of the shady character of their accusers.

The Defense Ministry rotates most army regional and zonal commanders on a regular basis, which gives these men a chance to conceal shady deals. Naval commanders receive, at best, a day or two advanced warning before being transferred to another post.[91]

In contrast to army officers, many more naval leaders speak English, and some marry women from the United States and other countries. Men and women in blue are more likely to be middle-class and cosmopolitan than their lower-class brothers and sisters in olive drab, who often come from Oaxaca, Guerrero, and other impoverished states. The relatively small size of the navy, one-fourth the personnel of the army, contributes to coherence. In contrast to the army, the navy gives lower-ranking officers important assignments and encourages them to use their initiative. Woe be the army lieutenant or captain who launched an action without the permission of a superior.

Analysts praise the navy's superior intelligence service, which cooperates smoothly with its U.S. counterparts. These skills go back Alfredo Wilfredo Robledo Madrid, who helped established CISEN, headed the AFI, and served as head of the Mexico State Security Agency (ASE). Since the 1970s Admiral José Luis Figueroa had focused on intelligence and espionage.[92] He also served as an advisor to the Presidential General Staff, instructing such younger officers as Wilfrido Robledo, Rafael Macedo de la Concha (President Fox's attorney general), and Jorge Carrillo Olea (a shadowy officer who served as governor of Morelos during a period of corruption). He also had a notable effect on Jorge Tello Peón, who worked on security matters under Calderón. In her book *Los cómplices del presidente*, which was published in late 2008, Anabel Hernández claimed that during the Echeverría presidency (1970–1976), Figueroa placed Robledo in the EMP's Section 3, which concentrates on intelligence.

And there is no discounting the Semper Fi élan of the marines, who especially loathe Los Zetas. This hatred emanates from the Arturo Beltrán melee. Only one Marine, 3rd Petty Officer Melquisedet Angulo Córdova (who was 30 years old), died in this raid, and he received a stirring public tribute in which the navy secretary presented his mother with the flag that was draped on her son's coffin. The following week, the BLO's allies, Los Zetas, went to the young man's home in Paraíso, Tabasco, and killed his mother, sister, brother, and aunt. Not even the Sicilian Mafia takes revenge against the families of fallen military men. The late August 2012 ambush in Morelos by 14 federal police officers of an embassy SUV carrying two CIA operatives and a Mexican navy captain may reflect the underworld's animus toward the ever-stronger links between the United States and the Mexican Navy.

An accord between Los Zetas and the Beltrán Leyvas enhanced the latter's ability to revenge the capture of their brother (Alfredo) against El Chapo Guzmán Loera, the Zambada brothers, and Nacho Coronel. Before his December 2010 death, Arturo Beltrán Leyva is also believed to have sought assistance from Treviño Morales in importing 23.5 tons of cocaine. The navy and customs officers found the shipment among containers on a Hong Kong–flagged vessel that had arrived at Manzanillo, Colima, from Buenaventura, Colombia.[93]

The navy had fewer deserters between 2007 and 2012 (4,671) compared with the army and air force (50,458).[94] The navy attracts many more middle-class applicants for the Heroic Naval Academy in Veracruz, carefully vets these men and women, conducts follow-up tests once they are on active duty, and enjoys more prestige as a service. In addition, there are fewer obstacles to reaching the upper echelons of the service.[95]

The Navy has shown greater readiness to innovate and to work with private contractors. In 2004 it began to deploy Spot ERMEXS satellites not only to track the movement of criminal organizations, but also to detect marijuana and poppy fields in Nayarit, Jalisco, Campeche, Quintana Roo, and Veracruz. Naval officials are now negotiating with three technology firms—Geo Eye, Digital Globe, and Imágenes Satelitales, SA—to enhance its ability to combat narco-trafficking.[96]

In April 2009 the Mexican Navy joined counterparts from 10 other countries in Unitas 50-09, a maritime exercise sponsored by the United States and held off the coast of Mayport, Florida. This marked the first time in the 50-year history of the event that the Mexicans had taken part as full contributors to this multilateral venture.[97] The following year the

Mexican Senate authorized the navy's participation in the POA-12, an exercise in Florida that homed in on narcotics trafficking, humanitarian assistance, regional coordination, and command and control skills. Mexico contributed an amphibious warship carrying a 150-member crew, a three-man helicopter team, and 43 marines.[98] Table 6.8 illuminates major differences between the army and the navy.

CONCLUSIONS

Several conclusions flow from this analysis.

First, President Calderón gave the Mexican military an assignment for which it was not trained, prepared, or equipped. The more than 47,000 drug-related deaths during Calderón's tenure are more an indictment of dirty incompetent civilian police agencies than of the armed forces, which have managed to capture dozens of important traffickers. The drug war and new tasks have expanded the army's budget, size, and stock of equipment. Regrettably, contact with the underworld has corrupted numerous enlistees and officers.

Second, as it amplifies current functions, the army (and to a lesser extent the navy) will have greater contact with civilians. While military personnel may not socialize widely with civilians, it remains to be seen whether their status as a caste marginal from the rest of society will diminish.

Third, Peña Nieto promised to gradually return thousands of soldiers to the barracks, replacing them with military-trained civilians in a Gendarmería Nacional (GN), modeled on its French counterpart. As will be discussed in Chapter 7, this force came a cropper for lack of careful planning, successful recruitment of cadres, and financial resources. SEDENA and SEMAR will remain key forces in combatting cartels, gangs, and other criminal organizations, even though the army in particular would like a diminished role in the combating DTOs in light of NGO criticism of human rights abuses and corruption, as well as the prevalence of mental illness among troops.[99]

Fourth, the military will pursue its public relations campaign to downplay the corruption arising from interaction with cartels. The services will continue to employ media advertisements, survey research, and special events to ingratiate themselves with the public, which supports men and women in uniform despite highly publicized bribe-taking, thefts, misallocation of funds, and human rights violations.

Fifth, mutual security concerns will lead to more numerous but lower profile contacts between the U.S. military and security agencies and their Mexican counterparts even as SEDENA and SEMAR reach out to Canada, Colombia, France, Spain, and other countries for training, specialized

Table 6.8

Comparison of Army and Navy/Marines

Elements of Comparison	Army	Navy/Marines
Secretary	General Salvador Cienfuegos Zepeda (born January 19, 1946, in DF); a dyed-in-the-wool traditionalist; oldest general eligible to be defense secretary	Admiral Vidal Francisco Soberón Sanz (born May 17, 1953, in DF); extremely progressive; youngest admiral eligible to be navy secretary
Number of members	200,000+	50,000 (18,000 marines in 30 battalions)
Combat Forces	80,000 to 100,000 (including air force, which forms part of the army)	15,000 marines—with special "SEAL"-type units
Organization	12 regions (45 zones)	1 headquarters in Mexico City 2 naval forces (Gulf, Pacific) 7 regions 13 zones 14 sectors
Rotation of commands	Every 12 to 18 months—with fixed periods	Every 12 to 18 months—without prior notification
Education of aspiring line officers	Heroico Colegio Militar (cheating sometimes tolerated to build an esprit de corps)	Heroica Escuela Naval Militar (cheating not condoned—with emphasis on merit)
Intelligence capability	Gathers lots of information, but mediocre analysts in DF; resists cooperating with other agencies, even the navy	Long tradition of prowess in intelligence gathering, which is still improving; cooperates well with U.S. agencies
Budget	55,610 million pesos in 2012	19,538 million pesos (2012)
Transparency	Minimal but improving	More transparent than the army as evidenced in the websites of the two branches

Image	Enjoys "revolutionary" mystique, as well as a reputation for valor in Mexican-American War (niños héroes)	Lower profile; ports of Tampico and Veracruz were attacked successfully by the United States, but naval personal don't carry chips on their shoulders
Desertions rate	50,458 (army/air force) between 2006 and 2012	4,671 (navy/marines) between 2006 and 2012
Corruption	High and growing as a result of its role in the war on drugs; key examples are Morelos and Northern Tamaulipas	Relative low
Nepotism	Significant	Exists but less than in army
Charges of human rights abuses	High and growing	The CNDH reports as many complaints about marine abuses on a per-capital basis as the army
Judicial structure	Fueros	Fueros
Social standing in eyes of middle class	Low	Acceptable
Social origins of officers	Lower middle class	Middle class
Attitude toward United States	One third of officer corps is progressive; one third traditional; and one third in between	Much more cosmopolitan and open; many members of the navy have traveled abroad; for example, participated in Unitas 50-09 in Mayport, Florida (2011) and in POA-12, an exercise in Florida (2012)

(continued)

Table 6.8 (*continued*)

Elements of Comparison	Army	Navy/Marines
Attitude toward U.S. intelligence agencies	Suspicious ("Give us the information and we will get back to you . . . a week later.")	Eager to cooperate ("Give us our assignment and we will carry it out.")
Political involvement	Several retired officers serve in congress; they typically head committees related to defense	Occasionally officers must take a leave of absence and do not lose seniority; retired officers head up some law enforcement agencies, e.g., CENAPI

Sources: "Recibe Semar 468 mdp para defensa," *Reforma*, August 7, 2011; Zósimo Camacho, "Más de 55 mil deserciones en las Fuerzas Armadas," *Contralínea*, June 6, 2013.

arms, intelligence, and instruction in cyber security. As suggested earlier, the U.S. Northern Command (NORTHCOM) can also be helpful by furnishing language instruction, information, radar, night goggles, and other used surveillance equipment to the U.S. Customs and Border Patrol (CBP) and other organizations such as the Texas Department of Public Security. The responsibilities of both agencies have mushroomed with the southward cascade of weapons and the accelerated flow of drugs and drug merchants across the 2,000-mile binational frontier.[100]

Operation Nimbus epitomized an effective Joint Task Force initiative supervised by NORTHCOM. In mid-February 2012 active-duty soldiers from Fort Hood and Fort Bliss deployed to southern New Mexico and Arizona to bolster CBP's security efforts. In the past National Guard units have successfully bolstered protection of porous, vulnerable areas. Operation Jump Start, which involved a two-year assignment of guardsmen to the Yuma Arizona sector, won praise from then-governors Arnold Schwarzenegger (California), Bill Richardson (New Mexico), and Janet Napolitano (Arizona), who wanted the mission extended.[101]

Finally, just as U.S. politicians turn to the public schools to solve such Herculean problems as teen pregnancies, drug abuse, hunger, poor health, and latchkey kids, their Mexican counterparts have turned to the military to perform functions they can't address successfully. While costly in lives, the drug war has forced the armed forces to acquire skills that are foreign to their training. The next chapter explores whether Peña Nieto can configure new agencies led by civilians.

CHAPTER 7

Peña Nieto's Approach to Combating Cartel Violence

INTRODUCTION

After its 12-year exile from Los Pinos presidential residence, Peña Nieto and his Mexico State and Hidalgo-dominated entourage were determined to convince a skeptical public that a "new PRI" had emerged. He insisted that the revolutionary party had long since abandoned the Jurassic Park where self-serving political dinosaurs roamed the terrain dispensing handouts and graft to ensure electoral triumphs, jobs for family members and cronies, Midas-sized wealth, and suppression of foes. "The country must be transformed without delay," he reiterated.

This chapter examines (1) the A-team in the president's entourage, as well as the sensational and symbolic arrest of Elba Esther Gordillo; (2) the importance of the new Telecommunications Law and the outlook for regulatory agencies; (3) the withering criticism of Calderón's security policy; (4) the proposed reorganization of the governing system, including security matters, under El Pacto por Mexico, or The Pact for Mexico; (5) political and social issues embedded in this manifesto; and (6) the likelihood that Peña Nieto will make good on forging a new PRI government during his *sexenio*, or 6-year term.

1. THE A-TEAM

The president configured a triangle of walk-through-fire devotees to guide his promised makeover. The A-team embraces Finance Secretary Luis Videgaray Caso, who fashions economic policy, including petroleum and tax reforms; Government secretary and former Hidalgo governor Miguel Ángel Osorio Chong, who is responsible for political and security issues in league with his undersecretary Luis Miranda Nava; Attorney General Jesús Murillo Karam; Eugenio Ímaz Gispert, who directs the Center for Investigation and National Security (CISEN), Mexico's anemic version of the CIA; and undersecretary of the Ministry of Social and Human Development (SEDESOL), Ernesto Nemer Álvarez, who will distribute social funds with a view to gaining both legitimacy for the regime and votes for the PRI.

Another important figure is Los Pinos's Media and Communications Officer David López Gutiérrez, a war horse who deftly handled public relations in the incumbent's presidential campaign. According to a confidential source, early in Peña Nieto's administration, hot-shot trainees in public relations from ITAM, a first-rate university, demonstrated innovations in communications techniques. They showed multicolor graphics, sophisticated PowerPoint presentations, and exotic moving video displays. López Gutiérrez said, in effect: "I want to thank you guys, but this is not a stock market presentation where securities rise and fall and make a visual impact on viewers. This is the area of presidential communications and here we control information and generate what interests the media."

In addition, Chief of the Presidential Office Aurelio Nuño Mayer, a protégé of Videgaray, who developed effective contacts with the international media and worked on transparency issues; legal counsel to the president is Humberto Castillejos Cervantes, another Videgaray disciple, who lent a hand in the telecommunications reform; Peña Nieto's private secretary Erwin Lino Zarate, who functions as gate-keeper for those who desire to enter the president's sanctum sanctorum. Although not intimates of the president, two other men who can advance or retard the administration's goals are Manlio Fabio Beltrones Rivera, one of Mexico's most astute dealmakers, a competitor with Peña Nieto for the PRI presidential nomination, and PRI chief in the Chamber of Deputies; and Senator Emilio Gamboa Patrón, a veteran politico, Beltrones Rivera's soul mate, and a Salinas loyalist. Of course, different committee chairs will zero in on legislation in their domains. A case in point is David Penchyna Grub, who as head of the Senate energy committee will perform the heavy lifting on the proposed modernization of the petroleum sector.[1] Peña Nieto's operators in the Senate include Raúl Cervantes Andrade, Enrique Burgos García, and former PRI secretary general María Cristina Díaz Salazar. Their House counterparts are Manuel Añorve Baños, Héctor Gutiérrez de la Vega, and Marco Antonio Bernal.

No doubt elder statesmen will proffer advice. Among these notables are Salinas, former finance secretary Pedro Aspe Armella (Videgary's mentor), as well as Alfredo del Mazo González (Peña Nieto's uncle) and other former Mexico State governors who comprise the quasi-political, quasi-social Atlacomulco Group.

In late March 2013 Peña Nieto announced the formation of five specialized cabinets, presumably chosen to increase government efficiency and reduce duplication.

To bind Peña Nieto even closer to the ruling party, he has become a member of the PRI's most powerful committees whose memberships have been halved: the 54-person Permanent Political Commission (Comisión Política Permanente (CPP), which enters into dialogues with other parties, formulates policy, and sets priorities for PRI legislators; and the 680-person National Political Council (CPN), which keeps abreast of PRI public servants and makes recommendations on their conduct. In another effort to cultivate and control its adherents, the revolutionary party in Nuevo León followed the example of its counterpart in Coahuila, issuing membership credentials with which the cardholder can obtain discounts at commercial establishments.[2]

The objective is to recentralize much of the power vested in the revolutionary party by Lázaro Cárdenas, which the president-government-PRI troika impelled in its heyday. The blueprint for accomplishing this goal crystallized in the Pacto por México.

2. THE NEW TELECOMMUNICATIONS LAW

Just as President Cárdenas ousted governors in thrall to Plutarco Calles, President Salinas wasted only six weeks before, in early 1989, incarcerating Joaquín "La Quina" Galicía Hernández, the redoubtable "moral leader" of the Oil Workers' Union, and Peña Nieto acted with dispatch to arrest the haughty, corrupt Elba Esther Gordillo, known as "La Maestra" or "The Teacher." The attorney general charged her with embezzling nearly $200 million in assets of the National Syndicate for Educational Workers (SNTE), and an investigation is underway into other possible wrongdoing by Gordillo, her family, and her friends. "The resources of unions belong to their members, not to their leaders. They must be used to benefit the workers," affirmed the chief executive after La Maestra's February 26, 2013, arrest.[3]

Observers alleged that these funds were only the tip of an iceberg that covered multiple mansions, cosmetic surgeries, jet planes, lavish gifts to lackeys, and a wardrobe that would have been the envy of former Philippine first lady Imelda Marcos. Attorney General Murillo Karam said the monies were destined to settle credit card debts and make deposits in Switzerland and Liechtenstein. "It's worth mentioning that Elba Esther Gordillo Morales declared [to Mexico's version of the IRS] earnings from 2009 to 2012 for 1,100,000 pesos ($88,000)." The PGR head said in a statement on February 27: "A number that [she reported] is much lower than those financial transactions and deposits cited for those same years."[4]

This bold strike, which may have been orchestrated by Videgaray, sent a message to trade union caciques, media titans, the business community, governors, mayors, and other officials that there was a new sheriff in town. A medley of factors—poor performance of students on standardized examinations, hyper-arrogance, alienation of major party leaders, the pressure she exerted on governors to add to the education budget in their states—facilitated the "*elbazo*," as the incarceration was labeled. No one appeared happier than Education Secretary Emilio Chuayffet Chemor, who personally despised Gordillo and was eager to implement the legislation for sweeping education reform that was approved in late 2012. This measure, backed by the PRI, PAN, and PRD, stipulates rigorous teacher assessments by an independent National Institution for the Evaluation of Education in lieu of capricious, self-serving hiring by the SNTE. "The State has not had the upper hand since Jesús Reyes Heroles [distinguished late education secretary] who described the Education Ministry as a rheumatic elephant that could barely move in the sense of defining an education policy. And it has gradually and persistently faced a deterioration of quality, coverage of the country, relevance, and equality," stated Chuayffet.[5]

Still, the arrest was less a vendetta than a determination to embellish the administration's identity as the ballyhooed new PRI. If convicted as charged, Gordillo can expect to spend a brief period behind bars. Born in 1945, she was 68 years old when imprisoned. Although she could receive a sentence of up to 30 years, Mexican law grants home arrest once prisoners turn 70. In addition, she has serious renal problems that are accentuated by the donation of one of her kidneys to her first husband. In March 2013 it was claimed that two birth dates have been recorded in her hometown of Comitán, Chiapas, near the Guatemalan border. One indicates that she came into the world on February 6, not June 2, 1945; if the former date proves correct, she could gain release four months earlier. How ironic that a woman who has paid a king's ransom on ironing out wrinkles, excising crows' feet, and expunging puffiness from her face should benefit by being older!

Whether Gordillo's removal as union ringleader will improve the nation's public education in the short to medium run is dubious. Many of her toadies preside over the SNTE's 54 locals around the country, while others serve as state secretaries of education. Teachers, especially in poor rural states, go on strike at the drop of a hat. For example, educators in Guerrero and Michoacán shuttered schools attended by 540,000 students for 40 days in 2013 at a daily cost to the government of 1,759 million pesos ($139 million). Even more militant is the National Coordination of

Educational Workers (CNTE), which aggressively participates in marches, sit-ins, and the storming of government buildings in Mexico.[6] In August 2013, 20,000 CNTE firebrands invaded the DF. They surrounded the nation's giant TV networks to demand airtime, blocked access to the airport, and chased members of the Chamber of Deputies out of their legislative hall in a vain move to quash the education initiative. Peña Nieto wisely avoided battling the thugs to avoid creating martyrs.

Salinas not only apprehended La Quina, the supposedly "untouchable" don of the oil workers' union, but federal police subsequently jailed four prominent stockbrokers on charges of illegal trading arising from the October 1987 collapse of the Mexican stock market. The most prominent was Eduardo Legorreta Chauvet, director of Operador de Bolsa, the nation's second-largest brokerage firm. The securities managers stood accused of selling worthless Mexican Treasury bills and investing clients' resources without their consent; yet, Salinas's motive in taking the financial barons into custody was to simulate even-handedness; not only was he nailing corrupt union bosses, but he was also lowering the boom on illegal machinations by well-known business gurus.

In 2013 Peña Nieto adhered to a similar game plan. Once Gordillo was behind bars, he mustered the political capital to gain passage of a constitutional amendment reforming the nation's telecommunications law.[7] This proposal gives authority to a regulatory body to break up phone and TV networks that control half the domestic market—a blow aimed at Carlos Slim Helú, the world's richest man, whose TELMEX controls 80 percent of the country's landlines and whose América Móvil cell phone corporation dominates 70 percent of the wireless market. Finance Secretary Videgaray estimated that greater competition would add 1 percent to gross domestic product.[8] Not only is trust-busting popular with average citizens who pay sky-high rates for third-world telecommunications service, but the initiative may have signaled revenge against Slim for allegedly having donated generously to López Obrador's 2012 presidential candidacy. Companies considered monopolies could be forced to rent parts of their holdings to rivals. The legislation would also increase foreign participation in media from 49 to 100 percent in television; and from zero to 49 percent in radio. The bill would also affect the TV conglomerates Televisa and Azteca, owned by billionaires Emilio Azcárraga Jean and Ricardo Salinas Pliego, which have a "TV duopoly." The initiative envisages auctioning off two new TV channels, including one similar to PBS in the United States, and three new radio frequencies.[9]

Rather than a panacea, this legislation forms part of an élan to strengthen the central government. The law replaces the Federal Communications Commission (COFETEL), on which Calderón appointee Mony de Swan Addati has energetically championed tough regulations, with the Federal Telecommunications Institute (IFETEL), whose

Table 7.1

Social Welfare Reforms Launched or Modified by the Pact for Mexico

Program	Purpose	Responsible Agency/ Agencies	Agency Head	Estimated Budget
National Crusade against Hunger	Provide food for 7,404,177 Mexicans who go to bed hungry	SEDESOL* SHCP	Rosario Robles Berlunga; former Brazilian president Luiz Inácio Lula de Silva, who championed "Hambre Cero" when in office ***	95,251 billion pesos for existing SEDESOL projects plus the crusade
Stipend for adults age 65 and older	The minimum age was formerly 70	SEDESOL	Rosario Robles Berlunga	26 billion pesos (included in SEDESOL budget)*
Life insurance for female heads of households	New program	SEDESOL	Rosario Robles Berlunga	400 million pesos (included in SEDESOL budget)
New National Housing Program	Construct 500,000 new houses	SEDATU	Jorge Carlos Ramírez Marín	Not Available
Education constitutional reform and subsequent regulations	Establish rigorous standards for recruiting and evaluating teachers; eliminate the 22,000 "commissioned teachers" who hold government posts (at a cost of 3,149 million pesos in 2010)**	SEP	Emilio Chuayffet Chemor	Not Available

(continued)

Table 7.1 (continued)

Program	Purpose	Responsible Agency/Agencies	Agency Head	Estimated Budget
National Program of Social Prevention of Violence and Crime	Create jobs for teenagers; recapture public places; diminish intrafamily violence; create recreational opportunities; focus on the 110 high-risk municipalities	SEGOB, SHCP, SEDESOL, SEP, SSA	Subsecretary of Gobernación Roberto Campa Cifrián	2.3 billion pesos

*Each older adult without social security will receive 525 pesos per month.

**Existing SEDESOL-sponsored programs such as Opportunities (Oportunidades/36,177 billion pesos); Food Assistance (Apoyo Alimentario/ 4,224 million pesos); Rural Sustenance (Abasto Rural/1,858 million pesos); and Social Provision of Milk (Abasto Social de Leche/1,086 million pesos) will continue to be funded. See Claudia Salazar, "Replica Sedesol los subsidios," *Reforma*, February 17, 2013.

**Sonia Del Valle, "Meten ampara contra pago a comisionados," *Reforma*, February 12, 2013.

***Itzaro Artela, "Anuncian visita de Lula por cruzada," *Reforma*, April 2, 2013.

commissioners will be pressured by politicians hunting lucrative contracts for themselves and cronies. Peña Nieto also anticipates the creation of a Telecommunications Ministry; politicians will scramble to fill executive posts within what will be an organization of great importance to multiple firms that are trying to gain greater access to the market.

In the same vein, Peña Nieto and his stalwarts are attempting to reconfigure the nine-member Federal Electoral Institute (IFE), which is supposedly made up of respected, impartial citizens who act autonomously. However, opposition parties charged that PRI and its electoral running-mate, the shady Mexican Green Ecological Party (PVEM), had triangulated with the MONEX financial giant to issue 7,851 electronic debit cards to woo voters. Because of a conflict of interest, former PRI cabinet member and IFE counselor Sergio García Ramírez pledged to abstain on whether to fine the revolutionary party just over 3 million pesos for this transgression. His failure to vote precipitated a 4 to 4 tie; in a second round on January 23, 2013, he cast his ballot in favor of exonerating the PRI and PVEM, and amid a furor, stepped down from his position. This resignation and rotation of counselors from the once-venerated body opens positions on IFE to be filled in 2013. To avoid future cliff-hangers, the PRI is wheeling and dealing to insert several partisans on the powerful electoral council.[10]

Also under an intense fusillade is the dynamic Federal Institute for Access to Information (IFAI), which enforces the country's freedom-of-information act enacted under the Fox administration. Sigrid Arzt and others among the five commissioners have poked and prodded sacred cows. Among other things, they have demanded that the Defense Ministry disclose security accords with the United States, that the navy make known the terms of its contracts for Blackhawk helicopters and other weapons, and that the ministry of Gobernación reveal its earthquake reaction plans. In addition, they have importuned the Attorney General's Office to indicate the 37 "most wanted" criminals, the National Banking and Stock Commission (CNVB) to provide data on money laundering cases, and the National Forestry Commission (CONAFOR) to pinpoint where the most deforestation occurred between 2007 and late 2012.[11] Of course, governors have co-opted most of the state IFAIs, one of the subjects in Chapter 8.

Meanwhile, IFAI discovered that the politically sensitive Federal Competition Commission (CFC) failed to collect some 865.9 million pesos in fines from entities that flouted the nation's antitrust law between 2007 and 2013. Among those giant firms that had used legal artifices to block payments were TELCEL, TELMEX, Eli Lilly laboratories, TELEVISA, and Cementos de México (CEMEX).[12] The last multinational corporation invariably ranks first or second in cement output, even as it sets overly high prices in Mexico.

Civil society has challenged politicians endeavoring to defang IFAI and other agencies mandated to shed sunlight on the expenditure of public monies. Seventy-eight NGOs have formed an Accountability Network (RRC), which is coordinated by Professor Mauricio Merino Huerta and sponsored by the Center of Research and Economic Teaching (CIDE), a world-renowned university in the Federal District. Constituted mainly of young people, the RRC has generated tens of thousands of tweets on behalf of open institutions, with their initial focus on the Senate because it has far fewer members (128) than the chamber of deputies (500).

Meanwhile, Murillo Karam has also diminished openness. In late March 2013, without previous notice, he abolished the Citizens' Participation Council (CPC). This body enabled civil society to have a behind-the-scenes peek at one of the nation's most obscure institutions. The CPC sprang to life in late February 2011 to promote the "efficient, transparent, and effective use of public resources, enhance budgetary discipline in expenditures, and impel a [professional] Federal Public Administration."[13]

A change in the amparo law (a blend of injunction and habeas corpus) also gives the government leverage over certain special interests, including radio and television stations. In the past an individual could obtain an amparo against the government that blocked, say, a construction project that he was undertaking. The judicial action would be "suspended" while the petitioner sought to have the amparo reversed, most likely by a superior court. Once applicable only to government agencies, the new legislation pertains to telecommunications, financial entities, mineral concessions, and national waters. The issuance of an amparo prevents enjoining of an official act while the petitioner appeals his case.[14]

3. WITHERING CRITICISM

The episode with "La Maestra" provided ammunition for Calderón's critics, who alleged that the former president should have discovered the blatant laundering of SNTE monies. PAN senator Ernesto Cordero Arroyo, the ex-president's chief contact among Mexican politicians, told questioners that as finance minister from 2009 to 2011, he knew nothing about "anomalous" transactions accomplished by Gordillo and her union.[15]

As early as mid-December 2012, Osorio Chong attended a session of the National Public Security Council (CNSP). At this gathering, he lambasted Calderón's kingpin approach, saying that it "provoked a fragmentation process of groups with different goals: we passed from a period of vertical to horizontal leadership, giving rise to much more violence and danger." In addition, the official declared that the capture of dozens of capos, which Calderón trumpeted as a success, boomeranged and "the rate of increase in homicides places us among the highest in world ... In recent years, because of the violence linked to organized crime, thousands of people have died and thousands of people have disappeared." Public-opinion polls indicated that one of every three households in the country had been affected by violence or criminal activity.[16]

Attorney General Murillo Karam claimed that some 70,000 people had died and 9,000 were missing during the last sexenio—a figure substantially higher than the 47,268 victims reported by *Reforma*[17] and the 26,121 disseminated by Gobernación (SEGOB). Although not providing evidence, the nation's top prosecutor asserted that large, medium, and small cartels had exploded to between 60 and 80 in recent years. The PRI contended that the mushrooming of organized crime occurred in "a truly impressive [manner] and in large part, the responsibility ... [lay] with the previous regime."[18]

Critics have also blistered Calderón's hard-charging secretary of public security Genaro García Luna, a no-nonsense engineer who worked closely and effectively with his U.S. interlocutors, for questionable spending on his watch. Since June 2012 the Fraud Section of the U.S. Justice Department's Criminal Division has allegedly been investigating possible graft and money laundering related to at least 17 businesses that, *inter alia*, sold patrol vehicles and safety equipment to the ministry of Public Security or SSP, the now-disbanded agency that García Luna headed. Whether this is a witch hunt or a valid accusation remains to be seen.[19] Appendix K describes the law-enforcement agencies that existed when Peña Nieto took office.

4. PACT FOR MEXICO

Traditionally, PRI regimes have governed alone, occasionally reaching out to small, client parties for the critical mass of votes required to pass a bill. As discussed in this book's introduction, a major exception took place under Carlos Salinas when he entered into *concertacesiónes* (understandings) with the PAN in the late 1980s and early 1990s. Similarly, in the vaunted Pact for Mexico, Peña Nieto persuaded the leaders of the three major parties to agree to 95 compromises in five policy areas to promote the country's growth and prosperity.

Then-PRI secretary general Díaz Salazar, now a senator, eagerly signed the document that advanced her chief executive's agenda. For his part, Jesús Zambrano Grijalva saw the Pact as a means to change the image of his Democratic Revolutionary Party (PRD) from a collection of warring, rabble-rousing tribes to a responsible, center-left organization that could accentuate the positive rather than continually opposing modernizing proposals. He especially wanted to distance the PRD as far as possible from López Obrador, who is lofting the banner of his own National Regeneration Movement (Morena), a hodge-podge of embittered radicals, corrupt union bosses, university dissidents, debtors' groups, CNTE flame-throwers, and other firebrands. True to form, leftist militants have railed against measures to open to private capital the oil industry, which Lázaro Cárdenas placed in state hands 75 years earlier. They also bemoan increasing the value-added tax and modifying the penal code, which, they assert, could eliminate "human rights and liberties secured in the DF."[20] Morena's messianic chieftain has continually castigated as "traitors" responsible leftists who support elements of Peña Nieto's agenda. In contrast, Osorio Chong said upon affixing his name to the document in the Chapultepec Palace, "The parties demonstrated that democracy not only implies popular representation. Today, we demonstrated with action that democracy entails accords, permanent negotiations, and responsible and respectful collaboration."[21]

The PAN's Gustavo Madero Muñoz sought to bring cohesion in a party that emerged from the presidential contest hemorrhaging members, abounding in programmatic differences, and reeling from acrimonious personal conflicts. To promote his goal, he bit his lip while Peña Nieto's loyalists excoriated the crime fighting efforts of Calderón and his entourage. "Citizens regard the manifesto as positive. Why do I say this? Because it is against monopolies, corruption, and privileges."[22] The narrow victory of the candidate jointly backed by the National Action Party and the Democratic Revolutionary Party in the mid-year 2013 gubernatorial contest in Baja California persuaded Madero and Zambrano to stick with the Pact. Nevertheless, they decried blatant fraud practiced by the PRI in Baja California and 13 other states where voters also went to the polls on July 7. The opposition party presidents demanded cleaning up the political process. Several currents within the PRD insisted that in light of PRI skullduggery their party abandon the accord. Especially vocal was ex-DF mayor Marcelo Ebrard Casaubón, an erstwhile PRI member who was angling to replace Zambrano as PRD's president as a stepping stone for a presidential bid in 2018.[23]

While detractors pilloried Calderón for his dogged commitment to the kingpin strategy, Peña Nieto proposed a "Sky's the Limit" approach. The Pact may turn out to be either a careful holistic policy or a short-lived hodge-podge of uncoordinated objectives designed to divert public attention from the carnage afflicting the nation and loft the PRI's standing.

ORGANIZATION

In theory, the Organizing Council for the Pacto por México (CRPM) sets the agenda, establishes the rules for negotiations, fixes objectives, and determines the working groups. This pro forma body is composed of three representatives of the executive branch, and three members from the major political parties. To no one's surprise, Peña Nieto named *Priístas*

Osorio Chong, SEGOB undersecretary Felipe Solís Acero, and Attorney General José Murat Casab to represent the presidency—with Osorio Chong functioning as executive director; the PAN's members are party president Gustavo Madero, Santiago Creel Miranda, and Juan Molinar Horcasitas; and the PRD's participants are party chief Zambrano, Jesús Ortega Martínez, and Carlos Navarrete Prida. Appendix L presents the full composition of the council.

With a rosary of social and political reforms, Peña Nieto and his inner circle have sought to divert attention from the bloodbath afflicting their country. Unlike Calderón, who continually talked about the drug war, the current president acts as if there were no narco-violence. During the first nine months of his administration, his speeches emphasized universal health care, public works, youth opportunities, housing construction, transparency, entrepreneurship, international relations, the probity of public servants, economic development, and above all, the "Crusade against Hunger," which is analyzed later in this chapter.

Even as Peña Nieto and his image-makers endeavored to change the national dialogue, the president fortified SEGOB, which became a shadow of its former self under the PAN. Osorio Chong holds the reins. Yet, the ministry's number two is Luis Miranda, who has the right of *picaporte* (direct access) to Los Pinos because of his role of troubleshooter for the president when he served as governor of Mexico State. Veteran politician Roberto Campa Cifrián serves as the newly created subsecretary for Social Prevention of Violence and Crime. In this position, he controls funds for projects with municipalities.

Solís Acero, an ally of über-politician and congressional leader Manlio Fabio Beltrones, is subsecretary for Political Accords. CISEN is once again under SEGOB's umbrella with Hidalgo native Eugenio Ímaz Gispert, a friend of Osorio Chong and Murillo Karam, heading the intelligence agency.

Lía Limón García, an ex-*panista* who backed Peña Nieto's campaign, functions as subsecretary for Judicial Affairs and Human Rights; David Garay Maldonado, former DF police chief, heads the Unidad de Gobierno; Paloma Guillén Vicente, sister of the EZLN's Comandante Marcos, occupies the post of subsecretary for Media Norms; and Eduardo Sánchez Hernández, former director of Grupo MVS media company, acts as the SEGOB's spokesperson. In addition, Gobernación will assume the daunting responsibility for operating the nation's nine maximum-security prisons, which are convulsed by intra-institutional violence, bribery, and escapes.

In addition to increasing from five to six the number of subsecretaries, Peña Nieto has also almost doubled (from 28 to 55) the number of administrative units in Gobernación, with more personnel devoted to political accords, human rights, risk management, and administrative efficiency. "The new structure will help achieve a decrease in violence, prevention and deterrence of crime, advancing the goal of a secure State," said a Gobernación spokesperson.[24]

SEGOB's overall functions include:

A. **Planning:** Reduce violence, restore peace and tranquility—with the focus on murders, kidnappings, and extortion—and pledge to make public the results in each area.

B. **Prevention:** Combat addiction, rescue public places from crooks, increase the number of full-time schools, impel productive projects. The 2013 budget is 115.625 million pesos; and the goal is to create an Inter-Ministerial Commission for Crime Prevention to coordinate activities and avoid duplication in this field.

C. **Human rights:** Establish a federal agency to reform human rights; instruct law-enforcement agencies in human rights; provide assistance to victims of abuse; restructure the National Migration Institute (IMN); employ genetic material and other databases to locate missing persons.

D. **Coordination:** Apportion the country into five regions to combat crime; the exchange of information available through the Mexican Platform, which has a database of criminal activities that is available to proper authorities throughout the country.

E. **Institutional transformation:** Assume responsibility for public safety, including the reorganization of the federal police and the possible creation of a new civilian law-enforcement agency.

F. **Evaluation:** Continuously assess programs using clear, credible, and transparent indicators.

GENDARMERÍA NACIONAL AND FEDERAL POLICE

On December 17, 2012, Peña Nieto announced his intention to create a Gendarmería Nacional (GN) modeled on Chile's quasi-military Carabineri,[25] Spain's Guardia Civil, and France's Gendarmerie Nacional. He emphasized: "This corps would form part of a territorial control body that allows the exercise of the sovereignty of the Mexican State [Government] in corners of the country, regardless of their distance, isolation or weak state."[26] At least 400 of the nation's 2,457 municipalities lack police forces. Appendix M indicates the major law-enforcement agencies in place or proposed at the outset of the Peña Nieto administration.

The chief executive, who, with his PRI brethren and the army, thought that Calderón was far too close to the United States, met with French interior minister Jean Marc Ayrault about the project. The government earmarked 117.4 million pesos for getting the agency off the ground, with a proposal to have 10,000 cadres from the armed forces (8,500) and navy (1,500). These numbers were slated to climb to 40,000 by 2015 when the unit was fully operative. Although military police would have done much of the initial training, the government intended to exclude current

Table 7.2

States in Zones of Responsibility for the Proposed Gendarmería Nacional

Zone	States
Northwest	Baja California, Baja California Sur, Chihuahua, Sinaloa, Sonora
Northeast	Coahuila, Durango, Nuevo León, San Luis Potosí, Tamaulipas
West	Aguascalientes, Colima, Guanajuato, Jalisco, Michoacán, Nayarit, Querétaro, Zacatecas
Center	DF, Mexico State, Guerrero, Hidalgo, Morelos, Puebla, Tlaxcala
Southeast	Campeche, Chiapas, Oaxaca, Quintana Roo, Tabasco, Veracruz, Yucatán

Source: Benito Jiménez, "Definen zonas regionales de coordinación," *Reforma,* January 10, 2013.

law-enforcement officers in light of deeply embedded corruption. Rather than attempt root-and-branch changes in the Federal Police (PF), the aim was to attract talented civilians in whom it could inculcate the practices, ideals, and values of the GN. As depicted in Table 7.2, this force would have been assigned to five zones where its members would work in concert with local law enforcement agencies, elected officials, and military personnel. The object was to respond rapidly and efficiently to prevent and combat high-impact crimes like robbery, murder, extortion, rape, and kidnapping, which engender nightmares for many Mexicans.

As the force expanded, members of the armed forces would have returned to their barracks or headquarters. The Gendarmería was slated to assume some functions of the scandal-torn Federal Ministerial Police (PMF), a dependency of the PGR, which would retain responsibility for investigating criminal cases, guarding and transferring prisoners, and undertaking arrests as directed by the attorney general's office.[27]

The commissioner of national security (CNS) and head of the PF, Manuel Mondragón y Kalb, was third in SEGOB's pecking order after Osorio Chong and Miranda Nava. Along with academic advisers, Mondragón y Kalb and David Javier Baeza Tello, the CNS coordinator with the PF, backed the idea of the Gendarmería Nacional. A physician as well as a karate and fitness devotee, the dome-headed retired admiral is praised not only for his physical prowess, but also for his effectiveness during four decades in public service. Amid an epidemic of killings, kidnappings, and extortions, in mid-2008 Mayor Marcelo Ebrard, with the required approval of Calderón and the Senate, elevated Mondragón from health secretary to secretary of public safety.

Under his leadership, local officials lauded plummeting crime rates, which enabled the PRD to pile up a landslide in the capital's 2012 mayoral race. However, Mondragón y Kalb had two advantages: (1) Mexico City has the nation's largest police force and (2) the cartels, with which the new security secretary had no experience, carry out relatively few operations in Mexico City, where the families of many capos live. To his credit, Mondragón was not cited in the notorious sub rosa activities consummated by the DF police bureaucracy for purchasing uniforms, vehicles, communications devices, and armaments. Indeed, he boasts broad support, as indicated by the promise by López Obrador, Peña Nieto's main rival for the presidency, to name the retired admiral secretary of public security.[28]

The octogenarian's responsibilities include national security, criminal policy, commanding the federal police, and serving as president of the National Conference of Public Security Secretaries. His office assists state and municipal authorities, the PGR, and the judiciary with respect to penal institutions, crime prevention, intelligence, and other tasks previously performed by the Ministry of Public Security, abolished by Peña Nieto, over its dozen years of existence. Mondragón may perform better in martial arts than in personnel selection. Alberto Amador Leal resigned soon after accepting the post of PF intelligence director. The former CISEN director and longtime PRI activist explained that his action was due to "the disorder and lack of leadership that exists within this agency."[29] Several other directors also left the post before the controversial Ramón Eduardo Pequeño, a veteran security official, assumed the intelligence position. The fact that PF chief Enrique Galindo Ceballos failed one polygraph test before passing another while working in law enforcement in San Luis Potosí has presented Mondragón with yet another headache.[30]

Much to Mondragón's dismay, the acclaimed Gendarmería Nacional turned out to be more of a campaign ploy than a serious initiative. The army and navy demanded a one-for-one replacement of their personnel entering the proposed outfit. Finance Secretary Luis Videgaray may have axed the project because of the cost required to double the number of cadres fighting cartels, gangs, and common criminals. Security maven Alejandro Hope, who heads the Mexican Institute for Competition (IMC), proved an effective and outspoken critic of the project. "There are doubts over what the Gendarmería is going to be, what will be its functions, and how will it relate to existing institutions?" he queried. Amid a firestorm of criticism from NGOs, the GN disappeared from the government's National Development Plan (2013–2018), known as the PND,[31] although the name may be applied to yet a new, smaller force to save face.

FEDERAL POLICE

In an early 2013 visit to the Command Center of the Federal Police, Mondragón took special interest in the agency's capabilities in intelligence, technological development, training, and vehicles and aircraft.

He stressed the important of "zero tolerance" for corruption, strict discipline, and instruction in intelligence, tactics, technology, human rights, and proper legal procedures. He looked closely at the Special Operations Group, which has expertise in explosives and the handling of kidnapping cases. He also praised the Social Assistance and Rescue Unit for its protection of civilians and its response to natural disasters. Before leaving, he admonished his audience: "The Federal Police must occupy the class, the level, and the position that Gobernación, our institutions, and the citizenry demands."[32] In late March 2013 Mondragón added 26 women and 176 men to the PF. [33] In the same month the federal police announced the installation of equipment with gamma and X-rays to inspect the interior of vehicles entering Mexico City via the Toluca–Mesón Viejo highway.[34]

The peripatetic Mondragón also introduced a hotline staffed by specialists in helping victims, managing stress, providing psychological advice, providing legal services, calling attention to demonstrations, and responding to emergencies. At times the call center can dispatch police to catch individuals in the act of committing crimes or at least render rapid attention to victims. Citizens could contact this Center of Attention of the Commissioner (CEAC) by Twitter, Facebook, email, and telephone 24 hours a day, 365 days a year. The center is modeled on a similar program that Mondragón introduced in Mexico City where callers could report anything from potholes to extortions.[35]

The PRI grew out of the army, with which it has a stronger rapport than it does with the navy. Even as he explored the GN, the president promised to increase compensation, improve medical services, enhance professionalization, and modernize the infrastructure of the army. "Your institutional loyalty demonstrates you are a force for the country's stability and democratic development," he said at a speech attended by the entire cabinet to celebrate the army's 100th anniversary. The centennial gave rise to a massive display of weapons in the Zócalo, an homage to the military in Congress, the issuance of a commemorative coin, and a plethora of activities in the states.[36] The chief executive also inaugurated a station called México Nueva Generación whose mission is to identify farming areas that reinforce the National Crusade against Hunger, a project discussed later in this chapter.

The army also received accolades for cooperating with the Mexico State Attorney General's Office to capture Martín Zacarías Pedro, the number three leader of La Familia Michoacán—a takedown that occurred in mid-February 2013 in Toluca.[37] For his part, Defense Minister Salvador Cienfuegos Zepeda praised the Pact as advancing "dissent and consensus with respect to ideological pluralism, the dilemmas of public administration, and legislative representation."[38]

What is the fate of the Mérida Initiative, a program identified with Calderón, who is persona non grata with the PRI? Campa insists that

Mérida Initiative funding will focus more on social programs and preven-tion. The lion's share of the $1.90 billion allocated through 2012 centered on intelligence, transportation, and police training.[39] How the initiative will mesh with Peña Nieto's security objectives remains to be seen. What effect will attenuating the Gendarmería have on U.S.-Mexican relations? During Calderón's tenure, Mexican military, intelligence, and law-enforcement personnel toured the Special Operations Command base at Fort Bragg, North Carolina, to observe how U.S. officers coordinate spe-cial air and naval missions. "U.S. officials stress that sharing this expertise does not mean U.S. special operations teams will be conducting raids against targets in Mexico, nor will they be entering the country with their own weapons," a former military officer said off the record.[40] Peña Nieto's reluctance to be overly identified with the U.S. military may end such conspicuous cooperation.

However, in mid-2013 the U.S. Congress had not approved the $234 mil-lion that President Obama requested for the Mérida program. Mexico's ambassador Eduardo Medina Mora pointed out that there would be more continuity than change in bilateral security relations, while placing more emphasis on economic matters—with a view to converting both countries into "the most competitive and dynamic in the world."[41] Their hesitancy will increase with the Mexican judiciary's handing drug czar Rafael Caro Quintero a "get out of jail free" card, an incident examined in Chapter 8. Meanwhile, officials of the U.S. Agency for International Development have been instructed to slow implementation of their programs.

The question of abuses continues to haunt Mexican security forces. Human Rights Watch has charged that upwards of 25,000 civilians have disappeared in the nation's shadowy drug fight. Researchers for U.S. NGOs probing the whereabouts of 249 missing people found credible evi-dence that the armed forces or police have participated in 149 of the disap-pearances. The victims included husbands and fathers who left home for groceries and never came back, and others dragged from their homes by uniformed men in the middle of the night. Many were seen being stuffed into military trucks and police vans. Since 2010 shopkeeper María Orozco has tried to locate her son who was abducted, with five friends, from a nightclub in Iguala, a bone-dry municipality south of the DF. "We used to see the military like Superman or Batman or Robin. Super heroes," said Orozco. "Now the spirit of the whole country has turned against them."[42]

"More and more Mexican military and security forces are involved in human rights abuses, and we should not be funding that. We should be condemning that," said Representative Jim McGovern, co-chair of the human rights commission in the U.S. House of Representatives.[43]

Peña Nieto is seeking cooperation from countries other than the United States. As indicated, the French showed interest in assisting with the Gendarmería Nacional, which is now in limbo. Mexico's president visited

China and Japan not to explore security issues, but to strengthen trade, aid, and economic ties in hopes of spurring GNP growth to help combat the poverty that spawns criminal behavior. He also met with leaders of the Dominican Republic, Uruguay, and Central American nations to forge closer cooperation in fighting crime and grappling with migrant flows. "We require a regional perspective to overcome as fast as possible the social ills that beset our countries; therefore, we must enter into a strategic dialogue about the challenges that face us and, united in a common front, we must overcome them; we need a close dialogue and good neighborliness to achieve peace, strengthen productivity, and create the wealth attain the well-being of our population," the Mexican leader affirmed.[44]

The archives of Mexico's Foreign Affairs Ministry overflow with such noble-sounding boiler-plate pronouncements concerning cooperation with neighbors to the south. In the final analysis, however, it's Uncle Sam that will be called upon to provide assistance. If requested, the Operations Command of the U.S. Northern Command (USNORTHCOM) in Colorado will continue to instruct Mexico's special operations troops in counterinsurgency as an outgrowth of the Mérida Initiative examined in Chapter 5.

This training arises from a September 2012 agreement with the Calderón government signed by Admiral William H. Raven, commander of the U.S. Special Operations Command, and General Charles H. Jacoby Jr., USNORTHCOM Commander. The accord will draw upon the interagency network that targeted al-Qaeda's Osama bin Laden. Headed by a colonel, the missions could range between 30 and 50 cadres.

USNORTHCOM has already helped Mexican authorities establish their own intelligence center in Mexico City to concentrate on criminal organizations. The center is based on U.S. experiences in Afghanistan and Iraq. As one critic asserted: "The creation of the new command marks another expansion of Adm. Bill McRaven's special operations empire as he seeks to migrate special operators from their decade of service in war zones in Iraq and Afghanistan to new missions, even as the rest of the military fights postwar contraction and multibillion-dollar budget cuts."[45]

NATIONAL INTELLIGENCE CENTER

Mexico's National Intelligence Center (CNI)—sometimes compared with the CIA and other times with the U.S. Homeland Security Administration—will coordinate and analyze information from all government agencies with intelligence functions. Other capabilities include forensic expertise, computer competence, voice definition, DNA analysis, and access to radar and drones that can detect underworld activities.[46] Among the organizations providing data are the army, navy,

PGR, CISEN, other federal entities, and special state and municipal forces involved in the drug war. This material will enhance the efficiency of elements on the front line that are combatting drug cartels. As CNI recruits and trains more civilians, it will slowly demilitarize these technical functions. The dearth of talent requires reliance on consultants from the United States. Most of the Mexicans are between the ages of 28 and 35 "and don't have the first idea" about sophisticated intelligence operations. While citizens are not blasé about drug smuggling, opinion polls indicate that the top priority for Mexico is safety in their homes, sidewalks, schools, workplaces, and neighborhoods. As a result, Peña Nieto will place far less emphasis on hounding drug big shots and more on preventing murders, kidnappings, and extortions or, at least, spinning the media to laud his security record.

SOCIAL WELFARE, POLITICS, ENERGY, AND COMMUNICATIONS

During the first six months of 2013, the Pact focused on 20 legal changes. One of the most important goals involves converting PEMEX from a quasi-state agency to a "productive public corporation characterized by increased exploration and production . . . [and] impelling competition in refining, petrochemicals, and transport. . . ." In a transparent gambit to win support from the Oil Workers Union, PEMEX made a 10-year, interest-free 500 million peso loan to the STPRM. The justification for this generous transaction, which was signed under Calderón (on August 17, 2011) but endorsed by Peña Nieto (on January 12, 2012), was the imperative to construct housing for workers. As of mid-February 2013, the union had not undertaken new housing projects.[47]

In terms of fair play, the Pact, which is outlined in Table 7.3, also examines the legality of independent candidacies, citizens' initiatives, popular consultation on controversial measures, rules for coalition governments, beginning in 2024 holding the presidential inauguration in September rather than December, and reexamining the status of the Federal District, which many observers believe should become a state.

In the social domain Peña Nieto sketched a program to transform the lives of the nation's 7.5 million poorest citizens. His plan, which is redolent of Salinas's National Solidarity Program (PRONASOL), will concentrate on the 400 most impoverished of Mexico's 2,456 municipalities, embrace greater community action, accentuate local government initiative, and boost agricultural production. The Ministry of Social Development (SEDESOL) is at the forefront of this National Crusade against Hunger, designed to benefit the millions of Mexicans who go to bed hungry. The dynamic Rosario Robles Berlanga, a former PRD interim

Table 7.3

Significant Political Reforms Included in the Pact for Mexico

Program	Purpose	Responsible Agency/Agencies
Re-election	Study possibility of re-electing legislators	Congress
Reduce from 5 to 2 months the period between the presidential election and his or her inauguration	Administrative efficiency	Congress
Examining status of DF, as well as that of the mayor and city council (ALDF)	Determining whether it should become a state	Congress
Citizen initiatives and popular consultations	Give citizens a role in decision making	Congress
Independent candidates	Now banned	Congress
Create a national electoral institute	Replace the 33 IFEs with an agency that registers voters, oversees contests, and provides a preliminary vote count	
Grant the president the constitutional right to govern with a coalition	Enhance stability	Constitutional amendment
Campaign financing with sanctions	Reduce spending by parties via greater transparency with strict sanctions on entities that violate legal limits on media outlays and other vote-getting mechanisms	Congress
Eliminate the "Fuero" that protects from arrest officeholders accused of crimes	Prevent suspects from using political offices as shields	Constitutional amendment

mayor of Mexico City, heads SEDESOL. PAN and PRD legislators have urged the venture to steer clear of political goals. In theory, use of the initiative for electoral purposes will carry a prison sentence of up to nine years, and Secretary Luis Videgaray pledged that the Finance Ministry would keep a sharp eye on planning, execution, and accountability of the program.[48] As observed in the fraud-tarnished mid-July 2013 elections, the PRI and other parties seem to have a gene for vote-buying in their DNA. Furthermore, the head honcho at SEDESOL is Ernesto Nemer, who is skillful at earmarking social resources to garner votes. In addition to the crusade, SEDESOL purportedly will direct funds to the two-thirds of its current 35 programs that receive subsidies. Peña Nieto has also announced a new national housing scheme that aims to construct 500,000 comfortable two-bedroom homes available with furniture and at subsidized mortgage rates. Jorge Carlos Ramírez Marín, secretary for Rural, Urban, and Territorial Development Secretaria de Desarrollo Agrario, Territorial y Urbano (SEDATU) is responsible for implementing this ambitious initiative based on the premise that "a [dignified] house enables one to have a better home."[49]

The chief executive has also announced pensions for people 65 years of age and older—an extremely popular concept that López Obrador employed when he was Mexico City's mayor (2000–2005).

The Peña Nieto administration also envisages a National Program for the Social Prevention of Violence and Crime (PNPSVD). This multi-ministry venture will target the 110 municipalities with the highest levels of misconduct by those teenagers known as "ni nis" because they neither study nor work. In theory, several agencies—Gobernación, Finance, Education, Health, SEDESOL—will co-operate to diminish violence, unemployment, intrafamily conflicts, and gangs taking over public spaces.[50]

VICTIMS' RIGHTS

Even before the debate on the pact commenced, in January 2013 Peña Nieto promulgated the General Law for Victims, which aims to provide reparations as well as legal, medical, and economic aid to those who have suffered at the hands of criminals. The legislation anticipates creating an Integral Help, Assistance, and Repair Fund (FAAPI) to finance the program; however, as is the case with so many ballyhooed undertakings, the source and amount of funds available has yet to be announced.[51]

Furthermore, a new penal code will be proposed that will be complemented by a Code of Penal Procedures and a new statute covering amparos, a complicated, versatile, often abused Mexican version of the protective injunction.

The UN's High Commissioner for Human Rights, Rupert Colville, praised the law, saying, "Its promulgation is one of the principal commitments in human rights by President Peña Nieto." In contrast, businessman Alejandro Martí, who formed SOS after his son was abducted, tortured, and executed, indicated that he favored a General Law of

Victims, but not Peña Nieto's version, which, he said, would re-victimize participants because of "an interminable series of procedures" embedded in the legislation. He also cited the lack of financial, judicial, and institutional resources available to those who have suffered.[52]

During a February 2013 visit to Central America, Peña Nieto signaled the Costa Rican court system as a possible model for Mexico, but, as indicated in Chapter 8, more rhetoric than reality surrounds serious judicial reform.

SEGOB will also assume the daunting responsibility of operating the nation's nine maximum security prisons, which have suffered a plethora of intra-institutional violence and escapes. Meanwhile, Mayor Miguel Ángel Mancera has appointed María Mayela Almonte Solís, a veteran corrections administrator, to take charge of prisons in Mexico City. [53] In an effort to diminish reliance on the United States, Gobernación will receive a budget of more than 62 billion pesos, which exceeds the funds allocated to the armed forces.[54]

Although announced earlier, the ambitious and costly social programs fall under the rubric of the National Development Plan that Peña Nieto presented on May 20, 2013. The goals, which emerged from a survey of the priorities of 200,000 citizens, will be discussed in five national and 32 state forums, as well as conclaves for women, indigenous communities, people with disabilities, young people, and mayors. The original iteration of the documents keyed on an inclusive Mexico, quality education for all, prosperity, and his country as a responsible global actor. [55]

CHALLENGES FACING THE PACT

Laying the groundwork for a civil discussion of major issues has merit, particularly in light of the intolerance that typically prevails between and within political parties. The first question that arises is how the government will pay for such an expensive and ambitious agenda. Even if the funds materialize, what is the chance of compensating, say, prison guards enough so that they will not be co-opted by the inmates? In late 2013 there was turmoil in the valley—characterized by CNTE gansterism, record kidnapping, anti-oil reform demonstrations, and cartel violence. Moreover, bitter intraparty strife beset both the PAN and the PRD. The likelihood that either or both will change presidents in 2013 may bring to office individuals who do not share Madero's and Zambrano's commitment to the bold plan. After all, there are no penalties for failure to comply with the pact, which is a highly publicized "gentlemen's agreement." If the gentlemen change, the agreement may also.

On August 12, 2013, the president announced a timid energy reform that would compensate with cash, not oil, private companies that

Table 7.4

Pros and Cons of the Pact for Mexico

Pros

- The placement of the Gobernación Ministry in charge of the security elements of this initiative enhances accountability in a controversial arena.
- Finance Minister Luis Videgaray provides extremely competent financial management.
- By arresting Elba Esther Gordillo and opening the telecommunications sector to new players, the president made clear that he was prepared to take charge the national agenda.
- Attention to social-welfare issues, especially in high-risk municipalities, will address the security of a neglected segment of the population.
- Tolerance is the pivotal requirement of democracy, and the Pact presents an opportunity for all major parties to overcome traditional inter- and intramural clashes
- It is an important first step toward injecting private capital into PEMEX, although the "energy reform" speaks of continuing state control over hydrocarbons under PEMEX as a "public firm."

Cons

- The budget for the pact will place a severe burden on Mexico's economy, which grew only 1.2 percent during 2013, after a 3.9 percent GNP increase in 2012.
- Elections in 14 states in 2013 strained, but did not eliminate, working relationships among the major parties, but the acid test will come when petroleum and tax reforms are unveiled; for example, the PRD has indicated that a national referendum must precede any effort to change Article 27, which guarantees state control over hydrocarbons.
- Mexico lacks trained professionals to launch a modern intelligence agency.
- It will require astute lobbying to mobilize PRI's 213 deputies and 54 senators to back the initiative, along with their PVEM electoral allies' 28 deputies and seven senators. In October the government abandoned the unpopular recommendation to extend the value-added tax (IVA) to food and medicine.
- López Obrador, whose stock has plummeted, will seize on any artifice remotely resembling privatization of PEMEX to stage assertive possibly violent mobilizations nationwide and promote his image as the people's savior.
- In light of the PRI's pronounced nationalism, it is unclear how any new security force will mesh with the Mérida Initiative, a term that has disappeared from the vocabulary of PRI officials.

the nation's hydrocarbons.[56] The PRD's Zambrano has said there should be a referendum on any changes in the oil industry. Nonetheless, the PRI and the PAN command the necessary votes to amend the constitution to implement the controversial measure. The major foes are not the Mexican people, althought they reflectively respond "no" to pollsters' questions about tweaking Article 27 to admit private capital's entrée into the energy sector. The major opponents are (1) top PEMEX executives, who have profited hugely from sweetheart contracts signed with mega-firms in Mexico and the United States, (2) international powerhouses such as the ICA construction conglomerate, Grupo R headed by Ramiro Garza Cantú, and Halliburton that have made billions of dollars providing goods and services to the monopoly, (3) the Oil Workers Union, (4) López Obrador who hopes to attract the CNTE and other zealots to rallies and marches, and (5) Lázaro Cárdenas and his followers in the PRD and the Workers' Party.

CONCLUSION

During the presidential campaign, critics often accused Peña Nieto of being a lightweight. He may not be Mexico's version of Joe "The Black Bomber" Louis, but he has an invaluable trait that Calderón lacked; he knows what he doesn't know. As a result, he has assembled a team comprised of traditionalists, which is split between political heavyweights (Osorio, Miranda, Nemer, Murillo Karam, Beltrones Rivera, and Gamboa Patrón) and ambitious technocrats (Videgaray, Foreign Secretary José Antonio Meade, Central Bank governor Agustín Carstens, and Central Bank deputy governor Javier Guzmán Calafell.)

To increase chances for propelling his programs, he has often named loyalists as ministers or seconds in command in such key secretariats as Gobernación and SEDESOL. Furthermore, he has followed a Salinasesque formula by jailing "untouchables" such as Gordillo, forcing competition on Carlos Slim and other plutocrats, strengthening Gobernación, heaping praise on the army, and ingratiating himself with the Church and intellectuals. Yet, Peña Nieto's security strategy ignores the drug war as he makes speeches on more than a dozen other topics. The major exception was the dispatch of federal police and the military to address the turbulence in Michoacán.

In contrast to campaign promises, the president has reduced transparency, manipulated IFE, and created new institutions that will be vulnerable to clientelism and political intrusion. Despite a weak economy, he has announced expensive social programs, apparently designed to yield corporatist constituencies that helped the unreformed PRI remain in power for 71 years.

The term "Mérida Initiative" has vanished from the vocabulary of Peña Nieto's entourage. Like all modern Mexican presidents, he will attempt to diminish his nation's reliance on Uncle Sam, which will be difficult now that the GN is on life-support. Peña Nieto may be the victim of his own promises. Meanwhile, the dialogue over the national development plan allowed the regime to examine options in vital areas, even as his entourage held out hope that the oil legislation would power an economic recovery.

CHAPTER 8

The Rule of Law

INTRODUCTION

Aficionados of black humor claim that honest Mexican judges should not buy green bananas because cartels are quick to lash out on behalf of defendants whom they convict. In late 2001 three couples were chatting outside Federal Judge José Manuel de Alba's sand-colored bungalow in seaside Mazatlán, Sinaloa. They were preparing to watch the hometown Venados (Deers) play baseball that balmy Sunday afternoon. Suddenly a red Chevrolet screeched to a halt; a man stepped out shouldering an AK-47 and sprayed the fans with bullets. Alba managed to escape by dashing into the garden. The other judges and one of the wives died immediately. This dramatic escalation of bloodshed made the survivor rethink his profession. "Until now, I hadn't thought about the danger, but now I am afraid," de Alba said as his hands trembled. "I have to be like a bullfighter controlling my fears. I have to have the courage to overcome this and try to serve society. Because if we let violence, not laws, govern us, then my security doesn't mean a thing."[1]

Appellate Judge Jesús Guadalupe Luna and District Judge Efraín Cazares López showed caution in handling cartel-related cases. In April 2008 Luna ordered the release of Iván Archivaldo "El Chapito" Guzmán Salazar, El Chapo's son, whom a lower court had sentenced to five years in prison for money laundering. In mid-2012 Luna upheld a lower court verdict to clear Sandra "Queen of the Pacific" Ávila Beltrán of organized crime despite a 2004 U.S. indictment as a suspect linked to the seizure of more than 9 tons of U.S.-bound cocaine on Mexico's Pacific coast. American authorities had sought the extradition of Ávila, a niece of

El Chapo, but were twice denied this opportunity. Only on August 10, 2012, was she required to face criminal charges in the United States. In mid-2012 marines captured one of Guzmán Loera's nine children, Jesús "Alfredillo" Guzmán. Chapito, as the young man is known, remains free along with his brother Ovidio Limón Guzmán López. However, the U.S. Treasury Department has placed them on the Kingpin List, which, as mentioned earlier, bars U.S. persons and companies from conducting financial or commercial transactions with the culprits, and freezes their assets in areas that are within U.S. jurisdiction.[2] Judge Efraín Cazares allegedly ignored evidence and released 12 of 35 officials detained in a mass May 2009 arrest of mayors and other public figures believed to be linked to La Familia Michoacán.[3]

Judge Luna and District Judge Cazares López were temporarily suspended from their duties by the seven-member Federal Judicial Council (CFJ), which recommends, evaluates, and disciplines members of the judiciary.

In light of such abuses, no wonder that during her early 2011 visit Secretary of State Clinton underlined the imperative to introduce the rule of law in Mexico. "A well-equipped, well-trained judicial system is essential. We stand ready to assist in that work," she said.[4] Her audience welcomed this comment in hopes that it meant more funds from the Mérida Initiative could be devoted to changing civil society rather than military-related affairs. Revamping Mexico's court system and its judicial culture constitutes a Sisyphean task. As the President Herbert Hoover said about the prohibition of alcohol, it represented a "noble experiment."

The U.S. attorney's office in Arizona held instructional sessions for Mexican federal prosecutors, investigators, and forensic experts on how to handle evidence and conduct oral trials. They also led workshops on the prosecution of money launderers and drug and firearms traffickers. With respect to the $500,000 to $700,000 of Mérida Initiative monies that funded the Rule of Law unit, Andrew Selee of Washington's Woodrow Wilson Center stated: "You are not going to solve the problem of drug violence in Mexico until you have a legal system that makes it hard for them [the cartels] to operate."[5] As part of the Mérida Initiative, the U.S. State Department earmarked approximately $2 million for Mexican law students to hone their skills through national oral moot trial competitions.[6]

This chapter (1) explores briefly Mexico's traditional judicial culture; (2) examines a sweeping judicial reform passed by Congress in 2008; (3) discusses the obstacles that it faces; (4) analyzes vigilante eruptions, including one that occurred in the Mexico City's Tláhuac neighborhood; (5) presents data on trends in *linchamientos* in Mexico; and (6) identifies an increasing number of groups that have organized to combat the drug cartels and other criminal organizations.

JUDICIAL CULTURE

Mexican courts frequently admit as credible evidence information derived as the result of electric shocks and other coercive interrogation techniques. "In America, prosecutors investigate, but the judge and jury decide the facts," said human rights lawyer Santiago Aguirre Espinoza. "Here, statements made to prosecutors are facts. There is no cross-examination or right to confront accusers. If a Mexican confesses to a prosecutor, that is considered sufficient evidence for a detention—so there is an inherent incentive to obtain confessions."[7] A rigorous survey found that 71 percent of convicted defendants never saw a judge before they were sentenced. About 47 percent of inmates in Mexico City's prisons are serving sentences for robbery involving sums of fewer than $20, law professor Ana Laura Magaloni said. "Those who fall into the system are often subject to arbitrary treatment."[8] Although half a dozen states have begun to implement judicial reform, Mexico's Congress has been stingy with funds for the ambitious initiative.

Some high-ranking jurists, tough military officers, business executives, moviemakers, foreign investors, and NGOs have decried the venality of the judicial system. In a presentation to the Mexican Senate, Jorge Mario Pardo Rebolledo, the newest member of Mexico's Supreme Court, recognized the discontent with imparting justice in México. ". . . [We] perceive that society is not satisfied with judicial decisions," he said in an understatement worthy of the *Guinness Book of Records*.[9]

Retired general Aponte Polito, alluded to in Chapter 6, who fought drug traffickers hammer-and-tongs in Baja California, publicly lambasted the local police, prosecutors, judges, and representatives of the attorney general's office, immigration agents, and customs officials for their ties to organized crime. "Corruption is the evil of all evils in our country . . . along with the lack of justice, impunity [for law breakers], irresponsibility, ineptitude, and demagogy," he told a reporter.[10]

In the same vein, entrepreneur Alejandro Martí, who agonized over the kidnapping, torture, and murder of his 14-year-old son in 2008, implored Mexico's chief justice to "impose exemplary punishments on corrupt judges and magistrates," adding that "an enormous lack of prestige characterizes our judicial authorities, our judges." Martí highlighted the infamous Guadalupe Luna, who released a former PGR official who had been sentenced to a 19-year term for kidnapping.[11]

Between 1995 and 2007 the Federal Judiciary Council (CJF) removed 22 judges and magistrates for irregularities; however, 41percent of these men and women were reinstated. The most notable case involved Guadalajara and the removal of magistrate Fernando Alonso López Murillo, who in 2002 was suspended for rendering decisions favorable to El Chapo and his allies El Güero Palma and Óscar Malherbe. Like Mexico's other 960 judges and magistrates, he had the right to challenge these sanctions. The Supreme Court reversed the CJF's decision, and López Murrillo not only returned to the bench, but sought 14 million pesos (well over $1 million) in compensation.[12]

In 2009, 2010, and 2011 the CJF penalized only 153 magistrates and judges—with the greatest number of actions affecting personnel in the DF, Mexico State, Quintana Roo, Guerrero, and Jalisco. The offenses included lack of professionalism, dishonesty, misappropriation of funds, sexual harassment, and abuse of power. Most offenders received private or public reprimands, suspensions, and fines. Only 30 were relieved of their duties.[13]

The Federal Judicial Council resembles an old boy's club—indeed, one insider called it a "mafia"—more than a group of distinguished professionals who swear to "guarantee the autonomy, independence and impartiality" of the judicial system. The appointment process politicizes the body. The chief justice presides over the CJF, which in itself constitutes a conflict of interest; the Supreme Court selects three other counselors from magistrates and district judges, the senate designates two, and the president names one. Except for the presiding officer, the other CJF members serve staggered five-year terms. Their salaries are among the highest for public officials and are well above that of President Peña Nieto. Including a plethora of benefits, the chief justice earns 5.9 million pesos, just under $48,000 per month, while the compensation for members who joined the council after 2011 is also 5.9 million pesos.[14]

Politicians and CJF counselors often directly or indirectly make contacts on behalf of litigants in cases in lower courts, whose judges are under the microscope of the judicial council. Legal clans linked and often beholden to senior judicial and political figures abound among Mexico's federal jurists, most of whom are men. As one humorist opined: "There is more incest in the Federal Judicial Council than there was in the Incan royal family."

Yet, conviction rates remain low. An analysis by the Monterrey Institute of Technology and Higher Education (ITESM) found that of the 7.48 million crimes committed in 2010, only 1 percent of offenders were convicted. The study indicated that citizens reported only 64,000 crimes, about 15 percent of which were investigated. However, the length of investigations has fallen from 269 days in 2006 to 130 days. In the same vein, CNDH president Raúl Plascencia Villanueva claimed that wrongdoers enjoy impunity in nearly 98 percent of the crimes carried out. Statistics for the past 10 years indicate, he said, that citizens report only 1.5 million of the 13 to 15 million offenses that take place annually. Of these reported infractions of the law, courts hand down just 150,000 sentences. These alarming statistics explain why residents increasingly take action on their own.[15]

However, Mexican politicians continually indulge in the assumption that passing a statute, enacting a constitutional amendment, or signing a treaty will cure an intractable problem, even though these formal actions represent no more than window dressing.

In early 2009 legal specialists, with the help of U.S. attorneys, attempted to iron out the provisions in the judicial reform, which will not be implemented, if at all, in the 31 states and Federal District before 2016. The momentum for change has slowed, and "we work with the same system that was used during the Spanish Inquisition," avers Alberto Barbaz Sacal, Mexico State's former attorney general.[16]

Two Good Samaritans hefting a video camera exposed Mexico's Byzantine criminal justice system. Roberto Hernández, a graduate student in public policy at the University of California and his wife Layda Negrete, a lawyer conversant in Mexico's dysfunctional legal system, made the award-winning documentary *Presumed Guilty*. The video portrayed how in 2005 police picked up 26-year-old street vendor Antonio Zúñiga, threw him behind bars, and slapped him with a murder charge. Even the absence of physical evidence and the presence of multiple witnesses who said the young man was elsewhere at the time of the crime did not deter the judge from sentencing him to 20 years in prison. Only a technical error—the defendant's first lawyer had a fake license—opened the way for a second trial and Zúñiga's gaining his freedom. Perhaps they will make a second film about the broken judicial system after an August 7, 2013, decision by a panel of judges to free drug racketeer Rafael Caro Quintero from prison, 12 years short of his 40-year sentence for

Table 8.1

Confidence in Judges and Magistrates

Date	Much or Some Confidence in Judges and Magistrates (%)	Little or no Confidence in Judges and Magistrates (%)	Change in Confidence (%)
July 2006	35	55	−20
May 2006	34	58	−24
June 2005	34	62	−28
May 2004	22	65	−43
August 2003	26	68	−42
May 2003	30	64	−34
June 2002	24	64	−40

Source: Parametría, "Encuesta Nacional en Vivienda,"http://www.parametria.com.mx/, 2006.

participating in the kidnapping, torture, and execution of DEA Agent Kiki Camarena, discussed in Chapter 1. The jurists justified their verdict on the grounds that the capo should have been tried originally in a state, not a federal, court—a rationale that ignited cries of corruption in both Mexico and the United States.[17] Table 8.1 indicates the public's confidence in judges and magistrates from 2002 to 2006, the only years for which data could be found.

ELEMENTS OF PROPOSED REFORM

In March 2008 Mexico's Congress approved a constitutional amendment to replace secretive proceedings and shadowy techniques with Anglo-U.S.-style adversarial proceedings. The changes include open trials, the admission of recorded phone calls into evidence if one of the participants agrees, presumption of innocence, the right of the defendant to face his or her accuser, and evidence-based proceedings—with a greater emphasis on forensics and meticulous fact-gathering. "In what experts say is nothing short of a revolution, Mexico is gradually abandoning its centuries-old Napoleonic structure of closed-door, written inquisitions—largely a legacy of Spanish colonial rule—that had long been criticized as rife with corruption, opaque decisions, abuse of defendants, and red tape that bogged down cases for years."[18] In most cases, money and influence trumped evidence, and prosecutors were allowed to hold organized crime suspects without charges for up to 80 days.[19] Professors Matt Ingram and David Shirk have provided an excellent summary of significant elements of the reform:

- Strengthening victim rights (reparation/restitution and restorative justice)
- Enhancing defendant rights, including the presumption of innocence
- Having access to a lawyer
- Employing efficiency measures, including prosecutorial discretion and alternative mechanisms of dispute resolution
- Ensuring Miranda rule protection against self-incrimination
- Implementing adversarial procedures based on oral hearings in all court procedures, including the public explanation of sentences
- Limiting pretrial detention except in the case of serious offenses, violent crimes, and the likelihood of prisoner flight; segregating defendants awaiting trial from the general prison population
- Appointing special judges for different phases of the proceedings (pretrial, sentencing, and sentencing implementation)
- Introducing plea bargaining
- Ensuring that one or more judges will be in the courtroom to hear the case[20]

The states have acted with glacial speed in implementing the reform. As a result, the Supreme Court's Chief Justice Juan N. Silva Meza has

Table 8.2

States and the Judicial Reform

States That Have Implemented the Reform	States That Have Partially Begun the Process	States That Have Yet to Act
Chihuahua, Mexico State, Morelos	Aguascalientes, Baja California, Chiapas, Pueblo	Aguascalientes, Baja California Sur, Campeche, Coahuila, Colima, DF, Guerrero, Jalisco, Michoacán, Nayarit, Sinaloa, Querétaro, Quintana Roo, San Luis Potosí, Sonora, Tabasco, Tamaulipas, Tlaxcala, Veracruz

Source: Instituto Mexicano de Doctrina Social Cristiana, "Plazos a la justicia en México: la reforma," Mexico City, May 18, 2012.

voiced concern about the situation. "We can't permit that the judicial reform remains anchored in idealism; we must think of the tangible, daily reality of our citizens . . . [o]ur commitment and efforts must be reinforced by the other Federal Branches and other levels of government."[21] Table 8.2 indicates the status of the states with respect to this penal initiative.

But these provisions do not become a reality until state and federal governments enact implementing legislation to craft rules and regulations for the new criminal justice system, primarily in the form of new codes of criminal procedure. The constitutional amendment also stipulates that state reforms must be implemented by June 17, 2016, which opened an eight-year window for implementation to take place.

PROSPECTS

Many judges, prosecutors, law professors, law students, clerks, and other relevant personnel are ambivalent about the changes. In 2011 the Trans-Border Institute surveyed by telephone 2,800 sitting judges, prosecutors, and public defenders in nine states. Of the 276 respondents, 47 percent said the proposed changes would not decrease criminality. However, the vast majority (70 percent) believed that oral trials would speed up criminal proceedings, and 84 percent said they would reduce corruption in the judicial sector. The response level was low (22.4 percent), and it would have been politically incorrect to oppose the changes, at least in a telephone conversation from an unknown interviewer.[22]

Clerks, rather than judges, often handle the paperwork in many criminal and civil cases. Judges who preside over a complex Anglo-U.S.-style proceeding may make or overlook errors that could reverse their decision, a possibility obviated when they act behind closed doors. In addition, they will probably have to work harder. Sad to say, but many corporate and labor interests enjoy the favor of their "own" judges (or judges they "own") and recoil at the prospect of a fair resolution of their disputes. In addition, judges and clerks who make the "right" decisions often receive bribes for their opinions. If they reject the payola, their lives—or those of their families—may be in jeopardy.

An optimist, Professor Ingram concluded that "In sum, 2012 offered some good news in terms of the approval of new laws relevant to criminal procedure reform. However, the real operation of these laws is still behind schedule, and 2012 continued to highlight some persistent weaknesses in both the implementation of the reform and in the ability ... to track this progress effectively ..." A key challenge continues to be the unavailability of systematic data on institutional changes; the paper by Ingram and colleagues that surveyed judges and lawyers highlighted this weakness, but their measures contribute to ameliorating this shortcoming.

Although it appears unlikely that all states will have adversarial proceedings by 2016, such an effort has obvious advantages, as pointed out by Ingram and Shirk. In addition, extremely well-paid jurists will have to appear physically in court and, presumably, disclose the rationale for their decisions. Law-enforcement officers will be queried on techniques used to obtain evidence and confessions. Crafty, well-connected lawyers who represent capos and other criminals will also have to show their faces in a public forum. Disputes should be resolved quicker, and so-called oral trials encourage parties to settle disputes privately subject to the approval of magistrates and judges.

Then there are pragmatic issues. Even if the new legislation is successful, are there enough judicial personnel to preside over oral trials? What is the source of funding for this new approach, particularly in light of the peril facing judges who convict dangerous felons? Can poorly paid public defenders go toe-to-toe with veteran barristers—a serious issue even in U.S. courts? How do the "uses and customs" practiced in hundreds of indigenous communities in Oaxaca and elsewhere jibe with the new system? While a start, the new proceedings cover only criminal cases, and by mid-2013 politicians had yet to approve a new penal code that would remove the mishmash of state laws and apply uniform definitions of crimes and national sentencing standards. The reform does not apply to administrative actions, labor disputes, and civil controversies. In the absence of a Mexican version of the American Bar Association, there is no professional body to monitor and assess the behavior of attorneys, many of whom have forged or bought licenses to practice law. The *Reforma* newspaper, the U.S. Agency for International Development, foreign investors, the redoubtable Monterey Group of industrialists, international organizations, and dozens of NGOs back the oral proceedings. Still, widespread opposition comes from many notables in the judicial establishment, some law school deans, lawyers who prefer to work in the shadows, capos who hold sway over judges, and politicians who take advantage of their influence over the Federal Judicial Council and, at times, even the Supreme Court. In the final analysis, the success of the innovation depends heavily on the magistrates and judges, who will still be chosen, supervised, and evaluated by the politically sensitive CFJ.

There is little consistency in implementing the reform in the several states that have taken the lead: Chihuahua, Oaxaca, and Nuevo León—with Chihuahua providing a laboratory. The most publicized case in that state took place in August 2008 and involved the late Rubí Marisol Frayre Escobedo, whose boyfriend admitted in open court that he had assassinated the 16-year-old and revealed where she was buried in Ciudad Juárez. The confession notwithstanding, the judges in Ciudad Juárez exonerated him for lack of probative evidence. The defendant's family sent death threats to Rubí's activist mother warning her not to pursue her campaign to reverse the decision. Her crusade ended when she was shot point blank while protesting in front of the Government Palace in Chihuahua city, the state capital.[23]

VIGILANTIISM

The fraud, cronyism, secrecy, and payoffs infusing the formal criminal justice system combined with police corruption have found citizens stepping into the legal void—sometimes acting as vigilantes. This term does not refer to white-hooded Ku Klux Klansmen clamoring after terrified, sweating African Americans to demonstrate their ugly sense of racial superiority.

Rather, the Spanish term *linchamiento* (lynching) describes situations when local residents spy a perceived wrongdoer committing a crime *"in flagrante."* Tolling church bells alert dozens, possibly hundreds, of citizens to the perceived danger of their neighbors. Although it has no law-enforcement authority, the assembled group seizes the suspect, beats and tortures him or her, and may even administer the coup de grâce by publicly burning, hanging, stoning, or mutilating their prey. The perpetrators, who are so numerous and/or so geographically isolated, realize that they can administer punishment with impunity—in many instances because the police steer clear of "rough justice," lest they become targets of the mob's fury.

In the 1976 film *Network*, the main character, a broadcaster who has had a nervous breakdown, urges his audience to throw open their windows and scream into the streets: "I'm mad as hell, and I'm not going to take this anymore!"—a plea that sparked a cacophony of protests from angry viewers from coast to coast. Many Mexicans share this sentiment. The pent-up frustration has incited some men and women to punish suspected offenders.

Their motivation to strike out at perceived delinquents is especially great in Oaxaca, Guerrero, Chiapas, Morelos, Michoacán and other poverty-stricken states with large vulnerable indigenous populations. They are reacting to the failure of states and municipalities to provide security in their homes, streets, schools, and workplaces. Suspected criminals who run afoul of these enraged citizens endure the brunt of a skewed version of grassroots justice.[24] Professor Rossana Reguillo Cruz, a militant who studies crime and violence at the Jesuit University of Guadalajara, echoed this conclusion, saying, "This is not something that has always been around in Mexico. It is a new phenomenon that has been growing since 2000."[25] Meanwhile, in late 2009 security specialist Sylvia Longmire argued that "Citizens are growing tired of drug-related violence, thievery, and other crimes—tired enough to take matters into their own hands."[26]

Although often poor, individuals in a throng may feel a sense of equality in carrying out their dark mission. This behavior, resembles Vigiles Urbani the night watchmen of Ancient Rome who fought fires and kept an eye out for thieves and runaway slaves. Seventeenth-century playwright Lope de Vega highlighted their exploits in his masterpiece *Fuenteovejuna*. The plot involves the royal commander, Fernán Gómez de Guzmán, who mistreated humble villagers of Fuenteovejuna. As a result, they joined together and killed their overlord. When King Ferdinand II of Aragon dispatched a magistrate to investigate, the townspeople—even when threatened with torture—responded in unison: "Fuenteovejuna did it." In other words, when everyone is responsible, no one is responsible in the anonymity of crowd action.

Such action signifies a distressing retreat from civility. The apprehended individual cannot defend himself; indeed, he may be innocent, having ventured into the wrong place at the wrong time. Even if he has engaged in criminality, the penalty meted out is often grossly disproportionate to the misdemeanor or felony. For instance, Mexican law does not permit capital punishment. In general, the targets are young males with some education, who are more likely to be seized in the evening, at night, or in early morning hours. Many linchamientos occur place around Christmas when people have *aguinaldos* (bonuses), free time, and may drink more than usual. Most of the cases take place in rural enclaves near Mexico City or other urban areas, and the local residents—men and women—frequently respond to the sound of church bells. Seldom do the perpetuators use firearms; they are more likely to pick up objects at hand—stones, bottles, and crude clubs.[28]

Citizens in the north have also spearheaded protests against foul play meted out by drug cartels, which often work hand-in-glove with local police. In the case of Ciudad Mier, Tamaulipas, residents abandoned their homes in search for safety, and in public opinion surveys, they have shown their disdain for politicians. All told, at least 120,000 people have fled the country—with the greatest exodus taking place in Chihuahua, Durango, Coahuila, and Veracruz.[27]

Mexico has achieved the dubious distinction of leading Latin America in the number of kidnappings—a crime second only to drug sales in generating income for criminal organizations. An astute analyst of Latin American affairs wrote: "No longer a cottage industry targeting the privileged few, today nearly everyone, rich to middle class to those of lesser means, faces the threat of kidnapping by organized gangs or the unorganized. Kidnapping for ransom is tailored to the victims, and if family or friends lag in paying even small amounts they may be sent crudely amputated body parts as a sign of worse to come."[28] Expert Barnard R. Thompson made this analysis in mid-2004.[29] Since then abductions have soared, possibly reaching 8,750 cases a month. Victims and their families report few of these crimes because of concern that the police may be accomplices.

THE CASE OF TLÁHUAC[30]

The most sensational case of informal justice in recent years took place on November 23, 2004. Inhabitants of San Juan Ixtayopan, a quaint community of 35,000 people tucked in the pine-covered hills in Tláhuac, erupted.[31] People in this borough on the DF's eastern fringe were enraged that only a dozen police officers—one for about every 3,000 men, women, and children—were assigned to preserve order in their largely rural community. They were particularly upset at criminals whom they believed to be stalking children, with a view to kidnapping and molesting them. One of three men in a grey sedan began filming the premises of the Popol Vuh primary school, where 380 youngsters were winding up classes. Fearing that the outsiders were predators, residents activated dozens of crude rooftop bullhorns that serve as alarm devices in some poor areas. Some 2,000 people quickly gathered, surrounded the unknown vehicle, overturned it, tied up and beat the occupants with metal pipes, splashed two men with gasoline, and set them on fire. A third man escaped and made it to the Central Military Hospital.

It turned out that the car's occupants, Víctor Mireles Barrera, Édgar Moreno Nolasco, and Cristóbal Bonilla Collín, were plainclothes detectives with the federal preventative police on the look-out for small-time drug dealers. Although they showed their credentials, two of the officers (Mireles and Moreno) were seized, tied up, and set afire. In a black comedy of errors, it took riot police three hours and 35 minutes to reach the horrifying scene, while television cameras and radio journalists were disseminating the incredible episode throughout the country.

Immediately upon witnessing the fracas on television, mayor López Obrador contacted Marcelo Ebrard, then the city's chief of public security and subsequent mayor (2006–2012). A man known for his rigid authoritarian personality, the ambitious Ebrard was ensconced in his hideaway office on Liverpool Street giving a television interview to reporters from *Proceso* magazine. He ordered his staff not to disturb him under any circumstances. As a result, his subordinates feared taking the initiative without a green light from their chief to the point of not even passing him a note.

Subsequently, President Fox fired Ebrard and his second in command for their dereliction.[32] Still, López Obrador, who opposed the chief executive on every front, trotted out excuse after excuse for failing to accomplish a rescue even as they deplored the chief executive's "premature" ousting of the security chief. Ebrard responded: "The president ... is afraid of what I could say about the happenings at Tláhuac and thus decided on my arbitrary dismissal."[33] Official justification for the tragedy included the terrain in Tláhuac was inhospitable for helicopters, people jammed the narrow streets where the violence took place, and cell phones weren't picking up signals in this remote area. Inside the halls of government, authorities claimed that guerrillas belonging to the People's Revolutionary Armed Forces (FARP) orchestrated the macabre episode.[34] At no point did senior decision makers point out that a contingent of DF preventative police was barely a kilometer away from ground zero, that the trucks carrying journalists had no trouble reaching the scene, and that even if helicopters couldn't have landed, their crews could have dispersed the rabble with water cannons, gunshots, and tear-gas canisters.

López Obrador did not want a blemish on his mayoral record, as he was preparing to run for president. He downplayed the affair and alluded to the inevitability of poor people from indigenous backgrounds resorting to traditional *usos y costumbres* of their native communities. In a message that seemed to invite vigilantism, the mayor stated: "It's better not to get involved in the traditions and beliefs of [indigenous] people."[35] In response to this advice, then-senator Diego Fernández de Cevallos, harrumphed: "There are still imbeciles in power that speak of usos y costumbres and that justify displays of mob violence ... arguing that mob violence is never wrong ... [Such statements are] disgusting."[36]

"Law enforcement is a joke," stated Daniel Flores, a 21-year-old engineering student who said he had stumbled into a major gang fight in his neighborhood a few months earlier but could not get the police to break it up.[37]

Meanwhile, at the request of electronic media journalists, the executioners shoved the bleeding, puffy-faced victims in front of TV cameras and radio microphones so that they could be interviewed. Videos of the crowd showed anger on the faces of some observers; others appeared serene, as if pent-up frustrations of daily lives—poverty, homelessness, disease, joblessness, divorce—were released through the blow-up. One expert spoke in terms of a catharsis of the "darker elements" of the viewers' beings.[38] "Onlookers cheered and shouted obscenities as the agents were splattered with blood." Other average people casually milled around the charred bodies left bleeding in the street.[39]

Normally the Tláhuac incident would have been dismissed by López Obrador as an example of the poor carrying out traditional justice. However, the involvement of federal police combined with media attention triggered an investigation of the episode. In mid-2009 nine suspects received lengthy sentences for the horrendous crime.[40] Additional individuals were subsequently convicted.

LITTLE RATS OF TEPIC

YouTube videos captured another especially grisly episode. These films featured five scruffy teenagers wearing blue jeans and tee-shirts who were slouched against a dark wall. Suddenly, a fist slammed into one boy's jaw. Next, the barrel of an automatic rifle pierced the frame, exciting unvarnished terror on the minors' faces.

"Why are you here?" demanded a sinister off-screen voice.

"For robbing," sobbed the baby-faced captive named Édgar Eduardo.

"You see. You were little rats and now look at you," snarled the questioner.

This episode took place in the fly-specked city of Tepic, capital of Nayarit state, 1,300 miles south of San Diego, in October 2009. The boys allegedly had robbed the luxury apartment of a shadowy figure. The dwelling's owner didn't bother to call the cops. Rather, he and his cronies collared the presumed thieves, took them to an abandoned house, shaved their heads, beat them with fists and gun butts, and forced them to French kiss each other.[41]

In the background the assailants are heard vowing to cut off their hands and sodomize the captives if they refused to engage in this humiliating gesture. To add to insult to injury, the adolescents were dumped jaybird naked on the street.

The event depicted in "Little Rats of Tepic," a video that was quickly withdrawn from circulation, excited mixed responses among *tepicanos*, especially because one of the boys claimed that they had been arrested by the state police and turned over to their four purported torturers, who were subsequently arrested.

Guillermo Huicot Rivas Álvarez, then-president of Nayarit's Human Rights Commission, deplored the act: "Opening the door to justice by your own hand is an enormous step back to a state of barbarism and lack

Table 8.3

Outcome of Linchamientos, 1988 through early 2005

Location	Subject Killed	Vigilante Acts Thwarted	Total
Mexico City	11	29	40
Mexico State	5	26	31
Morelos	14	13	27
Oaxaca	16	2	18
Guerrero	8	10	18
Chiapas	8	4	12
TOTAL	62	84	146

Source: Raúl Rodríguez Guillén, "Violencia y delincuencia: los linchamientos en México," in José Luis Cisneros and Everardo Carballo Cruz (eds.), *Pensar el futuro de México* (Mexico City: Universidad Autónoma Metropolitana, 2011), 181.

of culture," he asserted, adding, "In a democratic state crime can never be used to combat crime."[42]

Others disagreed. "In Mexico, we need death squads to hunt and exterminate rats and kidnappers without further expense to society and without . . . [do-gooders] getting in the way," wrote a contributor on the website of the Mexico City newspaper *El Universal*.[43] "I recognize that this is not the correct way to administer justice but I can't deny that it makes me happy that this type of thing happens," stated another reader.[44] As with a growing number of citizens, he blithely ignored Article 17 of the Mexican Constitution, which states that "No person can mete out justice on his own nor engage in violence to take the law in his own hands." Based on data compiled by Mexican scholars and presented in Table 8.3, just over 42 percent of vigilante acts analyzed between 1988 and 2005 ended in the deaths of the suspects.

ORGANIZED GROUPS

In the absence of trustworthy police and judges, more and more citizens have taken the law into their own hands. They have begun organizing "self-defense" groups to counter the violence waged against themselves, their families, their neighbors, and their municipalities. On December 3, 2008, six masked men stopped the car of Jorge and César Muñoz Reyes, who were carrying cattle from their ranch outside Parral, a small city in Chihuahua State where assassins killed Pancho Villa in 1923.[45]

The culprits ordered the men out of their vehicle, shot César, and kidnapped Jorge. Their father had to mortgage his property to pay a 5 million peso ransom ($385,000) to obtain Jorge's freedom. Five days later local cattlemen began to meet with other business community members to discuss creating a self-protection force. The leader of the group spoke cautiously about the "possibility" of such a vigilante movement.

More outspoken have been members of the self-styled Citizen Command for Juárez (CCJ). This group sprang to life in the violence-plagued Ciudad Juárez, which lies across the Rio Grande from El Paso, Texas. In an email to the media, this shadowy organization claimed to be funded by local entrepreneurs outraged by kidnappings, murders, and extortion in the sprawling metropolis of 1.4 million people. The CCJ may have killed and piled up the corpses of six men in their twenties and thirties in October 2008, leaving behind this sign: "Message for all the rats: This will continue." Early this year, a body was found in the city along with the warning: "This is for those who continue extorting."[46]

An article in *El Universal* indicated that on January 15, 2009, the CCJ sent a communication to the media warning that it would kill one criminal every 24 hours. "The time has come to put an end to this disorder . . . if criminals are identified, information can be sent electronically about the 'bad person' who deserves to die." It was signed, "El Coma."[47]

Reuters news service reported that another group—Businessmen United, The Death Squad—aired a video on YouTube threatening to hunt down mafiosi in Ciudad Juárez. At least two other vigilante-style bands have dispatched statements to the media: one in the northern state of Sonora, which borders Arizona, the other in the Pacific state of Guerrero, home to the resort city of Acapulco. A black-clad woman calling herself "Diana the Huntress" has purportedly begun slaying Ciudad Juárez bus drivers who rape women.

The execution of Benjamín Le Baron, an anticartel activist in Galeana, Chihuahua, induced his law-abiding Mormon community to consider forming its own self-defense contingent. In May 2009 hit men kidnapped Le Baron's brother, prompting the 2,000 local citizens to stage demonstrations in the state capital of Chihuahua. They refused to pay a $1 million ransom. Even after the youth was released, residents—many of whom are dual U.S. citizens—held protests to plead for police protection in the remote desert lands of Chihuahua state.

On July 7 gunmen broke into Le Baron's home and tortured him in front of his family before absconding with him and his brother-in-law, executing them, and dumping their corpses in the nearby countryside.[48] At first Chihuahua's PRI governor, José Reyes Baeza, agreed to provide training and weapons for a security squad in Galeana. This proposal met with criticism from the president of the National Human Rights Commission, who insisted that arming citizens would indicate a "failure" of the political regime.[49]

Taxi operators in Mexico City's Magdalena Contreras borough decided to take revenge for crimes against them. They suffered multiple assaults and robberies by thugs, who were believed to be protected by the police. When local authorities failed to nab the culprits after three complaints, the drivers acted. They seized the presumed leader of the assailants, "El Perro" ("The Dog"), and bludgeoned him to death. Their goals were to send a message to the gangsters, to obtain the names of other members of the criminal band, and to "accomplish justice" on their own. On August 14 Ismael Quintero Oliver and Marcos Érik Pérez Mora, leaders of the informal "pacto de los choferes" ("drivers' pact") were arrested with El Perro's cadaver in the backseat of their Ford Aerostar.[50] The case has yet to be resolved.

ADDRESSING ROUGH JUSTICE IN GUERRERO

"The dirty war never ended in Guerrero," declares Rosario Cabañas, the niece of guerrilla marauder Lucio Cabañas, whom the Mexican military killed in 1974. Forty years later, the state is plagued by corrupt political bosses, drug cartels, paramilitaries, self-defense organizations, community police, the army, and vigilantes. Approximately 10 to 15 of the state's 81 municipalities suffer anomic violence. Some of the proponents of rough justice in Guerrero appear in Appendix L.

Each of a dozen states has its own array of irregular militias. In addition to the band found in Guerrero, the presence of the flame-throwing members of Local 22 of the CNTE exacerbates the violence in Oaxaca, a state that also abounds in auto-defense groups. In 2009 these teachers staged a 48-hour strike during which they blocked roadways and occupied offices. In addition, many affiliates of the distraught and mercurial Popular Assembly of the Peoples of Oaxaca (APPO) have thrust themselves into the fray. As mentioned in chapter 7, the CNTE, which created APPO, laid siege to the DF in the last half of 2013 in a doomed effort to kill an educational reform. Some of these groups are of recent vintage; others have been around for decades and behave in accord with uses and customs in their indigenous municipalities. They may or may not be related to drug syndicates.

In fact, areas in which informal justice erupts are seldom those where the government is battling cartels. The very presence of mafiosi, federal police, and the armed forces militates against spontaneous acts against perceived criminals. On the other hand, cartel triggermen may ally with a local organization to protect their municipality. Most elected officials oppose informal law enforcement. Still, Fredy Gil Pineda Gopar, the mayor of Santos Reyes Nopala, Oaxaca, dissolved the despised municipal police and entrusted their security mission to Social Communitarian Police. He decided to eliminate this force and reinstate the local police after the Oaxaca government promised to provide security and promote social programs in the Costa Chica municipality.[51] The government's reluctance to provide information about cartel killings may lead the press to focus more on irregular law enforcement, which flourishes when impoverished rural people feel insecure.

CONCLUSION

In the opinion of the late *New York Times* Pulitzer winner Antony Lewis: "No matter how mistaken or craven" a court might be, the judiciary provides the "ultimate safeguard of our democracy."[52]

The implementation of oral trials in Mexico has ruffled the feathers of groups who have a vested interest in the status quo. Only a latter-day Dr. Pangloss would believe they will be in place in all jurisdictions by 2016. Rather than enacting a homogenous structure, the performing states have created a farrago of procedures—an invitation for attorneys and prosecutors to engage in "forum shopping."

Only when Mexico—with assistance from other nations—establishes competent, modern, uncorrupt police, prosecutors, courts, and penal institutions will Mexicans of all classes have faith in the judiciary. Then, and only then, will the rural poor and indigenous communities diminish their reliance on rough justice. The turbulence plaguing the Costa Chica and other parts of southwest and western Mexico furnishes a compelling argument for revamping the country's criminal justice regimen to achieve uniformity, fairness, and equality. Regrettably, the crime rate has risen since Peña Nieto took office, and his campaign vow to halve the number of murders during his sexenio seems like a wil-o'-the-wisp.

CHAPTER 9

The Enablers

INTRODUCTION

Although not considered criminals, a number of "legitimate" groups derive benefits from assisting drug mafiosi. For example, some members of the Roman Catholic clergy accept alms, building materials, and sweat capital, from capos, many of whom are extremely religious. Then there are tens of thousands of entrepreneurs who cohabit with the under-world—selling SUVs and small aircraft, fortifying these vehicles, renting hotel suites, and providing investment advice on a cash basis. Many governors, mostly *priístas*, have cast their lots with organized crime. U.S. officials have also succumbed to bribery and threats.

ELITE ENABLERS OF DRUG TRAFFICKING: THE CHURCH

The Vatican and Mexico's Episcopal Conference (CEM), which includes some 100 bishops has continually deplored narco-commerce. A spokesman for Mexico City's Cardinal Norberto Rivera Carrera emphasized: "Our position is the Church's traditional one that categorically condemns drug trafficking as immoral. Their good intentions of change do not undo the damage they have done to thousands of people."[1] Outspoken men like Héctor González Martínez, Metropolitan Archbishop of Durango, and José Raúl Vera López, Bishop of Saltillo, Coahuila, have exhibited exceptional courage in the face of death threats because of vocal condemnation of El Chapo and his ilk. In 2010 Vera López told the *Los Angeles Times* that links to the cartels "make us accomplices after the fact. A steeple built with drug money has blood gushing from its rafters."[2]

For his part, Bishop Emilio Carlos Berlie Belaunzarán observed that the Church requires donations to finance its more than 200 projects, as well as

14 priests and seminarians studying in Rome. Nevertheless, he added, "We don't accept it [money from suspicious sources]. We are totally against drug trafficking. We cannot accept it; drugs mean the destruction of the human being. Their consumption destroys the human person."[3]

The Church has gone beyond pronouncements and publications in excoriating crime and those who foster it. In January 2013 Father Omar Sotelo Aguilar, under the auspices of the Catholic Multimedia Center, produced a dozen brief videos to combat "the decades-long threat of narco-trafficking that plagues the entire nation." Titled *Hermano Narco*, the film shows the evils of crime. The first installment depicts thugs who killed the parents but spared their children, including a 13-year-old daughter and her younger brother. The little girl Miri narrated the final segment of the production. Even though advised to seek revenge against the killers when she grew up, she remembered her mother's words that "we are all children of God" and embraced and pardoned the assassins.[4]

The bishop of the dioceses of Culiacán, Jonás Guerrero Corona, launched an evangelization program to persuade drug criminals to seek forgiveness for their sins and follow "the just road." He argued that if Judas could be converted, why not capos? "The Church must continue its work as instructed by Jesus, sowing the faith, sowing a new life, and making common cause the disinherited, the forgotten, and now those who lack security," Guerrero Corona added.[5]

Meanwhile, the bishop of the Diocese of Tehuantepec in southern Mexico removed the Reverend Alejandro Solalinde Guerra, who defied cartels and crooked police to protect Central American migrants in the Brothers of the Road migrant shelter in Oaxaca, near the Guatemalan border. Solalinde said that the bishop told him that his public complaints were garnering too much attention, that his life was in danger, and that he planned to assign him to parish duties. Such a reassignment, the crusading priest said, would "bury me in bureaucracy, administrative tasks, ceremonies, and take away my full-time dedication to the migrants."[6]

In early August 2010 President Calderón urged religious leaders to report to authorities the identity, location, and illegal activities of criminals. Some clerics complied. Other men of the cloth refused due to fear of reprisals, the secrecy of the confessional, or ties with the malefactors.[7] Los Zetas have even demanded, under threat of death, that priests from central Tamaulipas bless their trucks, arms, and equipment before they surge into battle, sometimes in the middle of the night.

JUSTIFICATION OF CHURCH'S NARCO INVOLVEMENT

In 1997 the canon of the Basilica of Guadalupe raised eyebrows in a homily in which he suggested that more Mexicans should follow the examples of kingpins Rafael Caro Quintero and Amado Carrillo Fuentes, who had made offerings of millions of pesos.[8] When politicians alleged that the cleric was putting his stamp of approval on illicit deeds, the Church's first response was that it was the responsibility of authorities, not churches, to investigate the origin of alms deposited in their coffers. Father Alberto Athié, executive secretary of the Social Pastoral Committee of the Episcopate, affirmed that the hierarchy does not accept beneficence from the "culture of death" and that the government was free to audit its accounts.[9]

Church-narco ties elicited attention in the 1990s when newspapers published photographs of the Lord of the Skies, Amado Carrillo, visiting the Holy Land in the company of Father Ernesto Álvarez Valenzuela of Culiacán and Father Benjamín Olivas. Álvarez Valenzuela explained his action as a token of appreciation for the drug baron's generosity to the Ciudad de los Niños (City of Children), an orphanage in the Sinaloa state capital.[10]

On February 4, 1997, Olivas officiated at a wedding for the Carrillo Fuentes clan in a village south of Guamuchilito, Sinaloa, where members of the family reside. Olivas again performed nuptials for the narco-family on November 24, 2001. Assisted by Father Epifanio Torres, he married Amado Carrillo Fuentes's son, Vicente Carrillo Leyva, to Celia Karina Quevedo Gastélum. The state's public security force was on hand—not to nab the dons, but to protect the newlyweds and their guests during the lavish ceremony in the Sagrado Corazón church. Following the nuptials, the couple and their families celebrated the event at Alameda Palace salon in nearby Navolato, a raucous party that lasted hours. Soldiers arrived during the festivities but made no effort to take into custody Amado Carrillo or his son.[11]

The nuptials had unintended consequences for the bridegroom. As indicated in Chapter 4, Vicente Carrillo Leyva changed his name, posed as a young businessman, and took up residence in an upscale Mexico City neighborhood. However, the failure of his wife to adopt a pseudonym enabled authorities to track down and capture her husband.[12]

The bishop of Aguascalientes, Ramón Godínez Flores, gained notoriety by conceiving a latter-day theory of alchemy, practiced in the Middle Ages; namely, that ill-gotten funds that benefit the Church's social mission are magically transmuted into legitimate resources.[13] He claimed: "Of course the cartels donate money," avowing that the priests have no control over who shares their largess and "don't investigate the origin of donations."[14] Indeed, the penal code does not list such financial gifts as money laundering, according to Kathya Martínez, an attorney in Ciudad Juárez. "Money laundering is doing legal business with illegal money, so unless authorities can prove that a priest conducted any type of business or lied to 'Hacienda' [the Finance Ministry] about the origin of the money you have no case."[15]

Carlos Aguiar Retes, bishop of Texcoco and then the president of the CEM, proposed that the government recruit as "counterspies" narco-traffickers who confess their sins, abandon wayward lives, and gather intelligence about DTOs. "They are very generous with the people in their communities, and in general they install electricity, telecommunications, highways, roads, paid for by them," Aguiar Retes affirmed. The narcos should be afforded a way of starting a new life through a witness protection program similar to one in Colombia, he added.[16] He also cited the example of Colombia, where guerrillas who had deserted the FARC assisted in the 2008 rescue of former presidential candidate Ingrid Betancourt.

Meanwhile, anticartel crusader, poet, and father of a slain son Javier Sicilia flew to the Vatican on the eve of Pope Benedict XVI's March 23, 2012, visit to Mexico. He and four other activists met with Italian bishop Mario Toso, secretary of the Pontifical Council for Justice and Peace, to present a letter to the Pontiff that described the situation at home. The text stated, in part, that "Mexico and Central America are a body, like the body of Christ that has borne all the weight of criminal forces and omissions, and serious corruption by the government and Church hierarchy that keeps a complicit silence ... this unfortunate body sheds tears of blood and seeks, as Christ did in Gethsemane and Golgotha, the response of the Holy Father."[17]

Heriberto Lazcano even placated his mother by remodeling her place of worship. She lived in his native Hidalgo and owned a restaurant in Pachuca, the state capital.[18] The Zeta kingpin, who used to dispose of enemies by feeding them to lions and tigers, provided manpower and funds in 2009 to reconstruct the San Juan de los Lagos chapel. The sanctuary is located in El Tezontle, a neighborhood of 10,000 residents south of Pachuca, 300 meters from a base of the 18th Military Zone. The Executioner's mother procured the contribution, and a plaque on the brightly colored, flower-filled building recognized her son's generosity.[19]

The tablet read: "Lord, hear my prayer, listen to my cry for mercy; in your faithfulness and righteousness come to my relief," a message referring to Psalm 143. It described the facility as the "Center of Evangelization and Catechism of John Paul II. Donated by Heriberto Lazcano Lazcano." Just over a half mile away The Executioner directed the construction of a majestic sepulcher in the San Francisco Pantheon, which may one day hold the erstwhile Zeta leader's remains that his comrades snatched from a funeral parlor in Coahuila in 2012.[20]

A spokesman for the Archdiocese of Tulancingo, where the San Juan de los Lagos chapel is located, told CBS News that it was a community project completed in 2009 without money from the Church—a falsehood that embarrassed his superiors. More candid was Domingo Díaz Martínez, archbishop of Tulancingo and the bishopric embracing the place of worship, who said hypocritically: "Of course, we knew of the aid [provided by Lazcano], the error was having permitted the installation of a marker."[21] This brings to mind the cavalier attitude of Church elites with respect to sexual abuse of children.

A more sensational situation involved the Arellano Félix Organization, which was believed to have showered substantial amounts of money on Tijuana's Bishop Berlie Belauzarán, who later stood accused of shielding child molesters.[22] Berlie arranged a private meeting with the Mexican Apostolic Nuncio Jerónimo Prigione, who "thanked them for their generosity." Later, authorities accused AFO hit men of pumping 14 bullets into Guadalajara's Cardinal Posadas and six others at the city's airport on May 24, 1993, an event covered in Chapter 4. The shooters claimed that their target was El Chapo, who was also on the scene. The hoodlums escaped on an Aeroméxico flight to Tijuana. Two weeks later the Guatemalan army apprehended Guzmán Loera in the mountains of Guatemala; he was extradited to Mexico and sentenced to a 20-year term. In another version of the takedown, a respected Coahuila newspaper reported that El Chapo was seized by local guerrillas, who wanted to use him as a bargaining chip with the DEA.[23]

With respect to the death of Cardinal Posadas, the mother of the Arellano Félix clan prevailed upon Father Gerardo Montaño Rubio, the family's former parish priest and rector of Our Lady of the Sacred Heart in Tijuana, to allow her sons to disavow any role in the killing. Montaño Rubio, Berlie Belauzarán's protégé, arranged for Ramón (December 1993) and his brother Benjamín (January 1994) to meet with Prigione in an attempt to absolve themselves of responsibility for Posadas's death. After a telephone conversation with Salinas—Prigione had a direct line to Los Pinos on his antique desk—the chief executive opted not to meet with members of the crime family.

Montaño Rubio claimed that he did not know "what kind of business [the Arellano Félix brothers] were managing." Jorge Carpizo MacGregor, the attorney general at the time of the homicide and the author of a book on the subject, scoffed at the priest's statement. "That's as if someone living in Chicago in the 1920s was saying that they didn't know who Al Capone was."[24] After this action, the Church transferred Berlie Belauzarán, who became an archbishop, to Yucatán, and Montaño Rubio to Ensenada.

Some desperados place their faith in non-Christian figures.[25] Jesús Malverde has become most famously identified as "The Narco Saint."[26] During the dictatorship of Porfirio Díaz (1877–1911), bandits flourished in Mexico's jagged mountains and pockmarked back roads. The mustachioed Malverde, distinguished by alabaster-colored skin, became a folk hero. Like Robin Hood, he allegedly stole from the rich and gave to the poor. His admirers insist that agents of the caudillo hung the bandit and left him to rot on May 3, 1909, the anniversary of which is celebrated every year at the roughly hewn Malverde shrine in Culiacán.

Historians have found no concrete evidence that Malverde existed, and he is likely the amalgam of two outlaws—Heraclio Bernal from western Sinaloa and Felipe Bachomo from the north. "If he lived, faith in him is a remarkable thing," said dramatist Sergio López Sánchez, who has written and researched the life of Malverde. "If he never lived, it's even more remarkable because people have created this thing to achieve the justice that is denied them." Journalist and author Sam Quiñones reports that "Smugglers come to ask Malverde for protection before sending a load [of drugs] north. If the trip goes well, they return to pay the shrine's house band to serenade the bandit, or place a plaque thanking Malverde for 'lighting the way.' "[27]

Other narco-traffickers seek the good offices of Santísima Muerte (Saint Death), especially in Tepito in the heart of Mexico City's thieves' market and along the border with the United States. She takes the form of a clothed skeleton squeezing a scythe with her bony hand; from a distance, some say she resembles the Virgin of Guadalupe. "The narco-traffickers have always been very religious; they are not atheists." To the contrary, they are extremely superstitious, related University of Nuevo León psychologist José María Infante. "She [Santísima Muerte] is a figure who accords with their activities where life and death are closely intertwined," he added.[28]

As journalist Reed Johnson wrote: "In the tough Tepito neighborhood, where poverty, corruption and violence are daily realities, there is a beloved 'saint' who understands and forgives the frailties of all human flesh. Her domain is a labyrinth of grimy streets lined with auto body shops and humble mom-and-pop stores. From her perch behind a glass-encased altar adorned with candles, decayed flowers and shot glasses of tequila, she watches scruffy curs pick through garbage while a constant stream of pilgrims lays offerings at her feet."[29]

In March 2009 bulldozers crushed chapels built to venerate Malverde and Santísima Muerte. The faithful pledged to rebuild the shrines. While Tijuana Mayor Jorge Ramos Hernández denied any role in leveling the crude sanctuaries, he expressed opposition to anything that promoted narco-violence in the city. A similar sentiment lay behind the government's decision to deploy backhoes to obliterate more than 30 shrines of the ghostly skeleton spread throughout the border city of Nuevo Laredo. David Romo, founder and high priest of the Santísima Muerte church, urged his 5 million followers to take to the streets to protest this blatant "religious intolerance."[30]

It is not just religious figures who give rise to myths. Pancho Villa, born Doroteo Arango, earned fame because he continuously eluded the punitive expedition of General John J. "Blackjack" Pershing after the hard-riding freedom fighter attacked Columbus, New Mexico, in March 1916. Some nine decades later, Joaquín Guzmán shares elements of a mythic image similar to the revolutionary hero. El Chapo is everywhere—but nowhere. One of his *corridos* (ballads) alludes to his hiding in caves, something that the hunted Pancho Villa was forced to do as he lost influence. The authorities seem unable to capture El Chapo. His apologists have suggested that his claiming to have been born on Christmas Day has invested him with supernatural powers. As longtime Mexican watchers indicated: "Part Al Capone and part Jesse James, Mr. Guzmán has become a narco folk hero."[31]

Many criminals, aware that they may die before their normal ages, hedge their bets by embracing Christian and non-Christian "deities." Their generosity may be "a message to the community via the church on who has the economic power there. What better way to win over a community, their loyalty and their silence through *limosnas* [offerings]," commented award-winning journalist Alfredo Corchado.[32] In many cases, the drug lords supply timber, nails, concrete, gravel, shingles, and other building materials for churches and other public buildings rather than cash.

While a predominantly Catholic nation, Mexico now finds Protestants making inroads, especially along its northern and southern borders. Evangelicals, who are flourishing, lament coercion by the cartels. The Reverend Oscar Moha Vargas, president of the sect In Favor of Religious Freedom, pointed out that in 2012 thirty-two pastors of his denomination suffered theft, express kidnapping, and extortion. For example, Los Zetas forced payment of 35 million pesos to agree not to hurl grenades into a fundamentalist religious rite in Monterrey that attracted 25,000 believers.[33]

BANKING AND BUSINESS

Although ostensibly law-abiding, important financiers and businessmen often collaborate directly or indirectly with narco-traffickers. The February 1993 indictment of U.S. bankers cast light on the Gulf Cartel's ventures. U.S. authorities prosecuted the American Express Bank International for laundering millions of dollars of Gulf Cartel funds through its boutique branch in Beverly Hills, California. The money cascaded through a labyrinth of financial institutions in Mexico and the United States, Switzerland, the Cayman Islands, back to Mexico, and finally the United States. The bank forfeited $25 million in laundered funds, paid a $7 million penalty, and agreed to spend $3 million on a compliance program that constituted no more than window dressing. "This case quietly rocked the U.S. banking and financial communities, for it was the first time the depth of the emerging symbiosis between the legitimate financial sector and international organized crime was officially acknowledged."[34]

Gulf Cartel boss Ábrego García also laundered money through three exchange houses in the north. When the PGR froze 200 million pesos in 1994, the Monterrey Chamber of Commerce petitioned the government to release the funds because of the seizure's negative impact on business.

In 1989 the Gulf Cartel top banana, gave millions of dollars in drug earnings to assistant Ricardo Aguirre Villagómez, known as "Kenny Rogers" because of his resemblance to the entertainer. Using a foreign currency center in Monterrey, Aguirre crammed $50 and $100 bills into duffel bags, jetted to Texas, and squirreled away the loot in a local bank. Antonio Giraldi and María Lourdes Reatagui, then employed by Bankers Trust, opened accounts at Swiss banks and in New York to hold the money even as they created Cayman Islands companies to control the accounts.[35]

A higher-profile case involved HSBC Bank USA and HSBC México. According to the U.S. Department of Treasury, these giant financial institutions helped the Sinaloa Cartel and Colombia's Norte del Valle cartel launder some $881 million between 2006 and 2010. Bank chairman Douglas Flint admitted that "HSBC has made mistakes in the past, and for them I am very sorry." Stuart Gulliver, HSBC's CEO, was even more contrite: "We accept responsibility for our errors of the past. We have said that we are profoundly sorry for these, and we have changed. HSBC is now [a] fundamentally different organization [than] when the errors were committed."[36] After paying a $1.9 billion fine, the bank formed a specialized unit, including James B. Comey who now heads the FBI, to supervise executives on fraud and security-related matters. It will help the global institution satisfy tax transparency and compliance standards to squelch activities associated with illegal drugs.[37] Since mid-2000, the U.S. Treasury Department's Office of Foreign Assets Control (OFAC) has identified 1,100 businesses that have worked hand-in-glove with cartels in areas such chemicals, real estate, and construction.[38] One of the most entrepreneurial capos is El Azul Esparragoza Moreno, who was introduced in Chapter 4. Among his holdings are the Urbanizadora Nueva Italia real estate firm in Guadalajara and Socialika Rentas y Cateromg, an event planning company in Cancún. He has a trove of assets in Tjajomulco de Zuñiga near the Guadalajara Airport, including homes in Provenza Residential, Provenza Center shopping mall, and La Tierra Parque Industrial.[39] OFAC has also investigated Mexico Caja Amigo Express, Operadora de Caja y Servicios, Julticaja Tijuana Strong Link de México (an auto armoring service), Corrales de San Ignacio (a livestock firm), Grupo C.L.P. Constructora, Constructor Inmobiliario Pacar, and Cimientos de La Torre.[40]

The use of false identities makes it difficult to determine who has financed the building boom near Cancún's tourist zone; the construction of world-class resorts in Boca del Río, Veracruz; the erection of the Torres Gemelos (Twin Towers) in Acapulco; and the proliferation of expensive hotels on the Riviera Maya.

The violence has also turned the creation of private security firms into a bonanza. Of the 6,600 that have sprung to life, half operate in an irregular manner. Only 50 percent are registered with the state or federal government, and just 3 percent have been certified as meeting industry standards. To place a classified ad in a newspaper such as *Reforma*, an individual offering protection services has only to present a birth certificate, an official credential, and a letter of recommendation. The absence of reliable enterprises is prejudicial to citizens, gives legal firms a bad name, spurs unfair competition, and produces conflicts with authorities, lamented Santiago Jiménez Dueñas, vice president of the National Association of Vehicle Protection Companies.[41]

The point is that private firms that win multi-million dollar contracts greatly benefit from drug trafficking.

CORRUPTED U.S. PERSONNEL

Just as Mexico's drug-related violence doesn't come to a screeching halt at the Río Grande, neither does corruption—with the result that there is growing concern in Washington that Midas-rich cartels are successfully bribing U.S. officials.

The most attention has focused on the ballooning size of the U.S. Customs and Border Patrol (CBP), which grew to 21,394 men and women during the past five years in response to Congress's efforts to secure the 2,000-mile long binational frontier. Republican senators insist on elevating the number of agents to 40,000 as part of the immigration reform legislation before congress in 2013.[42]

"There is a concerted effort on the part of transnational criminal organizations to infiltrate CBP through hiring initiatives and compromise our existing agents and officers," stated James Tomsheck, the agency's assistant commissioner for internal affairs.[43]

The Government Accountability Office (GAO) disclosed that since 2005, there have been 150 customs officers, immigration agents, and border patrol members arrested or indicted on charges of drug dealing, alien smuggling, money laundering, and conspiracy. The GAO found that not only is corruption a nightmare, but Customs and Border Patrol lacks adequate controls to detect wrongdoing such as polygraph examinations for new hires and follow-up tests for employees after they join. While demanding a crackdown on illegal aliens and drug couriers crossing into the United States, representatives and senators have not appropriate sufficient funds to carry out the screening of new hires. Only 10 to 15 percent of recruits were given polygraph tests before receiving their assignments. Of those who have been subjected to lie detectors, 60 percent have been rejected for employment, noted Tomsheck, who estimated that 50 full-time examiners would have to be employed to test law-enforcement newcomers.[44]

Intensifying the problem is the failure to conduct background checks on 19,000 veteran employees every five years as the law requires. Such vetting is designed to ensure that agents who were once purer than Cesar's wife remain untainted. Are their bank accounts bulging? Are they zipping around in expensive foreign cars? Have they built lavish homes far out of proportion to their incomes? Are they wearing Rolexes so heavy that they require a sling to hold up their arms? Some 10,000 men and women are overdue for reinvestigation.

Reuters reported the arrest of U.S. Border Patrol agent Reynaldo Zuniga as he was schlepping a bag of cocaine up from the Rio Bravo. The cunning Zuniga waited until colleagues in the Harlingen, Texas, office were buried in paperwork before surreptitiously making pickups at the river.

"We've seen a sharp increase in investigations along the border over the past three years," affirmed Andy Black, who oversees the FBI-led Border Corruption Task Force in the San Diego area. "We are talking about a minority of agents but they are a very significant threat, a weak link in efforts to secure the border."[45]

Unlike embezzling or forging documents, turning a blind eye to drug smuggling doesn't involve an overt action. A border official has only to blithely wave through, say, a green Ford SUV with California tags at 3 p.m. Most of the new hires are honest, but many of them have relatives in Mexico. The mafiosi do not hesitate to reward or punish Mexican family members in accord with the behavior of an American brother, sister, or cousin.

While concerned about drug and human smuggling, the FBI is even more worried about criminals providing large sums of cash—or free access to prostitutes—for allowing terrorists to gain entry into the United States.[46] A recurring nightmare is al-Qaida or another terrorist outfit commandeering access to one of the many sophisticated cross-border tunnels constructed by the Sinaloa Cartel, Los Zetas, and other syndicates.

An especially blatant U.S. offender was Richard Padilla Cramer, a 26-year veteran of the drug war, who held high-profile positions in the United States and Mexico in the U.S. Immigration and Customs Enforcement agency. He even taught ethics courses at the DEA's El Paso Intelligence Center. After retiring in 2007, he went through the Correctional Officers Training Academy in Tucson. Upon graduation, he received a citation for professionalism and took a job at the Santa Cruz County Detention Center.[47]

The judicial brief filed against him asserted: "Cramer was responsible for advising the [drug traffickers] how U.S. law enforcement works with warrants and record checks as well as how [the] DEA conducts investigations to include 'flipping subjects,' or recruiting informants."[48] The 57-year-old "secret ally of drug lords" was convicted of investing $15,000 to $20,000 in 660 pounds of cocaine, as well as selling sensitive law-enforcement databases for up to $2,000. Cramer pleaded guilty to obstruction of justice, and received a two-year prison term. The U.S. district judge justified the light term on the convict's Vietnam military service and three-decade law-enforcement career.[49]

A judge showed no such leniency in the case of former Customs officer Margarita Crispin. On July 25, 2007, she was sentenced to 20 years behind bars for accepting $5 million in bribes to facilitate the importation of more than 1,000 kilograms of marijuana. She made border inspections at the El Paso crossing. In mid-2007, a truck in the lane assigned to her was found to be packed with 1,500 pounds of marijuana. The seizure of the vehicle, an analysis of Crispin's finances, an inspection of her telephone records, witness interviews, and documented surveillance yielded a federal indictment and her imprisonment. [50]

GOVERNORS

What is the relationship between decentralization, democracy, and corruption?

Mexico presents a paradox. Article 40 of the nation's oft-amended 1917 Constitution stipulates that the political system is a "federal republic integrated by states which are free and sovereign in order to organize their internal regimes." Nevertheless, power has traditionally emanated from Mexico City[51]—with presidents from PRI (1929–2000; 2012–) often acting as "semidivine father-figure[s] to the people, inherently good in caring for his children. He is never directly challenged, as for example in the press, because that would shake the very basis of secular government. He is the *jefe* of *jefes* [chief of chiefs], who makes all final decisions."[52]

Since the late 1990s, however, executive-legislative deadlock in Mexico City created a political vacuum, which was filled by the mass media, corporatist entities such as the SNTE, the CNTE, and the STPRM, NGOs, and, in large part, by the 31 governors and the mayor of Mexico City.[53] As a result, the governors have delighted in surging political clout. They live extravagantly and either turn a blind eye to narco-trafficking or collude with the cartels.

GROWING POLITICAL STRENGTH OF GOVERNORS AND THEIR IMPUNITY

National and international media shed some light on irresponsible federal officials, but governors tend to run their states like medieval

Table 9.1

Indebtedness of Selected Mexican States (in millions of pesos)

Entity	2013 (June)	2011	2010	% Change
Mexico City	54.9	56.2	52.6	4.37
Nuevo León	40.0	38.9	34.0	15.00
Mexico State	38.3	38.2	38.2	0.3
Coahuila	36.5	36.5	27.1	25.75
Veracruz	26.7	27.9	21.5	19.48

Source: Ministry of Finance. See "Aumenta 24.1% nominal deuda de gobiernos estatales en 2011: SHCP," *La Jornada*, February 8, 2012. The dollar-peso exchange rate was 12.97 (January 2010), 12.38 (December 2010), 12.12 (January 2011), and 13.75 (December 2011). For the first quarter of 2012 the accumulated deficits of these entities, in millions of pesos, were 55,778.3 for Mexico City; 37,937.9 for Nuevo León; 38,578.4 for Mexico State; 36,503.9 for Coahuila; and 28,122.9 for Veracruz.

barons ruled their feudal holdings. As indicated earlier, they have taken advantage of the federal legislative-executive stalemate since the last half of Ernesto Zedillo's administration in 1997. Several factors contribute to their enviable positions. Congress gives them princely budgets; and federal lawmakers acquiesce in the hugely distended deficits they compile, as seen in Table 9.1.[54] In addition, they forge bonds with local power brokers, and they dominate state legislatures with large salaries and copious benefits. Moreover, they control local transparency agencies, electoral institutes, and police forces. They also ingratiate themselves with the local media via government advertising, and direct the department of the Integral Department of Families, Women, and Infants (DIF). The last agency, which is charged with safeguarding children, assisting people with disabilities, and aiding the adoption process, is typically headed by the governor's spouse at a salary that in some states approximates $100,000.

In addition, state leaders have concealed sources of wealth. During 30 years in public service, Arturo Montiel Rojas, who governed Mexico State from 1999 to 2005, earned approximately $2.5 million (26.4 million pesos). Meanwhile, his wife at the time, Maude Versini, a French woman whom he married soon after winning the statehouse, received a yearly payment of $88,889 as head of the state DIF. He accumulated lucrative properties, including a condominium in Paris ($1.51 million); a getaway in Careyes, Jalisco ($5.56 million); as well as half a dozen homes in Toluca, Mexico State's capital, the Valle de Bravo, Acapulco, and elsewhere. When Versini divorced the ex-state executive in 2007, she demanded a settlement of 300 million pesos, but the amount she received in the messy proceedings has yet to be made public.[55] Montiel's case reflects the way that politicians accumulate wealth far in excess of their official income.

Especially vexing is the short shrift that state executives give to state and national transparency laws. Not only is Mexico's freedom-of-information statute riddled with loopholes, but obtaining compliance is a migraine for the highly regarded Federal Institute for Access to Information.[56] Even if they possessed sophisticated code-breaking skills, analysts would find it a formidable challenge to determine salaries, *aguinaldos*, travel outlays, other stipends, the collection and allocation of taxes, the presence and role of quasi-official agencies, the specifics of contracts and subcontracts, and the number of staff members on a state's payroll.

For years Oaxaca's government refused to publicize the earnings of its former governor, the unscrupulous Ulises Ruiz Ortiz (2004–2010). One scholar found that he failed to specify the purpose of expenditures amounting to 39 billion pesos (approximately $325 million).

While Mexico has a more plural regime, the PRI remains the 800-pound gorilla in terms of governorships. Until 2010 the self-described "revolutionary party" has never lost the statehouses in Campeche, Coahuila, Colima, Durango, Hidalgo, Mexico State, Nuevo León, Puebla, Tabasco, Tamaulipas, or Veracruz—states that boasted 31,377,089 (35.8 percent) of the nation's 84,781,114 registered voters.

Governors and Capos

Most governors either work with kingpins or turn a blind eye to their transgressions. It's tempting to justify nepotism, sweetheart deals, and jet-set behavior as "politicians all over the world do it," "corruption is an engrained part of Mexican culture," and "some of the payola benefits drivers, doormen, maids, and other lower-income workers." What cannot be rationalized, however, are the roles of state executives in fomenting drug dealing and other crimes that precipitate widespread bloodshed. U.S. authorities found former Quintana Roo governor Mario Ernesto Villanueva Madrid (1993–1999) guilty of collusion with the notoriously venal Juárez Cartel. The mid-1997 setback to the syndicate ignited a powder keg that turned Ciudad Juárez into a flaming battleground.

In the same vein, ex-Veracruz chief executive and erstwhile presidential aspirant Fidel Herrera Beltrán (2004–2010) turned his state into a haven for the sadistic Zetas, who called themselves La Compañía in his jurisdiction. A journalist who covers the crime beat wrote that Veracruz's officials "have permitted Los Zetas to control practically all activities related to organized crime, from the sale of drugs to the robbery of gasoline from PEMEX, including kidnapping, extortion, and traffic in illegal immigrants."[57]

Herrera Beltrán denied ties to La Compañía and other criminal organizations, asserted that the federal government should do more to safeguard the monopoly's infrastructure, and pointed out that there were 8,680 miles of pipeline in Veracruz.[58]

Petroleum rustlers have invaded other parts of the country. Pemex reported that in 2012 there were 1,749 clandestine thefts of oil, 34 of which were in Oaxaca, particularly in the Isthmus of Tehuantepec. A favorite target was 16-inch pipelines leading from the Salina Cruz refinery. Tanker trucks were also stolen.[59]

It is an open secret that the messianic, Bible-pounding La Familia, a lion's share of whose members bolted to form the Knights Templars in 2011, dominates the west-central state of Michoacán's port of Lázaro Cárdenas, which leads the nation in container off-loadings. NAFTA proved a boon to Mexico's macroeconomy. Yet, with the phasing out of subsidies, quotas, and other protective measures, imports from the United States and Canada dealt a blow to farmers living on communal farms and small-scale independent producers who provided food to the domestic market. Some of these people, along with deracinated, jobless young men who had flocked to Lázaro Cárdenas, joined La Familia Michoacán, later to become the Knights Templars.

In May 2009 Calderón ordered federal authorities to incarcerate a dozen mayors and other Michoacán public officials for alleged involvement in narco-trafficking.[60] As discussed earlier, the arrests generated a thunderous blow-back from the nation's political nomenklatura. It was one thing for the government to pursue criminals; quite a different thing was rounding up public officials who co-operated with narco-traffickers. For politicians, it was the policy version of jailing jaywalkers.

Before the Knights Templars came on the scene, La Familia homed in on Michoacán politicians, especially municipal officials, along their trafficking routes. A protected witness averred that in the 2009 election the criminal band contributed 2 million pesos ($155,000) to favored mayoral candidates who, if elected, would receive a stipend of 200,000 pesos ($15,000) per month. The same anonymous source swore that Leonel Godoy Rangel, who won the governorship in 2007, raked in $300,000 from each of La Familia's leaders—a charge he strenuously denied.[61]

Equally revealing is the case of Tamaulipas, a northeast state tucked below Texas, where three erstwhile governors are currently under criminal probe for ties to narcotics traffickers. A flagrant example is Tomás J. Yarrington Ruvalcaba, who occupied the statehouse from 1999 to 2004 and was a "compadre" of President George W. Bush, who feted him as a guest of honor at the White House.[62] In his last year in office, an opposition deputy accused the PRI governor, who had previously served as mayor of Matamoros, of being joined at the hip with the Matamoros-based Gulf Cartel. Yarrington, who rejected the accusations, has evaded capture, and Interpol has issued warrants for his arrest in 150 countries. The insidious corruption combined with a lethal battle between the

Sinaloa Cartel, the Gulf Cartel, and the Knights Templars on one side, and Los Zetas on the other drove drug-related murders in the state from 89 in 2007 to 675 in 2011—with 296 reported through mid-October 2012.

Colima's former governor Silverio Cavazos Ceballos (2005–2009) was determined to name his successor. Not only did he fend off party president Beatriz Paredes Rangel's attempt to block the nomination of his fair-haired boy, he also succeeded in electing his favorite, Mario Anguiano Moreno. At the time of the inauguration, the new state executive's brother Humberto Anguiano languished in a Mexican prison for drug dealing, while his cousin, Rafael Anguiano, had been arrested in Los Angeles in a 1997 sweep that dismantled methamphetamine and cocaine trafficking rings across the United States, according to the Associated Press. When Anguiano success-fully ran for mayor three years earlier, there was little interest in his family's exploits. Yet, during his gubernatorial campaign, this issue became salient. One banner proclaimed: "Welcome to Colima! Soon to be territory of our boss of bosses, Mario Anguiano Moreno. The Zetas support you, and we are with you until the death."[63]

National and international media shed some light on irresponsible federal officials, but governors tend to run their states like medieval barons ruled their feudal holdings.

CONCLUSION

The Roman Catholic Church must be brought into the struggle against organized crime. Wheedling and cajoling are fine, but the hierarchy should open its books to government auditors to expose the relatively small number of clerics in thrall to the capos.

If Peña Nieto is serious about curbing the assistance that business com-munities in both countries lend to the cartels, he must strengthen the Finance Ministry's Financial Intelligence Unit (UIF) and encourage it to cooperate fully with its U.S. counterpart OFAC.

Other active and former U.S. officials are likely to play ball with the car-tels, which have increasingly infiltrated America's law-enforcement agen-cies. In some cases, the money is irresistible, and threats to family members in Mexico provide a powerful lever to recruit turncoats amid tighter border surveillance. Above all, Congress's penchant for demand-ing a crackdown at the border and a sound immigration policy without appropriating adequate funds exacerbates the challenge. For instance, the GAO estimates that 40 percent of migrants enter the United States on a valid visa only to disappear into the population. DHS has no means to track whether and when they have left the country.

The dispersal of power to the states has further insulated key decision makers from the people, militating against regional development programs that are crucial to social mobility for the one-third of the population who live as rag-pickers in fetid slums or on postage stamp–sized farms. As such, it represents a major reversal in Mexico's attempt to transcend electoral democracy. It remains to be seen if Peña Nieto and his confidants can deploy the carrot and stick to recapture power lost by the executive branch and rein in governors who have become the nation's new viceroys and, in many cases, active or passive collaborators with the underworld.

Dependency on the federal budget would be an important means to gain cooperation from state leaders in fighting crime. Secretary Videgary is strongly urging the latter-day powerbrokers to help reduce violence in their jurisdictions and put their financial houses in order. If intractable, they could face budget cuts, the elimination of sought-after public works, and the steering of foreign investors to other states. Moreover, the president could ostracize them by refusing to visit their bailiwicks and not inviting them either to Los Pinos or on trips abroad. Mexico's most powerful politicians could use the mass media to highlight sins of commission and omission of intractable state chiefs. As a very last resort, Los Pinos and Gobernación could demand that the president of the local congress launch an impeachment proceeding against any governor who failed to commit himself to Peña Nieto's effort to reduce bloodshed.

CHAPTER 10

Conclusions

INTRODUCTION

Detractors heaped scorn on Peña Nieto during the campaign. When questioned about the price of a kilogram of tortillas, the country's staple, he froze like a deer caught in the headlights of an on-rushing tractor-trailer. He said he did not need to know because he was not the "woman of the house." At a literary fair in Guadalajara, the PRI nominee could not name three books that affected his life. Humorists said that he had "read the *Dialogues of Plato* but could not remember who wrote them." Nonetheless, he devoured the writings of *Martin Burger King.* Critics derided him as a "know-nothing" and "airhead." Lobbyist James R. Jones gave him more credit: "I would put Peña Nieto in a similar category as Ronald Reagan," said the former envoy to Mexico, referring to the actor-turned-president's early portrayal by Democrats as a dolt. "Reagan was not analytically smart, but he had good political instincts. He chose people around him who knew how to run a government."[1]

Much like López Mateos, the last president from Mexico State and a role model for the incumbent, Peña Nieto has recruited men and women to fill the gaps in his background. Some choices were wise; others questionable.

The president has forged an astute economic team led by Finance Secretary Luis Videgaray. Meanwhile, Gobernación secretary Osorio Chong failed to manage the CNTE aggression, even while at a loss to fashion a new security plan. It's too early to judge the effectiveness of Ernesto Nemer, the SEDESOL undersecretary who dispenses social resources to benefit the downtrodden, while enhancing the legitimacy of the president and mobilizing votes for the PRI. The Pact for Mexico was an inspired move to encourage the PRI, PAN, PRD, and PVEM,[2] renowned for intermural and intramural brawls, to discuss a broad array of issues. This accord is as fragile as a month-old Easter egg, especially given the deep fissures besetting the PAN and PRD. At the same time, these divisions furnished incentives for party leaders Madero and Zambrano to remake their organizations' images and gain credibility by espousing constructive measures. Moreover, Madero wants to supplant Senator Cordero as the number-one interlocutor with Calderón, who, as a fellow at the Harvard's Kennedy School in 2013, attempted to stage-manage the PAN from Cambridge. The Pact survived the controversial July 2013 elections but encountered tensions when Congress grappled with opening PEMEX to private capital and overhauling the tax system. The PRD hierarchy vowed that it would not vote to amend Article 27, which affirms state control over hydrocarbons. Proposed tax and oil reforms were also anathema to Mexico's other elements of the left, nation-alistic opinion leaders, PRI greybeards, and López Obrador and his ram-bunctious naysayers.

STRENGTHENING THE GOVERNMENT'S HAND

The incarceration of Elba Esther Gordillo combined with an educa-tional reform enacted in the waning days of the Calderón administration may eventually improve the country's abominable educational system, but La Maestra's imprisonment is no cure-all, as her disciples and the CNTE have pummeled root-and-branch changes. A sweeping telecom-munications bill, signed by the president in March 2013, could stimulate robust competition in the media, and underlines the government's will-ingness to face-down media Goliaths Carlos Slim and Emilio Azcárraga Jean.

A revision in the amparo legal artifice also strengthens the govern-ment's hand vis-à-vis media conglomerates, mining companies, and other state concessionaires. In a document titled *La Voz del CCE*, Gerard Gutiérrez, president of the powerful Business Coordinating Council (CCE), said that Peña Nieto's actions had generated worries in some quar-ters, although "in general [there is] an obvious change in expectations that are more favorable for the country."[3]

Even as segments of the private sector registered misgivings about the new team's assertiveness, the chief executive built bridges to Roman Catholics, who make up 84 percent of the nation's population of 114.5 mil-lion people. For 133 years, most PRI governments regarded the Church with misgivings, if not hostility, owing to its allegiance to the nebulous concept of Revolutionary Nationalism. Unlike President Salinas who threw his weight behind expunging constitutional restrictions on the Church, Peña Nieto is a Roman Catholic. Like Salinas, he reached out to the Vatican by attending, with his wife, Pope Francis's inaugural Mass on March 19, 2013. Apart from the public relations aspects of his trip to Rome, the chief executive looks to the Church for assistance on key policies, particularly ventures to assist the poor and discourage clerics from accepting the largess of capos. In yet another step reminiscent of the Salinas presidency, Peña Nieto has continuously praised the armed forces, as discussed in Chapter 6.

The president has also ingratiated himself with intellectuals, with whom he met privately in late March 2013. Among those present were historians Miguel León Portillo and Rafael Tovar y de Teresa, and ComArte director general Lucina Jiménez López. In addition, he welcomed to Los Pinos filmmaker Jorge Sánchez Sosa, composer Mario Lavista Camaco, physicist and astronomer Julieta Fierro, philosopher and poet Jaime Labastida Ochoa, and anthropologist Eduardo Matos Moctezuma. In this get-together, the chief executive recognized culture as a motor of economic development and reiterated his promise to promote, preserve, and disseminate the cultural wealth that lies at the heart of Mexico's identity.[4] At the same time, he spurned any mention of drug violence.

The *elbazo*, the Pact, the telecom bill, the revised amparo, the national development plan, the outreach to the Church and other constituencies, and overtures to the military indicated the PRI chief executive's attempt to frame the national agenda. He also sought to transmit the message that unions, corporations, governors, mayors, cabinet members, media moguls, and other special interests crossed swords with him at their peril. Senate leader Gamboa Patrón said that Peña Nieto "has changed the style of doing things though steadfastness and efficiency, with the determination to construct an inclusive México, thereby garnering a favorable attitude on the part of Mexicans and foreigners who have recognized the new government."[5]

The president also took pages from the playbooks of Salinas and López Obrador by unveiling a plethora of social programs encompassed in the Pact and the PND, the objectives of which are: (1) an inclusive society; (2) quality education for all; (3) prosperity, and (4) Mexico's playing a responsible global role. The development plan's blueprint emerged from AMLO-like opinion surveys. Throughout the latter half of 2013, the government held national and local public meetings—with special sessions for women, indigenous communities, young people, and the disabled.[6] The proposed schemes are as politically freighted as they are numerous. At the same time, they were designed to shunt attention from drug-related deaths, give rise to dozens of meetings, and buy time for Luis Videgaray to attain the vibrant growth that Peña Nieto promised on the hustings.

PUBLIC RELATIONS BLITZ

While efforts are made to address campaign promises, López Gutiérrez and Nuño Mayer have done a virtuoso performance of persuading the domestic and international Fourth Estate to extol Peña Nieto's accomplishments.

The Associated Press's Michael Weissenstein wrote, "Peña Nieto says his plan will make Mexico more democratic and competitive in the world economy, and his drive for reform is fueling international confidence about Mexico."[7]

Eager for foreign investment, image makers have concentrated on the financial press. The *Economist* heaped praise on the new chief executive. "If Mr. Peña succeeds, it [the PRI] will be able to argue that it is the only lot that can get anything done. Mexican consumers may see more competition under Mr. Peña. The opposition will have to work hard to ensure that Mexican voters do not see less."[8] The *Financial Times* joined in the love fest in a March 22, 2013, article that exuded optimism: "Recent reforms in Mexico have not gone unnoticed by the global investment community. Since taking office in December last year, President Enrique Peña Nieto appears to be on track for a year of big-bang reforms."[9]

Writing in *Forbes*, Mexican journalist Dolia Estévez gushed: "In his first three months in office, Mexican President Enrique Peña Nieto has surprised many with his determination to change the old rules of power by challenging Mexico's top billionaires and putting one of Mexico's most corrupt and powerful union leaders behind bars. By doing so he has asserted power in a way no Mexican President has since the 1990s."[10] The editors of the *Washington Post* wrote admiringly: "For more than a decade, Mexico's congress was mired in three-way gridlock, making passage of desperately needed fiscal, economic and social reforms almost impossible. Now, under new president Enrique Peña Nieto, Mexicans are proving that political grand bargains can happen—and that democracies can tackle their toughest problems."[11]

Such hyperbole masks the PRI's Machiavellian use of the media to make the case that the party has morphed from authoritarianism to democracy.

INABILITY OF CITIZENS TO INFLUENCE ELECTED OFFICIALS

Conventional wisdom holds that Mexico is a "democracy," thanks largely to alternations in power arising from Fox's defeat of the PRI in 2000 followed by Calderón's victory six years later. Proponents of this view include the mainstream media,[12] the State Department and other U.S. agencies, lobbyists, chambers of commerce, the AFL-CIO, most think tanks, the Roman Catholic Church and some Protestant denominations, ethnic interest groups, the Congressional Black Caucus, the Hispanic Congressional Caucus, and Democratic and Republican lawmakers eager to cultivate the Mexican-American community. An informal "Mexican Lobby" in Washington, New York, Chicago, Los Angeles and elsewhere continuously accentuates our neighbor's undeniable advances over the last 25 years. These include economic liberalization, sound macroeconomic policy, greater political openness, free speech, and ballot access to opposition parties. Also cited are the creation of IFE and IFAI, as well as the likelihood that national elections below the border are often more transparent than those held in the United States. At the same, the special pleaders downplay Mexico's formidable deficiencies. This paternalism springs, in part at least, from altruism. Also important are financial contributions from the U.S. government and Mexican and American corporations eager to propitiate Mexican-Americans and the denizens of their homeland. Yet, Mexico remains far from a democratic society. Why?

A congeries of constitutional provisions and electoral laws divorce the establishment from the masses. Average citizens are rarely able to influence the men and women who pledge to advance their interests. Further, there is a disconnect between formal rules and actual practice, impunity flourishes, corruption abounds, honest civil servants are at a premium, governors deploy resources to hold sway over mayors, and the criminal justice system is a nightmare, except for the wealthy.[13] No wonder average citizens feel impotent to affect policy. Nearly 80 percent of Mexicans rejected re-electing federal deputies because of their poor reputations, according to a late 2009 poll by Consulta Mitofsky.[14] A survey taken almost two years later revealed that four out of five respondents "believed that the people were not protected against official abuse."[15] The upshot is a chasm between the political elite and grassroots constituents, breeding in the latter a sense of political impotence.

A medley of elements gives rise to this situation. These include (1) a constitutional ban on re-electing chief executives, governors, mayors, and federal and state legislators; (2) the absence of a run-off for Los Pinos if no contender garners 50 percent plus one vote; (3) the denial of independent candidacies; (4) the prohibition on civic groups airing media ads during campaigns; (5) the dominance of party chieftains and governors in choosing nominees; (6) the use of proportional representation lists to select one-fourth of the Senate and two-fifths of the Chamber of Deputies; (7) the impunity of governors and most mayors; (8) a Kafkaesque judicial system that may or may not undergo reform; (9) the blatant self-serving behavior of politicians, and (10) the IFE's deluging political parties with resources.

These considerations combined with the fact that so many lawmakers lack defined constituencies militate against advancing the interests of average men and women. All the while, elected officials line their pockets with generous salaries, hefty fringe benefits, Christmas bonuses, travel funds, free medical care, office expense accounts, pensions, "leaving office" stipends, and many other ways to live the good life. For example, rather than drive vehicles used the year before, in early 2013 deputies acquired a fleet of new deluxe rental cars at a cost of several million dollars. In fact, leaders of party delegations received two automobiles. Meanwhile, Manlio Fabio Beltrones, the powerful PRI leader in the lower house, gave each of the 500 deputies ornate wood boxes containing valuable golden rings.[16]

For his part, Peña Nieto has not cut corners when it comes to spending on himself, his entourage, and goods and services at Los Pinos. Contracts for such items for the incumbent climbed to 646,292,870 pesos ($51,703.343) in 2013 compared with Calderón's outlays of 80,153,250 pesos ($6,412.260) during his last year in office. While disbursements for food for presidential personnel totaled 3.9 million pesos ($312,000) in 2012, his successor budgeted 6.7 million pesos ($536,000) for this category the following year. IFAI discovered that even the cost of Peña Nieto's official photograph ($29,733) was 60 percent higher than that of his predecessor, who, Priístas claim was less photogenic.[17] In all fairness, an administration's expenditures during the first months in office are invariably higher than in later years.

As alluded to, IFE lavishes monies on political parties—to the tune of nearly $294 million in 2013.[18] A harbinger of the PRI's intention to dominate the powerful institution came on January 23, 2013, when, as reported in Chapter 7, IFE counselor García Ramírez cast the deciding vote to exonerate the PRI for irregular spending during the presidential contest. Although highly regarded after its 1996 inception, IFE has become an unwieldy politicized bureaucracy rife with nepotism and corruption. Regrettably, for Mexico's future, it does a poor job of monitoring electoral laws, especially with respect to donations to candidates and parties.

Other acts belie the emergence of a PRI committed to democracy. Party bigwigs desperately want to micro-manage not only IFE, but IFETEL, which will interpret the new telecommunications law.

IFAI has raised the hackles of politicians, bureaucrats, and military officers because of its aggressive pursuit of transparency. Created on Christmas Eve 2002, the agency promotes freedom of information in a country where public bodies have turned opaqueness from an art form into an exact science. As evidence of this conclusion, in the 2012 "Corruption Perception Index," developed by Transparency International, Mexico came in 105th out of 176 countries examined.[19] In the context of responsiveness, former Sinaloa governor Juan S. Millán Lizárraga recounts the story of a PRI attorney whom the party recruited to run for deputy in

Jalisco. In his first appearance in the state, he confessed that he was in the contest because of his professional skills, not to respond to the requests of constituents for projects, favors, and resources. He wound up his brief speech in the town square by saying, "Take a good, long look at my face ... because this is the last time you are going to see it in this municipality." He kept his word—and he won.[20]

THE PEOPLE'S PRIORITY

Citizens are losing faith in their "democracy." Only 52 percent of respondents to a late 2012 poll said that with all the country's problems, "democracy was the best form of government." This figure was down from 59 percent when Calderón swore the presidential oath. In 2012, 40 percent of interviewees said that other forms of government could be as "good or better" than democracy—up from 29 percent in 2009. Meanwhile, 47 percent considered that Mexico had weak institutions, and 49 percent said that the country needed a strong hand at the helm of state (*mano fuerte*).[21]

As in the United States, presidential campaigns in Mexico begin the day after results have been announced for the last election. Even though a lot can change in five years, Mexico watchers are speculating that, given out-sized divisions in the PAN and the PRD, the PRI can retain Los Pinos in 2018. Among those likely to vie for their party's nomination are Finance secretary Videgaray Caso and Gobernación secretary Osorio Chong.

Neither will be in the running if the economy remains sluggish and narco-violence continues to escalate. Although dozens of capos have been arrested and extradited, the violence continues to mount even as deep fissures beset Los Zetas, the BLO, and the Juárez and Gulf Cartels as took place with the Medellín and Cali organizations in Colombia.

Public relations manipulation aside, there was no way to shelter the public from a late March 2013 scene in a central plaza in Uruapan, Michoacán, where seven corpses lay sprawled across white plastic chairs, some with notes pinned to their bodies with ice picks. In mid-2013, the greatest amount of blood flowed in Michoacán where the ascendant Knights Templars, bitter enemies of the Jalisco-based CJNG, terrorized municipalities, burned businesses, invaded homes, and beheaded foes. Exasperated townspeople resorted to forming auto-defense group to battle the cruel marauders. At the same time, many militias in Michoacán, Hidalgo, Morelos, Oaxaca, and Guerrero are linked to cartels. Vigilantes and community police poured more fuel on the raging fire, which also enveloped vast areas of Oaxaca and Guerrero. The bloodshed forced Peña Nieto to dispatch 2,000 additional troops and federal police to Michoacán, saying: "Michoacán has and will have the full support of the government to uphold the rule of law in every corner of the territory."[22] Such rhetoric offers little solace to the families of the 225 people who died in the state during the first seven months of 2013. As veteran reporter José Carreño told CNN: "In politics, there are no miracles, in economics, there are no miracles, and in security even less so. They are things that happen little by little, gaining ground piece by piece."[23]

Even if a miracle were to take place and traditional drug trafficking ceased, problems would still abound. The cartels, gangs, self-defense groups, cashiered law-enforcement agents, military deserters, and family murder squads have forged an infrastructure of criminality that embraces tens, perhaps hundreds, of thousands of men and women. In all likelihood, organized crime would ramp up kidnapping, extortion, the sale of pisos, murder-for-hire, and the shake-down of mayors for SEDESOL budgets. In addition, security expert Alejandro Hope pointed out that cigarette smuggling and boot-legging whiskey has already become a big business. He further believes outlaws could begin pushing Oxytocin and other opioid analgesics, launch cyber-attacks, infiltrate labor unions, and increase their piracy of films and other intellectual property.[24] Once a crook has the master version of a Hollywood film, he or she can duplicate it for three pesos a copy. And formidable barriers threaten the nation-wide implementation of an Anglo-Saxon judicial system. Even if the reform met with success, penitentiaries remain dangerous, chaotic, and perilous. Then there are the children who regard sharply dressed, bejeweled gunmen as role models. A woman told CNN México: "My son came into the house and told me: 'Mamá, I want to be like those [narco-traffickers]. They make a great deal of money.' " The child was nine years old. An even younger boy brought a gun to school because he wanted to "form a band of drug dealers and play at kidnapping children."[25] Young teenagers in Ciudad Juárez are emulating La Familia Michoacán by shaking down their classmates for a peso or two lest they be beaten, barred from using the bathroom, or have their backpacks or sneakers taken away. One child demanded money from a teacher. When she balked, he brazenly snatched her lunch as a chorus of rowdy friends chanted "Somos la Familia" ("We are La Familia Michoacán").

When researchers from the prestigious Facultad Latinoamerica de Ciencias Sociales asked youngsters in eight states what they believed their peers aspired to as a profession, 26 percent responded narco or gunmen—ahead of careers in business (17 percent), teaching (12.4 percent), police or military (10.7 percent), and government employee (4.4 percent). Only 1.4 percent indicated they wanted to migrate to another country. Nearly four out of 10 selected none of the options.[26]

Psychologist Rodolfo Salazar Gil, a champion of helping youngsters caught up in the conflict, said, "These boys and girls are missing their childhood and have no place to play. This war places in their imagination violence, hate, revenge, and rancor [that] displace beauty and the enjoyment of a sound life."[27]

MUTUAL RESPECT

On March 13, 2011, Calderón made a speech at the Woodrow Wilson Center for International Scholars in which he lambasted the weapons that pour across the U.S. border into his country. He was referring to the outlandish Operation Fast and Furious incident in which the U.S. Alcohol, Tobacco, Firearms, and Explosives agency allowed 2,000 guns to "walk" into the hands of suspected traffickers for Mexican cartels. The visitor's ire was justified and his facts correct, but his words belied Mexico's continual demand that the bilateral relationship be based on mutual respect. Apart from the ability of Mexican syndicates to purchase AK-47s and AR-15s on the international arms market or even rent them at the Tepito market in downtown Mexico City, Calderón blatantly interfered in U.S. affairs, and the audience gave him a thunderous round of applause.

What if President Obama were in Mexico and denounced corruption by governors? Even more sensitive would be his asking publicly why Mexico is lobbying the United States to give green cards to millions of its citizens at same time that it imports low-paid, exploited Guatemalans to work in Chiapas where unemployment is sky-high. The local press would berate him, and he would be asked to return to the United States quicker than a New York minute.

Under the Obama administration, cabinet members have bent over backward apologizing for the flood of guns entering Mexico and promise to mitigate this flow. Rather than making patronizing promises that can't be kept, wouldn't it be better to admit that powerful interest groups such as the National Rifle Association and its score of allies that have an expansive view of the Second Amendment dominate the U.S. Congress and many legislatures?

Just as Mexico has its doctrinaire beliefs such as "El Petróleo es el Nuestro" ("The Petroleum is Ours"), the United States has its own share of dogmas that may vex the population as a whole but that boast enormously strong and well-heeled advocates.

PRI nationalistic impulses aside, U.S.-Mexican cooperation will continue, even as the cartels's operatives waive fat bribes in the face of American officials. Peña Nieto's far-reaching plans may succeed, although he appears to have promised more than he can deliver. As an expert on Mexican affairs wrote: "Then-President Calderón also announced a very ambitious infrastructure spending strategy ... with plans to build a new port on the Pacific coast (Punta Colonet), a new Mexico City airport, thousands of kilometers of new highways and other expensive projects. Neither the port nor the airport was ever built ... so it's important to take the Peña Nieto [PND] announcement with a grain of salt."[28] His weak energy program reflects pandering to special interests.

Now the affluent live in princely mansions in cities like the DF, Guadalajara, Querétaro, and Puebla. They cocoon themselves from the worst of the hazards thanks to high walls, state-of-the-art security systems, bodyguards, skilled drivers, and the wherewithal to send their children to school abroad. In fact, more and more entrepreneurs are operating businesses from the United States, whose government gives green cards to those who create jobs by investing in high unemployment areas. At the same time, they pay little in taxes; provide only a widow's mite to cooks, maids, and handymen; and seek to send more of their countrymen to El Norte so that U.S. taxpayers can assume responsibility for their education, health care, retirement, security, and law-breaking. Advances in safety will only prosper when Mexico's nomenklatura commits itself to fighting organized crime. The administration's proposed budget contains taxes that weigh heavily on the middle class, thus offending the PAN and endangering the Pact.

The chief executive was extremely visible in the wake of tropical storms Ingrid and Manuel, which left thousands dead, missing, or homeless in September 2013. However, governors were not as active. For example, the state government acted so slowly that the notorious Gulf Cartel provided milk, juices, water, corn, and other foodstuffs to victims in Aldama and other municipalities in the southern area of Tamaulipas state.

Like the United States, Mexico faces other staggering challenges. Among these are a decrepit road system, an aging population, rampant deforestation and environmental degradation, contamination of rivers and lakes, severe coastline erosion, inadequate flood control, a failing drainage system in the DF and other large cities, and a mounting influx of illegal aliens.

Much like the Titanic's maiden voyage, Peña Nieto got off on a heralded start, with flags waving, Champagne flowing, and the rhetoric of change filling the air. Yet, the inexperienced captain and his crew proved to be administrators, not leaders. Instead of boldly acting to solve problems, they relied on public relations, threw money at their detractors, and cozied up to the PRD (until the next elections), which shares the PRI's appetite for costly social ventures crafted to win votes from new or existing groups. The president's entourage manipulated the media to downplay cartel killings and the 105,000 kidnappings accomplished by organized crime. Their fragile ship of state crashed into not one, but a series of political icebergs. These menaces included CNTE marauders, drug Mafiosi, PEMEX protectors, auto-defense groups, vigilante bands, locally spawned police, self-serving tycoons, venal functionaries, and other actors who recognize the ability to achieve their goals vis-à-vis a weak, gradually decomposing state, which lacks the genius of a strongman like Lázaro Cárdenas. Based on his first year in office, the chief executive's allusion to a new, effective PRI appears to be a chimera, not reality.

Appendices

APPENDIX A   History of Drug Activities

Date	Event/Action	Results
1804	German pharmacist Friedrich Sertürner refined raw opium into the so-called "miracle drug" morphine. The name of the substance was derived from Morpheus, the Greek god of dreams	Among other things, morphine reduced pain in medical procedures.
1858	Two U.S. scientists used a hypodermic needle to inject morphine directly into the bloodstream.	Increased the ease of using morphine for medicinal purposes.
1861–65	Confederate and Union doctors prescribed narcotics to treat wounds, abate suffering, and treat malaria, dysentery, and diarrhea.	Narcotics were legal.
	Sigmund Freud's technical paper "On Cocaine" popularized narcotics' use for treating nervous disorders, depression and his own morphine addiction.	Gave credibility to use of cocaine.
1909 and 1911	The International Opium Convention held conferences in Shanghai and The Hague that required signatories to suppress opiates and limit narcotics to medical purposes.	Required signatories to enact effective laws or regulations for the control of the production and distribution of raw opium; recognized the U.S.-initiated principle of restricting opium use to medical and scientific purposes; and sought to reduce trafficking in China.
1906	Pure Food and Drug Act passed.	Required accurate labeling of patent medicines sold in interstate commerce.
1910–1920	The International Opium Convention took force globally when incorporated into the 1919 Treaty of Versailles.	Universal attention to the dangers of opiates.

228

Date	Event/Action	Results
1914	Harrison Narcotics Tax Act enacted.	Regulated and taxed the production, importation, and distribution of opiates.
1919–1933	Prohibition of Alcoholic Beverages.	"A noble experiment"— Herbert Hoover
1930	U.S. Bureau of Narcotic Drugs (BND) created under the Treasury Department to combat the smuggling of opium and heroin.	This agency sought to consolidate federal drug enforcement and served as a precursor to the Drug Enforcement Administration (DEA).
1937	Congress passed the Marijuana Tax Act.	Struck down by the Supreme Court in 1969 because it violated the Fifth Amendment.
1942	Congress passed the Opium Poppy Control Act.	Prohibited the possession or growing of the opium poppy without a license.
World War II	Axis nations cut off supplies of opiates to the United States.	In a semisecret maneuver, the United States acquired heroin from Mexico for medicinal purposes.
1968	Creation within the Justice Department of a Bureau of Narcotics and Dangerous Drug (BNDD).	Although intended to reduce bureaucratic turf wars, tensions continued between the Bureau of Narcotics and Dangerous Drugs (BDNN) and the U.S. Customs Service.
1969 (September 21)	Operation Intercept.	Customs officers slowed to a crawl crossings between the United States and Mexico in an effort to gain greater cooperation from the latter on controlling marijuana flows.
1970	Congress passed the Comprehensive Drug Abuse Prevention and Control Act.	Consolidated previous drug laws; established five "schedules" for regulating drugs; and broadened the scope of "no knock" searches by law-enforcement agencies.

(*continued*)

Date	Event/Action	Results
1971 (June)	President Nixon declared the "war on drugs" in the wake of veterans returning from Vietnam as addicts and the emergence of "flower children."	Nixon's war crystallized in the Comprehensive Drug Abuse Prevention and Control Act of 1970, which continued drug prohibition policies dating to 1914.
1971 (September)	Operation Golden Flow Instituted.	Required urinalysis of all returning service personnel—only 4.5 percent of whom tested positive for heroin.
1972 (January)	Office of Drug Abuse Law Enforcement (ODALE) founded to spur joint federal-local task forces to combat street-level narcotics transactions.	A move to foster intergovernmental cooperation in addressing neighborhood drug crimes.
1972	"French connection" smashed.	U.S. and French authorities cracked down on the so-called French connection—a Marseilles-based heroin center controlled by Corsican gangsters and the U.S. Mafia; sharp reduction of heroin on the East Coast.
1973 (July)	Nixon created the Drug Enforcement Administration (DEA) as a "super agency" to concentrate on all aspects of the drug problem.	Consolidated agents from the BNDD, Customs, CIA, and ODALE.
1975 (September)	The Domestic Council Drug Abuse Task Force released a white paper that identified marijuana as "a low priority drug" in contrast to heroin, amphetamines, and mixed barbiturates.	Reorders list of priorities among controlled substances.
Late 1970s	"Cocaine cowboys" selling and using cocaine stormed Miami.	Alerted Washington to the power that Colombian drug dealers were accumulating.
1982- to 1999 (October 13)	Various initiatives—including the South Florida Task Force (1982–1989), Operation	Helped stanch the flow of cocaine into the Southeast United States; Colombians

Date	Event/Action	Results
	Impunity (1997–1999), and Operation Millennium (1998–1999)—cracked down on the influx of narcotics into the Southeast United States.	increasingly relied on Central America and Mexico as their avenue to U.S. consumers.
2000	Plan Colombia announced—with expenditures of $7.5 billion in the first 10 years.	Major U.S. commitment to fighting Colombian cartels.
2002–2010	Colombians elected Álvaro Uribe Vélez to two presidential terms.	Although cocaine still cascades from Colombia, Uribe waged war on the cartels and concentrated forces in cities to make them safer.
2007	Mexican president Felipe Calderón dispatched the armed forces and federal police to combat drug cartels.	Mexico's "kingpin strategy" sparked the capture and killing of two dozen or more drug big shots; yet, the death rate continued to rise.
2008	Mérida Initiative launched.	$1.6 billion allocated for Mexico, Central America, and the Dominican Republic.
2009 (February)	Major Latin American leaders called for the legalization and/or decriminalization of marijuana.	These presidents and ex-presidents included Ernesto Zedillo and Vicente Fox (Mexico), Laura Chinchilla (Costa Rica), Otto Pérez Molina (Guatemala), Juan Manuel Santos and César Gavaria Trujillo (Colombia), Rafael Correa Delgado (Ecuador), José Mújica Cordano (Uruguay), and Fernando Henrique Cardoso (Brazil).
2012	Enrique Peña Nieto elected president of Mexico.	Although criticizing his predecessor's kingpin approach, Peña Nieto, his Gobernación secretary, and his attorney general had yet to devise their own strategy by late 2013.

(*continued*)

(continued)

Date	Event/Action	Results
Recent years	Twenty-one U.S. states legalized the medicinal or personal use of marijuana.	Alaska, Arizona, California, Colorado, Connecticut, Delware, Hawaii, Illinois, Maine, Massachusetts, Michigan, Montana, Nevada, New Hampshire, New Jersey, New Mexico, Oregon, Rhode Island, Vermont, Washington, and the District of Colombia.

APPENDIX B Major Colombian Cartels

Cartel	Founders/Leaders	Major Criminal Activities	Subsequent Developments	Recent Colombian President
Cali (based in southern Colombia and the Cauca Valley)	Miguel and Gilberto Rodríguez Orejuela in association with José Santacruz Londoño (known as "Cali's Gentlemen")	Las Chemas, as they were first called, engaged in kidnapping and then expanded into marijuana sales before trafficking in cocaine via multiple independent cells; at their apex, they dominated 90 percent of the world's cocaine market; cells focused on narco-trafficking, bribing the military and police, forging ties with politicians, engaging in money laundering, "legitimate" business activities, and hiring lawyers and lobbyists to assist captured comrades	In mid-1995 authorities arrested six of the seven cartel heads: Gilberto and Miguel Rodríguez Orejuela, Henry Loaiza, Víctor Patiño Fomeque, Phanor Arizabaleta, and José Santacruz Londoño	Virgilio Barco Vargas (1986–1990); César Gavaria Trujillo (1990–1994); Ernesto Samper Pizano—dirty (1994–1998); Andres Pastrano Álvarez—inept (1998–2002); Álvaro Uribe Vélez—relatively clean, and crusader against cartels (2002–2010); Juan Manuel Santos Calderón—apparently clean (2010–present)

(*continued*)

(*continued*)

Cartel	Founders/Leaders	Major Criminal Activities	Subsequent Developments	Recent Colombian President
Medellín Cartel; amassed upwards of $60 million per day with sales of cocaine, much of which came from Peru and went to the United States, Canada, the Dominican Republic, and Europe	Ochoa Vázquez brothers (Jorge, Juan, David, and Fabio), as well as Pablo Escobar, Carlos Lehder, Jorge Luis Ochoa, Gonzalo Rodríguez Gacha, and Juan Matta Ballesteros	Heavily involved in cocaine smuggling and heavily armed; on August 18, 1989, murdered Luis Carlos Galán, leading presidential candidate, as part of a "total and absolute war" to prevent the extradition of their members; the syndicate unleashed a wave of assassinations	By 1993 the Colombian government—in collaboration with the United States, right-wing paramilitary groups, and the Cali Cartel, managed to dismantle this cartel; the coup de grâce came on December 2, 1993, when the PNC killed Pablo Escobar, who posed as Robin Hood and was ranked by *Forbes* magazine as the world's seventh wealthiest man, even as he masterminded savage acts; nearly two decades after Colombian cocaine kingpin Pablo Escobar died in a hail of bullets, his eldest son successfully sold designer tee-shirts plastered with photos of his father in Mexican states that are on the front lines of the country's deadly drug war	

North Valley Cartel			
	Founders	Activities	Outcome
Northern Valley of Cauca department	Jairo Ivan Urdinola Grajales and his brother Julio Fabio head a major drug trafficking organization associated with the so-called North Valley Cartel; the PNC arrested Ivan in April 1992, while Fabio surrendered to Colombian authorities in March 1994; the incarceration of the Urdinola Grajales, whose family is related by marriage to the Henao Montoya family. This clan includes Orlando "The Overall Man" Henao, Montiguéz "Monty" Franco, Diego "Don Diego" León Montoya Sánchez, Wilber "Jabón" Varela, and Juan Carlos "Chupeta"/"Lollypop" Abadía	Gained prominence in the latter half of the 1990s when the Cali and Medellín Cartels fragmented; exported multiton loads of cocaine primarily from Colombia's Pacific coast through the Cauca Valley to the United States and Europe; a rising number of extraditions prompted Hernando Gómez and Varela to try to cut a deal with the DEA; Montoya opposed this move, and a brutal internecine war erupted that took the lives of 100 assassins	Although Montoya was captured (September 10, 2007) and Varela killed (January 30, 2008), this cartel remains one of Colombia's strongest drug syndicates

Sources: Thomas A. Constantine, Administrator, Drug Enforcement Administration, DEA Congressional Testimony before Senate Foreign Relations Subcommittee, February 26, 1998; William E. Ledwith, Chief of International Operations, Drug Enforcement Administration, Testimony before the House Government Reform Committee, Subcommittee on Criminal Justice, Drug Policy, and Human Resources, February 15, 2000; "Colombia Takes Charge of Pharmacy Chain Linked to Cali Cartel," *USA Today,* September 17, 2004; U.S. Customs Service, "History of the US Customs Service Investigation into Colombia's Cali Drug Cartel and the Rodríguez-Orejuela Brothers," www.ice.gov/pi/news/factsheets/califs031105.htm; Peter Eisner, "Cocaine Trafficker Pablo Escobar in Colombia," *Newsday,* December 3, 1993; "Pablo Escobar T-Shirts a Hit in Mexican Drug War States," *Reuters,* October 2, 2012.

APPENDIX C Evolution of the Gulf Cartel and Los Zetas

Date	Event	Consequence
1992–1995	Jorge Eduardo "El Coss" Sánchez was a local police officer in Matamoros, the base of the Gulf Cartel	He learned the drug business at the grassroots level
January 14, 1996	Gulf capo Juan Ábrego García, nephew of infamous bootlegger Don Juan Nepomuceno Guerra (1915–2001), captured outside of Monterrey	Even though a minor player, El Coss befriended Osiel "The Friend Killer" Cárdenas Guillén and seized the reins of the cartel
March 14, 2003	Army captured Osiel Cárdenas Guillén, head of the Gulf Cartel	Top leader captured
March 14, 2003	Jorge Eduardo "El Coss" Costilla Sánchez assumed leadership	New leader assumes leadership
2004–2010	A troika evolved that was composed of El Coss, Antonio "Tony Tormenta" Cárdenas Guillén, and Zeta leader Heriberto"Z-3" Lazcano Lazcano	Even as the Gulf Cartel repelled efforts by El Chapo and his allies to invade the north, frictions multiplied among troika members
2005	Friction increased as Los Zetas indulged in grotesque cruelty and formed situational alliances with the Beltrán Leyva Organization (BLO), a rival cartel	The brutality was at odds with the profit orientation of the Gulf and Sinaloa Cartels
January 20, 2007	Mexico extradited Osiel Cárdenas to the United States	Co-operation with U.S. authorities*
February 24, 2010	A federal judge sentenced Osiel Cárdenas to 25 years in prison; he provided information to U.S. agents in exchange for a lighter term*	Zeta leader believed that Osiel had disclosed information about their tactics, leadership, and organization

Date	Event	Consequence
January 18, 2010	El Coss ordered Samuel "Metro 3" Flores Borrego to kill Sergio "El Concord" Peña Mendoza, a confidant of "El 40"	Animus evolves into warfare between the Gulf Cartel and Los Zetas
November 5, 2010	Navy killed Tony Tormenta after a fierce gun battle	Three of his bodyguards, known as "Los Escorpianos," were also killed, as were two members of the navy's Special Forces and a reporter
November 5, 2010	Osiel's brother Mario Cárdenas Guillén reluctantly assumed leadership	Another brother of Osiel comes to the fore
March 2011	Mario Cárdenas Guillén relinquished the reins of the cartel	Changing of the guard in the Gulf Cartel
March 2011	Rafael "El Junior" Cárdenas Vela, nephew of Osiel and former head of Matamoros plaza, took over	New leader takes over
September 2, 2011	Tortured and bound bodies of Flores Borrego and Eloy Lerma García, a high ranking local police officer, are found 13 miles south of Reynosa	Los Zetas got revenge for the death of Metro 3
October 11, 2011	Body of César "Gama" Dávila García, Tony Tormenta's personal accountant, was found in an abandoned house in Reynosa	Another event in intracartel battle for control
October 20, 2011	ICE captured Rafael "El Junior" Cárdenas Vela in Port Isabel, Texas; wearing pink shorts and loafers, he was heading toward his South Padre Island residence	El Junior's testimony helped convict Juan Roberto Rincón Rincón, the Gulf's plaza boss in Rio Bravo, Tamaulipas; Cárdenas Vela was living in the United States to escape revenge by Gulf Cartel rivals

(*continued*)

Date	Event	Consequence
October 26, 2011	U.S. Border Patrol arrested Juan Roberto "Comandante Primo" Rincón Rincón in Santa Maria, Texas	Former regional Gulf Cartel commander who said that one smuggler working for him moved 500 kilograms of cocaine into the United States each week
October 26, 2011	U.S. Border Patrol arrested José Luis "Comandante Wicho" Zuñiga Hernández in Santa Maria, Texas	Comandante Wicho was arrested along with Rincón as the men tried to escape rivals in the Gulf Cartel, Los Rojas
May 9, 2012	Gilberto Lerma Plata, former Tamaulipas police chief and cousin of ex-governor Manuel Cavazos Lerma and current senator, arrested in McAllen for smuggling drugs into south Texas for the Gulf Cartel	Confessed to charges and sentenced
September 3, 2012	Navy captured Mario Cárdenas Guillén in Altamira, Tamaulipas	Another setback to the cartel's ebbing strength
September 11, 2012	Mexican navy arrested Juan Gabriel "Sierra" Montes Sermeño in Guadalajara	Leader of Gulf Cartel's strike team known as the Kalimanes; captured with bodyguard Eusebio Horta Arguellos
September 12, 2012	Navy arrests "El Coss"	Cartel weakened even more; Homero Cárdenas,** a family member, became the the the leader of "Los Rojas" (pro-Cárdenas Guillén) wing of the Gulf Cartel; Mario Armando "El Pelón" Ramírez Treviño took charge of "Los Metros" (pro-Coss) faction of the cartel. He controls Reynosa through a wrestler called "El Simple" but often stays a few miles away in Río Bravo***

Date	Event	Consequence
October 7, 2012	Navy allegedly killed Zeta leader Heriberto Lazcano	Comrades stole his body from the funeral home and Rumors arbound that he is alive
November 26, 2012	U.S. Homeland Security agents apprehended gun traffickers Juan Ricardo Martínez Cárdenas and Daniel Blanco Avila in Roma, Texas	To avoid the Gulf Cartel, these men smuggled guns from Miguel Alemán, Tamaulipas, to Roma, Texas, before bringing them back to Miguel Alemán; Los Zetas paid them $1,200 every two weeks
January 15, 2013	Authorities found the corpse of Héctor "Metro 4" Delgado	Ruthless enforcer for Gulf Cartel
January 24, 2013	Jose Luis "El Wicho" Zuñiga Hernández sentenced to seven years in prison	Put behind bars a Gulf Cartel operative, captured by the U.S. Border Patrol in October 2011, and known for arms smuggling, kidnapping, and immigration violations
March 10, 2013	Miguel "El Gringo" Villarreal killed	He challenged El Pelón Ramírez Treviño for leadership of the Gulf Cartel
July 15, 2013	Marines captured El 40 Treviño Morales	Severe blow: authorities traced him via telephone numbers that he frequently called
August 18, 2013	Armed forces seized El Pelón Ramírez Treviño	May reopen wounds between two major factions of Gulf Cartel

*The seven years that he had served in Mexico reduced his 25-year term, which could be shortened even more for good behavior

**Homero Cárdenas, believed to be a cousin of Mario Cárdenas Guillén, is reportedly in line to take over the reins of the cartel; other allies of "El Pelón" included "Metro 4," Alfonso "Metro 7" Flores Borrego, and ex-Zeta Cruz Galindo Mellado, who realigned with the Gulf Cartel.

***El Chapo appears to be siding with Los Metros and reportedly has dispatched members of the Guadalajara-based Jalisco New Generation Cartel (CJNG) to assist them.

Sources: This appendix relies heavily on articles by the border's top criminal reporter, Ildefonso Oritz at *The Monitor* (McAllen, TX); "Gulf Cartel Commander Asks for Jury Trial in Brownsville," September 19, 2012; "Detainee: Zetas Smuggle Guns into US to Avoid Gulf Cartel" *The Monitor*, November 30, 2012; "Few Details Known about Quiet Fall of Feared Gulf Cartel Kingpin," *The Monitor*, January 27, 2013; "Gulf Cartel, Zetas Mark 3rd Anniversary of Bloody Rivalry," *The Monitor*, February 6, 2013; Jared Taylor, "Former Tamps: Police Chief, Cousin of Ex-Governor, Admits to Gulf Cartel Ties," *The Monitor*, March 3, 2013; Doris Gómera, "Ex-Comandante admite que fue cómplice del cártel del golfo," *El Universal*, March 5, 2013; Katherine Corcoran, "Mexico's New Government Follows Old Drug War Strategy," *Associated Press*, August 18, 2013.

APPENDIX D   Phases in the Development of the Arellano Félix Organization

I. **1989 Founding**: Whether it was Miguel Ángel Félix Gallardo, the Federal Security Directorate (DFS), or fortuitous events, plazas or territories were divided among the Sinaloans by "El Padrino."
   A. Arellano Félix Brothers wound up with Tijuana with Benjamín, the elder and the most feared vicious of the clan, emerging as the leader beginning in 1986.
   B. The AFO sought to move southward but was stymied by the Sinaloa Cartel, which became their archrivals along with the Gulf Cartel. They were at war with everyone but the Juárez Cartel's Amado Carrillo.
   C. 1989: Ramón Félix Arellano killed a close ally of El Chapo. In one of many acts of revenge, in 1993 the Sinaloa Cartel launched a spectacular attack against the Christine Discotheque in Puerto Vallarta where Javier and friends were partying. Although the target escaped, six people died in this brazen act. The Arellanos retaliated by striking at Sinaloan-controlled Guadalajara, hiring Alfredo "El Popeye" Araujo to mobilize elements of San Diego's Logan Heights gang to lead the assault. Conflict also erupted because El Chapo had dug a tunnel in AFO territory. Ramón died in a shootout with police in 2002.
   D. Mid-1990s: The military delivered a setback to the AFO. While commanding the 5th Military Region in Guadalajara, General Jesús Gutiérrez Rebollo won accolades for providing intelligence about AFO criminal acts—to the point that President Zedillo appointed him "drug czar." Much to the chief executive's chagrin, the senior officer was found to be on the payroll of the Juárez Cartel (in 1997).
   E. 1990s: Prospered by (1) selling large quantities of cocaine[*] and marijuana to the United States; (2) buying off police, politicians, and army personnel; and (3) unleashing sadistic acts of violence on their foes.

II. **1990s: Emergent Phase**
   A. May 24, 1993: Attempted murder of "El Chapo" Guzmán at Guadalajara Airport (the official line is that Cardinal Juan Jesús Posadas Ocampo was mistakenly killed while seated in a Mercury Grand Marquis).The assassins returned unmolested to Tijuana on a commercial flight.
   B. Violence also took the form of the attempted murder of Jesús Blancornelas, founder and director of the weekly publication *Zeta de Tijuana* (on November 27, 1997). On March 17, 2008, authorities arrested Saúl "El Ciego" Montes de Oca Morlett for this crime. David Barrón Corona, an AFO critical enforcer, died in the assassination effort.

---

[*]Estimated that once supplied 40% of cocaine to U.S., Robert J. Caldwell, "Spectacular Coup," *San Diego Union Tribune*, August 20, 2006.

C. September 17, 1998: Ramón Arellano Félix, the syndicate's chief enforcer, ordered the killing of 18 people on Ensenada.

D. 1998: AFO forged an alliance with the Sonora Cartel.

III. 2000–2008: Embattled Phase

A. March 12, 2000: Financial operator Jesús "Chuy" Labra Avilés was captured in Tijuana.

B. May 4, 2000: Operations director Ismael "El Mayel" Higuera Guerrero was captured in Ensenada and extradited to the United States (in January 2007).

C. February 10, 2002: Ramón was killed in Mazatlán.

D. March 9, 2002: Benjamín was captured in Puebla and extradited to the United States (on April 29, 2011). He was subsequently sentenced to a 25-year prison term.

E. June 22, 2004: Murder of Francisco Ortíz Franco, courageous longtime editor of the weekly publication *Zeta.*

F. August 14, 2006: Francisco Javier "El Tigrillo" was arrested aboard the *Doc Holiday* fishing boat by the U.S. Coast Guard on the open sea off Cabo San Lucas, BCS.

IV. 2008–2010 IV: El Teo and the Alienation of Civil Society

A. 2008: Break with Teodoro "El Teo" García Simental, his top enforcer Raydel "Crutches" Rosalio López, and other loyalists who challenged "The Engineer" for leadership of the AFO.

B. Although versed in many criminal pursuits, El Teo specialized in kidnapping, which he pursued with a ferocity characteristic of the new generation of Baja California capos.

C. As AFO expert Nathan Jones has indicated, the tsunami of kidnappings alienated the general public, the business community, the media, the military, and law-enforcement agencies.

Drug-Related Deaths in Baja California, 2006–2012

Year	Number of Drug-Related Deaths
2012	117
2011	142
2010	315
2009	320
2008	617
2007	154
2006	163

This figure benefits from Nathan Patrick Jones, *The State Reaction: A Theory of Illicit Network Resistance*, PhD Diss. University of California at Irvine, 2012.

V. 2010–2012: Deflated Phase

A. Crackdown by Tijuana police chief Julián Leyzaola.

B. Leyzaola, a retired general, worked extremely well with Zonal Commander Mújica.

C. PAN governor José G. Osuna Millán, Mújica, and Leyzaola successfully urged SEDENA to send first-rate troops to Tijuana.

D. There was improved coordination between U.S. and Mexican law enforcement, notably the San Diego Cross-Border Task Force's Luz Verde initiative, which, by January 2010, had indicted 43 AFO members.[2]

E. Civil society was repelled by El Teo's widespread brutal killings and kidnappings.

F. The army captured Eduardo "El Doctor" Arellano Félix in Tijuana (on October 26, 2008).

G. After the arrest and conviction of Francisco Javier Arellano Félix (on September 17, 2007), power passed to Luis Fernando "The Engineer" Sánchez Arellano (son of Alicia) and other members of the new generation of the family, who did not possess the know-how and skills of their uncles.

H. January 13, 2010: El Teo was arrested in La Paz, BCS; Rosalio López and other lieutenants were also apprehended.

VI. 2012—Present Subordinate Phase

A. Sinaloa Cartel dominates BC. El Chapo Guzmán, who believes that bloodshed is bad for business, has reached a modus vivendi with the AFO.

B. Thus, rather than decimate the AFO as it could, the Sinaloa Cartel pays a *derecho de piso* a transit charge for moving drugs into El Norte. The AFO continues to exert influence over corrupt police.

APPENDIX E Losses Suffered by the Arellano Félix Organization

AFO Leader	Function	Date/Place of Capture or Death	Force Responsible for Takedown	Comments
Francisco Rafael Arellano Félix	Chief executive officer before his arrest (eldest of the brothers)	August 7, 1980/San Diego; December 4, 1993/Tijuana (captured)	U.S. authorities and Federal Judicial Police	After imprisonment in Mexico, he was extradited to United States on September 16, 2006; released from U.S. penitentiary in El Paso after completing his sentence on February 2, 2008
Jesús "Chuy" Labra Avilés	Chief financial operator	March 12, 2000/Tijuana (captured)	Army	Extradited to United States on December 31, 2008
Ismael "El Mayel" Higuera Guerrero	Operations director	May 4, 2000/near Ensenada (captured)	Federal police	Benjamín's principal operator in Tijuana extradited to United States in January 2007
Ramón "El Min" Arellano Félix	Brutal chief enforcer	February 10, 2002/Mazatlán (killed)	Ministerial police	The most fiendish of the clan; analogous to Sonny Corleone in Godfather films
Benjamín Arellano Félix	Chief executive officer	March 9, 2002/Puebla (captured)	Army	Extradited to United States on April 29, 2011
Francisco Javier "El Tigrillo" Arellano Félix	Reckless gunslinger	August 14, 2003/open sea off Cabo San Lucas, Baja California (captured)	U.S. Coast Guard	Picked up on the Doc Holliday—a 43-foot-long deep sea fishing boat owned by the son of a former PRI governor

Name	Role/Description	Date/Status	Captured by	Notes
Marco Antonio "El Cris" García Simental	Joined cell of El Teo, his younger brother, in 2004; proficient drug smuggler; influenced by Higuera Guerrero	June 22, 2004/Mazatlán (captured)	Municipal Police	Known for viciousness; after the arrest of Higuera Guerrero, El Cris joined the cell of Efraín "El Efra" Pérez Pazuengos, an ally of El Mayel; took over eastern Tijuana communities of Cerro Colorado, El Florido, and Mariano Matamoros
José Jorge "El Cholo" Briceño López	Top AFO lieutenant	Late August 2008/Tijuana (presumed killed)	Unknown	Used beautiful women to assist in his kidnappings and murders
Eduardo "El Doctor" Arellano Félix	Weak leader	October 26, 2008/Tijuana (captured)	Army	Shared cartel's leadership with his cousin Luis Fernando "El Alineador" Sánchez Arellano
Jesús Alfonso "El Profe" Trapero Ibarra	Top lieutenant in Tijuana for Manuel "El Chiquis" García Simental, El Teo's brother; extremely brutal	February 24, 2009/Tijuana (captured)	Federal Preventive Police	Responsible for recruiting cadres, transporting narcotics to the United States, and controlling neighborhood drug dealers in Tijuana and Tecate
José Filberto "La Perra" Parra Ramos	Deadly operator for "El Teo" García Simental	June 10, 2009/Tijuana (captured)	Army	Top El Teo lieutenant, who participated in the 749 executions in Tijuana in 2008
Enedina Arellano Félix	Sister who runs minor business activities in Tijuana; managed real estate; may be involved in money laundering	No warrant for her arrest	Free	May live in southern California

(continued)

AFO Leader	Function	Date/Place of Capture or Death	Force Responsible for Takedown	Comments
Alicia Arellano		No warrant for her arrest	Free	Lives in Los Angeles area
Luis Fernando "The Engineer" Sánchez Arellano	Nephew of founding family; in charge of Baja California functions	Warrant issued for him in 2010		Son of Alicia Arellano; operates at pleasure of Sinaloa Cartel
Eduardo "The Doctor" Arellano Félix	Operated out of Los Angeles	October 26, 2008/Tijuana (captured)	Federal Police	Extradited to the United States on August 31, 2012
Eduardo Teodoro "El Teo"/"Tres Letras" García Simental	Vicious leader of a faction centered in Baja California Sur	January 13, 2010/La Paz, BCS (captured)	In a Mexican prison; the United States is seeking his extradition	Broke with AFO and sought alliance with Sinaloa Cartel

Note: Brothers Luis Fernando and Carlos apparently did not participate in criminal activities.

APPENDIX F Overview of Cartels (Xs indicate a cartel's involvement in the activities and concepts cited in the far left column)

Activities/Strengths	Los Zetas	Sinaloa Cartel	Gulf Cartel	Beltrán Leyvas	Knights Templars	AFO
Extreme Use of Fear and Intimidation	X **Systematic intimidation**		X **Tamaulipas and Nuevo León**		X **Systematic intimidation**	
Cohesion	Omar "El 42" Treviño Morales, Alejandro Chavarría Gallegos (finances)	Strong; Joaquín "El Chapo" Guzmán Loera, Ismael "El Mayo" Zambada García, Juan José "El Azul" Esparragoza Moreno (negotiator)	Low cohesion resulting from a division among Los Metros (Eduardo "El Coss" Costilla Sánchez) and Mario Piñon versus Los Rojos and Escorpios (allies of Mario Cárdenas Guillén)	Family based; Héctor and his half-brother	Claim to be acting in the "Lord's name"; practice a perverted form of muscular Christianity; may have recruited elements of the millenarian New Jerusalem cult	Severely weakened
Social Legitimacy	Hated because of sadistic acts	Relatively high where the cartel provides jobs		Low	Have generated marches against criminals and for human rights in Michoacán and Guerrero	
Contraband	X					

(continued)

(*continued*)

Activities/Strengths	Los Zetas	Sinaloa Cartel	Gulf Cartel	Beltrán Leyvas	Knights Templars	AFO
Corrupting Police/Judges/Politicians	X Past masters at corrupting local police	X Judges, police, and prosecutors, especially in Sinaloa	X Matamoros and Reynosa	X	X Michoacán	
Extortion	X		X Matamoros and Reynosa, Tamaulipas		X La Familia learned from Los Zetas	
Kidnapping	X	X (2007–2010): Period when the cartel needed money to fight Los Zetas in the north				
Murder for Hire*	X					
Petroleum Theft	X		X			
Street Blockades to Tie up	X		X			

	Traffic and Facilitate Attacks on Foes, Kidnappings, and Other Crimes**				
Narco-Banderas	X	X (2007–2010): Period when they sought to discredit Los Zetas	X	X	X
YouTube/Twitter	X	X (2007–2010): Period when they sought to discredit Los Zetas			
Smuggling Migrants	X Divest them of money, use them as slaves, or kill them	X Charge smugglers to take illegal migrants across areas that they control			

(continued)

(*continued*)

Activities/Strengths	Los Zetas	Sinaloa Cartel	Gulf Cartel	Beltrán Leyvas	Knights Templars	AFO
Alliances	Situational alliances with BLO, La Resistencia (Guadalajara), and possibly Mano con Ojos (Mexico State)	Co-operates with Gulf Cartel against Los Zetas	Co-operates with Sinaloa Cartel against Los Zetas	Los Zetas, Los Rojos (Morelos), the Independent Acapulco Cartel (CIDA), La Barredora (Acapulco), and Los Mazatlecos (Mazatlán)	Co-operates with the Sinaloa and Gulf Cartels against Los Zetas ***	

*For specific murders, cartels can contract a gunman from Hidalgo municipalities near Querétaro, Jacala de Lerma, and Huejutla, which have a tradition of killers for hire. For a modest sum, depending on the target, they will perform assassinations for gangs, cartels, businesspeople, or spouses who want to eliminate a wife or husband. A similar band, which works from Mexico City's sprawling, dangerous Tepito market, is believed to have killed the DF's acting police chief Edgar Millán Gómez on May 8, 2008.

**Los Zetas and the Gulf Cartel have bcome adept at scattering streets with *ponchallantes* (small, sharp metal stars that blow out tires), thus turning main streets into parking lots and facilitating kidnappings, murders, extortion, and other crimes.

***The Knights Templars have pledged to cease violent activities if the federal govenment crack down on other cartels in Michoacán. In August 2013, they were in the middle of a battle royal that pitted the Knights Templars against the CJNG and remnants of La Familia, auto-defense groups against the cartels, and ad hoc community pólice against cartels and gangs threatening their villages. This mayhem forced President Peña Nieto to dispatch 2,000 federal pólice and army personnel to the state.

Cartel	Founders and Organizational Structure	Major Asset(s)	Major Sources of Revenue	Nondrug Activities	Allies	Major Route(s) to United States	Chief Vulnerabilities
Sinaloa	Hub and spoke; shared leadership at the top: "El Chapo" Guzmán Loera and Ismael "El Mayo" Zambada García	Cohesion; bribery of politicians and police, judges, and prosecutors; dominates northwest plus routes through Central America; numerous portals for export, including Tijuana, Mexicali, Nogales, Ciudad Juárez, and Veracruz	Cocaine, marijuana, metham-phetamines, heroin	Investment in "legal" businesses in Sinaloa and elsewhere	Gulf Cartel (El Coss) faction; Jalisco New Generation Cartel CJNG the AFO	Baja California Sonora, Ciudad Juárez, and other parts of Chihuahua: controls 23,000 square miles of Mexican territory and operates in 78 U.S. cities, not to mention Central America and its vast international network	El Chapo's capture would invest instant credibility in the Peña Nieto administration

(continued)

Cartel	Founders and Organizational Structure	Major Asset(s)	Major Sources of Revenue	Nondrug Activities	Allies	Major Route(s) to United States	Chief Vulnerabilities
Gulf	Family	Corruption of local politicians and police	Cocaine Marijuana	Used-car trafficking, human smuggling, and eight-liners and other slot machines	Sinaloa Cartel; and Knights Templars	Frontiera chica (Miguel Alemán and Camargo); Matamoras, and Reynosa; before his 2013 capture, the cartel's Israel García Jr. moved 40 tons of marijuana a month to Florida in containers from the port of Brownsville	Division between Los Metros (Mario Armando "El Pelón" Ramírez Treviño) and Los Rojos (Homero Cárdenas)
Los Zetas	Originally a disciplined organization with a strong command and control structure; the death of "The Executioner" Lazcano and the capture of "El 40" Treviño Morales contributes to the group's fragmentation, as occurred with the	Instill fear in police, army, and civilians via sadistic violence; use of social media; penetration of 15 to 20 states plus Central America	Marijuana, cocaine—with extortion, kidnapping, and oil theft becoming ever more important sources of revenue	20 or more, including kidnapping extortion, murder for hire, contraband, oil theft, migrant smuggling, hijackings, loan-sharking, prostitution	BLO and La Resistencia (Jalisco); possibly Mano con Ojos (Mexico State)	Nuevo Laredo	Fragmentation after take down of top leaders

	Cali and Medellín Cartels in Colombia; Omar "El 42" Treviño Morales will attempt to take charge		Tijuana	Enemies of Los Zetas and CJNG
Knights Templars (KTs)	Religious cult; headed by the mercurial Servando "La Tuta" Martínez and the more pragmatic Enrique "El Kike" Plancarte	Fanaticism; sadistic violence; deep roots in Michoacán; control of local politicians; in March 2013 the KTs announced through narco-banners that they would withdraw from Michoacán and leave protection to official police agencies*	Methampheta mines, marijuana	La Corona, a gang that emerged in Zapopan, Jalisco, in November 2011; "Mano con Ojos" (Mexico State)
Beltrán Leyvas (BLO)	Lead by Héctor; organized on a family basis	Access to cocaine from Colombia, Peru, and Ecuador	Cocaine, marijuana; formerly human smuggling, money	Los Zetas; Los Rojos (Cuernavaca); the Independent	Severely weakened by death of Arturo and his top gunmen

(continued)

(continued)

Cartel	Founders and Organizational Structure	Major Asset(s)	Major Sources of Revenue	Nondrug Activities	Allies	Major Route(s) to United States	Chief Vulnerabilities
			laundering, extortion, kidnapping, murder, gun-running and control of major airports		Acapulco Cartel (CIDA), La Barredora; and Los Mazatlecos (Mazatlán)		
Arellano Felix Organización (AFO)	Family	Sinaloa Cartel now controls most of Baja California, including Tijuana and Mexicali	Marijuana		Dominated by Sinaloa Cartel	Tijuana	No access to cocaine; most chiefs either dead or in jail; a sister, Enedina, who may live in California, is the most visible member

*"En narcomantas, anuncian su repliegue Los Caballeros Templarios," _Proceso_, March 13, 2013.

APPENDIX H Prominent Kingpins Arrested/Killed during Calderón Administration

Name of Criminal	Affiliation	Date/Place Arrested/Killed	Agency Accomplish-ing the Arrest/Killing	Observations on Arrests and Killings
Heriberto Lazcano Lazcano "Z-3"	Leader of Los Zetas	October 7, 2012/Progreso, Saltillo/Presumed Killed	Navy/Marines	Critical blow to Los Zetas
Iván "El Talibán"/ "Z-50" Velázquez Caballero	Top leader of Los Zetas who was responsible for violence in San Luis Potosí, Zacatecas, and Coahuila	September 26, 2012/San Luis Potosí/Captured	Navy/Marines	A trusted lieutenant of Lazcano, who feuded with El 40 Treviño Morales, whom he blasted as a "traitor"
Eduardo Costilla Sánchez "El Coss"	Leader of the Gulf Cartel	September 12, 2012/ Tamaulipas/Captured	Navy/Marines	Intensified the fracture of the Gulf Cartel
Mario Cárdenas Guillén	Brother of Osiel Cárdenas, historic leader of the Gulf Cartel	September 3, 2012/ Altamira, Tamps/ Captured	Army	A weak leader who could not unify the Gulf Cartel
Erick Valencia Salazar "El 85"	Leader of the New Generation Jalisco Cartel	March 9, 2012/ Zapopan, Jalisco/Captured	Army	CJNG continues to thrive even in his absence
Flavio Méndez Santiago "El Amarillo"	Founding member of Los Zetas	January 18, 2011/Oaxaca/ Captured	Federal police	An important asset for Los Zetas

(continued)

Name of Criminal	Affiliation	Date/Place Arrested/Killed	Agency Accomplishing the Arrest/Killing	Observations on Arrests and Killings
Martín Beltrán Coronel "El Águila"	A top leader of Sinaloa Cartel	May 12, 2011/Zapopan, Jalisco/Captured	Army	
José de Jesús Mendez "El Chango" Méndez Vargas	Succeeded El Chayo as leader of La Familia Michoacán	June 21, 2011/Aguascalientes/Believed killed	Federal police	La Tuta Servando Martínez took advantage of his death to strengthen the breakaway Knights Templars
Francisco "El 2000" Hernández García	Beltrán Leyva Organization	November 4, 2011/Ciudad Juárez, Chihuahua/Captured	Federal police	Further weakened the BLO, especially in northern Mexico
Ezequiel Cárdenas Rivera "El Junior"	Nephew of Osiel Cárdenas and son of Ezequiel Cárdenas Guillén "El Tormenta"	November 25, 2011/Matamoros, Tamps/Captured	Army	
Raúl Lucio "El Lucky" Hernández Lechuga	A founding Zeta and ran its activities in Veracruz, Puebla, and Oaxaca	December 12, 2011/Córdoba, Veracruz/Captured	Navy/Marines	Deprived Los Zetas of a key regional leader
Teodoro García Simental "El Teo"	Arellano Félix Organization	January 12, 2010/La Paz, Baja California/Captured	Federal police	Took out of circulation a sadistic killer

Ignacio Coronel Villarreal "El Nacho"	Number three in the Sinaloa Cartel	June 29, 2010/Zapopan, Jalisco/Killed	Army	Nacho's death sparked a free-for-all in Guadalajara involving major cartels and their allied gangs
Édgar Valdez Villarreal "La Barbie"	Broke away from the BLO	August 30, 2010/Captured and ordered extradited to the United States	Army	One of major U.S.-born criminals who entered the Mexican underworld
Sergio Villarreal Barragán "El Grande"	BLO	September 12, 2010/Puebla/Captured	Navy/Marines	May 23, 2012; extradited to United States and may cooperate with the DEA
Ezequiel Cárdenas Guillén "Tony Tormenta"	Gulf Cartel leader	November 7, 2010/Matamoros, Tamps/Killed	Navy/Marines	Exacerbated fragmentation of Gulf Cartel
Nazario Moreno González "El Chayo"	Founder of La Familia Michoacán Cartel	December 9, 2010/Western Michoacána/Killed	Federal police	His protection was the responsibility of 12 gunmen he called the "Twelve Apostles"
Vicente Zambada Niebla "Vicentillo"	A key member of the Sinaloa Cartel	March 19, 2009/Mexico City neighborhood/Captured	Federal police	
Vicente Carrillo Leyva	Leader of the Juárez Cartel and son of legendary kingpin Amado Carrillo Fuentes	April 2, 2009/Mexico City/Arrested	Federal police	A weak leader

(continued)

Name of Criminal	Affiliation	Date/Place Arrested/Killed	Agency Accomplishing the Arrest/Killing	Observations on Arrests and Killings
Raymundo "El Gori 1" Almanza Morales	Zeta leader in the Cancún area and believed to have been involved with the murder of a general	May 22, 2009/Monterrey, Nuevo León/Killed	Army	Loss of an important and brutal Zeta operative
Arturo Beltrán Leyva "Jefe de los Jefes"	Leader of BLO	December 16, 2009/Cuernavaca/Morelos/Killed	Navy/Marines	Deprived the BLO of its most prominent capo
Alfredo "El Mochomo" Beltrán Leyva	Ally of El Chapo's Sinaloa Cartel	January 21, 2008/Culiacán, Sinaloa/Arrested	Army	Sharpened conflict between the BLO and the Sinaloa Cartel
Jesús Zambada García "El Rey"	Sinaloa Cartel operative for Central America	October 19, 2008; Mexico City/Arrested	Federal police	
Eduardo Arellano Félix	Youngest of the brothers who founded the Tijuana Cartel	October 25, 2008/Tijuana, Baja California/Captured	Army and SSPF	Extradited to the United States August 31, 2012

APPENDIX I   Clashes between Military and Civilian Police: 2007-2011

Date/Place	Police Agency	Military Agency	Nature of Conflict	Outcome
January 4, 2011 San Nicolás, NL	Municipal Police	Army	Police officers helped members of crime group escape by obstructing the military's chasing the armed suspects.	Three military personnel were hurt; a civilian killed.
March 25, 2011 San Luis Potosí	Municipal Police	Army	Mexican Army detained three police officers of San Luis Potosí DGSP for involvement in a robbery of two civilians; police allegedly took 32 mil 330 pesos.	
November 22, 2010 Apodaca, NL	Municipal Police	Marines	Suspicious activities; Marines investigated police officers.	Three outlaws and four policemen arrested.
October 26, 2010 Monterrey, NL	Municipal Police	Army	The Army stopped to investigate four policemen from Monterrey accused of following the military personnel of the the Public Security Ministry and the Federal Investigative Agency.	Only one police officer was taken into custody because he was carrying illegal radio equipment.
October 3, 2010 Monterrey, NL	Municipal Police	Army	Army investigated Guadalupe police officers for helping criminals escape after they threw a grenade into the city's main plaza.	Twelve people hurt.

(continued)

(continued)

Date/Place	Police Agency	Military Agency	Nature of Conflict	Outcome
August 20, 2010 Santiago, NL	Municipal Police	Army	Police accused of spying on, kidnapping, and killing Mayor Edelmiro Cavazos Leal.	Six municipal police arrested.
July 29, 2010 Veracruz	Municipal Police	Army	Federal judge in Veracruz ordered military to arrest 40 municipal police officers, 16 ministerial officers, and 6 former law-enforcement officials suspected of involvement in organized crime.	
January 13, 2010 Monterrey, NL	Municipal and State Police	Army	Police officer arrested for involvement in a kidnapping; after his incarceration, the suspect sought help from fellow officers, who stopped the army from taking the detainee to a military facility.	After exchanging verbal insults and stopping traffic, the police allowed the municipal officer to be taken to the Procuraduría General de Justicia (PGR); after the incident the general secretary of the state of Nuevo León, Javier Treviño, claimed that the state police arrived to support the military.

Date/Location	Police	Military	Description	Outcome
August 31, 2009 Monterrey, NL	Municipal Police	Army	Army detained an armed man with drugs and sought to take him to a military camp, but were stopped by police officers.	One police officer tried to flee the scene and shot in the leg by the army a. Man was transported to military camp; three police officers arrested a couple of days later.
September 2, 2009 Monterrey, NL	Municipal Police State and Federal.	Army	After an incident in August, military inspected documents of law enforcement agent.	Municipal cop incarcerated for not having proper ID.
June 16, 2009 San Pedro de la Garza, NL	Municipal Police	Army	Army took away firearms from the police officers of the Ministry of Public Safety.	
May 9, 2009 Cuernavaca, Morelos	Municipal Police	Army	Army arrested 27 police officers from Yautepec, including the secretary of Public Security; believed to be protecting drug sellers.	
May 5,2009 Aguascalientes	Municipal Police	Army	Police officers and military officers found associated with the Gulf Cartel. SIEDO stepped in to investigate the situation.	Six policemen and 12 military men arrested.

(*continued*)

(continued)

Date/Place	Police Agency	Military Agency	Nature of Conflict	Outcome
April 13, 2008 Municipal of Monterrey and Escobedo, NL	State Police	Army	The local police resisted an investigation that sparked a fight in Escobedo; on a different occasion, state Police resisted investigation and surrounded the four military units in Monterrey.	Six injured; during the second encounter, four police suffered injuries; Some state police were arrested; an arrangement was made: the police officers were freed, as military left the scene, police officers yelled insults. Police officers were later taken into custody to determine the sentence by a military tribunal.
April 8, 2008 Ciudad Juarez	Municipal police	Army	Army shot at a police vehicle after it failed to stop for inspection; police were attending to an emergency; Army arrested municipal cop.	One police officer received a gun shot in the head and was in critical condition. The other two Officers disappeared.

| June 6, 2007 Mexicali, BC international airport | PFP (Federal Preventive Police) | Army | Military took control of the airport; the PFP agents had allowed a smuggler to bring 26 kilograms of cocaine into the country; 14 people were investigated. | The military arrested seven officials of the PFP and three agents of Instituto Nacional de Migración (INM); suspects turned over to the Assistant Attorney General for Specialized Investigation of Organized Crime (SIEDO) in DF. |

Sources: "Ejército detiene a tres policías de SLP," ("Army Detains Three Police in SLP," *El Universal*, March 25, 2011; "Narcobloqueos en cuatro municipios de Nuevo León por la detención de un capo" ("Blockades by Municipal Police in Four Nuevo León Municipalities to Arrest Capo"), *La Jornada*, November 22, 2010; "Ejercito Mexicano detiene a 27 policias en Morelos" ("The Mexican Army Detains 27 Police Officers in the State of Morelos"), *Televisa*, Mayo 9, 2009; "Ejercito retira armas a policías de San Pedro Garza, NL" ("Army Takes Firearms Away from Police Officers of San Pedro Garza, NL"), *Televisa*, June 16, 2009; "Ejército revisa armas de 500 policías en NL" ("Army Inspects Firearms of 500 Police Officers in NL"), *El Universal*, November 28, 2011; "Policías y Militares se enfrentan en Nuevo León" ("Police and Soldiers Confront Each Other in Nuevo León"), *El Universal*, January 13, 2010; "'Cacería' de policías espías en la metrópoli" ("Hunt for Spying Police Officers in the City"), *revistacodigo21* magazine, October 26, 2010; "Investigan a policías por narcoterrorismo en Guadalupe; se recuperan heridos en granadazo" (" Police Investigated for Narcoterrorism in Guadalupe, Injured Recover After Granade Explosion"), *revistacodigo21* magazine, October 3, 2010; "Confirman autoridades detención de 56 policías" ("Authorities Confirm Detention of 56 Officers"), *El Mexicano*, July 29, 2010; "Reportan balacera entre policías y militares en Nuevo Leon" ("Shootout between Police Officers and Military Soldiers Reported in Nuevo León"), *El Informador*, August 31,2009; "Controlan los 'Zetas' a la policía de Aguascalientes," ("The Zetas control the Police in Aguascalientes"), *Entre Lineas*, May 5, 2009; "Enfrentamiento entre militares y policías en Monterrey deja seis heridos," ("Confrontation Between Military and Police in Monterrey leaves six wounded"), *Chihuahua al Instante*, April 13, 2008; "Militares balean a policías de Ciudad Juárez," ("Military Shoot Police in Ciudad Juárez"), *La Jornada*, April 8, 2008; "Arraigan a agentes federales adscritos al aeropuerto de Mexicali," ("Federal Agents Assigned to Mexicali Airport Detained"), *La Jornada*, June 6, 2007.

APPENDIX J Military Budgets and Desertions

Year	Budget (millions of pesos)	% Increased Pay for Combat Troops	Number of Desertions
1997	28,456	N.A.	11,122
1998	27,435	N.A.	18,861
1999	30,311	N.A.	19,849
2000	20,375	N.A.	22,205
2001	22,424	N.A.	15,870
2002	22,705	N.A.	15,503
2003	22,831	N.A.	14,744
2004	23,332	N.A.	18,267
2005	25,002	N.A.	20,224
2006	26,031	4,000 pesos	16,405
2007	32,200	26.9%	16,641
2008	34,861	41.2%	9,032
2009	43,632	68.6%	6,879
2010	43,632	92.2%	4,398
2011	50,039	118.5%	3,451
2012	55,610	N.A.	8,931
2013	77,127	N.A.	N.A.

Sources: The following URLs provide information, with page numbers, that the Federal Institute for Access to Information and Protection of Data (IFAI), Mexico's transparency institute, has received from SEDENA, http://www.sedena.gob.mx/pdf/ifai/2007/marzo_2007.pdf (20); http:// www.sedena.gob.mx/pdf/ifai/2011/febrero-2011.pdf (p. 21); https://www.infomex.org.mx/gobiernofederal/moduloPublico/rMedioElectP.action?idFolioSol= 0000700017811&idTipoResp=6# (p. 22); http://www.sedena.gob.mx/pdf/ifai/2011/junio-2011.pdf (23); Juan Arvizu and Andrea Merlos, "Este año van 18 mil: diputados," *El Universal*, December 4, 2008; Jorge Alejandro Medellín, "A la baja, reclutamiento para Ejército mexicano," *El Universal*, February 8, 2009. The number between January 2007 and June 2011 was 40,179, according to "Con mejor salario baja deserción en fuerzas armadas," *Milenio.com*, September 11, 2011; of this number, 17,758 were soldiers, 119 were officers, and eight were "jefes" (ranking officers). See "Más de 100 mil soldados han desertado en siete años, dice el Ejército," *Diario Las America.com*, January 23, 2008, www.diariolasamericas. com/news; Benito Jiménez, "Refuerza Ejército plan de reclutamiento," *Reforma*, February 7, 2008. Between 1995 and September 2008, 1,559 GAFES deserted. Between March 2009 and March 2011 some 121 Special Forces went AWOL. Between January 2007 and November 30, 2011, 92.43 percent of the 69,315 deserters were common soldiers, many of whom had no idea of the rigors of military life; "Recompensan a militares," *Reforma*, February 19, 2012; Zósimo Camacho, "Más de 55 mil deserciones en las Fuerzas Armadas," *Contralínea*, July 10, 2013.

APPENDIX K Mexico's Major Federal Law-Enforcement Agencies and Grassroots Forces at the Beginning of the Peña Nieto Administration

Agency	Commander	Number of Cadres	Responsible for Training	Base(s)	Functions	Innovations
Policía Federal	Enrique Galindo Ceballos	40,357	Military police; foreign advisers	Nation-wide Central Command (Iztapalapa, DF)	Protect such strategic assets as dams, hydroelectric plants, refineries, airports, and highways	Better recruitment; "zero tolerance" of corruption; strict discipline; enhanced training in intelligence, tactics, technology, human rights, and proper legal procedures; continuing education
Policía Federal Ministerial	Vidal Díaz Leal Ochoa	3,800		Presence in all 31 states	Formerly AFI/Investigative arm of Attorney General (PGR)	Point of contact for Plataforma México (law enforcement's major database) thanks to a new Communications Center funded by the Mérida Initiative
Mando Único	Typically the state public security secretaries; municipalities agree to place their police under a single state command	There are some 490,000 state and municipal police —with three quarters at the local level	Federal police, military police, private security firms	Decided by each state	Coordinate activities against criminals, especially in poor, vulnerable municipalities; economies of scale in acquiring equipment; encourage joint actions in other areas	By March 15, 2013, adopted by most municipalities in Aguascalientes, Mexico State, Morelos, NL, Chihuahua, Campeche, and DF

(continued)

Agency	Commander	Number of Cadres	Responsible for Training	Base(s)	Functions	Innovations
Community Police	Some enjoy the backing of municipal leaders, including those in the business community who seek protection; the Coordinadora Regional de Autoridades Comunitarias (CRAC) has worked in community policing for 17 years under the legitimate "uses and customs" practiced in 418 of Oaxaca's 570 municipalities; other grassroots militias like the Unión de Pueblos y Organizaciones del Estado de Guerrero (UPOEG), which Bruno Placido founded in January 2012, either turn criminals over to authorities or take justice into their own hands	There are hundreds, perhaps thousands, in the dirt poor Costa Chica of Guerrero and Oaxaca, who seek to end the lawlessness in the municipalities	On February 9, 2013, Interior Secretary Osorio Chong said the government will seek to "regularize their situation so that they can continue to assist authorities"			Protest against the failure of the government to provide security against ordinary criminals, cartels and vigilantes; even as Osorio Chong spoke of regularizing the community forces, the Knights Templars hung banners from bridges throughout Michoacán demanding that the government "put a stop to the farce of the community police," which it accused of working for the Jalisco-based CJNG cartel

Sources: Lorena López, "Estados más violentos de México, los que tienen menos policías," *Vanguardia*, April 21, 2011; Omar Aguilar, "Acuerdan México y Francia modelo de gendarmería anticrimen," *Noticias MVS*, October 17, 2012; Alejandro Hope, "Is It Worth Creating a Gendarmerie in Mexico?" *InSight Crime*, December 10, 2012; "Impulsan mando único policial en México," *Univisión*, February 2, 2013; "Grupos de Autodefensa reflejan inseguridad en México," *IFE*, February 12, 2013; Antonio Baranda, "Busca Mondragón renovar a la PF," *Reforma*, February 26, 2013; Antonio Baranda, "Alista Gobierno Gendarmería," *Reforma*, February 26, 2013; Francisco Nieto, "Se renovará la Policía Federal: Mondragón," *El Universal*, February 26, 2013; Rubicela Morelos e Israel Dávila, "Avanza la integración de los mandos únicos en Morelos y estado de México," *La Jornada*, March 4, 2013; "Some Mexican Vigilantes Set Aside Masks and Checkpoints, Seek to Form National Movement," *Associated Press*, March 14, 2013.

APPENDIX L   Advisory Council for the Pact for Mexico

The entire Consejo includes:
- Gustavo Madero Muñoz, president of the PAN
- Santiago Creel Miranda
- Marco Antonio Adame
- Sen. Rosa Adriana Díaz Lizama
- Alejandro Zapata Perogordo
- Juan Molinar Horcasitas, technical secretary

PRI
- César Camacho Quiroz, president of the PRI
- Martha Tamayo Morales
- Sen. Raúl Cervantes Andrade
- Dip. Héctor Gutiérrez de la Garza
- Arturo Huicochea Alanis, technical secretary

PRD
- Jesús Zambrano, presidente of the PRD
- Jesús Ortega Martínez
- Pablo Gómez Álvarez
- Eloí Vázquez López
- Alejandra Barrales Magdaleno
- Guadalupe Acosta Naranjo, technical secretary

Federal Government
- Miguel Ángel Osorio Chong, secretary of Gobernación
- Luis Videgaray Caso, secretary of Finance
- Aurelio Nuño Mayer, chief of the Presidential Office
- Felipe Solís Acero, Subsecretary of the Gobernación's coordinator with Congress and technical secretary

José Murat, Executive Coordinator

APPENDIX M Perpetrators of "Rough Justice" in Guerrero

Type of Group	Weapons	Number Involved	Relations with the Government	Motivation	Areas of Operation
Vigilantes	Bottles, sticks, stones	A handful to a busload of local citizens enraged over a perceived crime and/or police indifference	Anathema to government	Satisfaction that comes from striking out at an individual whose actions are perceived as evidence that the system fails to protect them	Throughout the nation but especially in remote areas where there are few police and many of them are corrupt
Popular Revolutionary Army (Ejército Popular Revolucionario EPR)	Automatic rifles and rocket launchers	A few hundred, at best	Attacks such government facilities as PEMEX pipelines	Marxist-Leninist "Prolonged War"	According to the navy, Guerrero, Oaxaca, Chiapas, Hidalgo, Guanajuato, Morelos, Michoacán, Puebla, Querétaro, Tlaxcala, Veracruz, and DF
Revolutionary—Army of Insurgent People (Ejército Revolucionario del Pueblo Insurgente ERPI)/broke with EPR (January 1, 1998)	Automatic rifles and rocket launchers	Dozens	Claims to protect local citizens from gangs, cartels, and abusive police and politicians	Marxist-Leninist (but less rigid than the EPR)	According to the navy, Costa Chica, Guerrero, and within a triangle of villages—Ayutla, San Marcos, and Copalano—approximately 100 miles from Acapulco

Union of Towns and Organizations of Guerrero (Unión de Pueblos y Organizaciones del Estado de Guerrero (UPOEG))	Uniforms, masks, and weapons; believed to be bargaining with the state government for money, uniforms, arms, and 500 radio and other communications equipment	Unknown	May receive funding from inept Governor Ángel Aguirre Rivera so that he, in turn, can seek more security funds from the federal government; Aguirre, who has handed out gifts in Ayutla, has asked the self-defense groups to incorporate themselves into the Secure Guerrero Operation, which is composed of the armed forces and PF	Formed to fight high electricity rates but evolved into a "community police" force in Ayutla de los Libres; has turned over prisoners to the legal authorities	Claims a presence in 41 towns in Guerrero
Regional Coordinator of Community Authorities (Coordinadora Regional ad Autoridades (CRAC))	Arms; do not wear masks		Elected in village assemblies; rejects negotiations with the government, insisting that its legitimacy comes from its own communities and popular assemblies	Promotes indigenous autonomy and the protection of their lands, especially from interests illegally harvesting timber and other natural resources.	Formed in 1995, undertakes policing pursuant to "Uses and Customs," which gives it greater legitimacy; operates in 128 indigenous communities in the Costa Chica and the Montaña regions of Guerrero.

(continued)

Type of Group	Weapons	Number Involved	Relations with the Government	Motivation	Areas of Operation
Community Police (Policía Comunitaria [PC]; this has become a portmanteau that covers a number of different organizations)	Typically have arms; boast support from local businesses	Created in scores of municipalities, especially in the south and southwest	In some states, governors support Community Police (e.g., Fausto Vallejo Figueroa/Michoacán); in other states these forces are opposed (Mario López Valdez/Sinaloa)		

Sources: Allison M. Rowland, "Local Responses to Public Insecurity in Mexico: A Consideration of the policía comunitaria of the Costa Chica and the Montaña de Guerrero," a paper prepared for presentation at the Latin American Studies Association, Dallas, Texas, March 27, 2003; "A Small Guerrilla Band Is Waging War in Mexico," *Los Angeles Times*, September 20, 2007; Alfonso Juárez, "Presenta Policía Comunitaria a detenidos," *Reforma*, January 31, 2013; "Tribunales Ciudadanos en Guerrero Violan la Constitución: CNDH," *Proceso*, February 3, 2013; Ezequiel Flores Contreras, "Grupo de autodefensa libera a cuatro detenidos en Ayutla," *Proceso*, February 14, 2013; "Malova, ahora presidente de la Conago, se pronuncia contra policía comunitaria; 'es tarea del Estado' dice," *Diario*, February 20, 2013; Clayton Conn, "Mexico: Guerrero's Indigenous Community and Self-Defense Groups," *Independent Reader*, March 11, 2013; "Vigilante Justice in Mexico: A State-by-State Guide," *Just the Facts*, March 13, 2013.

Notes

INTRODUCTION

1. Biographies: Lázaro Cárdenas del Rio, http:biographies- pavocavalry .blogspot.com/2009/01/lazaro-crdenas-d..., January 16, 2009.

2. Quoted in Enrique Krauze, *General misionero: Lázaro Cárdenas* (Mexico City: Fondo de Cultura Económica, 1987), 9.

3. Quoted in William Cameron Townsend, *Lázaro Cárdenas: Mexican Democrat* (Ann Arbor, MI: George Wahr, 1952): 44–45.

4. Enrique Krauze, *Mexico: Biography of Power* (New York: HarperCollins, 1997), 444.

5. Quoted in Victoriano Anguiano, *Lázaro Cárdenas*, 39; and found in Krauze, *Mexico: Biography of Power*, 453.

6. Helen Delpar (ed.), *Encyclopedia of Latin America* (New York: McGraw Hill, 1974), 108.

7. Richard B. Mancke, *Mexican Oil and Natural Gas: Political, Strategic, and Economic Implications* (New York: Praeger, 1979), 51.

8. Krauze, *Mexico: Biography of Power*, 446.

9. Ibid., 450.

10. The numbers vary widely; in any case, the nation's population declined from 15,160,369 (1910) to 14,334,780 (1921). See "Death Tolls for the Major Wars and Atrocities of the Twentieth Century," *Twentieth Century Atlas*, http:// necrometrics.com/20c1m.htm.

11. Quoted in Vikram K. Chand, *Mexico's Political Awakening* (Notre Dame, IN: University of Notre Dame Press, 2001), 14.

12. Portes Gil, quoted in Octavio Rodríguez Araujo, *La reforma política y los partidos en México* (Mexico City: Siglo Veintiuno Editores, 1983), 29–30; and found in

Dale Story, *The Mexican Ruling Party: Stability and Authority* (New York: Praeger, 1986), 21.

13. Quoted in Howard F. Cline, *The United States and Mexico* (New York: Atheneum, 1965), 217–18.

14. Krauze, *General misionero*, 89.

15. L. Vincent Padgett, *The Mexican Political System* (2nd ed.) (Boston: Houghton Mifflin, 1976), 37–38.

16. Quoted in *New York Times*, January 26, 1935, p. 1.

17. Hugh Thomas, "The Mexican Labyrinth," a study prepared for the Twentieth Century Fund, New York, November 1990, 75.

18. For the history and evolution of the PAN in the twentieth century, see Chand, op. cit.

19. Quoted in Joe C. Ashby, *Organized Labor and the Mexican Revolution under Lázaro Cárdenas* (Chapel Hill: University of North Carolina Press, 1967), 26.

20. Quoted in Kevin J. Middlebrook, *The Political Economy of Organized Labor* (Ann Arbor, MI: University Microfilms International, 1982), 66.

21. Cline, *United States and Mexico*, 222–23.

22. Quoted in Townsend, *Lázaro Cárdenas, Mexican Democrat*, 257.

23. Cline, *United States and Mexico*, 242.

24. This section relies on George W. Grayson, *The Politics of Mexican Oil* (Pittsburgh: University of Pittsburgh Press, 1980), 14–23.

25. Howard F. Cline, *Mexico: Revolution to Evolution, 1940–1960* (Westport, CT: Greenwood, 1981), 152.

26. George W. Grayson, *Mexico: from Corporatism to Pluralism?* (Fort Worth, TX: Harcourt Brace, 1998), 20– 21.

27. Anton Cermak, http://www.princeton.edu/~achaney/tmve/wiki100k/docs/Anton_Cermak.html.

28. Dale Story, *The Mexican Ruling Party* (New York: Praeger, 1986), 28.

29. Karl M. Schmitt, *Mexico and the United States, 1821–1973: Conflict and Coexistence* (New York: Wiley, 1974), 190.

30. This material, which originally appeared in the *San Diego Union Tribune*, was written by Don Freeman, "The Brave Belong, to All Countries, Not Just One," *Mexico File* newsletter, August–September 1997.

31. George W. Grayson, *The Mexico-U.S. Business Committee: Catalyst for the North American Free Trade Agreement* (Rockville, MD: Montross, 2007), 25.

32. Quoted in Alan Riding, *Distant Neighbors: A Portrait of the Mexicans* (New York: Alfred Knopf, 1985), 57.

33. President Miguel Alemán Valdés, "GlobalSecruity.org," www.globalsecurity.org/military/world/mexico/president-aleman.htm.

34. Quoted in *México y la revolución cubana* (Mexico City: Colegio de México, 1972), 107.

35. Documents containing the anticommunist warnings appear in National Archives, RG 59, 1060-63, Box 1510, Folder 712.00/4-262; and John F. Kennedy Library, National Security Files, Trips and Conferences: President's Trip to Mexico 6/62, 5/11/531/62, Box 237.

36. Agustín F. Legorreta, Banamex CEO, interview by author, Mexico City, January 11, 2003.

37. Jorge Fernández Menéndez, *Nadie supo nada, la verdadero historia del asesinato de Eugenio Garza Sada* (Mexico City: Grijalbo, 2006).

38. Legorreta, interview.

39. Juan S. Millán Lizárraga, who later served as governor of Sinaloa, was the PRI's delegate to Tamaulipas for this election. After marking his ballot for Salinas, Hernández Galicia showed it to Millán and said something like "Now I hope you are satisfied." Millán; interview with author, August 1, 1996.

40. Quoted in "Es detenido Joaquín Hernández Galicia 'La Quina,' líder del Sindicato de PEMEX," *Efemérides*, January 10, 1989.

41. Benito Jiménez, "Dobletea cargo líder y senador hasta el 2018," *Reforma*, October 22, 2012.

42. "Dispilfarro de Hija de Romero Descamps, Ícono de Corupción Priísta," *México News*, May 19, 2012.

43. Cuauhtémoc Ibarra, expert on the SNTE and former subsecretary of Education, interview with author, Mexico City, March 1, 2013; Arturo Cano, "Guerra sucia en el magisterio," *La Jornada*, August 31, 2002.

44. Óscar Conteras Latigue, "La Quina y Jonguitud," *Mañana*, November 27, 2011.

45. Marty Graham, "Luxury Villas, Designer Labels: Jailed Mexico Union Boss' U.S. Oasis," *Reuters*, March 3, 2013.

CHAPTER 1

1. Authorities found cartridges from handguns at the scene of a confrontation between Ernesto Fonseca Carrillo and the police.

2. Agustín Ambriz, "Arévalo Gardoqui: la Sombra del narco," *Proceso*, May 7, 2000.

3. "Sócrates Rizzo: PRI Presidents Oversaw Drug Trafficking," *Borderland Beat*, February 27, 2011.

4. Ibid.

5. "Se extienden los 'ajustes de cuentas' hacia las mujeres," *El Universal*, September 12, 2005.

6. "Querían darles 'lección' a plagiados del Heavens, *Reforma*, July 5, 2013.

7. "Sinaloa," History Channel, http://www.history.com/topics/sinaloa (accessed March 8, 2013).

8. Quoted in Malcolm Beith, *The Last Narco: Inside the Hunt for El Chapo, the World's Most Wanted Drug Lord* (New York: Grove, 2010), 41.

9. Quoted in Vincent J. Schodolski and John Crewdson, "Mexico's Drug Trade Has Friends in High Places," *Chicago Tribune*, December 19, 1989.

10. Originally quoted in *Proceso* and re-quoted in Luis Alejandro Astorga Almanza, *El siglo de las drogas: el narcotráfico, del Porfiriato al nuevo milenio* (Mexico City: Plaza Janés, 2005), 133.

11. James Creechan, "A Short History of Mexico's Narcocartels: Part 1," *Narco Mexico*, May 2009.

12. Quoted in Luis Astorga, *El siglo de las drogas*, 114. For a fascinating look inside this quasi-military organization, see Sergio Aguayo Quezada, *La Charola: Una historia de los servicios de inteligencia en México* (Mexico City: Grijalbo, 2001).

13. Peter Reuter and David Ronfeldt, "Quest for Integrity: The Mexican-US Drug Issues in the 1980s," *Journal of Interamerican Studies and World Affairs* 34, no. 3 (Autumn 1992): 102–3; and quoted in Vanda Felbab-Brown, "Peña Nieto's Piñata: The Promise and Pitfalls of Mexico's New Security Policy against Organized Crime," Latin American Initiative, Brookings Institution, February 2013.

14. Quoted in Luis Astorga, "Drug Trafficking in Mexico: A First General Assessment." Discussion Paper no. 36, January 22, 2009, www.unesco.org/most/astorga.htm

15. María Celia Toro, *Mexico's "War" on Drugs: Causes and Consequences* (Boulder, CO: Lynne Rienner, 1995), 12–13.

16. Richard Craig, "La Campaña Permanente: Mexico's Anti-Drug Campaign," *Journal of Interamerican Studies and World Affairs* (May 1978): 105.

17. Richard Nixon, "Remarks at a Bipartisan Leadership Meeting on Narcotics and Dangerous Drugs," Gerhard Peters and John T. Wooley, *The American Presidency Project*, www.presidency.ucsb.edu/ws/?pid=2280.

18. Craig, "La Campaña Permanente," 116.

19. Quoted in Luis Astorga, "Drug Trafficking in Mexico."

20. Quoted in Luis Astorga, *El siglo de las drogas*.

21. *Noroeste* (Culiacán), February 8–10, 1977.

22. Elaine Shannon, *Desperados: Latin American Drug Lords, U.S. Lawmen, and the War America Can't Win* (New York: Viking Penguin, 1988), 63.

23. Quoted in Juan M. Vasquez, "Redoubling Battle, Mexico Says of Its Anti-Drug Drive," *Los Angeles Times*, March 24, 1985.

24. Luis Astorga, "Drug Trafficking in Mexico."

25. Ibid.

26. Marjorie Miller, "In Death, a Generous Rancher Emerges as 'Crazy Pig,' the Drug Lord: Trafficking; Somehow, He Avoided Detection and Arrest for Years until He Was Mysteriously Gunned Down in Guadalajara," *Los Angeles Times*, November 20, 1991.

27. Quoted in Astorga, *El siglo de las drogas*, 116.

28. Hector Tobar, "Mexico Protests Drug Statements Made on NBC," *Los Angeles Times*, January 11, 1990; Astorga, *El siglo de las drogas*, 141–42.

29. Quoted in Anita Snow, "Sentence Overturned for Convicted Killer of U.S. Drug Agent," *Associated Press*, April 25, 1997.

30. Quoted in Ioan Grillo, "Autumn of the Capo: The Diary of a Drug Lord," *Time*, May 20, 2009.

31. Philip L. Russell, *Mexico under Salinas* (Austin, TX: Mexico Resource Center, 1994), 13.

32. Marisa Taylor, "Mexican Drug Traffickers Wage PR War over Image," *McClatchy Newspapers*, September 2, 2008.

33. For an insight into the wealth of Félix Gallardo and other big shots, see Héctor Aguilar Camín, "Narco historias extraordinarias,"*Nexus*, May 2007.

34. "Family: Ailing Drug Lord Seeks Help," *USA Today*, April 16, 2008.

CHAPTER 2

1. This section draws heavily on Jake Bergman, "The Place Mexico's Drug Kingpins Call Home." *Frontline* PBS, www.pbs.org/wgbh/pages/frontline/shows/drugs/business/place.html.

2. Kevin B. Zeese, *"Nixon Tapes Show Twisted Roots of Marijuana Prohibition: Misinformation, Culture Wars and Prejudice"* (Washington, DC: Common Sense Drug Policy, updated July 9, 2009).

3. Nixon Tapes, May 13, 1971, between 10:30 a.m. and 12:30 p.m., Oval Office Conversation 498-5, meeting with Nixon, Haldeman, and Ehrlichman, http://www.csdp.org/research/nixonpot.txt.

4. "GI's in Vietnam High on Hope's Jokes," *New York Times*, December 23, 1970.

5. Zeese, *"Nixon Tapes Show Twisted Roots of Marijuana Prohibition."*

6. "Thirty Years of America's Drug War: A Chronology," *Frontline* PBS, www.pbs.org/wgbh/pages/frontline/shows/drugs/business/chron.

7. William John Cox, "Richard Nixon's Vengeful War on Marijuana," *Consortium News*, September 16, 2010.

8. Quoted in Zeese, "Nixon Tapes Reveal Twisted Roots of Marijuana Prohibition."

9. Ambassador (ret.) Myles R. R. Frechette, email to author, November 25, 2012.

10. Carl Hiassen, "Flamboyant Cocaine Dealer Bids Farewell," *Houston Chronicle Archives*, June 28, 1985.

11. Ibid.

12. Francisco Alvarado, "Miami: See It Like a Drug Dealer," *Miami New Times*, October 13, 2005.

13. David Ovalle, "'Cocaine Godmother' Griselda Blanco Gunned Down in Colombia," *Miami Herald*, September 3, 2012.

14. "All 107 Aboard Killed as Colombian Jet Explodes," *New York Times*, November 28, 1989; Tom Wells, "Cocaine Cartel Chief Charged with Presidential Candidate's Assassination," *Associated Press*, September 25, 1990.

15. Bruce M. Bagley, "Drug Trafficking and Organized Crime in the Americas: Major Trends in the Twenty-First Century," published in *Agrarian Ideas for a Developing World*, March 24, 2011, http://agrarianideas.blogspot.com/2011/03/essay-on-drug-trends-by-bruce-bagley.html; Adam Thomson, "Colombia 'Mafia Links' Boost Cocaine Exports," *Financial Times*, November 29, 1999.

16. Ibid.

17. Frechette, email to author.

18. Larry Rohter, "Colombian Turncoat Tells Miami Court Samper Took Drug Money," *New York Times*, July 25, 1997.

19. Ibid.

20. "El adiós del cardenal Pedro Rubiano; se dedicará a viajar, a leer y a escribir sus memorias," *El Tiempo*, July 11, 2010.

21. Frechette, email to author.

22. Quoted in Douglas Farah, "Stung by U.S. Decertification, Colombia May Cut Cooperation," *Washington Post*, March 2, 1997.

23. Ibid.

24. Frechette, email to author.

25. Testimony by William E. Ledwith, Chief of International Operations, DEA, before the House Government Reform Committee, Subcommittee on Criminal Justice, Drug Policy, and Human Resources, February 15, 2000.

26. Steve Ambrus, "Fighting the New Drug Lords," *Newsweek*, February 20, 2000.

27. Ibid.

28. "Una visita de estado con dividendos para Colombia," *ELTIEMPO.com*, December 24, 1998.

29. Dr. Bruce Michael Bagley, "Drug Trafficking, Political Violence and U.S. Policy in Colombia in the 1990s," paper presented at the School of International Studies, University of Miami, Coral Gables, FL, January 5, 2001, FN 73.

30. "Pastrana, Clinton Defend Colombia Aid Package," *CNN World*, August 30, 2000.

31. Quoted in Clifford Krauss, "Colombian Port Dresses Up for Clinton Visit," *New York Times*, August 28, 2000.

32. Frechette, email to author.

33. Luis Torres de la Llosa, "La ayuda de Estados Unidos ira contra las FARC si trafican droga," *El Nuevo Herald*, January 27, 2000 and cited in Bagley, "Drug Trafficking, Political Violence and U.S. Policy."

34. Quoted in Office of Press Secretary, The White House, "Press Conference by President Clinton, President Pastrana of Colombia, House Speaker Dennis Hastert, and Senator Joseph Biden," Cartagena, Colombia, August 30, 2000.

35. Frechette, email to author.

36. David Gollust, "Clinton-Colombia," *Voice of America*, August 24, 2000.

37. "The FARC's Moment of Truth," *Economist*, January 17, 2002; Commander Christiana quoted in Jeremy McDermott, "Colombia Changes Tactics in Drugs War," *BBC News*, August 31, 2000.

38. McDermott, "Colombia Changes Tactics."

39. "The FARC's Moment of Truth."

40. Frechette, email to author, March 13, 2013.

41. Frechette, email to author, November 25, 2012.

42. Ibid.

43. Ibid.

44. Ibid.

45. Quoted in Frances Robles, "Colombia Leader Ending Term without Peace," *Miami Herald*, August 5, 2002.

46. "Profile: Alvaro Uribe Velez," *BBC*, March 29, 2010.

47. Frechette, email to author, November 25, 2012.

48. Latin American Working Groups, "The Other Half of the Truth," June 2008.

49. Quoted in "The Man behind Colombia's Miracle," *Commentary*, March 1, 2010.

50. Brian Fitzpatrick, "Colombia Stumbles towards Peace, but Belligerence Still the Currency in Strife-torn Land," *The Scotsman*, November 2, 2012.

51. Frechette quoted in *Latin America Advisor*, Inter-American Dialogue, August 16, 2011.

52. Quoted in "Colombian Drug Suspect Pleads Not Guilty in New York," Associated Press, July 10, 2013.

CHAPTER 3

1. Cory Molzahn et al., *"Drug Violence in Mexico: Data and Analysis through 2012,"* Transborder Institute, University of San Diego, February 2013, pp. 33–34. This excellent study contains a graph of drug-related arrests from 1988 to 2011 (p. 34).

2. U.S. Office of the U.S. Trade Representative, "North American Free Trade Agreement (NAFTA)." http://www.ustr.gov/trade-agreements/free-trade-agreements/north-american-free-trade-agreement-nafta, archived July 11, 2013.

3. Victoria Bruce and Karin Hayes with Jorge Enrique Botero, *Hostage Nation: Colombia's Guerrilla Army and the Failed War on Drugs* (New York: Knopf, 2010), 47.

4. U.S./Mexico Joint Working Committee on Transportation Planning, "Commercial Border Crossings and Wait Time Measurement at Laredo World Trade Bridge and the Colombia-Solidarity Bridge," Final Report Prepared for the Texas Department of Transportation, March 31, 2012.

5. "Mexico Drug Smugglers Make Jesus Statue of Cocaine," *Reuters*, May 30, 2008; Philip Caulfield, "Drug Catapult Seized at U.S.-Mexico Border; 9-Foot Hurler Used to Launch Pot into Arizona,"*New York Daily News*, January 27, 2011.

6. Dora Gómora, "DEA: mueve narco drogras en torpedos," *El Universal*, December 20, 2011.

7. Quoted in Sheila Steffen, "Drug Smugglers becoming More Creative U.S. Agents Say," *CNNJustice*, April 16, 2009.

8. Ábrego is one of several key players on the Mexican drug scene who was born in the United States; see, Ildefonso Ortiz, "Some Cartel Bosses Are Born in the U.S., but Work in Mexico," *Monitor* (McAllen, TX), June 23, 2013.

9. Peter Lupsha, "Transnational Narco-Corruption and Narco-Investment: A Focus on Mexico," *Transnational Organized Crime Journal*, Spring 1995.

10. Peter Lupsha, "Transnational Narco-Corruption and Narco-Investment: A Focus on Mexico." *Frontline* PBS, www.pbs.org/wgbh/pages/frontline/shows/mexico/readings/lupsha.html.

11. Chris Eskridge, "Mexican Cartels and Their Integration into Mexican Socio-Political Culture." An earlier version was presented at the International Conference on Organized Crime: Myth, Power, Profit, October 1999, Lausanne, Switzerland, p. 10, www.customscorruption.com/mexican_cartels_integr.htm.

12. Lupsha, "Transnational Narco-Corruption."

13. Ibid.

14. See Terrance E. Poppa, *Drug Lord: The Life and Death of a Mexican Kingpin: A True Story* (2nd ed., rev. and updated) (Seattle: Demand Publications, 1998).

15. Quoted in "Poison Across the Rio Grande," *Economist* (London), November 13, 1997.

16. Jiménez, "Identifica el Ejército tres rutas de cárteles."

17. John J. Bailey and Roy Godson, *Organized Crime and Democratic Governability: Mexico and the U.S.-Mexican Borderlands* (Pittsburgh: University of Pittsburgh Press, 2001), 48; Mark Fineman, "Mexican Drug Cartel Chief Convicted in U.S.," *Los Angeles Times*, October 17, 1996.

18. Tracy Wilkinson, "Mexican Navy Says It Captured Cartel Leader," *Los Angeles Times*, September 5, 2012.

19. Aracely Garza, "Capturan a presunto líder del cartel del Golfo Cadereyta," *Excélsior*, September 29, 2012.

20. "Caen banda ligada al Cártel del Golfo," *Reforma*, February 1, 2013.

21. Ildefonso Ortiz, "Gulf Cartel Infighting Reignites with Reynosa," *The Monitor*, March 18, 2013.

22. Notimex, "Capturan a 'El Tatanka' instructor de 'Los Zetas,' " *Noticieros Televisa*, April 25, 2009.

23. Alfredo Corchado, "Drug Cartels Operate Training Camps near Texas Border Just inside Mexico," *Dallas Morning News*; Carlos Coria, "Entrenan a zetas en Texas," *Excélsior*, May 22, 2009.

24. Dane Schiller, "Los Zetas entrenan en un rancho que mantienen en Texas, según el FBI," Houston Chronicle (Spanish ed.), May 27, 2009.

25. An impeccable, but confidential source, revealed that 22 tons of cocaine were captured.

26. "Mexico's Violent Zetas Cartel Sees New Leader Emerge," *Fox News Latino*, August 23, 2012.

27. "Mexican Journalist Dismembered, Burned, Officials Say," CNN World, March 1, 2010.

28. Dane Schiller, "Mexican Crook: Gangsters Arrange Fights to Death for Entertainment," *Houston Chronicle*, June 11, 2011; and "Invasion of the Body Snatchers," *Reuters*, March 9, 2007.

29. During this period, thieves penetrated 4, 679 oil and gas ducts; see Benito Jiménez, "Gastan 5 mil mdp en reparar ductos,"*Reforma*, March 30, 2013.

30. "Audita Coahuila ventas de carbón," *Reforma*, November 1, 2012.

31. Randy Kreider and Mark Schone, *ABC News*, October 9, 2012.

32. E. Eduardo Castillo, "Heriberto Lazcano's Relatives' Bodies Exhumed after Dead Drug Lord's Body Stolen," *Huffington Post*, October 22, 2012.

33. Quoted in Melissa Stusinski, "New Zeta Drug Lord 'Violent to the Point of Sadism,' " www.inquisitr.com/362503/new-zetas-drug-lord-violent-to-the-point-of-sadism/

34. Quoted in Yeillin Blanco, "Las bandas de narcos son empresas en México," January 22, 2010 www.minuto59.com/2010/01/las-bandas-de-narcos-son empersa.

35. "The Eerie Logic of the Zetas Cartel's Most Infamous Acts," *ABC News*, October 10, 2012.

36. John P. Sullivan and Samuel Logan, "Los Zetas: Massacres, Assassinations and Infantry Tactics," *Homeland 1*, November 24, 2010.

37. "Crecen Zetas en frontera sur," *Reforma*, February 17, 2013.

38. Irene Savio, "Anuncia Guatemala operativo con México," *Reforma*, February 17, 2013.

39. Ildefonso Ortiz, "Detainee: Zetas Smuggle Guns into US to Avoid Gulf Cartel, *Monitor*, November 30, 2012.

40. "Polarización en el SNTE," *El Universal* ("Bajo Reserva"), July 28, 2007.

41. Quoted in Corchado, "Cartel's Enforcers Outpower their Boss."

42. "Falsos zetas se dedican a la extorsión," *Consejo para la ley y los Derechos Humanos, A.C.*, October 25, 2007.

43. "Dan 'Zetas' narcoconsejo," *Reforma*, May 4, 2008.

44. César Peralta González, "Ejecutan a falsos 'Zetas' en Reynosa, tenían un narcomensaje," *Milenio*, February 28, 2009.

45. "Reclutan Zetas a mujeres," *El Norte*, March 27, 2009.

46. Ximena Moretti, "Zetas utilizan mujeres como sicarios," *Ágora*, April 23, 2012.

47. Rafael Malthus Ruiz, "Destaca EU fallo contra José Treviño," *Reforma*, May 11, 2013.

48. "El sobrinos de uno de los líderes de 'Los Zetas' es detenido en Monterrey," *CNN México*, June 15, 2012.

49. "Atrapan a jefe Zeta," *Reforma*, July 16, 2013; and Ildefonso Ortiz, "Fall of Zeta Chief Spells Uncertain Future for Cartel," *The Monitor* (McAllen, TX), July 15, 2013.

50. "Usan drones de EU en captura de El Z-40," *La Jornada*, July 19, 2013.

51. "Los Zetas, el cártel más poderoso de México: Stratfor," *Proceso*, April 18, 2013.

52. For the quotations in this paragraph, see Randal C. Archibold and Ginger Thompson, "Capture of Mexican Crime Boss Appears to End a Brutal Chapter," *New York Times*, July 17, 2013.

CHAPTER 4

1. William Branigin, "Bodyguards' Eating Habits Eased Capture of Drug Kingpin," *Washington Post*, April 13, 1989.

2. Diego Enrique Osorno, "El Jefe de Jefe, Miguel Ángel Félix Gallardo, un 'capo culto,' " *Columnas*, March 30, 2009.

3. For an extraordinary book on the machinations of Acosta and other prominent players on the drug scene, see Terrence E. Poppa, *Drug Lord: The Life & Death of a Mexican Kingpin* (2nd ed., rev and updated); (Seattle: Demand Publications, 1998).

4. Reportedly, he prefers to be called "El Tío" or "The Uncle."

5. Malcolm Beith, *The Last Narco: Inside the Hunt for El Chapo, the World's Most Wanted Drug Lord* (New York: Grove Press, 2010), 38.

6. "Los Tres rostros de El Mayo Zambada," *El Universal*, June 7, 2007.

7. Olga R. Rodriguez, "Troops Kill Senior 'Capo' of Cartel," *Associated Press*, July 30, 2010.

8. Ibid.

9. "Ejército mexicano capturó al número dos del cártel de Sinaloa, Roberto Beltrán Burgos," *InfoRegion*, May 31, 2009.

10. "Mexican Army Kills Sinaloa Cartel Leader," *EFE*, October 13, 2012.

11. "Shorty Guzmán's 'security chief' arrested in Mexico," *BBC News Latin America & Caribbean*, February 10, 2013.

12. Beith, *Last Narco*.

13. Adriana Gómez Licón, "Mexico Angry That Drug Lord Joaquín 'El Chapo' Guzmán on *Forbes* billionaire List," *El Paso Times*, March 14, 2009; "The 2009 Times 100" *Time*, May 1, 2009.

14. Beith, *Last Narco*, 61.

15. Ibid., 71.

16. Ricardo Ravelo, "The Secrets of 'El Azul,' " *Borderland Beat*, May 18, 2012.

17. For this analogy, I am indebted to Nathan Jones, postdoctoral fellow in drug policy, James A. Baker III Institute, Rice University; telephone interview, January 2, 2013.

18. "Se refuerza el cártel de Sinaloa," *EFE*, August 10, 2005; Grayson and Logan, *The Executioner's Men*, 16–17.

19. Grayson and Logan, *Executioner's Men*, 16–17.

20. M. J. Stephey, "Joaquín Guzmán Loera: Billionaire Drug Lord," *Time*, March 13, 2009.

21. Juan Veledíaz, " 'El Azul' discrete, platicador y gentil," *El Universal*, June 15, 2008.

22. Alberto Morales, "PGR debe informar sobre los más buscados: IFAI," *El Universal*, July 1, 2013.

23. Ravelo, "The Secrets of 'El Azul.' "

24. "Deja su marca en Guadalajara," *Reforma*, August 10, 2013.

25. Ravelo, "The Secrets of 'El Azul.' "

26. "Top Cocaine Smuggler Nabbed, Mexico Says," *CNNWorld*, January 21, 2008.

27. Quoted in Ibid.

28. "Beltrán Leyva Organization," *Borderland Beat*, September 13, 2009.

29. Ibid.

30. "La cantan famosos a 'La Barbie,' " *Reforma*, January 6, 2013.

31. "Beltrán Leyva Cartel Boss Arrested in Mexico City," *Borderland Beat*, November 2, 2012.

32. "The Gang that Took on Chapo: Los Mazatlecos," *Borderland Beat*, July 28, 2012.

33. Rafael Núñez, "A Not-So-Secret History of Vice in Juárez," *Newspaper Tree*, March 6, 2006.

34. Ibid. the classic study of Acosta is Terrence E. Poppa, *Drug Lord: The Life & Death of a Mexican Kingpin* (Seattle: Demand Publications, 1998).

35. Rafael Nuñez, "Amado Carrillo Fuentes' Death: Revenge over the Death of Ochoa Uncle," *Borderland Beat*, July 9, 2012.

36. Quoted in Molly Moore, "Drug Lord Goes Home in Coffin," *Washington Post*, July 12, 1997.

37. Dave Axe, "Inside the Fortified Palaces of Mexico's Drug Lords," *Toronto Post*, October 22, 2012.

38. "Los narcocachorros," *El Universal*, June 28, 2009.

39. David Gibson, "Juárez Cartel Threatens to Kill 'One Officer Daily,' " *Borderland Beat*, January 28, 2012.

40. "U.S. Judge Sentences Mexican Drug Gang Leader to Life in Prison for Killings," *CNNJustice*, April 6, 2012.

41. Lourdes Cárdenas, "Alleged Juárez Cartel Leader Arrested," *El Paso Times*, July 22, 2012.

42. Fernando Reyes, "Violencia aflora en Chihuahua; ejecutan a 9 en la capital este fin de semana," *Rumbo de Chihuahua,* June 23, 2013.

43. The five decapitated men may have been involved in the murder of a waitress/prostitute who worked in the bar and who had been impregnated by a member of La Familia. A few days before the ghastly incident, she refused to have sex with them. They waited for her when the bar closed and then raped and killed her. La Familia began its own investigation and found these men guilty. This may explain why the death note indicated that they "do not kill women."

44. James C. McKinley Jr., "Mexican Drug War Turns Barbaric, Grisly," *New York Times*, October 26, 2006, www.nytimes.com.

45. "Toma 'La Familia' ley en Michoacán," *Reforma*, November 24, 2006.

46. Peter Chalk, "Profiles of Mexico's Seven Major Drug Trafficking Organizations," U.S. Military Academy, January 18, 2012.

47. Alejandro Jiménez, "Atentados en Morelia Investigan ligas entre alcaldías y 'Familia,'" *El Universal*, September 19, 2008; Sam Logan and Kate Kairies, "U.S. Drug Habit Migrates to Mexico," *Americas Policy Program Special Report*, February 7, 2007, www.americas.irc-online.org.

48. "La Familia: Society's Saviours or Sociopaths."

49. Rafael Rivera, "'Boom' carguero en Lázaro Cárdenas," *El Universal*, December 29, 2008; Secretaría de *Comuniciones y Transportes, Informe: Estadístico Mensual: de cargo, buques y pasajeros*, January–December 2011–2012.

50. Quoted in Ioan Grillo, "Crusaders of Meth: Mexico's Deadly Knights Templar," *Time*, June 23, 2011.

51. "Dominar al país, plan de la Familia," www.deyaboo.forumcommunity.net.

52. Quoted in Hannah Stone, "New Cartel Announces Takeover from Familia Michoacán," *InsightCrime*, March 14, 2011.

53. "Dan Templarios 'bienvenida' Peña," *Reforma*, December 20, 2012.

54. "Caballeros Templarios de Michoacán," *In Sight Crime* http://es .insightcrime.org/grupos-mexico/caballeros- templarios.

55. "Caen 'jefe de plaza,'" *Reforma*, October 5, 2012; "Cae El Chivo, jefe de homicidas de Los Caballeros Templares," *Terra*, July 13, 2011.

56. "Ingresan 'Templarios' a Jalisco por alianza," *Reforma*, February 7, 2013.

57. "Captura el Ejército a sobrinos de capo," *Reforma*, January 31, 2013.

58. Ioan Grillo, "Crusaders of Meth: Mexico's Deadly Knights Templar," *Time*, June 23, 2011.

59. "Michoacán: al borde del Estado fallido," *Reforma* (Enfoque section), May 26, 2013.

60. Quoted in Benjamin Wells-Wallace, "The Truce on Drugs," *New York Magazine*, November 25, 2012.

61. Quoted in Robert J. Caldwell, "U.S. Law Enforcement Captures the Head of Mexico's Most Violent Drug Cartel, the Arellano Félix Organization," *Union-Tribune* (San Diego), August 20, 2006.

62. "Feds Arrest Reputed Drug King on Fishing Trip," *USA Today*, August 17, 2006.

63. "Mexico Arrests Alleged Drug Cartel Hitman in 1993 Assassination of Catholic Cardinal," *Associated Press*, January 27, 2008.

64. "Atribuyen 400 sicarios a 'El Muletas,' " *Reforma*, February 10, 2010.

65. "Empresarios y funcionarios protegían al Teo," *Zeta* (an independent weekly newspaper published in Tijuana), www.zetatijuana.com/html/ EdicionActual.

66. "New Drug Cartel Generation Emergences in Tijuana," *Borderland Beat*, December 3, 2009.

67. Quoted in Wallace-Wells, "The Truth on Drugs."

68. Ibid.

CHAPTER 5

1. Quoted in Alberto Nájar, "¿Quién conoce a Felipe Calderón?" *La Jornada*, November 6, 2005.

2. Quoted in Donald J. Mabry, "Father of a Mexican President: Luis Calderón Vega," www. historicaltextarchive.com/sections.pho?op=viewarticle&ar id=759, October 2, 2006.

3. "De Castillo Peraza a Calderón: "Tu naturaleza, tu temperamento es ser desconfiado has de tu sobra," *Etcetera*, July 22, 2009.

4. *Houston Chronicle*, February 13, 2006, and quoted in "Felipe Calderón," *Encyclopedia of World Biographies*, http://www.notablebiographies.com/supp/ Supplement-Ca-Fi/Calder-n-Felipe.html.

5. James C. McKinley, Jr., "Feuding President and Mayor Eclipse Mexican Campaign," *New York Times*, April 7, 2006.

6. James C. McKinley Jr., *New York Times*, January 26, 2006 and quoted in "Felipe Calderón," *Encyclopedia of World Biographies*.

7. Author's interview with former deputy Agustín Basave Benítez, August 3, 2011, Mexico City.

8. Dave Graham, "Mexico Opposition May Work with Criminals: Calderón," *Reuters*, October 16, 2011.

9. James C. McKinley Jr., "Mexican Drug War Turns Barbaric, Grisly," *New York Times*, October 26, 2006.

10. Quoted in "Acapulco Rocked by Gang Violence," *Sydney Morning Herald*, August 13, 2005.

11. Based on Mexico's 2012 National Survey on Victimization and Perception of Public Security. See Claire O'Neill McCleskey, *InSight Crime*, September 28, 2012.

12. Luis Hernández Navarro, "Joaquín Villalobos, el intellectual del calderonismo," *La Jornada*, January 26, 2010.

13. Tracy Wilkinson, "A Top Salvadoran ex-Guerrilla Commander Advises Mexico's Conservative President," *Los Angeles Times*, October 22, 2010.

14. Wilkinson, "A Top Salvadoran ex-Guerrilla Commander."

15. Quoted in White House, "Presidents Bush and Berger of Guatemala Participate in Joint Press Availability," Guatemala City, March 12, 2007.

16. Quoted in Peter Baker, "Calderón Admonishes Bush on Thorny Issues," *Washington Post*, March 14, 2007.

17. The White House, "Joint U.S.-Mexico Communiqué," March 14, 2007.

18. U.S. Embassy (Mexico City), Fact Sheet: "The Mérida Initiative: An Overview," Mexico City, May 2012; Eric L. Olson, "El futuro de la cooperación entre México y Estados Unidos. Iniciativa Mérida," in *Atlas de la seguridad y la defensa de México 2012*, eds. Sergio Aguayo Quezada and Raúl Benítez Manaut (Mexico City: Casede, 2012).

19. Government Accountability Office, "Mérida Initiative: The United States Has Provided Counternarcotics and Anticrime Support but Needs Better Performance Measures," Report to Congressional Requesters, July 2010.

20. "Mexico Still Waiting for U.S. Aid," *Borderland Beat*, December 7, 2009.

21. William Booth, "U.S. Lagging in Sending Anti-Drug Aid to Mexico, GAO Says," *Washington Post*, December 4, 2009.

22. Quoted in Ibid.

23. See, for example, Andrew Selee, *Overview of the Mérida Initiative* (Washington, D.C.: Woodrow Wilson International Center for Scholars, May 2008); Diana Negroponte, "Pillar IV of 'Beyond Merida:' Addressing the Socio- Economic

Causes of Drug Related Crime and Violence in Mexico"; Working Paper Series on U.S.-Mexico Security Cooperation, Woodrow Wilson International Center for Scholars, 2012; publications on the subject by the U.S. Congressional Research Service; Olson, "El futuro de la cooperación."

24. Quoted in "A 'New Phase' of the Mérida Initiative," *Just the Facts*, March 26, 2010.

25. Anquinette Crosby and Sari Horowitz, "'Fast and Furious' Takedown of AFT Head," *Washington Post*, August 30, 2011.

26. Phillip S. Smith, "Plan Mérida Focus to Shift to Border Region," *Alter Net*, August 20, 2011.

27. Quoted in "Ciudad Juárez redujo en 75% el número de homicidios en los últimos dos años," *EFE*, December 31, 2012.

28. Quoted in Joseph Kolb, "Ciudad Juárez Mayor Says US Drug War Aid Package Failed His City," *Fox News Latino*, May 24, 2012.

29. Cory Molzahn, Octavio Rodriguez Ferreira, and David A. Shirk, *Drug Violence in Mexico: Data and Analysis through 2012* (San Diego: Transborder Institute, University of San Diego, February 2013).

30. "Por abusos, se rebelan a la Policía Federal en Chihuahua," *Chihuahua Noticias*, August 15, 2012.

31. Quoted in Nathaniel Parish Flannery, "Why Is Mexico's Murder City Attracting Investors?" *Forbes*, August 27, 2012.

32. Quoted in "The New Juárez," *Deming Headlight*, October 4, 2012.

33. "Pierde Acapulco 80% de springbreakers," *Reforma*, March 12, 2012.

34. Ginger Thomson, Randal C. Archibold, and Eric Schmitt, "Hand of U.S. Is Seen in Halting General's Rise," *New York Times*, February 5, 2013.

35. Quoted in "Rechaza EU veto a General García Ochoa," *Reforma*, February 15, 2013.

36. Quoted in Ioan Grillo, "Mexican Leader Vows More Military Money," *Associated Press*, December 2, 2006.

37. Allan Wall, "Calderón, Mexico's Drug War Commander in Chief," *Mexidatainfo*, January 8, 2007.

38. Ibid.

39. Nathan Jones and Gary J. Hale, "Kingpin Strategy," *Borderland Beat*, October 28, 2012.

40. For a table detailing these antidrug operations, see George W. Grayson, *Mexico: Narco Violence and a Failed State?* (New Brunswick, NJ: Transaction Publishers, 2010).

41. Adam Thomson, "Transcripción de la entrevista: Felipe Calderón," *Financial Times*, January 23, 2007.

42. "Mexico Captures Díaz Parada Drug Cartel Leader," *Washington Post*, January 17, 2007.

43. Nathan Jones makes this point in "The Unintended Consequences of Kingpin Strategies: Kidnap Rates and the Arellano-Félix Organization," *Trends in Organized Crime*, forthcoming.

44. "Día de violencia deja 28 muertos en el puerto guerrense," *El Universal*, January 9, 2011.

45. Rolando Herrera, "Revela 'El Charro' división de cártel," *Reforma*, November 26, 2010.

46. "Cae presunto líder de cártel de Acapulco," *Reforma*, August 1, 2011.

47. The states most affected by these rivalries were Tamaulipas, Nuevo León, Coahuila, San Luis Potosí, Michoacán, Guerrero, Jalisco, Nayarit, and Colima. See "Arrecia 'narcoguerra' en norte y Pacífico," *Reforma*, June 21, 2011.

48. Grayson, *Mexico: Narco-Violence and a Failed State?* 127–32.

49. Quoted in "Mexican Judge Finds Ex-Drug Czar Had No Links to Cartel," *Fox News Latino*, April 16, 2013.

50. "La SIEDO va por más alcaldes de Michoacán," *Informador.com.mx*, n.d.

51. Tracy Wilkinson, "10 Mayors, Other Mexico Officials Detained," *Los Angeles Times*, May 27, 2009.

52. "Confirma PGR autenticidad de audio de Godoy Toscano y La Tuta," *Milenio*, www.milenio.com/node/553780.

53. "Se movilizan contra detención de alcaldes en Michoacán," *Informador .com.mx*,www.informador.com.mx/mexico/2009/106844/6/se-movilizan -contra-detencion-de-alcaldes-en-michoacan.htm.

54. For speeches and other messages by the defense secretary, go to http:// www.sedena.gob.mx/en/.

55. Secretaría de la Defensa Nacional, "*Discurso del C. General Guillermo Galván Galván, Secretario de la Defensa Nacional,*" Mexico City, February 9, 2011.

56. The full text of the speech appears in "Texto Íntegro Mensaje de Felipe Calderón por Sexto Informe," *El Universal*, September 3, 2012.

57. This section benefits greatly from Alejandro Hope, "Peace Now? Mexican Security Policy after Felipe Calderón," Working Paper, Inter-American Dialogue, January 2013.

58. "Sobran Generales," *Reforma*, October 12, 2012.

59. Elliot Spagat, "The Big Story: Mexican Extradited to US under New President," *Associated Press*, March 7, 2013. On March 7 the Peña Nieto government accomplished its first extradition,—César Alfredo Meza García, a suspected member of the Tijuana Cartel, who was sent to the United States.

60. Hope, "Peace Now?"

CHAPTER 6

1. "Critican militarización de zonas indígenas," *Reforma*, December 17, 2011; Lanza Sicilia condena a guerra," *Reforma*, September 16, 2011; "Repudian jóvenes militarización del País," *Reforma*, April 29, 2011.

2. Quoted in Antonio Baranda, "Niega Poiré militarización," *Reforma*, June 7, 2011.

3. Colonel (Ret.) Eric Rojo, an expert on security who is managing director of Magination Consulting International, remembers that in the 1950s, when he was a child in Mexico City, the population got along well with local police, known as the *Azules* ("Blues") or *Teocolotes* ("Owls"). Later, Police Chief Arturo "El Negro" Durazo Moreno thoroughly corrupted the force by creating a sweeping racketeering network that involved arms dealing, extortion, and murders. He was imprisoned from 1986 to 1992. Colonel Rojo, interview with author, March 15, 2012, Washington, D.C.

4. "Las cifras de la violencia, Ejecutómetro 2013," *Reforma*, October 6, 2013.

5. Roderic Ai Camp, "Armed Forces and Drugs: Public Perceptions and Institutional Challenges," in *Shared Responsibilities*, eds. Eric L. Olson, David A. Shirk, and Andrew Selee (Washington, D.C.: Mexico Institute, Woodrow Wilson International Center for Scholars and Trans-Border Institute, University of San Diego, 2010).

6. Doris Gómora, "Sedena: 5 años, 41 mil detenidos," *El Universal*, December 28, 2011; "Abate más criminals el Ejército," *Reforma*, January 21, 2012.

7. Juan Cedillo, "General toma posesión en SSP de Nuevo León," *El Universal*, February 4, 2011.

8. Lest this point be overstated, U.S. military personnel who have taken courses at Mexican Army institutions have told the author, off the record, that administrators and faculty condone cheating on the grounds that it forges an esprit de corps.

9. Marcelo Galán, "Militares, a cargo de la seguridad en 17 entidades," *El Universal*, February 28, 2011.

10. "Caen en NL 106 policías por narco," *Reforma*, January 22, 2012.

11. Secretaría de Hacienda y Crédito Público, "Proyecto de Presupuesto de Egresos de la Federacíon para el Ejercicio Fiscal." http://www.shcp.gob.mx/Paginas/default.aspx.

12. Olga R. Rodriguez and Julie Watson, "Mexican Soldiers Wary of Often Corrupt State Police," *Monitor*, November 9, 2009.

13. Quoted in Andro Aguilar, "Militarización sin resultados," *Reforma* ("Enfoque"), April 10, 2011.

14. "Caen 60% los homicidios en Juárez, estima Calderón," Informador.com.mx, May 21, 2012.

15. Quoted in Sanjuana Martínez, "Si agarro a un *zeta* lo mato; para qué interrogarlo?: jefe policiaco," *La Jornada*, March 13, 2010.

16. Quoted in "Por ordenes militares, Villa Castillo dejará Torreón," *La Jornada*, March 15, 2011.

17. Quoted in Rodriguez and Watson, "Mexican Soldiers Wary."

18. Quoted in William Booth, "WikiLeaks Discuss Notorious Mexican Drug Lord," *Star* (Toronto), December 26, 2010.

19. Alfredo Corchado, "Drug Cartels Taking over Government Roles in Parts of Mexico," *Dallas Morning News*, May 4, 2011. For an examination of Los Zetas, see George W. Grayson and Samuel Logan, *The Executioner's Men: Los Zetas, Rogue Soldiers, Criminal, Entrepreneurs, and the Shadow State They Created* (New Brunswick, NJ: Transaction Press, 2012).

20. Henia Prado, "Rehúsen jóvenes empleo de policía," *Reforma.com*, May 23, 2011.

21. "Entrenan mercenaries a soldados en País," *Reforma.com*, April 6, 2011; Bill Convoy, "U.S. Private Sector Providing Drug-War Mercenaries to Mexico," *Narcosphere*, April 3, 2011.

22. Verónica Ayala, "Quiere Santa Catarina Policía militar," *Reforma*, January 1, 2012.

23. "Alcaldesa de Monterrey Entrega ... a Jesucristo," *Vanguardia*, June 10, 2013.

24. "Solicitan apoyo al Ejército," *Reforma*, May 21, 2012.

25. Quoted in Randal C. Archibold, "Rights Groups Contend Mexican Military Has Heavy Hand in Drug Cases," *New York Times*, August 2, 2011.

26. Quoted in Maureen Meyer, with contributions from Stephanie Brewer, *A Dangerous Journey through Mexico: Human Rights Violations against Migrants in Transit* (Washington, D.C.: Washington Office on Latin America, December 2010).

27. Quoted in Iñigo Guevara Moyano, *Adapting, Transforming, and Modernizing under Fire: The Mexican Military 2006–11* (Carlisle, PA: U.S. Army War College, Strategic Studies Institute, 2011), 12.

28. Alejandro Moreno and María Antonia Mancillas, "Encuesta/Respaldan labor de Fuerzas Armadas," *Reforma*, December 1, 2011.

29. Héctor Raúl González, "Hacen meditación militares de Morelos, "*Reforma*, February 5, 2013.

30. "Encuesta: ocho de cada 10 mexicanos respondan al Ejército en las calles," *CNN México*, August 31, 2011; "Mexicanos ven al Ejército como la única fuerza para enfrentar narco,'" *El Debate*, January 5, 2012.

31. Instituto Nacional de Estadística y Geografía, *Boletín de Prensa Núm. 339/12*, September 27, 2012.

32. Pew Research Center, "Mexicans Back Military Campaign against Cartels," Pew Global Attitudes Project, June 20, 2012.

33. Horacio Jiménez, "PRI, autoritario y corrupto: Josefina," *El Universal*, June 18, 2012.

34. Quoted in Francisco Gómez and Doris Gómora, "Juegan a ser soldados," *El Universal*, February 5, 2011.

35. "Participará Ejército en película histórica," *Reforma*, April 1, 2012.

36. Quoted in Nurit Martínez Carballo, "Oran en Catedral por el Ejército Mexicano," *El Universal*, February 20, 2011.

37. "Realiza Ejército labor social en Juárez," *Reforma*, January 20, 2012.

38. "Ejército fatigada por lucha antinarco," *El Universal*, October 16, 2011; Secretaría de Defensa Nacional, "Unidad de Vinculación Ciudadana," October 28, 2011; "Las contradicciones del Ejército y Derechos Humanos en el caso Almanza," *CNN México.com*, June 22, 2010.

39. Guevara Moyano, *Adapting, Transforming, and Modernizing*, 14.

40. "Ejército Mexicano, la batalla de las mujeres," *Siglo de Torreón*, October 8, 2007.

41. "Se crea el Observatorio para la Igualdad entre Mujeres y Hombres en el Ejército y Fuerza Aérea Mexicanos," *Noneventagrados*, November 28, 2011.

42. "Pide diputada una mujer al frente del Ejército mexicano," *El Universal*, December 16, 2008; Jennifer Juárez, "'Adelitas' en el Ejército Mexicano," *CNN México*, September 19, 2010.

43. Henia Prado, "Admiten brecha de género en el Ejército," *Reforma*, March 8, 2012.

44. "Impulsan sin plazas a mujeres militares," *Reforma*, April 23, 2012.

45. Human Rights Watch, "World Report 2011: Mexico," www.hrw.org/world-report-2011/mexico; Silvia Otero, "Violaciones del Ejército son casos aislados: SRE," *El Universal*, August 18, 2009; "Realizan militares boda massiva," *Reforma*, July 28, 2012.

46. Jorge Alejandro Medellín, "Homosexualidad y Ejército," *Offnews.info*, October 21, 2010.

47. Quoted in Tracy Wilkinson, "Mexico High Court Rules Civilian Courts Should Handle Alleged Military Abuses," *Los Angeles Times*, July 13, 2011.

48. Corporal Vicente Ramírez Márquez quoted in Víctor Fuentes and Benito Jiménez, "Va military a Corte por Ejecución," *Reforma*, February 9, 2012.

49. Quoted in Ibid.

50. "Activists Accuse Mexican President of War Crimes in Drug Crackdown," *Guardian*, November 26, 2011.

51. "Justifica PRI freno a reforma militar," *Reforma*, April 29, 2012.

52. Benito Jiménez, "Juzca Ejército a 450 por delitos graves," *Reforma*, December 29, 2012.

53. "Pagaba a General narco en Coahuila," *Reforma*, February 18, 2012.

54. "Rinde el Ejército honores a Acosta," *Reforma*, April 22, 2012.

55. Andrea Merlos, "Detecta ASF errores en fondo de Sedena," *El Universal*, February 18, 2011.

56. Ricardo Gómez and Horacio Jiménez, "Sedena se niega a analizar detector," *El Universal*, October 14, 2011.

57. "New Mexican Presidential Aircraft, Double the Expense of the USA's Air Force One," *El Sol News*, August 10, 2012; Paul Lara and Aurora Vega, "Sedena negocia el nuevo avión presidencial," *Excélsior*, July 24, 2012.

58. President Calderón continually lauded the armed forces and provided them with higher salaries and more benefits, which can be found at the Defense Ministry's web site, www.sedena.gob.mx. See also "El gobierno mexicano anuncia aumentos en salarios y prestaciones de los soldados," *Terra*, February 19, 2011; "¿Que prestaciones tiene los soldados del ejercito mexicano?" http://mx. answers.yahoo.com/question/index?quid=2009120208383... "Mexico devela monument en honor a soldados caídos," *Associated Press*, November 20, 2012.

59. Benito Jiménez, "Recluta Ejército a campesinos," *Reforma*, July 3, 2011.

60. Quoted in "El gobernador de Chihuahua plantea servicios militar pagado para 'ni-nis,' " *CNN México*, March 28, 2011; "Gobierno prefiere que 'ni-nis' estudien a que vayan al servicio militar," *CNN México*, March 30, 2011.

61. "En México se incrementa el gasto en sistemas de seguridad," *América Economía*, October 14, 2010.

62. Guevara Moyano, *Adapting, Transforming, and Modernizing*, 20–21.

63. Quoted in Grace Wyler, "The Mexican Drug Cartel's Purpose-Built Tank," *Business Insider*, May 11, 2011.

64. "Paga Sedena 5 mmmdp por equipo para espiar," *El Universal*, July 16, 2012.

65. Quoted in Elliot Spagat, "Outspoken Mexican General Loses His Tijuana Post," *USA Today*, August 8, 2008. The text of Aponte Polito's letter to the Baja California attorney general appears in Julieta Martínez, "Carta íntegra del comandante Sergio Aponte Polito," *El Universal*, April 23, 2008.

66. Quoted in "Alto mando militar regaña a secretario de gobierno de BC por borracho," *La Crónica de Chihuahua*, September 20, 2011.

67. "Mexican Army Urged to Take Over Prisons," *USA Today*, August 1, 2005.

68. "Executan a 'zetas' en cárcel in Mazatlán." *Reforma*, December 14, 2008.

69. Daniel Venegas, "Diputados exigen alto a la extorsión desde cárceles," *Milenio*, October 19, 2008.

70. "Inhiben señal de celular en 4 cárceles," *Reforma*, December 31, 2008.

71. Quoted in Henia Prado, "Toleran autoridades drogas en penales," *Reforma*, November 16, 2008.

72. Icela Lagunas, "Detectan 119 kilos de mariguana en aduana del Reclusorio Sur," *El Universal*, December 15, 2008.

73. Arturo Rodríguez García, "Tamaulipas: la massacre del narcopenal," *Proceso*, October 29, 2008.

74. Llevan cárteles a penales guerra por territorios," *El Universal*, October 18, 2008; Claudia Bolaños, "Cárceles, infierno de pobres" ("Prisons, Hell for the Poor"), *El Universal*, May 16, 2009.

75. Rolando Herrera, "Saturan a estados con reos federales," *Reforma*, October 25, 2010.

76. Luis Brito, "Amotina el narco penales," *Reforma*, May 24, 2009.

77. "Reclutan cárteles en cárceles de NL," *Reforma*, February 27, 2012.

78. Arturo Rodríguez García, "Los Zetas, génesis de los conflictos en Topo Chico," *Proceso*, October 8, 2009.

79. Juan Cedillo, "Indagan 'atentado' en muerte de 14 internos," *El Universal.com.mx*, May 21, 2011.

80. "Édgar Ávila Pérez," "Ejército y PF toman penal de Veracruz," *El Universal*, June 9, 2009; "Ceresos bajo control: Ejército," *El Ágora*, August 17, 2009; "El Ejército asume el control de centros penitenciarios en Morelos" *Diariocrítico de México*, August 31, 2010.

81. For an analysis and summary of prison escapes and behind-bars violence, see "Cárceles: entre fugas, matanzas y excesos,"*El Universal*, December 29, 2011.

82. Sergio Caballero, "Nombran a militares en penales de QR," *Reforma.com*, April 26, 2011.

83. Patricia Salazar, "Asumen militares seguridad externa en penales de NL," *El Universal*, October 24, 2011.

84. "Cuidan militares centro de arraigo," *Reforma*, May 26, 2012.

85. Víctor Fuentes, "Teme Sedena narcoescapes en su prisión," *Reforma*, February 27, 2012.

86. Rosa María Méndez, "Mexicali: Ejército toma el control del aeropuerto," *El Universal*, June 12, 2007.

87. "Gastan en vigilar ¡boletas de 2006!," *Reforma* June 24, 2012.

88. "Rodolfo Torre Cantú, asesinado en Ciudad Victoria," *Univisión Noticias*, June 28, 2010.

89. José Antonio Román, "De 2006 a la fecha en el país han side asesinados 31 presidentes municipales," *La Jornada*, February 6, 2013.

90. "Capacitan Sedena a brigada de rescate," *ABC de Monterrey*, September 18, 2011.

91. "Reliability Tests Keep Officers away from Corruption—Mexican Navy," *BBC Monitoring Latin America*, November 16, 2008.

92. "El almirante Figueroa a la vida de los otros," *Reporte Índigo*, March 7, 2009.

93. "Investigan pactos de Beltrán con 'Zetas,' " *Reforma*, November 25, 2008.

94. Zósimo Camacho, "Más de 55 mil deserciones en las Fuerzas Armada," *Contralínea*, June 6, 2013.

95. "Reliability Tests Keep Officers away from Corruption."

96. Jorge Alejandro Medellín, "Negocian servicios de satelite militar privado," *El Universal*, January 27, 2009.

97. "Mexican Navy Will Join US Navy in Multinational Maritime Exercise," *Mexico Times*, April 7, 2009.

98. "Armada de México autorizada a participar en ejercicios en EE. UU.," *RT Actualidad / Actualidad*, September 5, 2012.

99. The military has recognized posttraumatic stress disorder among soldiers at least since 2005. See Jorge Alejandro Medellín, "El Ejército detecta trastornos por estrés en soldados," *El Universal*, October 17, 2005.

100. Staff Sargent Keith Anderson, "JTF-North Deploys Soldiers to Support Border Patrol in N.M., Ariz." *Border Narcotics*, March 18, 2012.

101. Sean Holstege, National Guard Wrapping up its U.S.-Border Duty: Region's Governors Want 2-Year Mission Extended, " *Arizona Republic*, June 12, 2008.

CHAPTER 7

1. Mexico's first-rate analyst reports that Norway's Statoil produces, with 6.6 times more workers, 78 barrels per employee compared with scarcely 25 barrels for PEMEX. See Luis Rubio, "El costo de las vacas," *Reforma*, July 21, 2013.

2. Ariadna Garcia, "Inegra PRI a Peña Nieto a directive," *El Universal*, March 2, 2013; "Inicia PRI credencialización de sus miembros," *Milenio*, July 30, 2011.

3. Quoted in Santiago Wills and Esteban Roman, "What Elba Esther Gordillo's Arrest Means for Mexico's Other Power Brokers," *ABC News*, March 1, 2013.

4. Quoted in Ibid.

5. Germán Canseco, "Systema educativo actual educa para la frustración: Chuayffet," *Proceso*, December 11, 2012.

6. Lilian Hernández, "Se perdieron 1,759 mpd por los niños sin clases," *Excélsior*, July 6, 2013; Jesús Guerrero, "Evalúa CNTE paro indefindo para abril," *Reforma*, March 27, 2013.

7. For the text of the legislation, see Presidencia de la República, "Reforma en Telecomunicaciones," March 11, 2013.

8. Michael O'Boyle and Dave Graham, "Mexico's Planned Telecoms Shake Up Threatens Slim, Televisa," *Reuters*, March 12, 2013.

9. Dolia Estévez, "Will Mexico's Proposed New Telecom Law Affect Slim's 'World's Richest Man' Status?" *Forbes*, March 11, 2013.

10. "Con un voto de diferencia, exonera IFE al PRI y PVEM por caso Monex," *Notimex*, January 23, 2013.

11. Larry Villagran, "Transparency in Mexico: Information Doesn't Come Easily," *Christian Science Monitor*, September 2, 2012; Jacqueline Peschard, "Desafíos de la transparencia a 10 años de IFAI," *El Universal*, July 6, 2013; Ivonne Melgar, "PRI frena reforma sobre transparencia," *Excélsior*, July 5, 2013.

12. Verónica Gascón, "Evaden empresas multas millonarios," *Reforma*, July 5, 2012.

13. Quoted in "La PGR elimina el Consejo de Participación Ciudadana," *Informador.com.mx*, March 26, 2013.

14. "Cambios a Ley de Amparo afectarán a la banca and concesionarios," *Veracruzanos.Info/Notimex*, February 13, 2013.

15. Leticia Robles de la Rosa, "Con Calderón no hubo reportes anómalos de Gordillo: Cordero," *Excélsior*, February 28, 2013.

16. Quoted in Mayolo López, "Disacredita Osorio estrategia de Calderón," *El Diario.mx*, December 18, 2012.

17. "Ejecuciones 2012," *Reforma*, January 8, 2013; E. Eduardo Castillo and Michael Weissenstein, "Mexico's New Government Offers Blistering Critique of Predecessor's War on Drug Cartels," *Associated Press*, December 17, 2012.

18. Quoted in "70 mil muertos en los últimos 6 años y mas de 60 cárteles nuevos," *El Comercial* (Buenos Aires), December 18, 2012.

19. Patricia Dávila, "García Luna, en la mira del FBI," *Proceso*, January 26, 2013.

20. "Tribu del PRD denucia negociación secreta entre gobierno de EPN and Bejarano," *Aristeguinoticias.com*, January 15, 2013.

21. Quoted in "Discurso Miguel Ángel Osorio Chong. Firma Pacto por México," GrupoFormula, December 2, 2012.

22. Quoted in Mayolo López, "Defiende Madero el pacto con Peña," *Reforma*, March 16, 2013.

23. Antonio Baranda and Claudia Guerrero, "Confirman PAN y PRD permanencia en Pacto," *Reforma*, July 17, 2013; "Acotan a Zambrano para seguir en el Pacto," *Reforma*, July 19, 2013.

24. Antonio Baranda, "Dejan a Osorio supersecretaría," *Reforma*, April 3, 2013.

25. For an analysis of the Carabineros, see Martz K. Cartalina, "Experiencia Comparada en La Organización y Administración de Fuerzas Policiales: Alemania, Canada, Chile, España, Estados Unidos e Inglaterra y Gales," Fundación Paz Ciudadana, Santiago, February 2000.

26. Alejandro Hope, "Is It Worth Creating a Gendarmerie in Mexico?" *Insight-Crime*, December 10, 2012.

27. "Gendarmería operará en 2015; reclutamiento inicia en Enero," Excélsior, December 24, 2012.

28. Ebrard's evinced his ire at Mondragón y Kalb's having accepted a key position in the PRI administration by refusing to deploy DF police for crowd control at Peña Nieto's inauguration—a task that fell to the Federal Police.

29. María Idalia Gómez, "Alberto Amador Leal renuncia a la Dirección de Inteligencia de la PF," *PuebloOnline.com*, January 24, 2013.

30. "Encargado del despacho de la policía federal reprobó examines de confianza," *LasNoticiasMexico.com*, January 4, 2013.

31. "ONGS piden debate público sobre Gendarmería Nacional," *El Universal*, March 27, 2013; and "'Disaparece' la Gendarmería del Plan Nacional de Desarrollo," *Chihuahua.noticias.com*, May 21, 2013.

32. Quoted in "Recorre Mondragón Centro de Mando de PF," *Reforma*, January 13, 2013.

33. "Recibe PF a 202 nuevos elementos," *Reforma*, March 23, 2013.

34. Sandra García, "Vigilan vía con rayos gamma," *Reforma*, March 19, 2013.

35. "Crea CNS centro para recibir denuncias," *Reforma*, March 18, 2013.

36. "Cumple 100 años el Ejército mexicano," *Aristegui Noticias*, March 15, 2013.

37. "Cae tercero al mando de La Familia Michoacana en el Edomex," *Proceso*, February 21, 2013.

38. "Congratula a Ejército el Pacto por México," *El Siglo de Torreón*, February 10, 2013.

39. "Mexico Wants US Aid to Focus More on Social Programs in Bid to Quell Drug Violence," *Associated Press*, February 14, 2013.

40. "Wikileaks: EU entrena militares mexicanos que se integran a los 'Zetas,' " *CNN México*, January 23, 2011. Silvia Garduño, "Atoran Iniciativa Mérida," *Reforma*, February 17, 2013.

41. Quoted in Silvia Otero, "En seguridad, renovado enfoque: Medina Mora," *El Universal*, May 4, 2013.

42. Quoted in Gabriel Stargardter "Mexican Security Forces Abducted Dozens in Drug War: Rights Group," *Reuters*, February 20, 2013.

43. Quoted in Nick Miroff, "Mexican Forces Linked to Abductions," *Washington Post*, February 21, 2013.

44. Quoted in "Erika Hernández, "Prioriza Peña diálogo cercano con CA," *Reforma*, February 20, 2013.

45. Quoted in Kimberly Dozier, "US Commandos Boost Numbers to Train Mexican Forces," AP, January 18, 2013.

46. "Centro de Inteligencia mexicano, similar a CIA: diputado," *El Universal*, January19, 2013.

47. Rolando Herrera, "'Presta' 500 mdp Pemex a sindicato," *Reforma*, February 14, 2013.

48. Érica Hernández and Claudio Guerrero, "Defiende Sedesol método de cruzada," *Reforma*, February 11, 2013.

49. "Peña Nieto va por 500 mil viviendas," *Informador*, February 12, 2013.

50. Antonio Baranda, "Prioriza a jóvenes plan antiviolencia," *Reforma*, February 11, 2013.

51. "Ley General de Víctimas Íntegral," *Excélsior*, January 10, 2013.

52. Quoted in "Alejandro Martí reprueba la Ley General de Víctimas," *Informador.com.mx*, January 9, 2013.

53. Diana Martínez de Luis Cruz, "Nombran a nueva titular de reclusorios," *Reforma*, January 11, 2013.

54. J. Jesús Esquival, "En sigilo, crea el gobierno una CIA a la Mexicana," *Proceso*, January 12, 2013.

55. Francisco Reséndiz, "Peña Nieto presenta el Plan Nacional de Desarrollo 2013–2018," *El Universal*, May 20, 2013; for the text of the plan, see Presidencia de la República, *Plan Nacional de Desarrollo: 2013–18*, Mexico City. http://pnd .gob.mx/

56. Dolia Estévez, "Investors Unimpressed with Mexican President Peña Nieto Energy Reform," *Forbes*, August 13, 2013.

CHAPTER 8

1. Quoted in Kevin Sullivan, "Mexican Judges' Climate of Fear," *Washington Post*, November 19, 2001.

2. William Booth, "Mexican Marines Capture Son of Cartel Figure 'El Chapo,' " *Washington Post*, June 21, 2012.

3. Adriana Gómez Licón, "Mexico Drug Cases Federal Judges Suspended for Possible Irregularities," *Huffington Post*, June 2, 2012.

4. Quoted in Nacha Cattan, "Why Hillary Clinton Flagged Judicial Reform as Essential to Mexico's Drug War," *Christian Science Monitor*, January 25, 2011.

5. Quoted in Brady McCombs, "US to Aid Mexico's Judicial Reforms," *Arizona Daily Star*, September 27, 2010.

6. Varalakakshmi Pulugurtha, "$2 Million Funding Available for Oral Trial Moot Court Competition of Mexican Law Students,"*Targeted News Service*, March 19, 2013.

7. Quoted in Guy Lawson, "The Making of a Narco State," *Rolling Stone*, March 11, 2009.

8. Hector Tobar, "Judicial Overhaul in Mexico OKd," *Los Angeles Times*, March 7, 2008.

9. Quoted in Ricardo Gómez and Elena Michel, "Rebolledo reconoce fallas en sistema de justicia," *Universal.com.mx*, February 10, 2011.

10. Quoted in "General: policías y jueces, corruptos," *Universal.com*, September 14, 2010.

11. Carlos Avilés, "Martí pide castigo para jueces corruptos," *El Universal*, October 15, 2008; Iván González, "Liberan a secuestrador de Carlos Antonio Pilgram," *Noticieros Televisa*, August 26, 2008.

12. Claudia Bensassini Félix and Arturo Caro Islas, "Anula la Corte Castigo de Jueces," *Medios Mexicos*, Konrad Adenaur Stiftung (A German NGO), December 2008.

13. María de la Luz González, "Poder Judicial sanciona a 108 de sus miembros," *Universal*, March 24, 2011. For more information about the Federal Judicial Council, see www.cjf.gob.mx.; Lauren Villagran, "Drug Lord Walks Free, and Spotlight Turns on Mexico's Troubled Legal System," *Christian Science Monitor*, August 12, 2013.

14. Claudia Benassini Félix, "Salarios millonarios para ministros, magistrados y consejeros electorales," *Medios Mexico*, Konrad Adenauer Stiflung, September 2011.

15. Cited in Nathan Jones, "Measuring Reforms to Mexico's Broken Justice System," *InsightCrime*, June 28, 2011.

16. Quoted in Randal C. Archibold, "Mexican Prosecutors Train in U.S. for Changes in the Legal System," *New York Times*, April 24, 2010.

17. "'Presumed Guilty' Sheds Light on Failures of Mexico's Justice System," *Los Angeles Times*, August 19, 2010; Lauren Villagran, "Drug Lord Walks Free, and Spotlight Turns on Mexico's Troubled Legal System," *Christian Science Monitor*, August 12, 2013.

18. Quoted in Archibold, "Mexican Prosecutors Train in U.S. for Changes in the Legal System."

19. Matt Ingram and David A. Shirk, "Judicial Reform in Mexico: Toward a New Criminal Justice System," Justice in Mexico Project, Transborder Institute, University of San Diego, May 2010.

20. Ibid.

21. "Preocupa a Poder Judicial que solo 3 estados han puesto en march el sistema penal y acusatorio: Juan Silva Meza," *Diario Jurídico*, June 5, 2012.

22. Matthew C. Ingram et al., "Justiciabarómetro [Judicial Barometer] Surveys Judges and Lawyers about Mexico's Criminal Justice Challenges," Justice in Mexico Project, Transborder Institute, University of San Diego, May 31, 2011.

23. "Matan a la activist que pedía justicia por su hija," *Informador.com.mx*, December 18, 2010.

24. Quoted in Sean Goforth, "Vigilante Justice," *Foreign Policy Blogs*, October 29, 2009.

25. Quoted in Ioan Grillo, "Vigilante Justice Spreads across Mexico," *Globalpost*, October 28, 2009; updated March 18, 2010.

26. Sylvia Longmire, "The More Deadly Side of Growing Vigilantism in Mexico," *Mexidata.info*, November 2, 2009.

27. Verónica Sánchez, "Destierra violencia a 120 mil," *Reforma.com*, March 25, 2011.

28. Quoted in Solutions Abroad, "Kidnappings in Mexico" www.solutions abroad.com/en./security.

29. Barnard R. Thompson, "Kidnappings Are Out of Control in Mexico," *Mexidata.info*, June 14, 2004.

30. The following sections draw heavily on George W. Grayson, "Threat Posed by Mounting Vigilantism in Mexico," Strategic Studies Institute (Carlisle Barracks, PA: U.S. Army War College, September 11, 2009).

31. This paragraph draws on Traci Carl, "Lynched: Mexican Agents Search for Leaders of Mob That Burned Two Officers Alive,"*Associated Press*, November 25, 2004.

32. The president appoints the DF's police chief.

33. Quoted in "Remueve Fox a Ebrard y Figueroa," *El Siglo de Torreón*, December 6, 2004.

34. "En Ixtayopan los policías investigaban ligas de las FARP," *La Jornada*, November 27, 2004.

35. Quoted in *La Jornada*, July 28, 2001.

36. Quoted in "Explota 'Jefe Diego' vs, usos y costumbres," *EsMas*, November 25, 2004.

37. Quoted in Richard Boudreaux, "Vigilantes' Fatal Fury in Mexico: Angry Mob Burns 2 Officers to Death," *SFGate.com*, November 25, 2004.

38. Dr. Luis de la Barreda Solórzano, Director, Instituto Ciudadano de Estudios sobre la Inseguridad, AC, interview with author, March 9, 2011, Mexico City.

39. Quoted in Traci Carl, "Mexican Agents Search."

40. Mario López, "Sentencian a nueve por linchamiento en Tláhuac," *Noticieros Televisa*, May 13, 2009.

41. "5 Jóvenes adolescentes son Humillados por Rateros," *nolachingues.com*, December 6, 2009.

42. Quoted in Ioan Grillo, "Vigilante Justice Spreads in Mexico," *Global Post*, October 28, 2009, updated May 30, 2010.

43. Mae López, "Conmociona a Nayarit tortura a 5 adolescentes," *El Universal*, October 24, 2009.

44. Ibid.

45. Ernesto Julio Teissier, "Reporte sobre política: Ahora, el vigilantismo brotese en DF, Juárez, Parral," *El Diario*, January 27, 2009.

46. Quoted in Julian Cardona, "Shadow of Vigilantes Appears in Mexico Drug War," *Reuters*, January 19, 2009.

47. Luis Carlos Cano, "Investigan a Comando Ciudadano por Juárez," *Universal*, January 21, 2009.

48. "Matan a Bejamín Le Barón, activista contra secuestros," *El Universal*, July 8, 2009.

49. Jorge Ramos Pérez, "CNDH cuestiona presencia del Ejército en las calles," *Universal*, July 11, 2009.

50. "Asesinan taxistas a asaltante," *Caracol Radio*, August 19, 2009.

51. "Crece la autodefensa," *Reforma*, February 12, 2013; Virgilio Sánchez, "Pactar dissolver autodefensa en Oaxaca," *Reforma*, February 13, 2013.

52. Max Frankel quoted in Adam Liptak, "Anthony Lewis, 'Supreme Court Reporter Who Brought Law to Life, Dies at 85,' " *New York Times*, March 25, 2013.

CHAPTER 9

1. Quoted in Laurence Iliff, "Mexico Drug Traffickers Are Financing Churches, Bishop Says," *Dallas Morning News*, April 5, 2008.

2. Quoted in Gustavo Aguirre Borderzine, "Drug Cartel Alms Funding Mexican Catholic Church," *Tucson Sentinel*, January 3, 2013.

3. Quoted in "Mexican Archbishop Denies Church Receives Money from Drug Trafficking," *Catholic News Agency*, March 9, 2006.

4. "Iglesia busca contrarrestar al narco con cortometrajes," *Milenio*, January 27, 2013. sipse.com/mexico/iglesia-busca-contrarrestar-al-narco-con-cor. . ., January 29, 2013.

5. "Intentarán evangelizer a los narcos; capacitan sacerdotes," *Excélsior*, August 8, 2012.

6. "Crusading Mexican Priest, Who Defies Drug Cartels and Corrupt Officials, Facing Reassignment," *New Haven Register*, August 8, 2012; Mark Stevenson, "Church Wants to Reassign Mexico Activist Priest," *Associated Press*, August 8, 2012.

7. Cecilia Barría, "Curas amenazados por narcotraficantes," *BBC Mundo*, April 21, 2009; Pepe Flores, "Calderón pide a los sacerdotes delatar al narco," *Vivir México*, August 5, 2010.

8. Alonso Garza Treviño, bishop of Piedras Negras, stated that drug baron Osiel Cárdenas Guillén contributed tons of food for the victims of floods that washed across Coahuila in 2006. See Leopoldo Ramos, "Rechazan que el narco financie a la iglesia,"*El Siglo de Torreón*, October 21, 2006. In 1997 Raúl Soto, the canon of the Basilica of Guadalupe, suggested in a homily that more Mexicans should follow the example of kingpin Rafael Carol Quintero and Amado Carrillo Fuentes, who had given millions of pesos to the church. See Carlos Fazio, "Polémica con la Iglesia en México por narcolimosnas," *Clarin.com*, September 25, 1997.

9. Carlos Fazio, "Polémica con la Iglesia en México por narcolimosnas," *Clarin.com* (Buenos Aires), September 25, 1997.

10. "Monseñor de oro," *Milenio.com*, December 19, 2008.

11. "Guardan Silencio de 'narcoboda' de los Carrillo Fuentes," *Noticeros Televisa*, December 12, 2001.

12. "Apellido de la esposa delató a Carrillo Leyva," *Milenio*, July 28, 2013.

13. Miguel Ángel Granados Chapa, "Plaza Pública: Bendito lavado de dinero," *El Diario*, April 7, 2008.

14. Quoted in Borderzine, "Drug Cartel Alms."

15. Quoted in Ibid.

16. Iliff, "Mexico Drug Traffickers."

17. The text of the letter appears in José Gil Olmos, "Pide Sicilia al Papa intercede para que Iglesia en México no sea cómplice de la narcoguerra," *Proceso*, March 17, 2012.

18. The Mexican military does not allow its soldiers to patronize this eatery lest they fall prey to Zeta spies.

19. Marcos Muedano, "Festejan 2 años de temple construido por 'El Lazca,' " *Universal.com.mx*, February 3, 2011; "Fetejan 2 aniversario del templo donado por el Lazca," *AlertaPeriodista*, February 4, 2011.

20. "Líder de 'Los Zetas' edifica su última morada," *El Universal*, February 12, 2012.

21. Susana Moraga, "Sabían en Hidalgo de 'limosna': CEM," *El Diario.mx*, October 24, 2010.

22. Scott Farwell, "2 Area Priests Moved to Mexico: Cases: One was Convicted of Molestation," *BishopAccountability.org*, May 10, 2002.

23. "Ventana a la Historia: Guerrilla capturó a 'El Chapo,' " *Vanguardia*, June 17, 2013.

24. Quoted in Chris Kraul, "Priest's Link to Drug Lords Fuels Concern," *Los Angeles Times*, May 26, 2002.

25. This section draws heavily on Grayson, "*Mexico: Narco-Violence and a Failed State*," 125–26.

26. For an extended analysis, see James H. Creechan and Jorge de la Herrán García, "Without God or Law: Narcoculture and Belief in Jesús Malverde," *Religious Studies and Theology*, 24, no. 2 (2005).

27. Sam Quinones, "Jesus Malverde," *Front Line: Drug Wars*, PBS, www.pbs.org/wgbh.

28. "El culto a la Santísima Muerte, un boom en México," *Terra*, www.terra.com/arte/articulo/html/art9442.htm.

29. Quoted in Reed Johnson, "A 'Saint' of Last Resort," *Los Angeles Times*, March 19, 2004.

30. "Destruyen 'narcocapillas' in BC," *Reforma*, March 25, 2009; Olga R. Rodriguez, "Mexico Targets Death Saint Popular with Criminals," *Associated Press*, April 18, 2009.

31. David Luhnow and Jose de Cordoba, "The Drug Lord Who Got Away," *Wall Street Journal*, June 13, 2009.

32. Quoted in Borderzine, "Drug Cartel Alms."

33. "Denuncian iglesias ataques del crimen," *Reforma*, January 11, 2013.

34. Lupsha, *Op. cit.*

35. Allen R. Myerson, "American Express Unit Settles Laundering Case," *New York Times*, November 22, 1994.

36. Luis Alonso Pérez Chávez, "Según el Departamento de Tesoro de Estados Unidos y la DEA," *Zeta*, December 17, 2012; Howard Mustoe and Gavin Finch, "HSBC Apologizes for Compliance Failures," *Bloomberg*, July 30, 2012.

37. Steve Slater, "HSBC Hires U.S. Expert on Drug Cartels after Mexico Lapses," *Reuters*, January 30, 2013.

38. J. Jesús Esquivel, "Liga EU con el narco a dos empresarios mexicanos y 16 empresas," *Proceso*, April 13, 2012.

39. U.S. Treasury, Esparragoza Moreno Organization, July 2012, www.treasury. gov/resource- center/sanctions/Programs/Documents/20120724_esparragoza_ moreno_org.; and "EU señala a empresas vinculados con el narcotráfico," *CNI* (Channel 40), October 10, 2012.

40. Juan Balboa, "Investiga PGR a personas físicas y empresas ligadas con los cárteles del narcotráfico," *La Jornada*, July 14, 2006.

41. Zósimo Camacho, "Seguridad Privada: 50% de empresas irregulares," *Contralínea*, May 21, 2013; *El Diario.mx*, August 10, 2012.

42. Ted Hesson, "What Doubling Border Patrol Agents Would Mean," *ABC-Univisíon News*, June 20, 2013.

43. Quoted in "The Border, the Cartels, and the Corruption of US Officials," *Forbes*, September 15, 2010.

44. Ibid.

45. Quoted in Robin Emmott, "Drug Smugglers Bribing U.S. Agents on Mexican Border," *Reuters*, July 15, 2008.

46. Kolb, "Study Finds Corruption on Rise among Border Agents, Rep Says Security 'at Risk.' "

47. Michael Marizco, "High Ranking Homeland Security Official Arrested on Trafficking Charges," *Border Reporter*, September 4, 2009.

48. Tracy Wilkinson, "U.S. Probing Drug Lords' Ties to Key Retired Official," *Chicago Tribune*, September 17, 2009.

49. "ICE Agent Gets 2 Years in Drug Smuggle Case," *NBC* (Miami), February 18, 2010.

50. Mark Potter, "Nearly 80 Have Been Arrested in the Last Five Years; Hundred More under Investigation," *NBC News*, April 7, 2011; Federal Bureau of Investigation, "Abuse of Trust: The Case of a Crooked Border Official," June 8, 2009.

51. Agustín Basave Benítez, *Mexicanidad y esquizofrenia* (Mexico City: Oceano, 2010): 101–14.

52. Padgett, L. Vincent, *The Mexican Political System* (2nd ed.) (Boston: Houghton Mifflin, 1976), 187.

53. Televisa, TV Azteca, and other media networks, multinational firms, drug cartels, and such boss-ridden corporatist labor organizations as the Oil Workers Union (STPRM) and, before Gordillo's arrest, the National Educational Workers Union (SNTE), have also taken advantage of the stalemate to expand their influence.

54. See Secretaría de Hacienda y Crédito Pública, http://www.shcp.gob.mx/ Estados/Deuda_Publica_EFM/2012/Paginas/1erTrimestre.aspx.

55. "Arturo Montiel y Maude Versini: Un divorcio de 300 millones de pesos," *Vanguardia*, September 26, 2007.

56. "Indespensable elevar transparencia en telecom: IFAI," Prodigy.MSN, February 2, 2012.

57. Jorge Carrasco Araizaga, "El cártel 'La Compañia' somete a Veracruz," *Proceso*, February 6, 2010; "Investigación liga a Fidel Herrera con Los Zetas," *Vanguardia*, December 13, 2011.

58. "Destaca Fidel Herrera medidas contra robo de combustibles," *Terra*, August 2, 2009.

59. Pedro Matias, "Detecta Pemex mil 749 tomas clandestinas en 2012; ubican 34 en Oaxaca," *Proceso*, February 14, 2013.

60. María De la Luz González, "PGR solicita arraigo a detenidos en Michoacán," *Universal*, May 29, 2009.

61. "Dicen que 'La Familia' apoyó campañas," *Reforma.com*, May 27, 2009.

62. Víctor Solís, "Tomás Yarrington, el 'compadre' de Bush," *El Universal*, May 23, 2012.

63. "Drug War Plays Big in Mexico Election," *Associated Press*, June 19, 2009.

CHAPTER 10

1. Nacha Cattan, "Peña Nieto Property Vow for Mexico Means Mastering the PRI," *Bloomberg*, July 2, 2012.

2. For the provisions of the pact, see *pactopormexico.org*. In 1993 Jorge Emilio González Torres founded the PVEM (Mexican Ecological Green Party), which is a fiefdom of the González family and makes self-serving alliances, most recently with the PRI.

3. "El Sector Empresarial: Los 100 días de Enrique Peña Nieto, balance opuesto de PRI, PRD y PAN," *Hechos de Hoy*, March 12, 2013.

4. "Diseñará Peña Nieto con intelectuales una política cultura," *Sintesis*, March 31, 2013.

5. Ibid.

6. "Peña Nieto presenta el Plan Nacional de Desarrollo 2013–2018," *El Universal*, May 20, 2013.

7. Michael Weissenstein, "Mexico's President Gathers Power Pushes Reform," *Associated Press*, March 19, 2013.

8. "Sacred Cows No More," *Economist*, March 16–22, 2013.

9. Patricia Oey, "Reform Momentum in Mexico Could Be Positive for This EFT," *Financial Times*, March 22, 2013.

10. Estévez quoted in "The Evolution of Mexico President Peña Nieto's Soap Opera Politics," *Forbes*, March 21, 2013.

11. "Mexico's Grand Bargaining," *Washington Post*, March 29, 2013.

12. Typical of news reports is the contention that "Democracy will survive in Mexico, too, even if the PRI moves back into power in three years." See Tim Padgett, "Swine Flu: the Political Stakes for Mexico's Government," *Time* [World edition], April 29, 2009.

13. These and other valuable items appear in the World Bank Group, *Decentralization and Subnational Regional Economics* (Washington, DC: World Bank, 2001).

14. "Rechazan relección 80% de mexicanos," *Universal*, January 26, 2010.

15. *Boletín UNAM-DGCS-494 2011*.

16. Claudia Salazar, "Dan más autos y más caros a diputados," *Reforma*, January 30, 2013; "Recibirán ¡2 coches! Monreal, Anaya," *Reforma*, February 2, 2013; "Se dan fistol de oro los 500 diputados," *Reforma*, December 6, 2012. In addition to their normal salaries ($6,657/month), deputies receive a Christmas bonus (*aguinaldo*; $35,905); funds for legislative assistance ($3,715/month); resources

for constituent service ($2,334/month); money to buy Christmas presents ($380); MetLife health insurance for themselves and their families ($1,477/year); compensation to off-set income tax payments ($3,035/year in 2007); contributions to a savings fund ($758/month); funeral expenses for deputies and close family members ($6,113); free airline tickets to return to their home state each week; low-interest loans up to $32,453; the 45 committee chairs and secretaries are allotted an extra stipend as well as funds to hire five staff members; and party leaders have monies to use as they see fit (e.g., the PRI received $39.4 million in 2013). The auditing of these expenditures is more fiction than fact.

17. Erika Hernández, "Eleve gasto en servicios Presidencia," *Reforma*, March 31, 2013; "Foto official de Enrique Peña Nieto costó más de $29 mil dólares," *Univisión*, March 8, 2013.

18. Instituto Federal Electoral (IFE), www.ife.org.mx/docs/IFE-v2/DEPPP/PartidosPoliticosyFinanc.

19. Transparency International, www.transparency2013.

20. Juan S. Millán Lizárraga, interview with author, July 8, 2004, Mexico City.

21. "Menos mexicanos confían en la democracia: Parametría," *Animal Político*, October 9, 2012.

22. Quoted in Nick Miroff, "West Mexico Sees Flare in Drug Violence," *Washington Post*, July 26, 2013.

23. Quoted in Catherine E. Shoichet, "A Grisly Crime Surges into Spotlight as Mexico Shifts Drug War Strategy," *CNN*, March 2013.

24. Hope, Interview with author, July 2, 2013, Mexico City.

25. "Los niños de las ciudades fronterizas ven a narcotraficante como modelo," *CNN México*, May 17, 2010.

26. "Adolescentes aspiran a ser narcos: encuesta," *El Universal*, January 16, 2013.

27. Quoted in Sanjuana Martínez, "Mil 400 niños asesinados en la guerra al narco; desinterés official frente a la tragedia,"*La Jornada*, October 9, 2011.

28. Andrés Rozenthal Gutman, "Is Peña Nieto's Infrastructure Program on the Right Track?" *Inter-American Dialogue's Latin America Advisor*, July 25, 2013.

APPENDIX D

1. Marjorie Miller and Sebastian Rotella, "Mobs Battle for Tijuana Drug Springboard: Major Share of Lucrative U.S. Market is the Prize," *Los Angeles Times*, June 5, 1993.

2. Nathan Jones, "Tijuana Cartel Survives, Despite Decade-Long Onslaught," *InsightCrime*, June 19, 2012.

Selected Bibliography

Aguayo Quezada, Sergio. *La Charola: Una historia de los servicios de inteligencia en México*. Mexico City: Grijalbo, 2001.

Ashby, Joe C. *Organized Labor and the Mexican Revolution under Lázaro Cárdenas*. Chapel Hill: University of North Carolina Press, 1967.

Astorga, Luis. *El siglo de las drogas: El narcotráfico del Porfiriato al nuevo milenio*. Mexico City: Plaza Janés, 2005.

Bagley, Bruce M. (ed.), and William O. Walker III. *Drug Trafficking in the Americas*. Coral Gables, FL: North-South Center Press, University of Miami, 1995.

Bagley, Bruce M., and Sergio Aguayo Quezada (eds.). *Mexico: In Search of Security*. Coral Gables, FL: University of Miami North South Center, 1993.

Bailey, John J. *Governing Mexico: The Statecraft of Crisis Management*. New York: St. Martins, 1988.

Bailey, John J., and Sergio Aguayo (eds.). *Strategy and Security in U.S.-Mexican Relations*. La Jolla, CA: Center for U.S.-Mexican Studies, University of California–San Diego, 1996.

Bailey, John J. (ed.). *Organized Crime and Democratic Governability: Mexico and the U.S.-Mexican Borderlands*. Pittsburgh, PA: University of Pittsburgh Press, 2001.

Bailey, John J., and Jorge Chabat (eds.). *Transnational Crime and Public Security: Challenges for Mexico and the United States*. La Jolla, CA: Center for U.S.-Mexican Studies, University of California–San Diego, 2002.

Basave Benítez, Agustín. *México mestizo: Análisis del nacionalismo mexicano en torno a la mestizofilia de Andrés Molina Enríquez*. Mexico City: Fondo de Cultura Económico, 2002.

Beith, Malcolm. *The Last Narco: Inside the Hunt for El Chapo, the World's Most Wanted Drug Lord*. New York: Grove, 2010.

Bolívar Moreno, Gustavo. *Sin tetas no hay paraíso*. Bogotá: Quinteros Editores, 2005.

Cameron, William Townsend. *Lázaro Cárdenas, Mexican Democrat*. Ann Arbor, MI: George Wahr, 1952.

Castellanos, Laura. *México Armado, 1943–1981*. Mexico City: Era, 2007.

Chand, Vikram K. *Mexico's Political Awakening*. Notre Dame, IN: University of Notre Dame Press. 2001.

Cline, Howard F. *The United States and Mexico*. New York: Atheneum, 1965.

Corchado, Alfredo. *Midnight in Mexico: A Reporter's Journey through a Country's Descent into Darkness*. New York: Penguin, 2013.

Donnelly, Robert A., and David A. Shirk. *Police and Public Security in Mexico*. San Diego, CA: University Readers, 2009.

Fernández Menéndez, Jorge. *Nadie supo nada, la verdadera historia del asesinato de Eugenio Garza Sada*. Mexico City: Grijalbo, 2006.

Fernández Menéndez, Jorge. *La FARC en México: De la política al narcotráfico*. Mexico City: Nuevo Siglo, 2008.

González, Francisco E. *Dual Transitions from Authoritarian Rule: Institutionalized Regimes in Chile and Mexico, 1970–2000*. Baltimore: Johns Hopkins, 2008.

Grayson, George W. *The Politics of Mexican Oil*. Pittsburgh: University of Pittsburgh Press, 1980.

Grayson, George W. *Mexico: From Corporatism to Pluralism?* Ft. Worth, TX: Harcourt Brace, 1998.

Grayson, George W. *The Mexico-U.S. Business Committee: Catalyst for the North American Free Trade Agreement*. Rockville, MD: Montross, 2007.

Grayson, George W. *Mexico: Narco Violence and a Failed State?* New Brunswick, NJ: Transaction Publishers: 2010.

Grayson, George W., and Samuel Logan. *The Executioner's Men: Los Zetas, Rogue Soldiers, Criminal Entrepreneurs, and the Shadow State They Created*. New Brunswick, NJ: Transaction Publishers, 2012.

Grillo, Ioan. *El Narco: Inside Mexico's Criminal Insurgency*. New York: Bloomsbury, 2011.

Gutiérrez, Alejandro. *Narcotráfico: El gran desafío de Calderón*. Mexico City: Planeta, 2007.

Krauze, Enrique. Mexico: *Biography of Power*. New York: Harper Collins, 1997.

Langton, Jerry. *Gangland: The Rise of the Mexican Drug Cartels from El Paso to Vancouver*. New York: Wiley, 2011.

Logan, Samuel. *This Is for the Mara Salvatrucha: Inside the MS-13, America's Most Violent Gang*. New York: Hyperion, 2009.

Longmire, Sylvia. *Cartel: The Coming Invasion of Mexico's Drug Wars*. New York: Palgrave, 2011.

López Obrador, Andrés Manuel. *Un proyecto alternativo de nación*. Mexico City: Grijalbo, 2004.

Molloy, Molly, and Charles Bowden (eds.). *El Sicario: The Autobiography of a Mexican Assassin*. New York: Nation Books, 2011.

Osorno, Diego Enrique. *La guerra de los Zetas: Viaje por la frontera de la necropolítica*. Mexico City: Grijalbo, 2012.

Padgett, L. Vincent. *The Mexican Political System*. 2nd ed. Boston: Houghton Mifflin, 1976.

Poppa, Terence E. *Drug Lord: The Life and Death of a Mexican Kingpin*. Seattle: Demand, 1998.

Preston, Julia, and Samuel Dillon. *Opening Mexico: The Making of a Democracy.* New York: Farrar, Straus and Giroux, 2004.

Ravelo, Ricardo. *Osiel: Vida y tragedia de un capo.* Mexico City: Grijalbo, 2009.

Reveles, José. *El cártel incómodo: El fin de los Beltrán Leyva y la hegemonía del Chapo Guzmán.* Mexico City: Grijalbo, 2010.

Riding, Alan. *Distant Neighbors: A Portrait of the Mexicans.* New York: Alfred A. Knopf, 1985.

Russell, Philip L. *Mexico under Salinas.* Austin, TX: Mexico Resource Center, 1994.

Scherer García, Julio. *La reina del pacífico: es la hora de contar.* Mexico City: Random House Mondadori, 2008.

Schmitt, Karl M. *Mexico and the United States, 1821–1973: Conflict and Coexistence.* New York: Wiley, 1974.

Scott, Peter Dale, and Jonathan Marshall. *Cocaine Politics: Drugs, Armies, and the CIA in Central America.* Berkeley and Los Angeles: University of California Press, 1998.

Shannon, Elaine. *Desperados: Latin American Drug Lords, U.S. Lawmen, and the War America Can't Win.* New York: Viking Penguin, 1988.

Shirk, David A. *The Drug War in Mexico: Confronting a Shared Threat.* New York: Council on Foreign Relations, 2011.

Story, Dale. *The Mexican Ruling Party: Stability and Authority.* New York: Praeger, 1986.

Thomas, Hugh. *The Mexican Labyrinth: A Study Prepared for the Twentieth Century Fund.* New York: Twentieth Century Fund, 1990.

Toro, María Celia. *Mexico's "War" on Drugs: Causes and Consequences.* Boulder, CO: Lynne Rienner, 1995.

Wornat, Olga. *La Jefa: Vida pública y privada de Marta Sahagún de Fox.* Mexico City: Grijalbo, 2003.

Wright, George. *Mexico City: Heart of the Eagle; Democracy or Inequality.* Ottawa, ON: RCW, 2004.

ARTICLES

Cox, William John. "Richard Nixon's Vengeful War on Marijuana," *Consortium News*, September 16, 2010.

Craig, Richard. "La Campaña Permanente: Mexico's Anti-Drug Campaign." *Journal of Interamerican Studies and World Affairs* (May 1978).

Creechan, James and Jorge de la Herrán García, "Without God or Law: Narcoculture and Belief in Jesús Malverde." *Religious Studies and Theology* 24, no. 2 (2005).

Kurtz-Phelan, Daniel. "The Long War of Genaro García Luna." *New York Times Magazine*, July 13, 2008.

Lawson, Guy. "The Making of a Narco State," *Rolling Stone*, March 11, 2009.

"Menos mexicanos confían en la democracia: Parametría," *Animal Político*, October 9, 2012.

"Mexico Still Waiting for U.S. Aid," *Borderland Beat*, December 7, 2009.

"Nixon Tapes Show Roots of Marijuana Prohibition: Misinformation, Culture Wars and Prejudice." *Common Sense Drug Policy*, March 2002.

"Nixon Tapes Reveal Twisted Roots of Marijuana Prohibition," *Common Sense for Drug Policy*, updated July 9, 2009.

Reuter, Peter and David Ronfeldt. "Quest for Integrity: The Mexican-US Drug Issues in the 1980s," *Journal of Interamerican Studies and World Affairs* 34, no. 3 (Autumn 1992).

Thompson, Barnard R. "Kidnappings Are Out of Control in Mexico," *Mexidata.info*, June 14, 2004

Wells-Wallace, Benjamin. "The Truce on Drugs: What Happens Now That the War Has Failed?" *New York Magazine*, November 25, 2012.

BOOK CHAPTERS

Camp, Roderic Ai. "Armed Forces and Drugs: Public Perceptions and Institutional Challenges," in Eric L. Olson, Donald A. Shirk, and Andrew Selee, *Shared Responsibilities*, eds. (Washington, D.C.: Mexico Institute, Woodrow Wilson International Center for Scholars, October 2010).

Olson, Eric L. "El future de la cooperación entre México y Estados Unidos. Iniciativa Merida," in Sergio Aguayo Quezada and Raúl Benítez Manaut (eds.) *Atlas de la seguridad y la defensa de México 2012*. Mexico City: Casede, 2012.

SCHOLARLY PAPERS

Bagley, Bruce M. "Drug Trafficking, Political Violence and U.S. Policy in Colombia in the 1990." Paper presented at the School of International Studies, University of Miami, Coral Gables, FL: January 5, 2001.

Bagley, Bruce M. "Drug Trafficking and Organized Crime in the Americas: Major Trends in the Twenty First Century." Published in *Agrarian Ideas for a Developing World*. March 24, 2011.

Eskridge, Chris. "Mexican Cartels and Their Integration into Mexican Socio-Political Culture." An earlier version was presented at the International Conference on Organized Crime: Myth, Power, Profit, October 1999, Lausanne, Switzerland.

Felbab-Brown, Vanda. "Peña Nieto's Piñata: The Promise and Pitfalls of Mexico's New Security Policy against Organized Crime," Latin American Initiative, Brookings Institution, February 2013.

Molzahn, Cory et al., "Drug Violence in Mexico: Data and Analysis through 2012," Transborder Institute, University of San Diego, February 2013.

GOVERNMENT SOURCES

Government Accountability Office. "Mérida Initiative: The United States Has Provided Counternarcotics and Anticrime Support but Needs Better Performance Measures." Report to Congressional Requesters, July 2010.

Ledwith, William E., Chief of International Operations, DEA, testimony before the House Government Reform Committee, Subcommittee on Criminal Justice, Drug Policy, and Human Resources, February 15, 2000, Washington, D.C.

Secretaría de la Defensa Nacional. "Discurso del C. General Guillermo Galván Galván, Secretario de la Defensa Nacional," February 9, 2011. Mexico City.

U.S. Embassy (Mexico City), Fact Sheet: "The Mérida Initiative: An Overview," May 2012, Mexico City.

White House, Office of Press Secretary, "Press Conference by President Clinton, President Pastrana of Colombia, House Speaker Dennis Hastert, and Senator Joseph Biden," August 30, 2000, Cartagena, Colombia.

White House, "Presidents Bush and Berger of Guatemala Participate in Joint Press Availability." March 12, 2007, Guatemala City.

INTERVIEWS AND E-MAILS

Álvarez Palafox, Fred. Interviews with author, January 10, 2012, October 5, 2012, February 28, 2013, and July 2, 2013, Mexico City.

Bagley, Bruce M. E-mails to author, October 3, 1913 and October 9, 1913.

Bailey, John J. E-mail to author, October 3, 2013.

Basave Benítez, Agustín. Interviews with author, October 4, 2012 and July 5, 2013, Mexico City.

Beltrones Rivera, Manlio Fabio. Interview with author, September 16, 2011, Toluca, Mexico State.

De la Barreda Solórzano, Dr. Luis. Director, Instituto Ciudadano de Estudios sobre la Inseguridad. Interview with author, March 9, 2011, Mexico City.

Derham, Ambassador (ret.) James M. Derham. Interview with author, April 28, 2012, Williamsburg, VA and E-mail to author, June 2, 2013.

Flores Velasco, Guillermo. Interviews with author, January 9, 2012, July 3, 2012 and July 3, 2013, Mexico City.

Frechette, Ambassador (ret.) Myles R. R. E-mails to author, November 23, 2012 and November 25, 2012.

Hope, Alejandro. Interview with author, July 2, 2013. Mexico City.

Ibarra, Cuauhtémoc. Interview with author January 8, 2012 and October 3, 2012, Mexico City.

Jones, Nathan postdoctoral fellow in drug policy, James A. Baker III Institute, Rice University. Telephone interview January 2, 2013.

Millán Lizárraga, Governor Juan S. Interviews with author July 8, 2004, Mexico City and July 3, 2008 (telephone).

Olmos Tomasini, Carlos. Interview with author, February 28, 2013, Mexico City.

Ortiz, Ildefonso, journalist with *The Monitor* (McAllen, TX). Telephone interviews April 15, 2011, August 10, 2012, March 15, 2012, July 12, 2013, and October 11, 2013.

Rojo, Colonel (Ret.) Eric, managing director of Magination Consulting International. Interview with author, March 15, 2012, Washington, D.C.

Valencia, Juan Gabriel. Interviews with author August 4, 2007, January 13, 2008, April 20, 2008, July 6, 2008, September 5, 2008, March 10, 2009, November 8, 2009, January 8, 2012, July 4, 2012, and October 6, 2012, Mexico City.

Index

About the Author

GEORGE W. GRAYSON is the Class of 1938 Professor of Government Emeritus at the College of William & Mary, and has made more than 200 research trips to Latin America. In addition, he is a senior associate at the Center for Strategic & International Studies, an associate scholar at the Foreign Policy Research Institute, a board member at the Center for Immigration Studies; and a life member of the NAACP. His recent books include *The Executioner's Men: Inside Los Zetas, Rouge Soldiers, Criminal Entrepreneurs, and the Shadow State They Created* (co-authored with Sam Logan; Transaction Publishers, 2012) and *Mexico: Narco-Violence and a Failed State?* (Transaction Publishers, 2009).